A WOMEN'S HISTORY OF THE
CHRISTIAN CHURCH

A Women's History of the Christian Church

Two Thousand Years of Female Leadership

Elizabeth Gillan Muir

UNIVERSITY OF TORONTO PRESS

Toronto   Buffalo   London

LIBRARY AND ARCHIVES CANADA CATALOGUING IN PUBLICATION

Muir, Elizabeth Gillan, 1934–, author

A women's history of the Christian church : two thousand years of female leadership /
Elizabeth Gillan Muir.

Includes bibliographical references and index.
ISBN 978-1-4875-9385-8 (hardcover).–ISBN 978-1-4875-9384-1 (softcover)

1. Women in Christianity—History. 2. Christian leadership—History.
3. Christianity—History. 4. Christian women—Biography. I. Title.

BV639.W7M85 2019   270.082   C2018-906257-6

We welcome comments and suggestions regarding any aspect of our publications—please feel free to contact us at news@utphighereducation.com or visit our Internet site at www. utorontopress.com.

North America
5201 Dufferin Street
North York, Ontario, Canada, M3H 5T8

2250 Military Road
Tonawanda, New York, USA, 14150

ORDERS PHONE: 1-800-565-9523
ORDERS FAX: 1-800-221-9985
ORDERS E-MAIL: utpbooks@utpress.utoronto.ca

UK, Ireland, and continental Europe
NBN International
Estover Road, Plymouth, PL6 7PY, UK
ORDERS PHONE: 44 (0) 1752 202301
ORDERS FAX: 44 (0) 1752 202333
ORDERS E-MAIL: enquiries@nbninternational.com

Every effort has been made to contact copyright holders; in the event of an error or omission, please notify the publisher.

The University of Toronto Press acknowledges the financial support for its publishing activities of the Government of Canada through the Canada Book Fund.

♾ Printed on acid-free, 100% post-consumer recycled paper with vegetable-based inks.

Printed in Canada

 Canada Council **Conseil des Arts**
for the Arts **du Canada**

 ONTARIO ARTS COUNCIL
CONSEIL DES ARTS DE L'ONTARIO
an Ontario government agency
un organisme du gouvernement de l'Ontario

Funded by the   Financé par le
Government   gouvernement
of Canada   du Canada   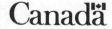 Canada

 MIX
Paper from
responsible sources
FSC   FSC® C016245
www.fsc.org

CONTENTS

ILLUSTRATIONS

ACKNOWLEDGMENTS

MANY MEN AND WOMEN in museums, archives, libraries, churches, in denominational offices and privately held collections have generously taken time to provide me with information or with assistance in other ways to make this book a reality. I apologize to those I have inadvertently omitted.

I would like to thank: Dr. Agnes Regina Murei Abuom, Rev. Dr. Gary Agee, Bishop Olga Lucia Alvarez, Kim Arnold, Iris Barta, Dr. Marion Best, Taylor Billings, Howard E. Bowers, Canon Janet Catterall, Peter Cheney, Bishop Michele Birch Conery, Marie-Claude Fortier, Christine Gordon, Terry Gregg, Kristine Greenaway, Jill Hetland, Rev. Dr. Susan Hood, Charlotte Howard, Dr. Stan Ingersol, Susan Jackson, Lisa Jacobson, Rev. Najla Kassab, Pavel Korsun, John Kutcher, Rev. Kathleen Macpherson, Caleb Maskell, Bishop Bridget Mary Meehan, Daphne Metcalfe, Christine Morris, Dr. Deidre Palmer, The Very Rev. Susanna Pain, Dr. Paul Peucker, Dr. Isabel Apawo Phiri, Dr. Elisabeth Raiser, Sr. Elizabeth Rolphe-Thomas, Karen Seaman, Rev. Dr. Janice Sevre-Duszynska, Rebecca Smith, Nic-Don Stanton, The Most Rev. Patricia Storey, Dr. Mary Theresa Streck, Rev. Suzanne Theil, Verana Thim, Dr. Philip L. Wickeri, and Cherylin Williams.

Others were kind enough to forward photographs: Ana Maria Borges, Dr. Eduardo Pereira da Silva, Mary Lee Berner Harris, Alaina W. Hébert, Jasmin Leckelt, Dr. Emilie Gagnet Leumas, Father John Matusiak, Paul Mortlock, Terri Rogan, Dr. Monika Triest, and the staff at Yoido Full Gospel Church.

As usual, when I delve into "computerland," my children James Muir and Dee Allaert have assisted enormously with technology. Dr. Phyllis Airhart and Dr. Mark Toulouse at Emmanuel College, Toronto, provided special assistance making this book possible. Cory Lemos helped with translation. I am grateful to all.

My editors and other specialists at the University of Toronto Press, a hard-working team, were led by Natalie Fingerhut and Julia Cadney, whose creative suggestions were tremendously helpful.

My thanks to all these kind men and women who are interested in the history of women in the Christian Church.

PREFACE

Those who cannot remember the past are condemned to repeat it.

George Santayana (1863–1952)

THIS BOOK GREW OUT of an International Women's Day event created and organized by female theological students in Toronto, Canada. Those of us invited to be panelists were asked to talk about a woman we admired in the history of the Christian Church. During our discussions, it became all too readily apparent that theological students were quite unaware of the rich history and extensive contributions of female leadership in the church over the centuries. Even church history specialists had little or no knowledge of female leaders apart from a few early martyrs.

The general public is of course even less aware. When I mentioned this project to one friend, she said, "Well, that will be a thin book." Another woman told me that she had heard of a monastic community in the Middle Ages that was supervised by women, but likely I would find it because it was unique.

This, then, is an attempt to make the thousands or millions of women leaders in the Christian Church over the centuries better known.

I have to confess, though, that even I was not fully aware of all the remarkable research that has been accomplished recently in this area and the many women who have been uncovered and brought back from obscurity. I was reminded of one of my New Testament professors when I was at graduate school, who wrote his dissertation on one aspect of the life and work of St. Paul. Wanting to be thorough, he said that he had decided to read everything that had been written about Paul. He began on one end of the relevant shelf in the library stacks, only to realize very soon that new books were being added on the other end faster than he could read through the works already written.

This was almost the case with the history of women in the church. My intention has been to distill and meld my own research with the results of other historians' research and produce women's 2,000-year story. Most of the research already completed has been necessarily restricted to one woman, or one community or denomination, or one time period or geographical location, and I believe that the whole story needs to be told to present a picture of all the women's work that has been undertaken. But I must apologize where I have had to omit some findings. There are so many studies. Dozens of female *and* male theologians and historians have produced innumerable works, most of it excellent, but it has not been possible to include everything that has been written in the number of pages allotted to this book. There is also the problem of hagiographical studies; much of that information is unfortunately suspect or at least lacking in human detail.

Since histories in the past have almost totally excluded women—half the adult population—it may seem fair and timely today to write a history of only women. But there are some dangers with this approach. First, it may give the impression that women have achieved more than they actually have, and that they were not as restricted as they often were. And second, there is the problem of bias and lack of objectivity. When I taught courses on women's history, I always began by stating that the course was totally objective. Never having been challenged on this point, I then had to confess that I believe there is no such thing as total objectivity. We are all biased to a degree, depending on our upbringing, where we've gone to school, what we've read, where we've lived, what churches we've attended, what our parents have taught us, and so on. But the important point is to know and acknowledge one's bias. My bias will probably become apparent as you read this story, although I have attempted to present different sides of various issues. I hope that you as a reader will understand and acknowledge your own bias. As my *koiné* or biblical Greek professor said to us once, "There are three Truths. My Truth, Your Truth, and The Truth." Simple perhaps, yet very profound, a dictum that could have avoided much of the violence, sexism, and discrimination that you will read about on the following pages if ecclesiastics and politicians had accepted this reality.

The next step, of course, is for a future historian to integrate all the following chapters into a complete history with equal attention paid to both men and women. There is also a need for an up-to-date history of feminist theology; and perhaps another historian could research LGBTQ members throughout the history of the Christian Church. This particular study, however, remains a history of female leadership, as much as can be recorded in the assigned number of pages.

One further note: as historians are aware, the way names are spelled and dates recorded varies tremendously over the centuries and even during a person's lifetime, sometimes even in the same document. Thus you may find discrepancies in spelling and dates on the following pages compared with what you may have read elsewhere.

May you applaud the many strong, determined, and extraordinary religiously affiliated women described in the ensuing chapters, whatever your bias or your belief.

Chapter 1

WOMEN IN THE EARLY CHURCH: PART I

IN THE NEW TESTAMENT

In 1955, the journalist Edith Deen published a ground-breaking work, *All of the Women of the Bible*, which included over 300 concise biographies of women found in the Old and New Testaments—"the major named figures in the foreground and the nameless women in the background of **Scripture**." Yet she missed one of the most important women in the New Testament: the Apostle Junia.[1]

It's not surprising that Deen missed her. Junia had been mentioned in the New Testament in Paul's Letter to the Romans (16:7), written about the year 57: "Greet Andronicus and Junia, my relatives, who were in prison with me; they are prominent among the apostles, and they were in **Christ** before I was." Evidently Junia had been a leader in the early Christian Church even before Saul the Jewish persecutor was converted and became Paul the great Christian saint and apostle. But somehow, one of the first Christians in Rome, the female apostle Junia became known as Junias, a man's name that didn't even exist in any extant inscriptions from that period. When Deen collected the women in the New Testament, in the biblical translation she used, Romans 16:7 had begun: "Greet Andronicus and Junias [two men]...."

How did that happen?

Over the centuries, several well-known male Christian **theologians** had recognized the woman Junia as an apostle, even some with little regard

FIGURE 1.1 The apostle Junia, pictured on the right-hand side of this image, is commemorated on 17 May in the Orthodox Church. Photo: Courtesy of the Orthodox Church in America. https://oca.org/.

for women, including the child prodigy and scholar Origen of Alexandria (185–254); Jerome (347–420), the father of the Latin Vulgate **Bible**; John Chrysostom (347–407), archbishop of Constantinople; Hatto or Atto (885–961), the **bishop** of Vercelli; Theophylact (1050–1107), a Greek archbishop; and the philosopher and **theologian** Peter Abélard (1079–1142). As the "Church Father" John Chrysostom noted, "How great the wisdom of this woman must have been that she was even deemed worthy of the title of apostle."

By the twelfth century, however, the woman Junia had been designated a male in the New Testament. Even later, many of the biblical translations from the twentieth century still translated the name as Junias. Most recent translations, however, clearly read the name as female. The journalist Rena Pederson analyzed Bibles from the twenty-first century and found that they were all using Junia.[2]

When Junia went to Rome, she must have been in her early 40s or 50s, if she had been present when **Jesus** was alive. Life expectancy in those days in Rome was about 60 to 65 if one escaped the illnesses of childhood, so

Junia would have been in her late middle years. She was likely brought up Jewish if she and Andronicus were "kinsmen" or relatives of Paul. If they had been imprisoned as Paul says, then they were very early Christians. It is estimated that there were only about 1,000 Christians in Rome at that time.[3]

Scholars think the name Junia means that she was a freed slave or a child of freed slaves of the prominent Junian family, which suggests that she would likely have been taught reading and writing. It might also mean that she and Andronicus survived prison because they had influential or well-to-do friends who brought them food in jail.[4]

Pederson spent months in Italy investigating how Junia got "lost," and eventually discovered that a thirteenth-century **archbishop**, Giles of Bourges or Aegidius Romanus (1247–1316), appears to have been the culprit, seemingly the first scholar to refer to the "honorable men" Andronicus and Junias. A contemporary of the **misogynist** Pope Boniface VIII (1235–1303), who wanted all nuns securely locked away in their **convents**, Giles may have been influenced by him, believing that no woman could rank as an apostle. Later, Pope Benedict XIV (1675–1758) had great admiration for Giles, styling him as *Dr. Fundatissimus* (best-founded teacher). He was indeed very literate. Upon his death, Giles's personal library of 18,000 books was bequeathed to an Augustinian school in Paris. Interestingly, a contemporary of Giles, the German Benedictine nun and mystic Gertrude the Great (1256–1302), a prolific writer, correctly translated Romans 16:7 naming Junia (feminine) an apostle.[5]

Apart from Gertrude, it was only in the sixteenth century that Junia reappeared. The renowned scholars Disiderius Erasmus (1466–1536) and William Tyndale (c.1494–c.1536) both translated the original Greek texts, recovering Junia's name. Curiously, about the same time, the Protestant Reformer Martin Luther (1483–1546) kept the male name in his German translation, referring to "men of note," Andronicus and Junias. From 1898 to 1920, Junia reappeared, although an even earlier 1863 *Dictionary of the Bible*, reprinted in 1920, listed the woman Junia "of note among the apostles." In 1927, committees translating the texts assumed it must be a male name and used Junias again. In 1989, however, the New Revised Standard Version of the Bible reverted to Junia, and now most translators of the Bible agree.

Tracing Junia's history was a complicated process, but Junia has now been recognized as a woman and an apostle. The **Orthodox Church** lists Andronicus as Bishop of Pannonia in what is today Hungary, where both he and Junia traveled and healed many people. Their feast day is celebrated on 17 May. The calendar of saints' days under the Emperor Basil Porphyrogenitus (958–1025) wrote of Junia: "Having with him (Andronicus) as consort and helper in godly preaching the admirable woman Junia, who dead to the world and the flesh, but alive to God alone, carried out her task."[6] Junia is still honored today; the hymn or *Kontakion* to Junia and Andronicus describes Junia as "all-wise," who "shone with righteousness."[7]

What did it mean to be an apostle? The term appears 79 times in the New Testament: 10 in the four **gospels**; 28 in the book of Acts; 38 in the Epistles; and 3 in Revelation. Apostles were appointed to a special function in the church, commissioned and empowered to proclaim the gospel to all nations. In Greek "apostle" meant messenger or one sent on a mission. Often it was used as one who knew and worked with Jesus. According to Pederson, in the Bible, apostles taught, worked miracles, forgave sins, ordained **presbyters** or **elders**, administered the sacred rites and made laws. In Ephesians 4:11, Paul mentions apostles first, of all the gifts of ministry. In the *Didache*, the earliest book on Christian church order, probably written in the first century, apostles were wandering missionaries; initially they did not need to be eyewitnesses to the life of Jesus.[8]

Generally we think of the 12 male disciples as being "the" apostles. But there were other apostles mentioned in the Bible besides the 12: Matthias, who replaced the traitor Judas Iscariot (Acts 1:26); Paul, the apostle to the Gentiles, who wrote many of the New Testament letters (1 Corinthians 15:8–9); Barnabas who disposed of his land to help the other apostles (Acts 14:4–14); Andronicus and Junia, Paul's **missionary** colleagues (Romans 16:7); James, brother of Jesus (Galatians 1:18); Silvanus, Paul's friend (1 Thessalonians 2); Timothy, Paul's companion (1 Thessalonians 2); perhaps two unknown Christians (2 Corinthians 8:23); and Epaphroditus (Philippians 2:25–30).

Some biblical scholars consider the 72 disciples that Jesus sent out as early missionaries (Luke 10:1–20) to be apostles as well; Origen of Alexandria believed that Andronicus and Junia were part of that cohort. And according to 1 Corinthians 15:6, some 500 men and women saw Jesus after his resurrection; most of them were still alive when Paul wrote that letter. Paul believed he was an apostle because he had seen Jesus on the road to Damascus during his conversion experience, so the 500 could be considered apostles, too.

OTHER WOMEN

Paul's Letter to the Romans contains a wealth of names of women leaders in the early church besides Junia, although there is little information about them. Thirty-four per cent or 10 out of 29 people that Paul commends by name are women, and as the theologian Jouette Bassler points out, only three of the functions that Paul mentions—**deacon**, patroness, co-worker, host, laborer, apostle—are performed by men, but seven of those women mentioned were in those roles.[9] The early conservative Christian theologian, Hippolytus, Bishop of Pontus (170–235) wrote:

> Lest the female apostles doubt the angels, Christ himself came to them so that the women would be apostles of Christ and by their obedience rectify the sin of the ancient Eve.... Christ showed himself to the [male] apostles and said to them ... It is I who appear to these women and I who wanted to send them to you as apostles.[10]

The **minister** Phoebe (Romans 16:1–2) who carried Paul's letter from Cenchrea, the port of Corinth, to the new church in Rome also had her detractors. She was called a *diakonos* by Paul, a word which can be translated from the Greek as servant, helper, deacon, or minister. Often, Paul used it interchangeably with missionary or coworker for the same people. Generally when it referred to men, it was translated in Bibles as "minister," but when it referred to a woman such as Phoebe, it became downgraded to servant or helper. Phoebe was also referred to as *prostates*, meaning one who presides, or a woman who is set over others. Edith Deen referred to her as a deaconess, usually considered a little lower than a deacon administratively. However, Deen was convinced that "it was more of an honour to be referred to as a servant than as a deaconess." (In fact, it seems that the word deaconess did not come into use in the early church until the fourth century, and was used interchangeably with deacon.)[11]

Origen believed that Phoebe had been officially ordained, as did the noted preacher John Chrysostom, who was generally demeaning in his assessment of women. Chrysostom wrote: "You see that these were noble women [Junia and Phoebe], hindered in no way by their sex in the course of virtue, and this is as might be expected for in Christ Jesus, there is neither male nor female." Origen wrote that the passage about Phoebe taught him two things:

"Women are to be considered ministers in the Church and ... ought to be received in the ministry." The fact that Paul sent her as an emissary on his behalf signals that she was esteemed, and competent to represent him and his churches' interest.[12]

Indeed, Phoebe was widely known and admired. Bishop Theodoret of Cyrrhus (393–460) wrote that "[Paul] opened the world to her [Phoebe] and in every land and sea she is celebrated. For not only do the Romans and Greeks know her, but even all the barbarians."[13] In Jerusalem in the fourth century, an epitaph for the deacon Sophia read:

> Here lies the servant and bride of Christ
> Sophia the deacon, the second Phoebe,
> She fell asleep in peace on the 21st of the month of March
> In the 11th indiction.[14]

The Byzantine Ordination Rite of the Deaconess, an eighth-century prayer for the **ordination** of deaconesses used by the church in Constantinople, gives special recognition to Phoebe:

> Sovereign Lord, you who do not reject women offering themselves and desiring to minister in your holy houses ... receive them into an order of ministers, bestow the grace of your **Holy Spirit** also upon this your servant ... and fill her with the grace of the diaconate, just as you gave the grace of your diaconate for Phoebe, whom you called to the work of ministry.[15]

Another important husband and wife team in the early church, Prisca/Priscilla and Aquila (Romans 16:3; Acts 18:2, 18, 26; 1 Corinthians 16:19; 2 Timothy 4:19), tentmakers and teachers, left Rome when the Emperor Claudius (10 BCE–54) expelled the Jews. They lived in Corinth and Ephesus, traveling as missionaries for the fledgling church. Priscilla, thought to be related to the Roman senator Pudens, was the head of a house church in Rome (house churches were the early meeting places for Christians), and is commended for teaching a man called Apollos. Priscilla's importance is established not only through Paul's recommendations but by the fact that she was usually named first when reference was made to the couple, meaning that she was considered the more important of the two. It has even been suggested that she wrote the Letter to the Hebrews in the New Testament.

She evidently was instrumental in having Paul's letters copied and dispersed throughout the Roman Empire.[16]

Pederson notes that Priscilla is mentioned six times in the Bible:

> She helped start three house churches. To appreciate the magnitude of that effort, just imagine starting three churches from scratch in three cities around the world today. Then imagine starting three churches at a time when you could be flogged, stoned, expelled or imprisoned for doing so.[17]

Tradition tells us that both Prisca and Aquila perished in the general persecution of Christians around the year 64. Her house church in Rome was one of the first places of Christian worship in that city and on or near that site today is a lovely little church called Santa Prisca (short for Priscilla). In the **basilica**, there is an altarpiece painted by the Italian artist Domenico Cresti (1560–1636) showing Prisca being baptized by St. Peter. A seventeenth-century fresco on the wall by Anastasio Fontebuoni (1571–1626) depicts the martyrdom of a young woman, possibly their daughter with the same name, Priscilla.[18]

The Woman's Bible, published and edited in 1895 by the American suffragist Elizabeth Cady Stanton (1815–1902) and the Coalition on Women and Religion, was quite clear about Priscilla's and Phoebe's role in the early church! A member of the committee, deceased just before publication, author and suffragist Ellen Battelle Dietrick (1847–95) wrote:

> To one who uses unbiased common sense in regard to the New Testament records, there can be no question of women's activity and prominence in the early ministry. Paul not only virtually pronounces Priscilla a fellow-Apostle and fellow-bishop (Romans chap. 16, verses 3-5), but specially commends Phebe [*sic*], a Greek woman, as a minister (diakonos), which, as we have seen, may be legitimately interpreted either presbyter, bishop, or Apostle. That it was well-understood, throughout the whole church, that women had shared the labors of the Apostles, is evident by Chrysostom's eulogy thereupon. Phebe was the bishop of the Church in Cenchrea.[19]

There are numerous other women leaders mentioned in the New Testament, women who must have been considered so important in the development of the early Christian Church that they have escaped total erasure although we are given little information as to what they did.

The four unmarried daughters of Philip the **evangelist** (Acts 21:8–9) were **prophets** at Hierapolis in Asia, mentioned both in the New Testament and in the *Ecclesiastical History* written by the Greek historian Eusebius of Caesarea (260–340) sometime before 303, quoting Bishop Polycrates of Ephesus (125–96). In the early church, prophets **spoke in tongues**, offered prayer, provided guidance, interpreted scripture, and taught. Eusebius thought they should belong to the first stage of apostolic succession. *The Teaching of the Twelve Apostles*, or the *Didache*, notes that prophets provided instruction, presided over the **Eucharist**, and led prayers. They were considered the church's high **priest**s (13:3). The *Epistle of Barnabas* (4:9) written around 130, told the prophets that they should not shut themselves up in solitude but attend common meetings. An 84-year-old woman prophet, Anna, the daughter of Phanuel of the tribe of Asher (Luke 2:36–38), spent her days at the Jewish Temple, fasting and praying.

Both Elizabeth, Jesus' aunt, and Mary, his mother, were prophets; meeting when they were both pregnant, Elizabeth with John the Baptist and Mary with Jesus, they prophesied about their children's future (Luke 1:41–55). Revelation 2:18–23 mentions a woman prophet with a large following in Thyatira (located in present-day Turkey), encouraged by the local church but condemned by the author John as a "Jezebel" (referring to an ancient queen considered "bad" but whose only "sin" was worshipping the ancient goddess: Jeremiah 7:18). There are references to Ammia, a prophet in Asia Minor who is mentioned in non-biblical sources from 160 on. As the disciple Peter quoted from the Old Testament prophet Joel (Joel 2:28) on the first Christian Pentecost when men and women received the Holy Spirit:

> Then afterward
> I will pour out my spirit on all flesh;
> And your sons and your daughters shall prophesy,
> Your old men shall dream dreams;
> And your young men shall see visions,
> Even on the male and female slaves in those days,
> I will pour out my spirit.[20]

Prophets, of course, could not be regulated; their authority lay in their spontaneous ecstasy and inspired theological interpretation. As it is written in the *Shepherd of Hermas*, a literary work of the late first century or early second:

> When someone who has the Divine Spirit comes into the meeting of the
> righteous who have the faith of the Divine Spirit and intercession is made
> to God from the Assembly, then the angel of the prophetic spirit rests
> on the person and filled with the Holy Spirit the prophet speaks to the
> congregation as the Lord wills. (*Mandate* XI.9)

There would have been prophets in every early Christian center. It was only
when the church became institutionalized that this creative element could
be subordinated in favor of a controlled ministry, and prophets were often
replaced by bishops.[21]

Lydia (Acts 16:14–15, 40), a businesswoman in Philippi dealing in expensive purple cloth, became the first of **St. Paul**'s converts in Europe. Originally
she had come from Thyatira, where the woman prophet mentioned above
in Revelation came from. Thyatira was also where the muricid mollusk
flourished, the source of the purple dye Lydia used. Lydia had her whole
household baptized, beginning the first house church in Philippi. And
since the house church was in her home, and homes were the purview of
women, she would have been the leader. Women could legitimately teach
and preach in that context as it was safely in the private realm and not in
a public place. It also suggests that these women or their families owned
substantial resources if their houses were large enough to accommodate
groups of men and women.

House churches were also led by Mark's mother, Mary (Acts 12:12), who
had a maid and a large house separated from the street by a gate and a
courtyard; Nympha (Col. 4:15); and probably Apphia, wife of Philemon
(Philemon 1:2). Ignatius sent greetings to a woman called Alce and also to
Tavia and her household; they likely led house churches. Like Junia, Nympha
became known as a man in several early biblical translations, although again
the masculine name Nymphan is simply not found in inscriptions of that
period, whereas scholars have come across the feminine name Nympha more
than 60 times in early writings and archeological discoveries.[22]

Other prominent women leaders mentioned in the New Testament are
Euodia and Syntyche, two of Paul's co-workers in Philippi (Philemon 4:2),
active evangelists who "struggled" with Paul, spreading the gospel as preachers
and teachers; Claudia (2 Timothy 4:21) who is named along with two very
prominent male leaders; and Tryphosa and Tryphaena, two Greek women
mentioned as workers with Paul, likely twins (Romans 16:12). It is thought
that Tryphaena was a deacon.

It is interesting and significant to note that at least eight of the first Christian churches had known strong female leadership. There were so many women that Celsus, a second-century Greek philosopher, had ridiculed Christianity because it was a religion of women, children, and slaves. Origen agreed, but said that it also included "superior" people as well. Bishop Cyprian of Carthage (200–58) acknowledged that Christian maidens were so numerous in the churches that it was difficult to find husbands for all of them; Bishop Callixtus of Rome (?–222) tried to resolve that by giving women of the senatorial class permission to marry slaves or freedmen even though it was prohibited by Roman law. So it should not be surprising that women were prominent in several early churches:[23]

Rome: Ten of the twenty-eight people mentioned in Paul's Letter to the Romans were women, and Phoebe was to carry the letter to that church.

Jerusalem: Mary, the mother of John Mark, hosted a church there.

Philippi: The church was founded by Lydia, and Euodia and Syntyche were active in that place.

Corinth: The church had women prophets and start-up assistance from Priscilla and Aquila.

Caesarea: The church was ministered to by Philip's daughters.

Laodicea: A house church was run by Nympha.

Cenchrae: Phoebe was the deacon there.

Ephesus: Where Priscilla ministered along with Aquila.[24]

Martha and Mary of Bethany, sisters of Lazarus whom Jesus raised from the dead, were some of Jesus' closest friends, and there are several references in the New Testament to them. In one, Mary sat at Jesus' feet, listening to him teach, while Martha "was distracted with much serving" in the kitchen, irritated that she had to prepare dinner alone (Luke 10:38–42).

Exegetes are not unanimous in their assessment of the status of these two women. It has been suggested that Mary symbolized women who were allowed to study, called to the intellectual and spiritual life as men were, departing from the custom in Judaism at that time which generally prohibited women from receiving an education. Jesus was continually violating the social mores of his society in treating women as the equals of men, as he does in that instance with Mary. Yet Mary does nothing with Jesus' teaching. She does not speak out, but is simply a passive listener. As Jane Schaberg points out in The Women's Bible Commentary, Mary's attitude is that of a disciple, but she is not a disciple: "She is only an audience." Still, it is thought that it was Mary who anointed Jesus' head with expensive ointment while he was dining in Bethany in the house of Simon the leper. This earned her commendation from Jesus for her prophetic foresight, although she also received criticism from the other men present, some of whom were indignant about wasting so much money that could have been used to help the poor. "You always have the poor with you," Jesus told the other diners, "but you do not always have me ... she has anointed my body beforehand for burial" (Mark 14:3–9; Matthew 26:6–13; John 12:1–8).[25]

On the other hand, it has been suggested that Martha was a deacon or deaconess; the story may have been told to downplay women serving the Eucharist. Whatever the case, Martha is credited with recognizing Jesus as the **Messiah**, one of two women in the New Testament with such insight.

Another celebrated woman was Tabitha, or Dorcas, one of Jesus' disciples in Jaffa, raised from the dead by St. Peter (Acts 9:36–42), well known for sewing clothes for widows and helping the needy, perhaps a member of the order of widows herself. Later, women's Dorcas Sewing Societies would be established worldwide. Other women were Salome, a woman present at Jesus' **crucifixion** (Mark 15:40), and one of the many women who followed Jesus from Galilee; and Lois and Eunice (2 Timothy 1:5), Timothy's mother and grandmother, who taught the Christian faith to Timothy. Pederson notes how ironic it is that Paul's Letter to Timothy prohibits women from teaching.[26]

A woman convert in Athens, Damaris (Acts 17:34), a woman of "high standing," disappeared from a version of the New Testament, the Codex D (fourth or fifth century), but returned in later editions. Nereus' sister, the mother of Rufus; Julia; and Olympas are other women mentioned by Paul in Romans 16:15 as church workers or saints along with Mary (Romans 16:6).

Most of the women in the New Testament, though, are nameless or pushed to the background and demoted. The Roman Army and Navy Commander and philosopher, Pliny the Elder (23–79), who lived in Jesus' time, pointed out that information about women doctors was intentionally hidden, for women were supposed to be quiet and as inconspicuous as possible, "so that after they were dead no one would know that they had lived."[27] That obviously applied to women other than doctors. The American biblical scholar Bruce Metzger notes in his *Text of the New Testament* that in some biblical translations, in Acts 17:4, the phrase describing women who were "prominent in the community" was changed to "wives of leading citizens"; a wife would be considered a lesser person than a prominent woman. In Acts 17:12, the phrase "Greek women of the better class, and men, too" was altered to "a considerable number of men and women of the better class," perhaps not as great a shift in meaning.[28]

Jesus had four brothers whose names we know—James, Joses/Joseph, Judas/Jude, and Simon—but unnamed sisters in the New Testament (Mark 6:3; Matthew 13:55–56; Galatians 1:19). In non-canonical stories, however, the sisters are named Assia and Lydia, but they remain obviously of lesser importance than the men. The Samaritan woman whom Jesus met at the well (John 4: 7–42), who was later known as Photina, was left nameless in the Bible, although she has been considered the first Christian evangelist. When Jesus confessed that he was the longed-for Messiah, she ran to her Samaritan village of Sychar, told the inhabitants about him and they became believers because of her testimony. The woman with the issue of blood healed by touching Jesus' robe was later called Veronica, but again was left nameless in the Bible (Matthew 9:20–22; Mark 5:25–34; Luke 8:43–48).[29]

In the gospel accounts of the crucifixion after the male disciples fled, women remained at or near the foot of the cross. The women are named differently in the various gospels, but at least some of them are named. In John 19:25–27, Jesus' mother, Mary, his mother's sister Mary the wife of Cleophas, and Mary Magdala, were mentioned. The Markan account (Mark 15:40–41) lists Mary Magdalene, Mary the mother of James the younger and Joses, Salome, and many other women from Galilee. In Matthew 27:55–56, we read of Mary Magdalene, Mary the mother of James and Joseph, and the mother of Zebedee's sons, and, again, other women who had followed from Galilee. In Luke (23:49, 55), we find simply "the women who had followed him from Galilee."

The women who discover the empty tomb on the third day after Jesus was crucified are all named in three gospels, but not in Luke at first: Mary Magdalene and the "other" Mary in Matthew (28:1); Mary Magdalene, Mary the mother of James and Salome in Mark (16:1)—although earlier Mary Magdalene and Mary the mother of Joses had watched to see where Jesus' body was placed; "the women who had come with (Jesus) from Galilee," in Luke (23:55; 24:10)— though later Mary Magdalene, Joanna, Mary the mother of James and the "other women" play a role; and in John it is just Mary Magdalene (20:1).

We are also told of women who just didn't count, for example, in Matthew 14:21: "there were about five thousand men, not counting women and children"; and in 15:38: "[there] were four thousand men, not counting women and children." Then there were female "camp followers" as Jesus "made his way through towns and villages preaching." Mary Magdalene, Joanna the wife of **Herod**'s steward Chuza, Susanna, and several others were part of a group of "men and women" (Luke 8:1–3; Mark 15:40–41, Matthew 27:55–56) who traveled with Jesus and his 12 male disciples, surely an unusual phenomenon in their society at that time. Questions have been raised as to how Joanna was able to leave the protected and privileged state in which she lived in Herod's court; perhaps her husband had died. It has also been suggested that Joanna was the Jewish name for Junia, the apostle who got "lost"; they may be one and the same.[30] These women supported Jesus and the 12 male disciples, providing for them out of their own resources—although in *The Woman's Bible*, Elizabeth Cady Stanton strongly disapproves of women supporting men if the women needed the money themselves:

> to my mind there is nothing commendable in the action of young women who go about begging funds to educate young men for the ministry, while they and the majority of their sex are too poor to educate themselves, and if able, are still denied admittance into some of the leading institutions of learning....[31]

IN ECCLESIASTICAL ORDERS

Women in two ecclesiastical **orders** mentioned in the New Testament, widows and women deacons, would have been prominent in their early church communities as well. There are countless examples of women in these orders and other interesting references to women elders, presbyters, priests, and even bishops both in and beyond the New Testament, many of which will be examined in this chapter and the next. Virgins, too, were a separate group; their order was not fixed, although admission was formalized with guaranteed remuneration. They might live with their families or as members of female communities.[32]

Widows were not only the recipients of charity, but were one of the earliest groups of women leaders who were financially compensated by congregations. In 1 Timothy 5:9–10, Paul separates women who were widowed when their husbands had died, and the order of widows who devoted their lives to the Christian community. These latter women were to be over 60, married only once, and known for good works such as raising children, showing hospitality, washing the saints' feet, and helping the afflicted. Ignatius of Antioch (35–108) wrote to the Smyrnians mentioning the order of widows; Tertullian (155–240), the "Father of Latin Christianity," mentioned that there were virgins not yet 20, established as widows; and Polycarp, Bishop of Smyrna (69–155) also referred to this order. Widows were said to have banded about Tabitha whom Peter raised from the dead (Acts 9:40, 41).[33]

In the third-century church document *Didascalia*, some of the ministrations of widows appear to have been directed to helping men. The French **Jesuit** Cardinal Jean Daniélou (1905–74) believed that according to this statute directing widows to pray and lay on hands, they were involved in the administration of the **Sacrament** of the Dying, Extreme Unction for both men and women.

In fourth-century letters written by Pseudo-Ignatius, widows were said to be **altars**, and virgins were likened to priestesses of Christ. According to the *Statuta ecclesiae antiqua* C. 12, written in southern France in the fifth century, widows were to teach other women so that they could answer newly baptized Christian women's questions about their faith, and instruct them on how to live, but they were not to teach in church, or teach men, or baptize—as they may have been doing, if the church felt a need to prohibit these acts. As written in the *Didascalia* (15) and the *Constitutiones* II (9), it was "dangerous" for women to baptize, both for the baptizer and the baptized, "for it can lead to her downfall [the baptizer]; more it is contrary to custom and sacrilegious," although it is not clear what terrible thing would befall.

In another document from Syria written at the same time, *Testamentum Domini Nostri Jesu Christi*, originally in Greek, contrary to that regulation, widows were directed to sit at the front of the church and were referred to as female priests (*pro presbyteris [feminis] supplicemus*). They were to sit "within the veil" around the altar during the Eucharist along with the other clergy, and were ordained, elected by the people as were all clergy. The widows were to instruct the ignorant, convert and teach the prisoners, visit sick women, anoint women being baptized, and supervise deaconesses.

Father Sisto Scaglia in *Notiones archeologiae christianae* II (1) believes that widows had a chair just like the bishop's *cathedra* and presided in church assemblies. He notes that the *Corpus Inscriptionum*, a collection of early Christian epitaphs published in Berlin in 1905, provides several examples, and Tertullian mentions such a widow's seat in his *De virginibus velandis* VIII. Tertullian wrote that the church didn't allow women who had been married twice to be ordained or to preside in the Christian community. In two inscriptions, one from Terni and the other from the Basilica of St. Praxedes in Rome at the time of Pope Pascal I (?–824), the word *episcopa* (bishopess) is applied *apropos* of widows.[34]

The Shepherd of Hermas, written earlier, in about 148, asks that two copies of a manuscript be made, one for Bishop Clement of Rome (?–99) to share with the elders, and the other for Grapte "who shall **exhort** the widows and orphans." Who Grapte was is not known, but obviously she was in charge of the women while Bishop Clement was in charge of the men.[35]

Often, however, in their pronouncements the church tried to constrain the widows, instructing them to stay at home: "let a widow know that she is the altar of God ... the altar of God never wanders or runs about anywhere, but is fixed on one place ... they are talkative and chatterers and murmurers, they incite strife and they are bold and they have no shame." Widows who were visiting and giving theological instruction in homes had become "gossips," violating the virtue of chastity and silence by visiting various church members.[36]

After almost all gatherings of **ecclesiastics** from different Christian communities, decrees were issued that attempted to proscribe women's activities in the church. The Council of Nicea in 325, an organized attempt to develop a unified Christendom, decreed that women were no longer to be ordained for leadership roles, thus affirming that they were formerly being ordained; proscriptions were generally made to deal with actual behavior and not imaginary situations. The Council of Laodicea in 363 forbade women from the priesthood, presiding over churches, and approaching the altar, so likely women were involved in those activities. The Fourth Synod of Carthage in 397 forbade women to teach men in an assembly or to baptize; again, there had to be a reason for this order. The Council of Chalcedon in 451, attended by 250 bishops or their attendants, ruled that women had to be over 40 to be ordained as deacons; evidently, then, women were still being ordained in the middle of the fifth century.

Female deacons were important in the early church hierarchy. The office of deacon was well established by the time of Paul's Letter to the Philippians, probably in the year 62, and his First Epistle to Timothy written around 65, which noted that women deacons were to be serious, temperate, and faithful. Some have argued that Paul is referring only to male deacons' wives and not female deacons, but most contemporary scholars as well as the early Greek Fathers believe that this reference is clearly to women deacons. Tertullian observed "how many men and women there are whose chastity has obtained for them the honour of ecclesiastical orders." An early second-century letter from Pliny the Younger (61–113), the Roman author and governor of Pontus/ Bithynia to the Emperor Trajan (53–117), refers to two maidservants who were called deacons. They were apparently the two most knowledgeable persons and leaders in their local church, and although he tortured them, he received little useful information. Pliny wrote:[37]

> However they had abandoned [sharing in the **Agape**: Holy Communion] after the publication of my edict by which, according to your orders, I had forbidden…. I judged it so much the more necessary to extract the real truth, with the assistance of torture, from two female slaves who were styled ministers, but I could discover nothing more than depraved and excessive superstition.[38]

The theologian Clement of Alexandria (150–215) spoke of women deacons in his *Stromata* 3, 6:

> The apostles, giving themselves without respite to the work of evangelism … took with them women, not as wives but as sisters, so that they might serve as their co-ministers, serving women living at home; by their agency the teaching of the Lord reached the women's quarters without arousing suspicion. We are also aware of all the things Paul prescribed on the subject of women deacons."[39]

In the fourth century in the **East** and perhaps in the second century in the **West**, deaconesses were clearly ordained. According to the late fourth-century *Apostolic Constitutions* III.16.1, a collection of church orders, bishops were to ordain (*procheirisai*) women deacons who were "faithful and holy." Prayers were given for ordaining bishops, priests, deacons and deaconesses, sub-deacons, and lectors, followed by **confessors**, widows, virgins, and exorcists, who at that time were not ordained. Evangelos Theodorou, the Orthodox expert on women deacons, explains that the ordination of woman deacons in the sanctuary right in the heart of the Divine Liturgy ranks it among the orders of the higher clergy.[40] The long prayer for the ordination of the deaconess was similar to that for a deacon. The women received the same diaconal powers as the male deacon: "Concerning a deaconess … O Bishop, thou shalt lay thy hands upon her in the presence of the presbytery … O Eternal God … who also in the **tabernacle** of the testimony, and in the temple, didst ordain women to be keepers of thy Holy gates ... look down upon this Thy servant, who is to be ordained to the office of a woman deacon."[41]

The churches' Council of Nicea in 325 referred to deaconesses as clergy; however, gradually the office of deaconess or woman deacon is thought to have declined as future church Councils ruled against them. The Council of Orange in 441 stated: "Let no one proceed to the ordination of deaconesses anymore" (Canon 26). The Council of Epaone in 517 noted in Canon 21, "We abrogate completely to the entire kingdom the consecration of widows who are named deaconess"; and in 533 the Council of Orleans II ruled that "No longer shall the blessing of women deaconesses be given, because of the weakness of their sex."[42]

A rule was one thing, but the actual observance was another. Rules were usually made to stop a practice in existence. Indeed, legislation under the sixth-century Emperor Justinian I of Constantinople (482–565) attributed an equal legal position to men and women deacons. Graves outside Philippi from the fourth to the sixth centuries contain inscriptions on headstones of women as **deacons** and **canonesses**. For example, Agatha, buried at Extra-Muros in the fifth century with her husband John, a linen weaver and treasury official, was named a deacon, and Posidonia, another female deacon, was buried with a woman named Pancharia, a canoness. All were buried to the west of Philippi, not associated with any basilica. In Delphi in the fifth century we find:

> The most pious deaconess Athanasia
> Having lived a blameless life modestly
> Having been ordained a deaconess by the most holy bishop,
> Pantamianos, made this monument, in which lie her remains.
> If any other dares to open this monument, in which the
> Deaconess has been deposited, he will have the portion of
> Judas, the betrayer of our Lord, Jesus Christ.[43]

In *Ordained Women in the Early Church*, the historians Kevin Madigan and Carolyn Osiek have compiled a comprehensive collection of both literary and epigraphical references to deaconesses or women deacons, and to women presbyters as well, both in the West and East, most of them only up to 600. They discovered that the female diaconate continued to exist and develop for many centuries afterwards, mostly in the East, but also in the West, continuing at the same time as widows' groups. In their study, Madigan and Osiek did not include the order of virgins or women prophets as they were not considered church offices nor commissioned by ordination. They also found that there was more evidence for women presbyters in the West than in the East, some of them at least exercising a ministry at the altar even in the West.[44]

According to their sources, deaconesses or female deacons were involved in a host of activities: they anointed women's bodies with oil before their **baptism**, they visited women and gave religious instruction, they welcomed and maintained order among the women at assemblies, they traveled and sometimes represented their church, they were liaisons between the bishop and women visitors. Some of them poured the water and the wine in the chalice at the Eucharist in the absence of a qualified male; others read the Bible in women's groups. They blessed the paschal (Easter) candle at the Easter Vigil, acted as **cantors**, announced the various parts of the liturgy, dismissed the congregation. They received communion after bishops and presbyters, symbolizing their relative importance.[45]

Madigan and Osiek found more than 40 references to female deacons or deaconesses in literary works such as letters and stories from the East, along with many other notations in official church documents and **canons**, and 61 inscriptions still in existence ranging across the Eastern Mediterranean area, including epigraphical works such as funerary, votary, or *sarcophagus* inscriptions, on *stelae*, mosaics, plaques, in burial caves, and on monuments.

One of the more interesting literary references to a woman deacon is the *Dialogue on the Life of John Chrysostom* (16.179–90), written about 410 by the author Palladius of Galatia (363–430):

The deacon speaks: Now if it's not too much trouble, tell us about Olympias, if you have some knowledge of her.

The bishop: Which one? There are several.

The deacon: The deacon of Constantinople, who was the bride of Nebridius, the former prefect.

The bishop: I know her well.

The deacon: What kind of woman is she?

The bishop: Do not say "woman," but "such a person" (*anthrōpos*), for she was a man (*anēr*) despite her bodily appearance.

The deacon: How is that?

The bishop: By her life, her asceticism and knowledge, and her patient endurance in trials.[46]

High praise indeed, for "woman" symbolized weakness of the flesh and "man" stood for courage and strength, a concept looked at later. Olympias also worked with two other female deacons in Thyatira, named Pentadia and Procla.

The contemporary theologian John Wijngaards refers to 32 inscriptions concerning women deacons from the Byzantine Empire between 200 and 800, noting that few tombstones have survived destruction through war, vandalism, and other disasters. He posits that there must have been a minimum of 32,000 women deacons during that period, realizing that in the year 535, there were 40 deacons who ministered at Hagia Sophia Cathedral in Constantinople alone. The last reference to a woman's ordination as deacon that Wijngaards discovered was from the fourteenth century in the *Xenophon Codex* gr. 163 from the **monastery** of St. Xenophon on Mount Athos, in northeastern Greece: a prayer for the ordination ceremony.[47]

In the West, there were fewer references to women deacons. However, there were more references to women presbyters (ministers) than in the East. Two such are a medallion mosaic in the church of St. Augustine in Hippo, North Africa, probably after 431: "Guilia Runa the presbyteress, rest in peace, lived for fifty years"; and a fourth- or fifth-century funeral inscription from Tropea, Calabria: "Leta the Presbytera, Sacred to her good memory. Leta the presbyter[ess] lived forty years, eight months and nine days. Her husband made [this tombstone]. She preceded him in peace on the day before the ides of May."[48]

Others include an epitaph for a woman Epiktas, a *presbytis* from the third or fourth century, buried on the Greek island of Thera; an earlier inscription from Egypt: "Artemidorus ... fell asleep in the Lord, her mother Paniskianes being an elder [*presbytera*]"; an epitaph from Sicily in the fourth or fifth century referring to Kale the elder (*presbytis*); and a memorial for Ammion the elder (*presbytera*) set up in the third century by Bishop Diogenes. Arthur Frederick Ide claims that the distinction between priest/priestess and deacon/deaconess did not become clearly defined until Pope Gelasius I (?–496) ruled that the priestess "ministered the faith directly from Christ, while the deaconess ministered the faith for and through Christ," putting the priestess slightly higher than the deaconess.[49]

According to Gelasius, priestesses or women priests were being ordained in the fifth century; he noted "the gravity of the error and the destructive consequences that can rebound to the church from that abuse ... the gravest of these is the conferring of the sacrament of priesthood on women." In a long letter to all the bishops in Lucania in the south of Italy and in Sicily, he wrote in 494: "Nevertheless we have heard to our annoyance that divine affairs have come to such a low state that women are encouraged to officiate at the sacred altars, and to take part in all matters imputed to the offices of the male sex, to which they do not belong."[50]

Recently, the theologian and professor Gary Macy has added to our knowledge of female deacons. He discovered references to women's ordination in later papal, theological, and episcopal documents up to the twelfth century. He maintains that women bishops (*episcopae*), women priests (*presbyterae*), deaconesses, and **abbesses** led liturgies, distributed communion, heard confessions, and served at the altar, although some clergy couples may have co-ministered in churches in these positions, and the functions of deaconesses and abbesses appear to have merged by the tenth century. But there is evidence of women deacons up until 1000 in Asia Minor, Greece, Cyprus, Syria, and parts of southern Italy.

Macy examined the numerous references to *presbyterae* and found that some of the women were married to priests and would have received an honorary title; however, many were single, thereby earning the title because of their own work. There were inscriptions for women from Italy, Poitiers, and Croatia, from the fourth to the sixth centuries, and letters from ecclesiastics again complaining that some bishops were ordaining women to function as priests: "women are confirmed to minister at the sacred altars and perform all matters imputed only to the service of the male sex and for which women are not competent," one cleric wrote. In 511, three bishops from northern Gaul demanded of two priests in Brittany that "silly little women ... not pollute the holy sacraments by illicit assistance." These deaconesses were taking the chalice in their own hands and delivering it to the people, an action well beyond the officially accepted practice for women in the Church.[51]

In 747, Pope Zachary (679–752) was asked if nuns could read the Gospel or sing at Mass. He replied in the negative but added that he had heard to his dismay that divine worship had fallen into such disdain that women had presumed to serve at the sacred altars, and that the female sex were performing all the things that were assigned exclusively to men. Four years earlier he had ruled that "No one should presume to join himself physically to an abominable consort like a *presbytera*, deaconess, nun or female monk or a godmother."

The tenth-century *Roman-Germanic Pontifical*, a set of Latin documents, contains the complete liturgy for the ordination of a deacon and a deaconess.

When the bishop blessed the deaconess, he placed the *orarium* on her neck. The *orarium* was a stole worn by bishops, priests, and deacons when they prayed or preached. Bishop Atto of Vercelli (885–961) explained to a questioning priest named Ambrose that women were ordained in the early church because of great need, and *presbyterae* and deaconesses preached, taught, and baptized. He pointed out that since babies were being baptized and not adults any longer, there was not the same need for women to assist in that role.[52]

The Council of Paris in 829 railed against women who were distributing communion and "other things which it would be shameful to mention." Macy insists that women were still distributing communion in the tenth, eleventh, and even the twelfth centuries as texts for these services with prayers written with feminine word endings exist—one copied in the eleventh or twelfth century at the Abbey of St. Sophia in Benevento and another with its provenance unknown. And there is evidence that deaconesses existed in the diocese of Lucca, Italy, at least up until the time of Bishop Ottone of Lucca (?–1146) in the twelfth century.[53]

Macy points out that there are five known references to women bishops in Western Christianity. The most famous is Theodora whom the Catholic Church maintains holds only an honorific title as the mother of Pope Paschal (775–824). In the high arch over the door in St. Zeno's Chapel in the Basilica of Santa Prassede in Rome, there is a mosaic of four women: two female saints, Prassede and Prudentia, along with Mary the mother of Jesus, and a woman whose head is surrounded by a square halo, meaning that she was still alive when the mosaic was completed, probably in the ninth century. The inscription reads *Theoda Episcopa* or Bishop Theoda. The last letter "a" is defaced to make it look like an "o," an attempt to change a female name to a masculine one. It has also been suggested that Theodora's coif or hairstyle indicates that she is not married, and therefore the title of bishop could not have been honorific. The Roman Catholic Church, however, disputes that her hairstyle is that of an unmarried woman.[54]

John addressed his second letter in the New Testament to an "elect lady" (2 John 1:1); Arthur Frederick Ide believes the lady was just that—elected and waiting in the wings, as bishop-elect. Her children referred to in the Bible are either the members of the congregation or the churches under her dominion.[55]

A third reference to a female bishop is on a tomb found in Umbria in central Italy dated between the fourth and sixth centuries with the inscription to the "venerable woman, *episcopa* Q," possibly the wife of Pope Siricius

(334–99). There are numerous inscriptions to *presbyterae* in that area in the fifth century and it may be that there were several female leaders there at that time.

Brigid/Bridget of Dundalk, Ireland (453–523), was ordained a bishop, according to the ninth-century story *Bethu Brigte*. Brigid had established a cell in a giant oak tree at Croghan Hill for women and then a convent on that site for both men and women. She and seven other women wore a white cloak and white veil; they farmed the fields and spun and embroidered. They supported the arts and her monastery became famous for exquisite metalwork and illuminated manuscripts. Brigid became the Mother Abbess of all of Ireland's convents and the schools attached to the monasteries. She was a skilled horsewoman and constant traveler, unenclosed as were most of the Irish female monastics. It was said that she shared a bed with a female companion, Dar Lugdach (?–c.525), who succeeded her as an abbess, but whether they were lovers is not known.

Hildeburga, wife of Segenfrid (?–996), Bishop of Le Mans, in France, was also described as an *episcopissa* (bishop). Whether these were honorary titles is not clear (except for Brigid), although we do know that all these women administered church property, as did bishops.[56]

Macy notes that the wives of bishops, priests, and deacons were obliged by church law to separate from their husbands when the latter were confirmed in their new position. Both parties were expected to enter the religious vowed life. In this way, many wives of bishops, priests or deacons were able to become *episcopae, presbyterae*, and deaconesses, if they were suitable, although not all did, and not all bishops approved of them functioning in those positions or *ordo*.

Gregory the Great (?–604) referred to an abbess who lived all her life in the vestments that the priestesses or *presbyterae* wore. As the historian Charles R. Meyer points out, there were no special vestments for wives of priests, so she was a priestess "in her own right." Historian Girogio Otranto examined several references that clearly referred to women who were *presbytera* because they had earned the title, not because they were wives of ecclesiastics. In 425, Falvia Vitalia sold a cemetery plot in Salona, the ancient capital of Dalmatia, as a presbyter, and definitely not as the wife of a presbyter.[57]

By the eleventh and twelfth centuries, however, women were being denied ordination and ecclesiastical responsibility. As in the movie *The Perfect Storm*, several events collided that worked against women.[58]

First, the eleventh-century Gregorian reforms that insisted on celibacy for the priesthood and other ecclesiastics introduced a fierce misogyny, pushing women out of the church hierarchy. Roman law was being used selectively to enforce the idea that women were not capable of leadership, and the theories of the misogynist Aristotle that women were biologically and intellectually inferior reached the West at this time. Ordination became defined as something only for males. Women were denigrated as never before, such as in this passage by Peter Damian (1007–72), a reforming Benedictine monk and cardinal:

> I speak to you o charmers of the clergy, (women) appetizing flesh of the devil. That castaway from paradise, you (**Eve**, and hence all women), poison of the minds, death of souls, venom of wine and of eating, companions of the very stuff of sin, the cause of our ruin. You, I say, I exhort you women of the ancient enemy, you bitches, sows, screech-owls, night owls, she-wolves, blood suckers, ... harlots, prostitutes, with your lascivious kisses, you wallowing places for fat pigs, couches for unclean spirits.[59]

It was pointed out that the Latin word for woman, *mulier*, was derived from the words for softness of mind, *mollities mentis/mollior*, while the Latin word for male, *vir*, originated from *virtus animi*, strength of soul. "Soft or light-minded" women were the butt of a popular thirteenth-century lawyers' joke: "What is lighter than smoke? A breeze. What [is lighter] than a breeze? The wind. What [is lighter] than the wind? A woman. What [is lighter] than a woman? Nothing!" In the *Decretum Gratiani*, the laws collected in 1140 by Gratian, Causa 32, question 7, criticizing a ruling of Ambrose, read: "He must know that Ambrose does not call him 'man' on account of his male sex, but by the strength of the soul; and he should realize that 'woman' is not called so because of the sex of her body but because [of] the weakness of her mind."

As Macy points out, "The cumulative effect of a selective use of church laws, Roman laws, philosophy, and scripture combined to create an array of authorities, all in agreement on the natural incompetence, subordination, and danger of women. Men wanted to believe the worst about women, and so they found justification to do so."[60]

The celibate or ecclesiastical life was deemed to be infinitely holier than the lay married state, although early in the church's history, celibacy had already been a spiritual goal. As a result of being denied a leading role in the church, women entered convents in droves around this time, searching for some other form of deep spiritual expression. It was not much later that women participated extensively in non-conformist religious groups such as the Beguines, the Cathars, and the Guglielmites, where they assumed leading administrative and ecclesiastical roles; that may have been one reason these groups attracted women to such a degree. These and other communities will be examined in a later chapter.[61]

Macy comments that once women were not being ordained they were considered never to have been ordained; all references to their ordination were expunged or quietly dropped. The church mantra became, what wasn't being done, had never been done.

Little is known about the order of canonesses referred to earlier. Hypatius, a fourth-century bishop, designated a female canon responsible for burials, but Bishop Epiphanius of Salamis (c.310–403) wrote that the priestly functions of this order were forbidden to women. Letter 52 of Bishop Basil of Caesarea (329–79), however, written around 350, is addressed to *canonicae* and letter 173, written around 374, is addressed to a specific canoness named Theodora. The historian Annemarie Kidder reported that there were canoness houses headed by an abbess in Switzerland, France, and Germany from the ninth century on, one on the Rhine headed by the abbess Tengswindis. They followed what was called the "Aachen Rule," took no solemn vows, could own personal property and hire servants. They were celibate. They were engaged in charitable and liturgical services outside the convent, and claimed the orders of virgins and widows as their antecedents. In the ninth century, there were 18 of these houses in France and another 38 were formed between the tenth and eleventh centuries.[62]

Two women from the New Testament, Mary, the mother of Jesus, and Mary Magdalene (c.10 BCE–c.74), need a fuller treatment; their stories will be dealt with in another chapter.

FURTHER READING

PRIMARY

Bettenson, Henry, and Chris Maunder, eds. *Documents of the Christian Church*. Oxford: Oxford University Press, 2011.

Madigan, Kevin, and Carolyn Osiek, eds. and trans. *Ordained Women in the Early Church: A Documentary History*. Baltimore: The Johns Hopkins University Press, 2005.

The New Testament, The New Revised Standard Version. 1989.

Wijngaards, John. *Women Deacons in the Early Church: Historical Texts and Contemporary Debates*. New York: The Crossroad Publishing Company, 2002.

SECONDARY

Campbell, Joan Cecelia. *Phoebe, Patron and Emissary*. Collegeville, MN: Liturgical Press, 2009.

Deen, Edith. *All of the Women of the Bible*. New York: Harper & Row, 1955.

Fiorenza, Elizabeth Schüssler. *In Memory of Her: A Feminist Theological Reconstruction of Christian Origins*. New York: The Crossroad Publishing Company, 1983.

Ide, Arthur Frederick. *Woman as Priest, Bishop & Laity, in the Early Catholic Church to 440 A.D.* Mesquite, TX: Ide House, 1984.

Kraemer, Ross Shepard. *Her Share of the Blessings: Women's Religions among Pagan Jews and Christians in the Greco-Roman World*. New York: Oxford University Press, 1992.

Kroeger, Catherine. "The Neglected History of Women in the Early Church." *Christian History*, April 2016.

Macy, Gary. *The Hidden History of Women's Ordination: Female Clergy in the Medieval West*. Oxford: Oxford Scholarship Online, 2008.

Martimort, Aimé-Georges. *Deaconesses: An Historical Survey*. Translated by K.D. Whitehead. San Francisco: Ignatius Press, 1986.

Meyer, Charles R. "Ordained Women in the Early Church." *Chicago Studies* 4 (1965).

Newsome, Carol A., and Sharon H. Ringer, eds. *The Women's Bible Commentary*. London: Westminster/John Knox Press, 1992.

Pederson, Rena. *The Lost Apostle, Searching for the Truth about Junia*. San Francisco: Jossey-Bass, 2006.

Ricci, Carla. *Mary Magdalene and Many Others*. Minneapolis: Fortress Press, 1994.

Stanton, Elizabeth Cady, and the Coalition on Women and Religion. *The Woman's Bible*. New York: European Publishing Company, 1898.

Swidler, Leonard. *Biblical Affirmations of Women*. Philadelphia: The Westminster Press, 1979.

Torjesen, Karen Jo. *When Women Were Priests*. San Francisco: Harper Publishing, 1993.

NOTES

1 Deen, *All of the Women of the Bible*.
2 Pederson, *The Lost Apostle*, 18; Swidler, *Biblical Affirmations of Women*, 299.
3 Pederson, *The Lost Apostle*, 105.
4 Pederson, *The Lost Apostle*, 14.
5 Pederson, *The Lost Apostle*, 128. Giles of Rome was bested by Juana de la Cruz of Mexico (1651–1695) who had a library of 4,000 books as well as scientific and musical instruments.

6   Pederson, *The Lost Apostle*, 191f.

7   *Kontakion*, Orthodox Church in America.

8   Pederson, *The Lost Apostle*, 34f; Edgar Hennecke, "The Didache," *New Testament Apocrypha*.

9   As reported in Pederson, *The Lost Apostle*, 42.

10 As quoted in Pederson, *The Lost Apostle*, 47.

11 Deen, *All of the Women of the Bible*, 230f; Pederson, *The Lost Apostle*, 47; Abrahamsen, "Women at Philippi," 25. It is possible that Romans 16:1–23 was part of a letter for the church in Ephesus and later appended to a letter for the Roman church: see Campbell, *Phoebe*, 17.

12 As quoted in Pederson, *The Lost Apostle*, 47f; Origen, *Commentary*, 291.

13 "Working Women in the NT: Priscilla, Lydia and Phoebe," *New Life*, 5.

14 Kraemer, ed., *Maenads, Martyrs, Matrons, Mystics*, 221.

15 As quoted in Campbell, *Phoebe*, 51.

16 Chicago, *The Dinner Party*.

17 Pederson, *The Lost Apostle*, 48.

18 Pederson, *The Lost Apostle*, 209f.

19 Ellen Battelle Dietrick, "Epistle to the Romans," in *The Woman's Bible*, ed. Stanton, 154.

20 Acts 2:14, 16–18 in the New Testament.

21 Fiorenza, Lecture.

22 Kroeger, "The Neglected History."

23 Kraemer, *Her Share of the Blessings*, 128; Kroeger, "The Neglected History of Women in the Early Church."

24 "Women in the Heart of God (8): Women's Roles in the Early Church."

25 Jane Schaberg, in *The Women's Bible Commentary*, ed. Newsome and Ringer, 289.

26 Pederson, *The Lost Apostle*, 216.

27 Ricci, *Mary Magdalene*, 20.

28 Pederson, *The Lost Apostle*, 168.

29 Jesus' brothers are considered by some churches to be cousins in order to support Mary's perpetual virginity.

30 Richard Bauckham as quoted in Matt Slick, "Was Junia in Romans 16:7 a Female Apostle in Authority?" n.d., n.p.

31 Stanton, *The Woman's Bible*, 125.

32 Elm, *"Virgins of God,"* 147ff.

33 Tertullian, *De virginibus velandis* C.9 and Ignatius, *Letter to the Smyrnians* XIII.1 as quoted in Swidler, *Biblical Affirmations*, 306; Elm, *"Virgins of God,"* 229.

34 Meyer, "Ordained Women in the Early Church," 291.

35 Catherine Kroeger, "The Neglected History of Women in the Early Church."

36 Torjesen, *When Women Were Priests*, 148.

37 Swidler, *Biblical Affirmations of Women*, 313.

38 Ide, *Woman as Priest, Bishop & Laity*.

39 As quoted in Wijngaards, *No Women in Holy Orders*, 15.

40 Wijngaards, "The Ancient Diaconate of Women Was a Sacrament."

41 Swidler, *Biblical Affirmations of Women*, 309ff.

42 Swidler, *Biblical Affirmations of Women*, 314f; Wijngaards, *No Women in Holy Orders*, 19.

43 Kraemer, ed., *Maenads, Martyrs, Matrons, Monastics*, 223.

44 Madigan and Osiek, eds. and trans., *Ordained Women in the Early Church*.

45 Campbell, *Phoebe*, 52.

46 As quoted in Madigan and Osiek, eds. and trans., *Ordained Women in the Early Church*, 43.

47 Wijngaards, *No Women in Holy Orders*, 109; Wijngaards, *Women Deacons*, 187.

48 Madigan and Osiek, eds. and trans., *Ordained Women in the Early Church*, 193f; *The Didascalia 15* and *Constitutiones, III*, 6.

49 "Women in the Heart of God (8): Women's Roles in the Early Church"; Ide, *Woman as Priest, Bishop & Laity*, 51.

50 Rossi, "Priesthood, Precedent and Prejudice," quoting Giorgio Otranto, "Notes on the Female Priesthood in Antiquity."

51 Macy, *The Hidden History of Women's Ordination*, 13.

52 Macy, *The Hidden History of Women's Ordination*, 17.

53 Macy, "The Ministry of Ordained Women," 14.

54 "Women and the Early Churches," accessed 24 September 2018, http://www.augsburgfortress.org/media/downloads/0800638263_Chapter1.pdf?domainRedirect=true.

55 Ide, *Woman as Priest, Bishop & Laity*, 52ff.

56 Macy, *The Hidden History of Women's Ordination*, 6; Turpin, *Women in Church History*, 45ff; Dolan, "A Revival of Female Spirituality," 40.

57 Meyer, "Ordained Women in the Early Church," 295.

58 In 1991, three raging weather fronts came together to produce the fiercest storm in modern history. The movie *The Perfect Storm* told the story of the disaster on the eastern Atlantic.

59 As quoted in Macy, *The Hidden History of Women's Ordination*, 4.

60 Macy, *The Ministry of Ordained Women*, 14.

61 Macy, *The Ministry of Ordained Women*, 9.

62 Abrahamsen, "Women at Philippi," 25; Kidder, *Women, Celibacy and the Church*, 203.

Chapter 2

WOMEN IN THE EARLY CHURCH: PART II

BEYOND THE CANON

A young woman called Thecla (c.30–?), 18 years old and very beautiful, was engaged to Thamyris, a man in her home town of Iconium in Turkey. Just at that time, St. Paul arrived in her community, speaking next door to where she lived. Thecla was fascinated by his preaching but her mother forbade her from going to hear him, so she sat at her bedroom window and listened to every word. Night and day, she heard him talk about the new religion that emphasized chastity. Immediately committing to Christianity, Thecla broke off her engagement, deciding to live as a virgin. Thamyris and Theoclia, Thecla's mother, were so enraged that they asked the governor to have Thecla burned and Paul punished. Paul escaped. Thecla was tied to the stake and the fire lit, but an enormous storm put out the flames. Thecla ran off to find Paul and they traveled together to Antioch. There she rebuffed a Syrian who fell in love with her. His male ego bruised, he had her thrown to the lions and bears, but a female lion protected her, killing the other animals, being martyred itself in the fight. Wanting to be baptized, Thecla threw herself into a pit full of water and fierce seals, and baptized herself. The seals were miraculously killed before they could harm her. Other wild beasts were sent to tear her apart, but the women watching in the arena threw perfume, overpowering all the beasts by putting them to sleep. Thecla was then tied to a fierce bull

FIGURE 2.1 "Protomartyr and Equal of the Apostles," Thecla is commemorated on 24 September in the Orthodox Church in America. Photo: Courtesy of the Orthodox Church in America. https://oca.org/.

that was supposed to tear her apart, but a flame from heaven burned the cords that bound her, and she escaped again.

Thecla returned to Iconium, commissioned by Paul to preach the gospel. Afterwards she traveled to Seleucia, disguised as a man with her hair shorn. So many people were converted and healed through her ministry that the doctors lost patients and revenue. They plotted to rape her in revenge. This time, God opened a large crevice in a mountain where she could hide. She lived there as a monastic for 72 years, teaching, preaching, baptizing, and healing without permission or assistance from any male ecclesiastic.

The story of Thecla, written sometime in the first or second century in Asia Minor, circulated for years throughout the early Christian Church, especially along the Mediterranean. By the end of the fifth century, Thecla was being held up as an example of virginity and martyrdom, not only in Asia Minor but also in Italy, Gaul, Germany, North Africa, Armenia, Cyprus, Palestine-Syria, and Egypt, her story available in numerous languages. It is said that at one time the cult of Thecla rivaled that of the Virgin Mary. Thecla's story and image have been found on Greek and Coptic *papyri*, in parchment manuscripts, on wooden combs, terracotta oil lamps, textile fragments, limestone grave *stelae*, wall paintings, textile fragments, and **pilgrim** flasks fabricated as late as the seventh century. It has even been suggested that Thecla wrote some of the books in the New Testament. A *troparion* or hymn to her in the Antiochian Orthodox Christian Church praises her for her suffering:

> You were enlightened by the words of Paul, O Bride of God, Thekla,
> And your faith was confirmed by Peter, O Chosen One of God.
> You became the first sufferer and martyr among women,
> By entering into the flames as into a place of gladness.
> For when you accepted the Cross of Christ,
> The demonic powers were frightened away.
> O all praised One, intercede before Christ God that our souls may be saved.[1]

The theologian and teacher Origen of Alexandria considered Thecla's story on a par with John's Gospel and Paul's Letter to the Galatians. Athanasius, Bishop of Alexandria, visited Thecla's shrine at Seleucia, and held her up as a model for women, especially for the local nuns. Gregory of Nazianzus (329–90), Archbishop of Constantinople, hid out at her shrine to avoid an unwelcome ecclesiastical appointment. Sometime in the year 380, the well-known Spanish pilgrim, the nun Egeria, traveled to the **Holy**

Land with an entourage and visited Hagia Thecla, "only three nights from Tarsus…. Since it was so close we were pleased to travel there," she wrote.[2] Egeria was apparently of high social standing for she was "solicitously" attended by bishops, clergy, monks, and escorts of soldiers whenever she needed them. She reported in her travel account that at Thecla's shrine she found "innumerable" cells for men and women, a high wall to keep the Isauians out, and her friend Marthana, a deaconess who was in charge of the monastic cells of "apotactites" or "apostolics" who renounced all private property. Egeria stayed with them two days and then returned to Tarsus. It is likely that she belonged to a religious community in her home town in Spain.[3]

In the early fifth century, two **ascetic** women, Marana and Cyra from Beroea in Macedonia, made a pilgrimage to the shrine of the "triumphant" Thecla, traveling all the way there and back without any food. By this time, Thecla's shrine welcomed men and women from all over the known world.[4]

Not everyone, of course, accepted Thecla's story as orthodox. The historian Eusebius (263–339) found that it verged almost on the heretical and Jerome condemned it. Tertullian reported that the "presbyter" who produced the document had been "convicted" and "removed from office." The problem was not with Thecla's asceticism, but rather with what she did, operating in the sphere supposedly restricted to men.[5]

Recent excavations have uncovered the fifth-century remains of three basilicas, one measuring more than 80 meters in length, and a large public bath and several cisterns, believed to be a later complex on the same site as Thecla's monastery. Yet some historians and theologians doubt whether Thecla ever existed. Some elements of her story are certainly fanciful, but also symbolic, such as the support of all the women when she was thrown to the lions. Cutting one's hair and dressing as a man to travel freely was not uncommon for women in her day and escaping the subjugation of marriage and the dangers of childbirth were often the motivations for women entering convents or becoming **hermits**. Dictionaries of saints are full of stories of women who followed the same path, although Jerome warned his young friend Eustochium against women who dressed as men, and the Synod of Gangra in 340 condemned women who cut their hair and wore men's clothing as part of asceticism. Later, the Emperors Valentinian (321–75) and Theodosius I (347–95) decreed that women who cut off their hair, "contrary to divine and human laws … shall be kept away from the doors of the churches. It shall be unlawful for them to approach the consecrated

FIGURE 2.2 Sixth-century limestone roundel relief depicting a haloed St. Thecla surrounded by lions and angels. Photo: The Nelson Gallery–Atkins Museum, Kansas City, Missouri, United States.

mysteries, nor shall they be granted … the privilege of frequenting the altars which must be venerated by all."[6]

Any bishop who allowed a woman with a shaved head to enter a church was to be expelled from his office. However the bishop of Heliopolis is thought to have allowed Eugenia (?–258), an Egyptian noblewoman, to wear men's clothing and become a monk; she founded a convent in Egypt. It was said that women needed to be "manly" to be saved, celibate, and ascetic, but cutting their hair was evidently not part of the process. It was usurping men's style.[7]

The **Church Father** Cyprian (c.200–58) wrote to virgins urging them to remain unmarried and explaining the benefits of celibacy: "You do not fear the sorrows of women and their groans, you have no fear about the birth of children, nor is your husband your master, but your Master and Head is

Christ in the likeness of and in the place of a man; your lot and condition are the same [as those of man]."[8]

Prominent ascetic women were often called the "new Thecla." However, the *Acts of Paul and Thecla*, which introduced the story of Thecla, was not accepted into the **canon**—the list of approved books which formed the New Testament—even though Thecla's story was widely read in churches. The canon closed for the **Western Church** toward the end of the fourth century, and some time later for the **Eastern Church**.

The story of Nino, or Nina (c.296–c.335), is almost as amazing but not as well known as Thecla's. Nino grew up in a Greek-speaking family from Cappadocia, although some sources believe she was from Rome, or possibly Jerusalem, or even Gaul, perhaps the only child of a famous family. She received a vision of the Virgin Mary who gave her a grapevine cross and said: "Go to (the Georgian kingdom of) Iberia and tell there the Good Tidings of the Gospel of Jesus Christ … and I will be for you a shield against all visible and invisible enemies. By the strength of this cross, you will erect in that land the saving banner of faith."[9] The church **patriarch** blessed her and sent her off to preach the gospel "among the pagan nations." She joined a community of 37 virgins in the Kingdom of Armenia.

Unfortunately, all the women except Nino were killed by the Emperor Diocletian (244–311) who had wanted one of the virgins for his wife but she had refused his advances. Nino, however, survived; she had hidden among some wild rose bushes. About 320, after a long journey, she entered the Kingdom of Iberia, today known as Georgia, preached the gospel unceasingly, and healed many people, including Queen Nana, who immediately converted to Christianity along with her attendants. King Mirian, however, opposed Christianity until he was struck blind on a hunting trip. He prayed to the Christian God, the God of Nino, and was also healed. In 326, he made Christianity the state religion and built the first Christian church there.[10]

Archeological evidence and historical records indicate that there was a woman involved in the conversion to Christianity of the men and women in the eastern kingdom of Georgia. Today, there are almost 89,000 women over the age of 16 in that area whose name is Nino.

It is estimated that we have lost at least 85 per cent of the early Christian literature that was not in the canon. Some of this material has been recovered: numerous Gospels and Acts written in the second and third centuries contain stories of women who thronged around the disciples and other Christian evangelists as they traveled from town to town spreading the story of Christianity. Inspired by the preaching they heard, many of the women espoused a life of sexual continence. In the *Acts of Peter* (c.180–90), Peter is crucified because so many women leave their husbands to live a life of celibacy that the men rose up in arms. The story is similar in the *Acts of Thomas* and the *Acts of John* from the early third century, with the added feature in the latter that two women who converted to Christianity, Drusiana and Cleopatra, raised up the dead. Drusiana had a positive relationship with her fiancé in that he finally agreed to convert to asceticism with her. However, she later killed herself rather than be a temptation to a man who wanted to commit adultery with her.[11]

Most biblical interpreters find little or no evidence in the New Testament that Jesus encouraged the ascetic or celibate tradition for all his followers. His presence and support of the wedding at Cana (John 2:1–11) and the various dinners he attended suggest that he was not an ascetic; however, some followers interpreted various biblical passages as elevating asceticism and continence as a superior way of life. In Matthew 19:10, after Jesus laid down the principle of the indissolubility of marriage as a counter to the easy divorce in his society which was detrimental to women, the disciples responded, "If such is the case of a man with his wife, it is better not to marry"—apparently concerned with male freedom. In Mark 8:34, we read the words, "If any want to become my disciples let them deny themselves and take up their cross and follow me." Jesus also advised a rich young ruler to sell all his possessions and give the money to the poor if he wished to inherit eternal life (Mark 10:17–27; Matthew 19:16–30; Luke 18:18–23). Paul wrote in 1 Corinthians 7 of the superiority of virginity: "It is well for a man not to touch a woman ... to the unmarried and widows I say that it is well for them to remain unmarried as I am ... now concerning virgins ... it is well for you to remain as you are ... if a husband dies ... (a wife) is more blessed if she remains as she is." The Church Fathers inherited these attitudes and built on them. Jerome praised poverty and virginity and gathered celibate women around him; Gregory the Great, Pope Gregory I (?–604), influenced others in treating sexual relations as solely for procreation. Augustine of Hippo (354–430) suggested that "nothing so casts down the manly mind from its height as the fondling of woman and those bodily contacts which belong to the married state."[12]

Most scholars believe, however, that Paul's advice to remain unmarried was motivated by the early church's expectation of Jesus' imminent return and the end of the world as they knew it. Paul suggested that followers should have their minds and hearts fixed firmly on the coming of the Lord and not stressed or busy with other matters such as marriage. "I want you to be free from anxieties," he wrote (1 Corinthians 7:32). And Jesus' advice to the rich young ruler has been taken literally by many as advice applicable to all followers, although most **exegetes** understand the passage as advice to one person whose possessions totally consumed or possessed him.

Nevertheless, many people felt the need to get rid of everything that distracted them, all earthly goods and human contact, to pursue a relationship with God. As "The **Desert Mother**" Amma Syncletica (c.270–350) said, "Whatever we do or gain in this world, let us consider it insignificant in comparison to the eternal wealth that is to come."[13]

It has been suggested that asceticism became the new martyrdom. Men and women ascetics were called "white martyrs," contrasted with "red martyrs" who shed their blood. During spasmodic periods of persecution, women, and men, were killed simply because they adhered to the Christian faith. One such woman was the newly married young mother Vibia Perpetua (?–202), who, with the slave Felicitas and other new Christians, was put to death in the amphitheater in Carthage. It has been argued that she was a leader in the early church. She left a record of her time in prison, one of the earliest extant writings by a woman.[14]

After the Emperor Constantine (274–337) legitimized Christianity in 313 and the early sporadic persecution of Christians ceased, the church emphasized asceticism and chastity. Many within the Christian communities were disgusted at the increasing materialism in society and opted to find a simpler lifestyle by retreating from the world. Large numbers of women not only became ascetics, but many of them fled into the desert in Egypt, Syria, Persia, and present-day Turkey. In the preface to *The Paradise of the Holy Fathers*, the story of many of these desert monastics, Wallace Budge writes that the women were "as well able to live the life of the solitary as any man."[15]

We hear very little of the women's experiences, however, directly from them. Jerome's letters to several women were collected and preserved, but very few of their letters exist—for example those written by Paula (347–404), head of a women's community in Bethlehem; or Marcella (325–410); or Eustochium (368–c.419) and Blaesilla (c.364–84), two of Paula's daughters. There is one letter from Paula and Eustochium to Marcella that was published as Jerome's *Epistola* XL.VI/46, describing their pilgrimage. The same is true of Olympias (c.381–c.408) and John Chrysostom: we know about Olympias only through Chrysostom's writings. Perhaps even more curious is the example of Macrina (c.330–c.379), the sister of Basil of Caesarea (330–79) and Gregory of Nyssa (c.335–94), who was 12 when she decided to remain a virgin. Although we have a biography of Macrina written by Basil, not one of Gregory's 366 existing letters includes any mention of her. However, *On the Soul and the Resurrection*, written in 380, is thought to be Macrina's sophisticated theology, reported by Gregory.[16]

We know of other women desert ascetics such as Theodora, Sara, and Syncletica (c.270–c.350) because some of their sayings were fortuitously preserved in a collection of the Desert Fathers' sayings, *Apophthegmata Patrum* from the fifth century, and the *Historia Lausiaca* by Palladius of Galatia, Bishop of Helenopolis (363–c.430), a frequent traveler himself to the various monasteries. Palladius suggested that there were 2,975 women living in the desert. However, the historian Margot King, who has spent years researching the "Desert Mothers," easily found, in a short time, 1,100 named women and 900 anonymous female recluses who lived from the sixth to the fifteenth centuries, many of the later recluses in Gaul, Ireland, and Britain. King now believes that there were tens of thousands of such women.[17] She also notes that Christian monastic women existed even before Anthony (252–356), who was considered to be the first monastic hermit, escaped to the desert. He had already placed his sister in a community of virgins, according to Athanasius (c.296–373), Patriarch of Alexandria.

It is thought that male monasteries began with Pachomius (292–348) who founded a **coenobitic** community in 307 in Egypt. His sister Maria went to visit him but he wouldn't see her; he had a hut built for her near his monastery. She became the leader of one of two women's monasteries, along with nine for men, after Pachomius died.

Even though some of these chaste women became well known, building monasteries and being lauded for their asceticism, they still thought of themselves as second-class citizens and temptresses of men, responsible for the downfall of humanity, believing that was their lot in life. When Melania the Elder (350–410) visited the maid-turned-**anchoress**, Alexandra, who shut herself in a tomb in the desert, Melania asked her the reason for her lifestyle. Melania reported that "she called out to me through the opening: 'A man was disturbed in his mind because of me and so that I should not afflict or dishonor him, I chose to go into the tomb alive, rather than cause a soul made in the image of God to lapse.'"[18] Drusiana, mentioned above, committed suicide rather than commit adultery with an insistent male; in the *Acts of Peter*, Peter re-paralyzed his own daughter after he healed her so that she would not be a temptation to a man. In the same **apocryphal** work, there is also the story of a gardener's daughter who died rather than be seduced by a man. When the gardener prayed and his daughter was brought back to life, she was seduced.[19]

Most of these ascetic women accomplished an enormous amount of charitable work in spite of their lifestyle, or perhaps because of their response to Jesus' mandate to feed the hungry and care for the poor. A lot of their energy and attention, though, appears to have been directed toward their own future salvation.

Melania the Elder founded a convent in Jerusalem for about 50 nuns where she lived for 27 years, and a monastery for men. Reputed to be very learned and extremely wealthy, and known for her large collection of books, she was initially praised by Jerome, until he turned against her because of her support of Origen. He tried to expunge his earlier positive comments about her from his writings. Palladius wrote that she read every commentary on the Bible that was ever written, "not casually," but seven or eight times. Originally from Spain, Melania married a proconsul when she was 14 years old, was widowed when she was 22, and afterwards moved to Rome. When the Visigoths invaded the city in 410, Melania and others, including her granddaughter Melania the Younger, fled to Sicily and then to North Africa before continuing to Jerusalem. Later, Melania spent several months in the desert visiting various hermits; often the male ascetics blessed her. When she was 60, she rebuked a young man who washed his hands and feet in the blazing hot sun and rested on a sheepskin. Appalled, she said to him:

> … when I first took upon myself this garb water hath never touched more of my body than the tips of the fingers of my hands, and I have never washed my feet, or my face, or any one of my members. And although I have fallen into many sicknesses, and have been urged by the physicians, I have never consented or submitted myself to the habit of applying water to any part of my body; and I have never lain upon a bed, and I have never gone on a journey to any place reclining on a cushioned litter.[20]

Melania the Younger (c.383–439), reported to be a deacon, established monasteries in Africa and on the Mount of Olives after the deaths of her young children. Like Alexandra, she shut herself up in a box in her cell, but eventually got up and out and went on a pilgrimage to the Holy Land. Then she enclosed herself in a cell for another 14 years before traveling once again.

Married at 13, she and her husband decided to become monastics when she was 20, although her husband was hesitant at first. Both later founded convents and monasteries. She had said to him:

> If you choose to practice asceticism with me according to the fashion of chastity, then I recognize you as master and lord of my life. But if this appears grievous to you, being still a young man, take all my belongings and set my body free, that I may fulfill my desire toward God and become heir to the zeal of my grandmother whose name I also bear. For if God had wished us to have children, He would not have taken away my children untimely.[21]

Melania's wealth was reported to be enormous; she had properties in Sicily, Britain, Iberia, Numidia, Mauritania, and Italy. One of her properties was so large that she reportedly needed a staggering amount of staff—24,000 slaves—to look after it. She sold all the villages she owned around the world giving the money to the church and the poor. She ate once a day—although when she first became an ascetic, she had eaten only once every five days.

Olympias was the superintendent of a monastery in Constantinople, a deaconess-abbess and a major supporter of John Chrysostom, who regularly sought her advice. Widowed at 19, Olympias refused to remarry. The Emperor Theodosius (347–95) wanted her to marry a relative so that he could keep tabs on her money, but she said that she was "unsuited to the conjugal life and was not able to please a man," so Christ the King "freed him, Nebridius [her husband], from the bond and delivered [her] of this burdensome yoke and servitude to a husband, having placed upon her mind the happy yoke of continence." She noted that she was "preserved uncorrupted in flesh and spirit."

Olympias's wealth was also immeasurable. It is said that she donated so much money to the church that in today's currency it would be worth about us$900,000,000. She gave John Chrysostom 10,000 pounds of gold, 20,000 of silver, and all her real estate in Rome, together with the house of the tribune complete with baths and all the buildings near it, a mill, a house near the public baths of Constantinople, another house, and all her suburban properties. She owned all the houses and shops near the church she attended. She also supported other archbishops and bishops financially. Whether this was all part of the millions we do not know, but she evidently still had enough money to found a community of more than 250 deaconesses and virgins in Constantinople before 398; it became a center of prayer and charity and eventually included a hospital and an orphanage. She also bought hundreds of slaves, in order to set them free.

Chrysostom wrote many letters to Olympias while he was in exile as a result of criticizing the Empress Eudoxia (?–404), addressing them, "To my lady, the most reverend and divinely favoured deacon Olympias."[22] Olympias was later exiled and imprisoned herself for supporting Chrysostom. We know that at her request, Chrysostom had ordained three women relatives of hers as deacons, Elisanthia, Martyria, and Palladia, who "bade farewell to the ephereal and empty things of life" according to Jerome. Olympias had been ordained a deacon herself and her 50 chambermaids as well as her relatives, all "adorned with the crown of virginity and practicing the most exalted life which befits the saints." Olympias administered her monastic community herself as long as she could, turning it over to a woman called Marina, and she in turn handed it over to Elisanthia, one of Olympias's relatives. Olympias's garments were the worst that could be found, and the food she ate "was of such an inferior class that … it was rejected even by her servants." It is said that Olympias died in poverty and that at some point her charitable projects were shut down because she refused to support the new bishop who replaced John Chrysostom.[23]

There is an apocryphal story that when she was questioned about her duties "which belong fitly to a man," Olympias responded by inquiring: "When the flock are hungry and there is no shepherd, are the sheep to starve, and haven't women been shepherdess since time began? Is the faith of Christ so weak that it can be administered only by a man?"[24]

Paula's daughter Blaesilla (364–84), who became an ascetic when she was young, had studied Greek and Hebrew. For a while she enjoyed this life, but then she became quite ill. When she recovered, she adopted Jerome's lifestyle, but she soon died, as it was too much for her weakened body. Paula was distraught, but Jerome insisted that she was grieving overly much. Public opinion, however, was against him. Jerome, himself, had lived as a hermit in the desert but he found that lifestyle was not suitable for him. Yet he had no hesitation in encouraging an ascetic way of life for his women friends.

Eustochium (368–419), the oldest daughter of Paula (347–404), went to Bethlehem with Jerome to live in 385, after she and Paula had gone on a pilgrimage together that same year. It was becoming common for both wealthy men and women to travel to the Holy Land as a sign of devotion to God, and also to build monastic communities where they could practice asceticism. Women, then, were assured of multiple blessings because of their "manly" nature as a result of this new life. The church, however, was uneasy about women traveling. As Athanasius the Great (296–373) wrote in his "Second Letter to Virgins," to young women who were saddened when their pilgrimage to the Holy Land was over, "It behooves you to be enshrouded, set apart, and withdrawn in every way, with a steadfast will, and to be sealed up, just as you were sealed up by the Lord at the beginning as a servant." Throughout the centuries, the Church was troubled by women moving freely about as men could do.[25]

For the women who gathered around Jerome, however, every moment of their time was to be focused on God either through physical discomfort or scriptural study. Jerome held classes on the Bible that he called "The Church of the Household." He warned Eustochium not to "go from home to home to visit the daughters of a strange land." Eustochium and Paula supported Jerome financially and helped him translate the Bible from Greek and Hebrew into Latin. All the women around Jerome became so well educated that Augustine of Hippo (354–430) noted that "any old Christian woman was better educated than many a philosopher." One Christian woman called Catherine (?–307) was forced by Emperor Severus II (250–307) to debate 50 university scholars; she was so successful that she converted them all to Christianity, which enraged the emperor so much that he had all the men— and Catherine—killed.[26]

Paula noted the poverty of Bethlehem, contrasting it to the wealth of Rome, where she had been a member of Marcella's group of wealthy ladies who were attempting to follow a life of monastic severity. A high-born woman who had always been carried about by slaves so that her feet would never touch the ground, Paula followed Jerome to Bethlehem by boat as her young children stood weeping on the quay; she was supposedly torn between her love for her children and her love of God. Jerome described her departure:

> The vessel ploughed onwards and all her fellow-passengers looked back to the shore. But she turned away her eyes that she might not see what she could not behold without agony.... No mother, it must be confessed, ever loved her children so dearly.... She overcame her love for her children by her greater love for God.... Making up her mind to dwell permanently in holy Bethlehem ... three years in a miserable hostelry, 'til she could build the requisite cells and monastic buildings.[27]

Jerome quoted Paula as saying, "I desire to depart and be with Christ ... I keep under my body and bring it into subjection; lest that by any means when I have preached to others, I myself should be a castaway." Jerome admired Paula's self-control believing that as bodily appetites were conquered, they were transformed into spiritual appetites. Eventually, however, bodily weakness brought on by incredible abstinence and by redoubled fasting took its toll. Paula was frequently sick but proud that she never entered a bath except when dangerously ill. She also declared that she "must disfigure that (her) face ... now to please Christ." Paula gave away all her money and when she had none left, she borrowed, leaving her daughter Eustochium overwhelmed with a mass of debt.[28]

The male and female monastics in the monasteries that Paula established had their work and meals separately but worshipped together. All the sisters were clothed alike; they used linen only to dry their hands. "Could there be a more splendid instance of self-renunciation than that of this noble lady... [she] gave away so much of her wealth that she reduced herself to the last degree of poverty?" Jerome asked rhetorically. "She lived in vows of religion 5 years in Rome and 20 in Bethlehem." In front of the cavern (where she was buried) was written:

Seest thou here hollowed in the rock a grave,
'Tis Paula's tomb; high heaven has her soul.
Who Rome and friends, riches and home forsook
Here in this lonely spot to find her rest.
For here Christ's manger was, and here the kings
To Him, both God and man, their off'rings made.[29]

Macrina is recognized mostly because of her influence on her two famous brothers, Basil of Caesarea and Gregory of Nyssa. Thought to be the eldest of 10 children, she was incredibly well educated even theologically, which was unusual for a woman at that time. Her father had been an attorney and professor and likely emphasized education for all his children, encouraging Macrina to read Homer, Plato, Demosthenes, and the Greek tragedies as well as what we term the Old Testament, as was customary in boys' education at that time. Around 311, Macrina and her husband fled into the forest to escape persecution, living wild for seven years. Macrina was one of the first women to set up a religious community open to all women in Pontus (now in Turkey) around 355 while she was still in her 20s. Her brother Peter belonged to her community and perhaps other men as well. The convent was surrounded by woods and valleys and reached out to the community around it. A deacon, she taught, preached, and prophesied, and also founded a large hospital with different pavilions for different diseases and living spaces for nurses and physicians. Macrina literally went out to the streets and picked up women who were close to starvation, nursing them back to health. She gave all her money away to the poor as many of the other women did, so that on her deathbed, she had nothing to wear that was suitable; her brother Gregory covered her with his episcopal cloak. Her family's large estates were scattered throughout three provinces, so there must have been great family resources at one time. Macrina had added the name of Thecla to her baptismal name. Gregory wrote of her that, like Thecla, she "went beyond the nature of a woman." It is reported that she said, "The process of healing shall be proportioned to the measure of evil in each of us, and when the evil is purged and blotted out, there shall come in each place to each, immortality and life and honour."[30]

Marcella's father died when she was young, and she herself was forced to marry when she was in her teens. Her husband died in 340 after seven months of marriage, and Marcella rejected other suitors, deliberately going out only with her mother and a train of virgins and widows to discourage male attention. Beautiful and highborn like the other women attracted to Jerome—or perhaps it was the opposite, Jerome was attracted to supportive women—Marcella fasted but in moderation, giving up wine and flesh. According to Jerome, she seemed to be always singing or in private prayer in basilicas. She was apparently the first woman in the West to organize an ascetic community of notably well-to-do women, first in her villa on the prosperous Aventine Hill area in Rome, and then later in a large country residence and property outside the city.

Marcella and the other women in her group gave up their silk clothes, jewelry, and make-up, wearing brown goat's hair robes instead and sleeping on thin mats on the floor, if indeed they did sleep. For they often stayed up at night crying and praying. Jerome wrote extensively about the sin of women's fashionable clothes and adornments. Not only did he object to any such "prostitution" as make-up because this made women "displeasing to God," but he objected to wearing gold and silver because these minerals came from the mines, "deadly laboratories," where prisoners were sent to work. It was said that the women wore hoods "to avoid looking at each other." Often they would preach on the streets against materialism or debate some theological concept.[31]

In 410, Marcella was beaten by invading soldiers and her estate was destroyed. She died soon afterwards. On her death, Jerome wrote to her student Principia:

> How much virtue and intellect, how much holiness and purity I found in her
> I am afraid to say, both lest I may exceed the bounds of men's belief and I
> may increase your sorrow by reminding you of the blessings you have lost …
> whatever I had gathered together by long study, and by constant meditation
> made part of my nature, she tasted, she learned and made her own.[32]

Paula's daughter Eustochium was trained in Marcella's cell. According to Jerome, it was also Marcella "who originated the condemnation of the heretics … who showed how large a number they had deceived … she who called on the heretics in letter after letter to appear in their own defence, especially the Montanists." Jerome believed so highly in Marcella's intellect and abilities that he often referred church elders to her for **hermeneutical** or biblical interpretations. Jerome stayed in her palatial house for three years as he translated the Bible into Latin, and it was in Marcella's house that Jerome met Paula for the first time.[33]

Another well-known wealthy ascetic woman, Fabiola (?–399), converted by Marcella, divorced her husband even though divorce was generally a male prerogative, and traveled to the Holy Land around 395 to study scripture. It was said that she herself was a nurse, physician, surgeon, and teacher. She gave away all her possessions to the poor and was criticized for "robbing her own children."[34]

There is even a story of an eight-year-old girl called Susan from Armenia who ran away with a caravan of Christian pilgrims going to Jerusalem sometime in the fifth century. She had asked her parents to take her to the holy sites but her parents had laughed it off. She went on her own to Gaza to find a desert convent; she stayed there and became a leader of a group of ascetic women. One day, walking among the sand dunes, she found a cave, and refused to go back to her community for three years. "My sisters," she said, "leave me alone. I am with you for all the time; but because the Lord prepared this place for me, so that I might easily live in quietude here, go and stay in peace." The other women, however, regularly brought her food and water. Believing the story real, which it may have been, John of Ephesus (507–586) wrote about her: "This is a woman, but she is stone, and instead of flesh, she is iron." It is thought that she lived in the desert for 25 years.[35]

Amma Syncletica of Alexandria (c.270–350), a third- and fourth-century Desert Mother, well educated and wealthy, gave all her inheritance to the poor, and with her younger sister who was blind lived in a desert crypt among the tombs outside Alexandria as a hermit, although some say she lived beside a river. Soon other women clustered around her. Twenty-seven of her sayings are listed in the *Sayings of the Desert Fathers*; for example: "There are many who live in the mountains and behave as if they were in the town; they are wasting their time. It is possible to be a solitary in one's mind while living in a crowd; and it is possible for those who are solitaries to live in the crowd of one's own thoughts."[36] Syncletica also declared that "according to nature, I am a woman, but not according to my thoughts." Chastity and asceticism had made her "manly."

In *"Virgins of God,"* Susanna Elm writes that women left their families, villages, and communities in search of religious fulfillment in the desert. They did so on their own, undaunted by extremes of nature or fierceness of attacks by humans or demons. In the process, the women "became men" in the strength of their soul and the success of their ascetic achievement, and at times also in their outer appearance. Ascetic women were mothers, teachers, pilgrims, transvestites, and wanderers, but it was in the desert "they became most truly men." One anecdote tells the story of finding a monk dead, and when other desert monks took the body to bury it, they discovered that it was a woman.[37]

The fifth-century Desert Mother Amma Sarah never raised her eyes to look at the river she lived beside for 60 years. She said to the brothers that "it is I who am a man." Some monks of Scetis west of the Nile came and she put out a basket of fruit for them. They left the good fruit and ate the bad—"true monks."[38] Theodora, regarded as the ideal teacher by both the Desert Fathers and the Desert Mothers, is quoted as saying: "Let us strive to enter by the narrow gate. Just as the trees, if they have not stood before the winter's storms cannot bear fruit, so it is with us; the present age is a storm and it is only through many trials and temptations that we can obtain an inheritance in the kingdom of heaven."[39]

Admiring these ascetic women, the bishop and poet Venantius Fortunatus (530–607) wrote this poem for a friend describing the ideal woman:

She, frugal in food, surpassing Eustochium, and, she, abstinent, surpassing Paula,
She recalls the wounds which the leader Fabiola healed
Rivaling Melania in zeal, Blesilla [*sic*] in piety,

Having the strength to rival Marcella in devotion,

She restores Martha in obedience, and Mary in tears,

She, ever awake, wished to imitate Eugenia, she wished to be like Thecla in suffering.

Through these inclinations, she bears everything praised in these women:

I recognize these signs, which having been done previously, I now read.[40]

These are some of the most well known of the women who lived in or near the desert and built monastic communities, but there are many others in fifth and sixth century Gaul especially, who lived a similar ascetic life.

Genovefa (419–512), from an aristocratic family in northern Gaul, decided to remain a virgin and was consecrated with two other young women in Paris. She lived with her mother at home surrounded by other virgins, helping the poor. She was advised by Germanus, Bishop of Paris (c.490–576), to "have faith, my daughter and act manfully."

Radegund/e (520–587), queen of the Franks, is perhaps the best known. She built hospices for needy women, converted her private palace into a hospital, and donated her clothes to charity and wore a hair shirt instead. After an unstable childhood in which she was shunted back and forth between kingdoms depending on who had won the last battle, Clotaire I (497–561), king of the Franks, married her when she was 20, making her one of his six wives. She escaped this unpleasant marriage, founded a monastery for women in Poitiers as well as a leper hospital, and obtained a mass of relics including a fragment of the "True Cross." Bishop Médard of Noyon (456–545) appointed her a deaconess at her request but as he was hesitant to "veil the king's spouse," she entered the **sacristy**, put on monastic garb and proceeded straight to the altar, saying to the "blessed" Médard: "If you shrink from consecrating me, and fear man more than God, Pastor, He will require His sheep's soul from your hand." He obeyed. Radegund studied medicine, looked after the infirm, and ate almost nothing but legumes and green vegetables. She would secretly eat rye or barley bread while others ate cake. An extreme ascetic, she bound her neck and arms with three broad iron circlets, which fettered her body so tightly that they could only be removed with difficulty; her flesh was badly cut. On another occasion, she heated a brass plate in the shape of a cross and pressed it to her body. The abbess Caesaria II, sister or niece of Bishop Caesarius of Arles (471–542), warned against such ascetic practices for very practical reasons: an extreme ascetic might fall ill, need delicacies, and take time away from governing others.[41]

Evidently well educated, Radegund wrote poetry in Latin, and she and her nuns spent their days reading the scriptures, copying manuscripts as well as doing needlework and weaving. Several churches and other sites are named after her. One of the nuns who was educated under her wrote her biography, which was included in *The Acts of the Saints of St. Benoit*. The Roman poet Bishop Fortunatus (c.530–c.600) used to dine with Radegund and the abbess, claiming that they ate all kinds of delicacies surrounded by a profusion of flowers—so her life might not have been all discomfort and deprivation.[42]

Another Frankish queen, Chlothilde (475–545), married another king of the Franks, Clovis (466–511), whom she converted from belonging to a "heretical" sect to participating in mainstream Catholicism. After he died, she retired to an abbey at Tours, becoming involved in court politics. As queen, she had appointed bishops in her territory, and later funded projects for churches and monasteries. Another woman ascetic, Monegundis (?–570), left her husband with his permission and fled to Tours after her daughters died, and there founded a hermitage and later a convent for women.

All these women embraced asceticism. Gregory (538–94), bishop of Tours, noted that "not only men but members of the inferior sex … are not sluggish in fighting the good fight but full of manly vigor." The ascetic lifestyle provided an opportunity for women to escape their second-class position. Sufficient financial resources and perhaps even an aristocratic background certainly helped in their spiritual journeys, although most of them also helped to care for the poor and needy, participating in manual labor. Genovefa took part in the harvesting of the crops. Radegund/e baked bread for the poor, even grinding the flour herself. She swept floors and cleaned toilets.[43]

EARLY "HERETICAL" GROUPS

Several early groups that were declared "heretical" also allowed women great freedom and opportunity in their life and worship.

The Nestorians, who separated in the fifth century over the nature of Christ, allowed deaconesses to "minister the sacred bread and wine" to female communicants; the Monophysites, who also differed on Christ's nature, permitted women to preside over public prayer, to offer incense, and to present the bread and wine at the altar during the liturgy.[44]

FIGURE 2.3   Fresco of women breaking bread, from the catacombs of Priscilla, Rome, Italy. Photo: Bridgeman Photos.

Montanist churches in Asia, Phrygia, Southwest Asia Minor, and North Africa focused on spiritual gifts and visions, and made extensive use of female prophets. Founded by Montanus (fl. second century) with the female prophets Maximilla (?–c.179) and Prisca, high-born women who left their husbands to follow Montanus, these churches valued women's roles. It was written by their critics that women baptized, consecrated the Eucharist, and held the offices of priest and bishop. This happened regularly in the congregation at Pepuza in Phrygia, the home of Montanus. According to Epiphanius, bishop of Salamis, Maximilla, who took over the leadership after Montanus's death, is reported to have claimed that "the Lord sent me as a supporter of this task, forced to do it ... to be a revealer of this covenant, an interpreter of this promise to impart the knowledge of God."

Either Prisca or Quintilla (it is attributed to both) reported having a vision of the resurrected Christ in the form of a woman clothed in a shining robe. "Christ came to me [while I slept]," she reported, "and put wisdom into me and revealed to me that this place is holy. Jerusalem will come down from heaven in this location." Seemingly obsessive in his concerns about sexual relations, in his book *Treatise on Marriage and Remarriage*, the African Church Father Tertullian (c.155–c.240) elaborated on the "Blessings of Continence." He quoted "the holy prophetess" Priscilla as having said that "continence effects harmony of the soul, and the pure see visions and, bowing down, hear voices speaking clearly words salutary and secret."[45]

Tertullian himself was a Montanist early in his career. In the second or third century, he wrote about "a sister who has been favoured with the gifts of revelation." She communed with the angels and with the Lord, she "discern[ed] men's hearts," she obtained "directions for healing." Tertullian claimed that "all her communications are examined with the most scrupulous care, in order that their truth may be probed." He wrote that God was her witness, "and the apostle is a fitting surety that there were to be Spiritual gifts in the Church."

The theologian Hippolytus (170–235), however, referred to Maximilla and Priscilla as "wretched women" who were magnified "above the Apostles and every gift of Grace, so that some of them presume to assert that there is in them something superior to Christ." The Montanist women wrote books, but in 396, an imperial edict ordered all the Montanist writings burnt. Even as late as the ninth century, however, there was a complaint from a patriarch of Constantinople that something needed to be done about the Montanists, so they evidently lasted as a Christian organization for several centuries.[46]

According to Epiphanius, there were seven virgins who prophesied for the Montanists. Critical of several sects and divergent Christian groups, Epiphanius also claimed that the Marcosian women who followed the **Gnostic** Marcus, were told to open their mouths and "say any old thing and you will be prophesying." Bishop Irenaeus (130–202) confirmed that the Valentinian Gnostic Marcus surrounded himself with women whom he allowed in his presence to **consecrate** chalices containing wine. Epiphanius also referred in very negative terms to women bishops, presbyters, and prophets among the "heretical" Pepuzians, Artotyritai, Priscillians, Cataphrygians, and branches of Montanists. Hippolytus spoke of a woman named Marianne who began a Gnostic sect, and Firmilian, bishop of Caesarea Mazaca (?–269), wrote in 265 that a woman was baptizing and celebrating the Eucharist according to the ritual of the church, but the location is unknown.[47]

After he left the Montanists, Tertullian turned against them and spoke about a woman he called a "viper" because she was baptizing men and women. "These heretical women," Tertullian wrote. "How audacious they are. I mean they teach, they preach. They do all kinds of things they shouldn't do."[48]

Another early theologian, Jerome, was ambivalent about women. While he surrounded himself with learned chaste women, he abhorred other women to an incredible degree. He blamed the beginning of most of the groups or sects he considered "heretical" on women:

> It was with the help of the whore Helena that Simon Magus [?–65] founded his sect; troops of women accompanied Nicholas of Antioch, that inventor of pollutions; it was a woman that Marcion [85–160] sent as his precursor to Rome, to undermine the souls of men in readiness for his traps (possibly the prophetess Philoumene); ... Montanus ... used two wealthy noblewomen, Prisca and Maximilla first to bribe and then to subvert many churches; ... it was the resources of Lucilla that helped Donatus [?–c.355] to pervert many people throughout Africa with his filthy version of baptism.[49]

It was a different Helena who helped Simon Magus than Helena (246/50–327/30) the mother of the Emperor Constantine. The latter is credited with building the Church of the Nativity at Bethlehem as well as the Church of the Holy Sepulchre in Jerusalem. She was one of the first pilgrims to tour the Holy Land, and she restored many important Christian sites. There is no record of the Helena who helped Simon Magus or of the Lucilla who helped Donatus, and Montanism and Priscilla (Prisca) and Maximilla have already been mentioned.

Like many of the early Church Fathers, Jerome was at times obsessed with sexuality and this must have affected his relations with women and his attitudes to celibacy. He even set up a scale to determine one's devotion to God. Virginity received a spiritual value of 100, but marriage was worth a spiritual value of only 30.[50] In a letter to Eustochium, Paula's daughter, he wrote about the time he lived in the desert:

> Terrified by the thought of hell, I had condemned myself to this prison, my sole companion being wild beasts and scorpions. Often, however, a chorus of dancing girls cavorted around me. Emaciated, pale, my limbs cold as ice, still my mind boiled with desire. Lust's fires bubbled about me even when my flesh was as good as dead. Completely helpless, I would fling myself at the feet of Jesus, water them with my tears, wiping them with my hair.[51]

Jerome connected fasting to incontinence, which he wrote was especially a problem for women. "Chastity cannot be safe by other means than fasting," he said. He associated food with lust because eating was a bodily appetite:

"Nothing so inflames the body and excites the genital members unless it be undigested food and convulsive belching," he emphasized.[52]

Early Christianity was rife with different theological interpretations and practices, and theologians and ecclesiastics fought and discussed these subtleties, not always amicably, eventually leading to designating certain beliefs "heretical." In the end, heresies are defined by those in power, those who determine orthodoxy of belief. Women appear to have been extremely active in many of the groups considered heretical; and it may be that the acceptance and welcome of women in powerful positions as ecclesiastics in these sects resulted in naming the groups "heretical." In any case, it does show to what great extent women held leading and active roles in a variety of groups in the early Christian Church. It is sometimes difficult, however, to assess what communities and sects not in the mainstream actually practiced and believed, for **heresiologists** often invented the "facts" and developed stereotypes of "heretics," always negative and often scandalous.

As the historian Jennifer Kolpacoff Deane notes, "Heresy is an artificial category designed by authorities who regard themselves as orthodox." The word **heretic** comes from the Greek word *hairesis* or *haireisthai*, meaning "choice"; a heretic, then, is someone who chooses to believe something different. The well-known historian Karen King notes that terms such as orthodoxy and heresy simply indicate who the winners and losers were. "In practice," she notes, "heresy can only be identified by hindsight, instituting the norms of a later age as the standard for the early period." She states that "the logic of the story is circular: the New Testament and the Nicene Creed define orthodox Christianity, not only in the fourth century and beyond, but anachronistically ... as well."[53]

When one reads that an individual or religious group murdered babies and ate them, indulged in promiscuous and deviant sex, and practiced black magic or other such negative rituals, it should raise a red flag, alerting us that it is only the accusation of an opposing faction trying to discredit another group.

FRESCOES

Information about women's activities in the early church can also be gleaned from the frescoes in the catacombs where early Christians often buried their dead.

FIGURE 2.4 Fresco of *orans* or women praying, from the catacombs of Priscilla, Rome, Italy. Photo: Bridgeman Photos.

On the walls in the earliest catacombs in Rome, especially in the Greek Chapel, there are numerous frescoes of women praying with their arms uplifted. These praying women are called *orans*. While a few are male, the figures are overwhelmingly female; they are sometimes in a group, and often by themselves. The catacombs alone contain frescoes depicting at least 200 women praying in this manner. And there are *orans* on *sarcophagi*, rings, *stelae*, plaques, and other artifacts from the second century on. It is not known who they are, but in Corinth, as likely in other centers, women were prominent in the role of "pray-er." In the second century, Polycarp (69–155) proclaimed that the widow's service of prayer was an offering on the altar. According to the Letter to Timothy, widows were to pray without ceasing. The order of virgins was also associated with prayer. There is also a catacomb painting that shows an *orans* standing beside a Eucharistic altar, perhaps assisting at the Eucharist. Whatever the connection, it seems clear that prayer in the church setting was closely associated with women.[54]

In the Domitilla catacombs one can see a painting of the "12 apostles" sitting around Jesus. In the center there is a fresco of a woman praying, but who she was is unknown; the figure has been blacked out. Evidently some destruction of the early frescoes was carried out at the request of two popes—Innocent x (1574–1655) and Clement IX (1600–69). But there is still an unusually large number of frescoes depicting women praying, breaking bread, and featured in Bible stories, and many of the paintings are still in fairly good condition.[55]

FURTHER READING

PRIMARY

Hennecke, Edgar, Wilhelm Schneemelcher, and R. McL. Wilson, eds. *New Testament Apocrypha.* Vol. 1. Translated by R. McL. Wilson. Philadelphia: The Westminster Press, 1959.

Kraemer, Ross S., ed. *Maenads, Martyrs, Matrons, Monastics: A Sourcebook on Women's Religions in the Greco-Roman World.* Philadelphia: Fortress Press, 1988.

MacNamara, Jo Ann, John E. Halborg, and E. Gordon Whately, eds. *Sainted Women of the Dark Ages.* Durham, NC: Duke University Press, 1992.

McLure, M.L., and C.L. Feltoe, eds. and trans. *The Pilgrimage of Etheria.* London: Macmillan Co., 1919.

St. Athanasius of Alexandria. *The Paradise of the Holy Fathers: Volumes 1 & 2.* https://www.ecatholic2000.com/athanasius/untitled-208.shtml.

Wilson-Kastner, Patricia, G. Ronald Kastner, Ann Millin, Rosemary Rader, and Jeremiah Reedy, eds. *A Lost Tradition: Women Writers of the Early Church.* Lanham, MD: University Press of America, 1981.

SECONDARY

Castelli, Elizabeth. "Virginity and Its Meaning for Women's Sexuality in Early Christianity." *Journal of Feminist Studies in Religion* 2, no. 1 (Spring 1986): 61–88.

Davis, Stephen J. *The Cult of St Thecla: A Tradition of Women's Piety in Late Antiquity.* Oxford: Oxford University Press, 2001.

Elm, Susanna. *"Virgins of God": The Making of Asceticism in Late Antiquity.* Oxford: Clarendon Press, 1994.

Kim, Eunjoo Mary. *Women Preaching, Theology and Practice through the Ages.* Cleveland: Pilgrim Press, 2004.

MacDonald, Dennis Ronald. *The Legend and the Apostle: The Battle for Paul in Story and Canon.* Philadelphia: Westminster Press, 1983.

Rossi, Mary Ann. "Priesthood, Precedent and Prejudice: On Recovering the Women Priests of Early Christianity." *Journal of Feminist Studies* 7, no. 1 (1991): 73–94.

Swan, Laura. *The Forgotten Desert Mothers*. New Jersey: Paulist Press, 2001.

Wijngaards, John. *No Women in Holy Orders: The Women Deacons of the Early Church*. Norwich: Canterbury Press, 2002.

Williams, Manon. "From the Holy Land to the Cloister: The Decline of Female Ascetic Pilgrimages in the Early Medieval West (c.350–615)." MA thesis, University of Colorado, 2015.

NOTES

1 "Life of St. Thekla," Antiochian Orthodox Christian Archdiocese of North America.

2 Davis, *The Cult of Saint Thecla*.

3 Apotactics (meaning those who renounce) were ascetics, who rejected marriage and possessions, attempting to live the life of the early Christians. They are mentioned by Epiphanius, bishop of Salamis (c.310–403), in *A Lost Tradition*, ed. Wilson-Kastner et al., 76.

4 Davis, *The Cult of Saint Thecla*.

5 Muir, "Thecla and Friends."

6 Elm, *"Virgins of God,"* 218.

7 Chicago, *The Dinner Party*, 131.

8 Cyprian, "To Pomponius, Concerning Some Virgins," Epistle 61, New Advent.

9 "The Life of St. Nina, Equal to the Apostles, Enlightener of Georgia," *The St. Nina Quarterly*.

10 "The Life of St. Nina, Equal to the Apostles, Enlightener of Georgia."

11 Muir, "Thecla and Friends."

12 *Soliloquies* 1.10, quoted in Muir, "Thecla and Friends."

13 Howard, "Getting Away to It All," 6.

14 "The Martyrdom of Saints Perpetua and Felicitas."

15 Athanasius of Alexandria, *The Paradise of the Holy Fathers*.

16 "Helena, Egeria, Paula, Eustochium, Pega, Bridget, Guthrithyr, Margaret, Isolda, Birgitta, Catherine, Margery, Rose and Julia: The Bible and Women Pilgrims," accessed 24 September 2018, http://www.umilta.net/egeria.html.

17 King, "The Desert Mothers: A Survey of the Feminine Anchoretic Tradition in Western Europe."

18 Swan, *The Forgotten Desert Mothers*, 72.

19 "The Acts of Peter," in *New Testament Apocrypha*, ed. Hennecke et al.

20 Athanasius of Alexandria, *The Paradise of the Holy Fathers*, Chapter XLI, "Of the Holy Woman Melania the Great."

21 Lowther, *The Lausiac History of Palladius*, Chapter LXI, "Melania the Younger."

22 Kraemer, *Maenads, Martyrs, Matrons, Monastics*, 196ff.

23 Kraemer, *Maenads, Martyrs, Matrons, Monastics*, 195ff; Athanasius of Alexandria, *The Paradise of the Holy Fathers*, "Of the Blessed Woman Olympias."

24 Kraemer, *Maenads, Martyrs, Matrons, Monastics*, 134ff.

25 Athenasius as quoted in Williams, "From the Holy Land to the Cloister," 31.

26 Chicago, *The Dinner Party*, 127.

27 Jerome's "Letter to Eustochium" on the death of Paula, in 404.

28 Gail Corrington, "Anorexia, Asceticism and Autonomy," 56f.

29 Kraemer, *Maenads, Martyrs, Matrons, Monastics*; "Macrina the Younger (c.327–90)," *Tentmaker Ministries.*

30 Hammack, "Women of the Early Church"; Turpin, *Women in Church History*, 34f; Elm, *"Virgins of God,"* 41, 205.

31 Kraemer, *Maenads, Martyrs, Matrons, Monastics*, 178; Mar, "The Rebel Virgins and Desert Mothers Who Have Been Written Out of Christianity's Early History"; Tertullian, "On the Apparel of Women."

32 Rebenich, *Jerome.*

33 Kraemer, *Maenads, Martyrs, Matrons, Monastics*, 178.

34 Williams, "From the Holy Land to the Cloister," 29; Chicago, *The Dinner Party.*

35 Mar, "The Rebel Virgins and Desert Mothers"; Swan, "Blessed Hermit Susan," in *The Forgotten Desert Mothers*, 100.

36 Chryssavgis, *In the Heart of the Desert*, 29ff.

37 Elm, *"Virgins of God,"* 271, 281.

38 Kraemer, *Maenads, Martyrs, Matrons, Monastics*, 11.

39 Kraemer, *Maenads, Martyrs, Matrons, Monastics*, 123.

40 Williams, "From the Holy Land to the Cloister," 52.

41 Dolan, "A Revival of Female Spirituality," 52.

42 Macy, "The Ministry of Ordained Women," 21; MacNamara, Halborg, and Whatley, eds., *Sainted Women of the Dark Ages*, 76ff.

43 Williams, "From the Holy Land to the Cloister," 60ff; Brakke, *Demons and the Making of a Monk: Spiritual Combat in Early Christianity*, 194.

44 Meyer, "Ordained Women in the Early Church," 291.

45 Jerome, *Letters*, 133.4, quoted in Cloke, *"This Female Man of God,"* 9.

46 Cloke, *"This Female Man of God,"* 201; Carroll, *The Cult of the Virgin Mary*, 48.

47 Jennings, "Ancient and Medieval References to Montanism."

48 Kraemer, *Maenads, Martyrs, Matrons, Monastics*, 257; Bell, "A Royal Nun in the Sixth Century in France," in *Women: From the Greeks to the French Revolution*, 100.

49 Deane, *A History of Medieval Heresy and Inquisition*.

50 Deane, *A History of Medieval Heresy and Inquisition*, 2, 8; Epiphanius, *Panarion* 49.1; Jennings, *Ancient and Medieval References to Montanism*; Smith and Wace, eds., *A Dictionary of Christian Biography*, 939; Tertullian, "Treatise on Marriage and Remarriage," 10f.

51 Pederson, *The Lost Apostle*, 215; Torjesen, "The Early Christian Orans," 42, 51.

52 As quoted in Marjorie M. Malvern, *Venus in Sackcloth*, 71.

53 "#Refo Thursday," *Christian History Institute*, 10 August 2017.

54 King, *The Gospel of Mary of Magdala*, 160.

55 Corrington, "Anorexia, Asceticism and Autonomy," 55.

Chapter 3

THE RISE OF THE VIRGIN MARY AND THE DEVOLUTION OF MARY MAGDALENE

AROUND 47 BCE, BEFORE Herod the Great ruled over Judea, Joachim, a wealthy and pious farmer who lived in the country of Jericho and owned vast flocks of sheep and herds of cattle, married Anna, the daughter of another wealthy family who lived beside the Sea of Galilee. Anna and Joachim were so rich that they gave a third of all their revenues to charity, a third to the temple, and if anyone knocked on their door for alms, they gave to them, too. But they were not happy. Anna and Joachim were not able to conceive a child. It was thought that they must be out of favor with God.

One day, when everyone was going to the temple for a great festival, Joachim was not allowed in. The High Priest Reuben barred his way. "It is not fitting for you to offer your gifts," he said, "because you have begotten no offspring in Israel." Humiliated and angry, Joachim went off to the hill country with his shepherds and herdsmen and pitched a tent where he fasted and grieved. Anna, too, was sunk in despair, abandoned and shamed. In her grief she cried out:

Woe to me, who begot me,
What womb brought me forth?
For I was born as a curse before them all and before the children of Israel,
And I was reproached and they mocked me and thrust me out of the Temple of the Lord,
Woe is me ...[1]

God took pity on them, for an angel of the Lord came to Anna and said, "Anna, Anna, the Lord has heard your prayer. You shall conceive and bear, and your offspring shall be spoken of in the whole world." Happily, Anna replied, "As the Lord my God lives, if I bear a child, whether it be male or female, I will bring it as a gift to the Lord my God, and it shall serve Him all the days of its life."

The angel went to Joachim with the good news, too. Thus it was that they met and kissed at the Golden Gate, with this one act conceiving a girl child, Mary, assuring that child was free from the stain of original sin.[2]

When Mary was three, Anna and Joachim took her to the Jewish temple to stay and be taught as they had promised—or so the story goes, for girls would never have been kept in its precincts. There, she was honored as the one who would spin and weave the purple cloth for the curtains of the sanctuary. When Mary was 12, the priests were worried that she would pollute the temple if she stayed after she matured, so they sought a husband for her. The elderly Joseph was as amazed as anyone else when he was chosen by the Lord to be her partner. However, he took her to his home to be guarded by five virgins, Rebecca, Zipporah, Suzanna, Abigail, and Cael. They kept her company while Joseph was away as an **itinerant** carpenter.[3] It wasn't long until the angel of the Lord visited Mary with the news that she would bear a son (Luke 1:35–37): "The Holy Spirit will come upon you, and the power of the Most High will overshadow you; therefore the child to be born will be called holy; he will be called Son of God. And now your relative Elizabeth in her old age has also conceived a son; and this is the sixth month for her who was said to be barren. For nothing will be impossible with God."

When Joseph returned from his six-month journey, he found Mary pregnant. He was most upset. But the angel of the Lord came to him also and he knew then that Mary's child was God's. Mary's first-born, Jesus, was conceived without sin, without any physical contact between her and her husband Joseph.

This story of Mary's childhood is told only in second- to fourth-century apocryphal books considered spurious and not accepted into the canon. The story does, however, indicate the beginning of the belief in the immaculate conception of Mary. This concept first appeared in the Roman Catholic Church's formal liturgy centuries later in 1854 although a commemorative feast had begun in 1476.[4]

There are not many references to Mary in the four canonical gospels for such an important person, except in the stories of Jesus' birth. The most

FIGURE 3.1 The dedication of the Virgin Mary as a young child, a fresco painted by Giovanni da Milano (1325–70) in the Opera di Santa Croce, Firenze (Florence). Photo: Opera di Santa Croce.

elaborate account of Jesus' birth in the New Testament is found in the late first- or early second-century Gospel of Luke beginning with the pregnancy of Elizabeth, Mary's cousin, and then Mary's own pregnancy. Luke mentions Mary 12 times, the most of all the four gospels, but most of these references are in the infancy narrative where she is pictured as submissive, obedient, and self-sacrificing. There are references to her as Jesus' mother when she and Joseph took Jesus to the temple to be circumcised and then Mary and Joseph went to be purified (Luke 2:21–24); and later when Jesus was 12 and his mother and father found him in the temple listening to the teachers (Luke 2:41–51).

The Gospel of Matthew mentions Mary by name, again mostly in the story of Jesus' birth (Matthew 1, 2); once when Jesus rejected his own family in favor of his disciples (Matthew 12:46–50); and once when neighbors, listening to Jesus in his home town, were amazed that he was Mary and Joseph's son (Matthew 13:54–57)—not a good reflection on Mary and Joseph! But as Jesus himself said, "Prophets are not without honor except in their own country and in their own house": "Where did this man get this wisdom and these deeds of power? Is this not the carpenter's son? Is not his mother called Mary? And are not his brothers James and Joseph and Simon and Judas? And are not all his sisters with us? Where then did this man get all this?"

There are no birth narratives in the Gospels of Mark and John, and so mention of Mary in these gospels is very limited. The earliest gospel, the Gospel of Mark, only mentions Mary once by name in a story similar to the above, when Jesus amazes his neighbors in his hometown (Mark 6:1–6), and refers to her once when she and Jesus' siblings visited Jesus, but he refused to see them, noting that his followers were his real mother and brothers, and not his birth mother and siblings (Mark 3:31–35). The Gospel of John refers to her twice, once at the wedding in Cana where Jesus turned water into wine after Mary told the servers to listen to him and do as he said (John 2:1–12), and once at the foot of the cross where Jesus said to his mother, "Woman, here is your son," and to the Beloved Disciple, "Here is your mother" (John 19:26–27). In the New Testament Acts of the Apostles, Mary was gathered together with other disciples before the coming of the Holy Spirit after the death of Jesus (Acts 1:14).

In their study of Mary in the New Testament, Raymond Brown and other contemporary scholars noted a development in the depiction of Mary from the early Gospel of Mark to the later Gospel of Luke, "from the negative estimation of Mark to the positive one of Luke, with Matthew representing the middle term." However, it was centuries before her "elevation" was complete. The writer-psychologist Michael Carroll points out that popular devotion to Mary really only became widespread in the latter part of the fifth century, and from then onward, there was a steady increase in the Mary cult. Although Mary doesn't appear in the Easter morning stories in the four canonical gospels, by the sixth century when her cult was developing, the apocryphal *Acts of Thaddeus* claimed that Mary was the first to see the risen Christ, giving Mary primacy even over the male disciples.[5]

Early apocryphal writings from Egypt told of Mary's assumption into heaven, but these stories didn't reach the West until the late fifth century and they were condemned by Pope Gelasius I (?–496). In one story from *Pseudo-John the Evangelist*, "The Falling Asleep of Mary," Mary's body was carried away by angels to be preserved until the general resurrection. Another tale from *Pseudo-Melito*, the "Transitus Mariae," claimed that her body was carried to heaven after being resurrected by Jesus.[6]

John Damascene (676–749), a Syrian monk, reported that a similar story had been told in the fifth century at the Council of Chalcedon (451): in this version, Mary had died in the presence of the apostles, but when they opened her tomb they found it empty. The belief then spread that Mary had been taken up bodily into heaven. About the same time as that Council, an ancient hymn about Mary called the Akathist Hymn or *Akathistos* to the Most Holy Mother of God, referred to her story in 12 lengthy stanzas:

> The children of the Chaldees
> Seeing in the Virgin's hands him whose hands made men,
> And knowing him as Lord
> … cried out to her who is blessed:
> Hail! Mother of the unsetting Star.
> Hail! Splendor of the Mystic Day.…[7]

The Church Fathers and other early ecclesiastics weighed in about Mary. An Arabian group considered heretical, the Collyridians, who ordained women as priests and who persisted into the late **Middle Ages**, offered sacrifices of cakes to the goddess Mary. It is rumored that the group may have begun with the leadership of the historical Mary or it may be a remnant of the ancient Goddess religion. In the fourth century, in response to these women who worshipped Mary, Bishop Epiphanius said, "Let Mary be held in honor. Let the Father, Son, and Holy Spirit be adored, but let no one adore Mary."

Ambrose, bishop of Milan, agreed. "Mary," he said, "was the temple of God, not the God of the temple. And therefore he alone is to be worshipped who is working in his temple."[8]

Jerome, Augustine, and Ambrose all considered Mary the prime example of virginity. Jesus' siblings, however, were a problem that needed to be solved. Jerome suggested that Joseph was only the token husband of Mary, that Jesus' brothers (and presumably his sisters) were in fact his cousins, the children belonging to Mary, the wife of Cleophas. Others suggested that Jesus' siblings were earlier children of Joseph. John Chrysostom argued that if Mary had other children, Jesus wouldn't have had to entrust her care to the Beloved Disciple when he was dying on the cross; her children would have looked after her. In a book from the sixth or seventh century, *The History of Joseph the Carpenter*, Jesus is depicted as speaking of his mother as "virgin undefiled." Even as early as the fourth century most of the Church Fathers supported the concept of Mary's perpetual virginity and it was enshrined in church doctrine by the seventh century. The idea is still debated. The contemporary American evangelist and Baptist minister John Ankerberg points out that the Greek words for brother and sister as sibling are the precise words used in the Gospels when they refer to Jesus' siblings, and different words are used in other places in the New Testament Gospels when referring to cousins and kinsmen.[9]

The Catholic Church believed that Mary brought several benefits to Christian society. Irenaeus (130–202), bishop of Lugdunum in Gaul, suggested that Mary's obedience to God cancelled the disobedience of Eve in the opening book of Genesis in the Old Testament when she picked the apple from the tree; Mary made up for Eve's great sin. "For what the virgin Eve had bound fast through unbelief, this did the virgin Mary set free through faith…. Mary has become the cause of salvation, both to herself and the human race." This concept was later enshrined in the 1566 *Catechism* of the Council of Trent.

Cyril, bishop of Alexandria (378–444) attributed even more benefits to Mary:[10] "Hail Mary, Mother of God, majestic common-treasure of the whole world, the lamp unquenchable, the crown of virginity, the scepter of orthodoxy, the indissoluble temple, the dwelling of the Illimitable, Mother and Virgin … through whom Angels and Archangels rejoice, devils are put to flight … and the fallen creature is received up into the heavens."[11]

Arguments about just who Mary was, however, were more about the nature of Christ than about Mary. Should she be *Christotokos* or *Theotokos?*

Christ-bearer or God-bearer? In the end she became known as *Theotokos*, because the baby she bore in Bethlehem possessed a human nature mysteriously joined to the eternal nature of God. To describe her otherwise would have denied the full divinity of Jesus.[12]

From the twelfth century on, Mary became even more important in the lives of ordinary Catholics, and in the theology and practices of the church. Cathedrals were built in her honor, such as the Cathedral of Our Lady of Chartres, begun in 1145 although construction lasted for 16 years. Artists painted every aspect of her known and apocryphal life, focusing on the annunciation of the angel telling Mary that she would bear a son; the birth of Jesus; the flight of Joseph, Mary, and Jesus to Egypt to avoid Herod's wrath; and the crucifixion. There were illuminated manuscripts, prayer books, feast days, and fanciful legends. Mary herself was often depicted reading a book, likely the Bible, indicating her dedication and faith. One bishop complained that by the Middle Ages, Mariology had reached such heights that "in the thirteenth century, God changed sex."[13]

After the late Middle Ages, Mary became the representative of the church in heaven to whom prayer could be addressed, becoming a "Mediatrix," taking over some of her son's duties as she was invoked for healing and protection. However, a fragment of a prayer has been discovered from even before this, from the third or fourth century, perhaps the earliest prayer asking for Mary's intercession: "We flee to you for protection, O Holy Mother of God. In our needs do not disdain our prayer, but save us at all times from all dangers." The **rosary** was developed in the thirteenth century, a group of guided meditations called "Mysteries" on the lives of Christ and his mother, directing prayers to Mary. Even John Wycliffe (1330–84), one of the major forerunners of the sixteenth-century Protestant Reformation, said it would be "impossible that we should obtain the reward of heaven without the help of Mary."[14] The Reformer Martin Luther (1483–1546) feared Christ as a judge but Mary was his "mercy-seat" and so as a young man, he prayed to her to help him decide on his vocation.[15]

A late medieval story illustrates this easier access to Mary. In a vision, Brother Leo saw two ladders, a red ladder with Jesus at the top and a white ladder with his mother, Mary, at the top. When someone tried to climb the red ladder they fell back, but when they climbed the white ladder, Mary stretched out her hand to the person and they climbed quickly to heaven.[16]

Marian associations were formed—the first one the "Sodality of Our Lady" founded by the Jesuits in 1563; Marian Congresses were held around the

FIGURE 3.2 Mary, mother of Jesus, "The Virgin of the Paradise" (Virgem do Paraiso), a fourteenth-century ivory triptych from the Evora Cathedral Museum, Evora, Portugal. Photo: Courtesy of the Museum.

world; pilgrimages were made to Marian shrines. The policies of the Roman Catholic Counter-Reformation encouraged devotion to Mary, especially on the part of the Jesuits. Mary was praised for her charity, prudence, humility, patience, obedience, compassion, purity, truth, modesty, and poverty, mostly passive characteristics.[17]

Most medieval non-orthodox religious communities, though, denied the efficacy of Mary. In his study of the cult of Mary in medieval "heresies," the psychologist and writer Michael Carroll notes that the Cathars, the Waldensians, the Lollards, and the Hussites, groups that will be examined later, all denied that Mary had any intercessory power. Carroll notes that the Mary cult has been stronger in some parts of Europe than in others; it is especially intense in France and Italy, where women are more often found in the home as housewives than in careers outside the home.[18]

In 1950, Pope Pius XII (1876–1958) defined the dogma of the Assumption of the Blessed Virgin Mary into heaven, "where she is present in soul and body reigning, together with her only Son, amid the heavenly choirs of angels and Saints." He noted that it had been almost a century since Pius IX (1792–1878) proclaimed and defined the dogma that the great Mother of God had been conceived without any stain of original sin.

Then in 1954, Pope Pius XII proclaimed the Queenship of Mary in his *Ad Caeli Reginam* **encyclical**. Noting that he did not wish to proclaim a "new truth" he argued that Mary's queenly dignity was already found in ancient documents of the church and the "books of the sacred liturgy." He mentioned St. Ephrem (306–73), a Syrian deacon who prayed to Mary as "Majestic and Heavenly Maid, Lady, Queen"; St. Gregory of Nazianzus (329–90), archbishop of Constantinople, who called Mary "the Mother of the King of the Universe"; and the Roman Christian poet, Prudentius (348–413) who wrote that Mary had brought forth God as man, and even as Supreme King. By 1956, according to Pius XII, "the Most Blessed Virgin Mary was so indissolubly associated with Christ ... that our salvation proceeded from the love and sufferings of Jesus Christ intimately joined with the love and sorrows of His Mother." He noted that Mary reigned "with a mother's solicitude over the entire world"[19]

While Mary the Mother was the recipient of such worldwide devotion, another biblical Mary, Mary Magdalene (c.10 BCE–c.74), was being held up as the penitent prostitute *par excellence*. Her name graced penitential facilities such as the church-run prison-like Magdalene Laundries in Ireland, Australia, Canada, and England where thousands of girls and young women who had

FIGURE 3.3 The Magdalene Laundry on Stanhope St. in Dublin, Ireland, advertised as an "Industrial Training School for Orphans and Children of Respectable Parents," run by the Sisters of Charity with contracts from the state, forced girls and young women to work 12 hours a day, sometimes incarcerating them for life. Photo: News Dog Media.

been raped, girls who were too pretty "for their own good," single mothers, and other "wayward" women were incarcerated, often for life, under the pretense of being reformed. These laundries operated until the late twentieth century.[20]

But it wasn't always that way. Mary Magdalene was the most important woman in the Gospels of Mark, Matthew, and John, in that she was the first to see the resurrected Christ, and the first to be commissioned to tell all the others the "Good News" of Jesus' resurrection.

In Mark (16:1–11), Mary Magdalene, Mary the mother of James, and Salome found the stone rolled away in front of Jesus' tomb on Easter morning with a young man in a white robe sitting inside. He commanded the women to go and tell the other disciples that Jesus was risen. In the original ending to the Gospel, the women said nothing for they were very afraid. In an additional short ending, the women did tell the other disciples. In a later longer ending, Jesus appeared to Mary Magdalene alone who then told the other disciples, but because she was a woman, they did not believe her. Women were simply not qualified to be witnesses under Judaic law.

In the Gospel of Matthew, the story is similar. Mary Magdalene and the "other" Mary encountered an angel dressed in white at the tomb who commissioned them to tell the rest of the disciples that Jesus was "raised."

On the way to share the news, they met Jesus who spoke to them and again asked them to go and tell the rest of the disciples, a double commission (Matthew 28:1–10).

In the Gospel of John, the story became more involved and even more biased in Mary Magdalene's favor. Mary Magdalene went alone to the tomb and seeing the stone rolled away, ran to tell Simon Peter and the Beloved Disciple that Jesus' body had gone. Peter and the Beloved Disciple ran to the tomb, but then left. Mary stayed, weeping, and saw a man whom she supposed to be the gardener, but who turned out to be Jesus. As she went to embrace him, Jesus told her not to "hold on to me" because he had not yet ascended to the Father, and asked her to tell the other disciples.

The "Easter" story in Luke is somewhat different. Although Luke has more references to women than any of the other three Gospels, he was actually more supportive of the male disciples than of the women around Jesus. In fact, we begin to see what appears to be a leadership controversy, some sort of tension between Mary Magdalene and Simon Peter. Brilliantly analyzed by Ann Graham Brock in her book *Mary Magdalene*, the references to Peter are more positive in this Gospel than in the other three, and Mary Magdalene plays a subordinate role rather than the primary one she had in Mark, Matthew, and John. Mary Magdalene is not commissioned, and neither does she meet the risen Christ. Peter becomes the first to meet the resurrected Jesus.

The non-canonical material available displays competition and even outright hostility between Mary Magdalene and Peter. In the *Gospel of Thomas* from the first or second century, Peter wanted to expel Mary Magdalene from their group: "Let Mary leave us," Peter commanded, "because women are not worthy of life," but Jesus responded, "Look I myself shall lead her so that I will make her male in order that she too may become a living spirit." As has been seen in the lives of the ascetics, women could become as men if they denied their sexuality and lived ascetic and frugal lives.[21]

In the early Gnostic *Gospel of Mary*, Mary Magdalene was praised by Christ in a vision given only to her. Peter asked her to tell them what the Savior had said, only to attack her afterwards. Levi defended Mary, noting that Peter was acting like a rival. "Your hot temper is always with you," he told Peter, "and now you are questioning the woman as though an adversary to her." Peter asked, "Did he (Jesus) really speak with a woman without our knowledge, not openly? Are we to turn about and all listen to her?" And again in the third-century Gnostic *Pistis Sophia*, Peter complained about Mary Magdalene: "My Lord we are not able to suffer this woman who takes

FIGURE 3.4 Mary Magdalene instructs the 11 male disciples after Jesus' death. Photo from the St. Alban's Psalter. Dombibliothek Hildesheim, HS St. God. 1 (Property of the Basilica of St. Godehard, Hildesheim), Germany, p. 51.

the opportunity from us, and does not allow anyone of us to speak but she speaks many times." In the *Questions of Mary*, Mary Magdalene was so put down by Peter that she was reduced to tears. At one point in *Pistis Sophia*, Mary Magdalene expressed her fear of Peter: "My Lord," she said to Jesus, "my mind is ever understanding, at every time to come forward and set forth the solution … but I am afraid of Peter, because he threatened me and hates our sex."[22]

Also in the *Gospel of Mary*, after He had risen, Jesus sent Mary Magdalene to find the 11 disciples, "those wandering orphans," to bring them back from the banks of the Jordan where they had taken up their fishing nets again and were no longer fishers of men. Jesus told her to say to them that "it is your brother that calls you." Or if they refused to come back, she was to say, "It is your master," and if they refused that, she must say, "It is your Lord."[23]

In many of the apocryphal books, Mary was described as the Beloved Disciple; she was the one that Jesus loved most of all. In the *Gospel of*

Philip, written about 250, we read that "there were three who walked with the Lord at all times: Mary his mother, and her sister, and Magdalene, the one who was called his companion.... [But the Lord loved] her more than [all] the disciples [and used to] kiss her [often] on her [lips]." Some of the male disciples were jealous of Mary Magdalene: "Why do you love her more than all of us?" they asked Jesus. As Peter had said in the *Gospel of Mary*, "Sister, we know that you have been loved extensively by the Savior as no other woman."

The theologian Ramon Jusino makes an interesting and credible case that the Gospel of John was actually written by Mary Magdalene and later redacted to make it more acceptable, to make it look as though it were written by a man. He posits that Mary Magdalene was indeed the Beloved Disciple and the leader of the Johannine community. In those instances where reference is made to Mary Magdalene in the original Gospel of John before it was edited, the references were changed to "another disciple" thus making some sentences somewhat awkward.[24]

In the *Dialogue of the Savior*, 14 references to an individual disciple, or one-third of all the references, are directed to Mary Magdalene, noting that "she spoke this word as a woman who understood completely." Several times in *Pistis Sophia*, Jesus congratulated Mary Magdalene on her theological understanding and spiritual maturity as compared to the more obtuse male disciples:

> Miriam (Mary Magdalene), the blessed one, whom I will complete in all the mysteries of the height, speak openly, you are she whose heart is more directed to the kingdom than all your brothers.... Now it happened when Jesus heard these words he said: Excellent, Miriam, the blessed one, who will inherit the whole kingdom of the Light.[25]

Whatever the reasons for the tension between Peter and Mary Magdalene—because Mary Magdalene was a woman, because Jesus had a special relationship with her, or because she was especially intelligent and learned—there is no doubt that Mary Magdalene held primacy as a disciple in three canonical gospels and in many of the apocryphal works. She became known as the *apostolorum apostola*, the "Apostle to the Apostles," encouraging the other disciples when they were stymied or afraid, and teaching them when they failed to understand. "Do not weep, and do not grieve, and do not doubt; for his grace will be with you completely and will protect you," she told the others.[26] In the

Sophia of Jesus Christ, Mary Magdalene was one of seven women and 12 men gathered to listen to the Savior. At the end of his speech, he told them, "I have given you authority over all things as children of light," and they went forth to preach the gospel. In actual fact, in the ruins of house-churches from the third century, carved into plaster walls and in frescoes and on wooden doors from the first to the third centuries, one can still see Mary Magdalene with a torch in her hand, leading the others. By the eleventh and twelfth centuries, there were hymns that referred to her as *apostola*.[27]

We need to ask, then, what would the history of the Christian Church have looked like if Mary Magdalene had won over Peter?

It is also important to note that Mary Magdalene was *never* described as a prostitute or any other kind of "fallen" woman in any of the early gospels or supplemental materials. In 591, however, Pope Gregory the Great (?–604), preached a **sermon** identifying a composite Mary Magdalene as the penitent sinner who washed Jesus' feet and dried them tenderly with her hair, the woman taken in adultery (John 7:53–8:11), and Mary of Bethany; however, it has also been said that it was Odo, the second abbot of Cluny (878–942), in the tenth century who melded them together. Perhaps it was confusing because there were just too many "Marys" in the biblical stories. Someone has calculated that the name Mary is found 51 times in the New Testament.

In the sixteenth century, the theologian and biblical scholar Jacques Lefèvre d'Etaples (1455–1536) separated Mary Magdalene from the women prostitutes but he was excommunicated for that "heresy." It was only in 1969 that the Vatican officially corrected Gregory, sorting out the Marys that Gregory had identified as one, separating them from each other and from the penitent sinner. But by then Mary Magdalene had been irrecoverably identified as a sinner, if a penitent one. Her sin, of course, had been identified as sexual; the seven demons supposedly expelled from her could have been any illness, but they were considered to be of a sexual nature. It has even been suggested that the reason Jesus told Mary Magdalene not to touch him after she met him resurrected from the grave was that she was not worthy; she was the second Eve, guilty of sin.

Mary Magdalene also became mixed up with Mary of Egypt (344–421), who had been a prostitute for 12 to 17 years before she was converted and transformed, becoming a hermit in the desert for another 47 years living on roots, water, and two loaves of bread. It may not have helped either that Mary Magdalene was from Magdala, called Tarichea in Jesus' time, a town rich in trades and fishing. The historian Josephus (37–100) claimed that there were 40,000 inhabitants and a fleet of 230 fishing boats there. It had a bad reputation because of its wealth and consequent corruption. The town of Capernaum was close by; both were towns on the lakeside where Jesus often preached. It is interesting that Mary Magdalene was the only woman mentioned among Jesus' followers who was not characterized by a relationship to a male and was therefore likely unmarried. It may be that this was threatening to later church theologians.[28]

Rumors and legends built up around Mary Magdalene, as they did about all the major disciples. She was from a wealthy family; too much wealth had led her to a life of debauchery. Or she had been going to marry John the Evangelist or did marry him in the wedding at Cana, but John left her to become a disciple of Jesus, and in despair and anger, Mary Magdalene began to live "loosely." But she reformed after she met Jesus.

After the resurrection of Jesus, Mary Magdalene; Mary Jacobe, Jesus' aunt; Mary Salome, the mother of the apostles James the Great and John; Lazarus, the brother of Mary; Martha of Bethany; Maximian of the 72 apostles sent out at one point by Jesus; and Sarah, an Egyptian servant of Mary Jacobe; or some of them, depending on the version of the story, were put in a boat without sails or a rudder. However, they successfully made it to an island at the mouth of the Rhone River where Mary Magdalene began her conversion of the people of the French province of Provence, preaching and effecting miracles, eventually dying in a cave on a hill, La Sainte-Baume, where she lived for 30 years. She was given the Eucharist by angels as her only food. After her death, her remains were moved in the ninth century to Constantinople, and later to Rome, and then to France, where two churches claimed to house her body; or she went to preach in Rome, as was claimed in the *Gospel of Nicodemus*, chapter 11. Later she was said to have worked as a missionary at Ephesus and lived to be 84.[29]

Whichever version, Mary Magdalene has never lost the taint of being accused of prostitution. Paintings, festivals, statues, movies, musicals, novels, stained glass windows, and frescoes have all reflected a strong cult around her. Generally she can be recognized by her long red-gold hair and her scarlet gown—not so much because of her "sin," but because of the charity or love of God who forgave her. By the late Middle Ages, 200 churches had been dedicated to her and she was the first female saint to have a college named after her at Oxford. She has been named the patron saint or guardian of scent-makers, glove-makers, seamstresses, coiffeurs, shoe-makers, wool-weavers, drapers, and wine-producers, among other artisans. But she has always been

FIGURE 3.5 Mary the mother of Jesus reads, sitting on a donkey, while Joseph walks, carrying the baby Jesus on their flight to Egypt. From a Book of Hours, c.1475. Photo: Bibliothèque Royal Albert 1er, Brussels, MS IV 315, fol. 30. This theme was repeated in other paintings; for example, Mary reclines with a book while Joseph rocks the swaddled babe in an early fifteenth-century Northern French Book of Hours at Walters Art Gallery, Baltimore, United States, MS 10.290, fol. 69.

depicted as a penitent, and even language has been shaped by her supposed repentance: *maudlin* in French, from Magdalen, denotes tearfulness in English. Perhaps it is easier to relate to a reformed sinner than to a saint.[30]

The Virgin Mary, on the other hand, has always been a saint. Writing in *The Woman's Bible*, even the feminist Elizabeth Cady Stanton (1815–1902) felt that the Virgin Mary should not be criticized as an ordinary mortal, even though many of the early theologians had some harsh words to say about her. The Virgin Mary, Stanton agreed, had rightful authority over Jesus, but Archbishop Theophylact (1055–1107) criticized her for "vainglory," Tertullian accused her of "ambition," and St. Chrysostom said she was impious and disbelieving. And yet, Stanton wrote, "it ill becomes those who believe that she was the mother of God" to criticize her as they would another. [31]

Most recently at the 1959 Church Council Vatican II, however, Pope John XXIII (1881–1963) insisted that "the Madonna is not happy when she is placed before her son." The Pope warned against excesses in Marian devotion: to "equally avoid the falsity of exaggeration on the one hand and the excess of narrow-mindedness on the other." The result of this pronouncement was a near-cessation in Catholic preaching about Mary and fewer devotions in her honor. Statues of her disappeared from churches; rosaries were put away; gone, to a degree, was the uncomfortable scapular—the square piece of woolen cloth worn on the body, hanging both on the chest and the back, assuring certain benefits such as a speedy release from purgatory. Women who had found access to Mary easier than to Christ felt the loss. And many mourned the vanishing feminine face of God. Other women, especially Protestants, had realized that the concept of a virgin mother, perpetual or not, was a useless and impossible stereotype. The historian Marina Warner notes that this concept of Mary often resulted in a "hopeless yearning and inferiority for women."[32]

FURTHER READING

PRIMARY

Daley, Brian E., ed. and trans. *On the Dormition of Mary, Early Patristic Homilies.* Crestwood, NY: St. Vladimir's Seminary Press, 1998.

Jacobus de Voragine/Varagine. *Medieval Sourcebook: The Golden Legend*, Vol. 4, translated by William Caxton, 1275. First Edition 1483. Reprint, London: J.M. Dent & Sons, Temple Classics, 1900.

Mother Superior Lydia of the Convent of Portaïtissa. *Selected Acathistos Hymns in Honour of the Theotokos*, translated by Guram Kochibrolashvili and Marijcke Tooneman. The Hague: Gozolov Books, 2011.

"The Role of the Blessed Virgin Mary, Mother of God, in the Mystery of Christ and the Church." In *The Documents of Vatican II, VIII*, edited by Walter M. Abbott, S.J., translated by the Very Rev. Msgr. Joseph Gallagher, 85–96. New York: The America Press, 1966.

SECONDARY

Brock, Ann Graham. *Mary Magdalene, the First Apostle: The Struggle for Authority*. Cambridge, MA: Harvard University Press, 2003.

Brown, Raymond E., Karl P. Donfried, Joseph A. Fitzmyer, and John Reumann, eds. *Mary in the New Testament*. Philadelphia: Fortress Press, 1978.

Carroll, Michael P. *The Cult of the Virgin Mary*. Princeton: Princeton University Press, 1986.

Haskins, Susan. *Mary Magdalen: Myth and Metaphor*. London: Pimlico, 2005.

Horton, Adey. *The Child Jesus*. New York: The Dial Press, 1975.

Jansen, Katherine Ludwig. *The Making of the Magdalen: Preaching and Popular Devotion in the Later Middle Ages*. Princeton: Princeton University Press, 2000.

Jusino, Ramon K. "Mary Magdalene: Author of the Fourth Gospel?" Mwanza, Tanzania: St. Augustine University of Tanzania, 1998.

King, Karen L. *The Gospel of Mary of Magdala: Jesus and the First Woman Apostle*. Santa Rosa, CA: Polebridge Press, 2003.

Meighan, Janice. "Mary Magdalene, Partner or Prostitute: An In-depth Study of the Transformation of Mary Magdalene in Church History." York University, Toronto, March 2005.

Pagels, Elaine. *The Gnostic Gospels*. New York: Random House, 1979.

Warner, Marina. *Alone of All Her Sex: The Myth and Cult of the Virgin Mary*. New York: Alfred A. Knopf, 1976.

NOTES

1   Horton, *The Child Jesus*, 30ff, as found in the non-canonical *Protevangelium of James* written around 150 to early 300s, and in the early *Gospel of Pseudo-Matthew* with accretions from the Middle Ages.

2 Horton, *The Child Jesus*, 32ff.

3 Horton, *The Child Jesus*, 57ff.

4 Jeffrey, "Where'd That Come From?" 18.

5 Brown et al., eds., *Mary in the New Testament*, 266.

6 Ruether, *Mary: The Feminine Face of the Church*, 61.

7 Memling, "Did You Know?" 3, Stanza 9. Ur of the Chaldees is thought to have been the birthplace of Abraham.

8 Jeffrey, "Hail Mary," 20; Carroll, *The Cult of the Virgin Mary*, 43.

9 Jeffrey, "Hail Mary," 20; Ankerberg, "Should the Catholic Church Elevate Mary's Status to Co-Redeemer, Mediator of all Graces, and Advocate of Mankind?"; Perotta, *Saint Joseph*.

10 Webber, "Second Eve," 20.

11 Cunneen, *In Search of Mary*, 133.

12 Dahl, "That Most Familiar Story," 24.

13 Chicago, "Virgin Mary," in *The Dinner Party*, 140.

14 Jeffrey, "Hail Mary," 21.

15 Cunneen, *In Search of Mary*, 197.

16 Ruether, *Mary: The Feminine Face of the Church*, 65.

17 Cunneen, *In Search of Mary*, 75; Warner, *Alone of All Her Sex*.

18 Carroll, *The Cult of the Virgin Mary*, 4ff.

19 Pope Pius XII, *Ad Caeli Reginem*, 11 October 1954.

20 The story of these Laundries can be found in movies such as *Convents of Shame* and *Sex in a Cold Climate*, and in articles such as Niall O'Sullivan, "Magdalene Compensation Snub Is Rejection of Laundry Women," *The Irish Post*, 2 August 2013; Henry McDonald, "Magdalene Laundries: Ireland Accepts State Guilt in Scandal," *The Guardian*, 5 February 2013; "In Full: Enda Kenny's State Apology to the Magdalene Women," *The Journal*, 19 February 2013.

21 Brock, *Mary Magdalene*, 78.

22 Brock, *Mary Magdalene*, 84; Muir, "Thecla and Friends," 19; *Pistis Sophia*, ii.72.

23 Haskins, *Mary Magdalen*, 52.

24 Brock, *Mary Magdalene*, 89ff; Jusino, "Mary Magdalene: Author of the Fourth Gospel?"

25 Brock, *Mary Magdalene*, 94ff.

26 The Gospel of Mary as reported in Pagels, *The Gnostic Gospels*, 13.

27 Meighan, "Mary Magdalene, Partner or Prostitute," 19; King, "Women in Ancient Christianity," 3; Jansen, "Maria Magdalena," 63.

28 Meighan, "Mary Magdalene, Partner or Prostitute," 7.

29 Pederson, *The Lost Apostle*, 53ff.
30 Reames, "The Legend of Mary Magdalen, Penitent and Apostle."
31 Stanton, *The Woman's Bible*, 129.
32 Warner, *Alone of All Her Sex*, 333; Abbot, ed., *The Documents of Vatican II*, vol. 4, 67; Carroll, *The Cult of the Virgin Mary*, 68ff.

Chapter 4

THE NUN, THE ABBESS,
AND THE ANCHORITE

THERE WERE VERY FEW women's convents still open in England in 1536 when, desperately needing money, King Henry VIII dissolved the monasteries to get hold of their wealth.[1]

Eileen Power, an expert on English nunneries, has claimed that there were only 138 nunneries throughout all of England between 1270 and 1536, excluding the double houses of the Gilbertine order. One half of these were Benedictine, and about a quarter belonged to the **Cistercians**; the rest belonged to several different orders. Twenty-one were large abbeys with an abbess in charge; the balance were smaller priories, managed by a **prioress**. Altogether, these nunneries would have held only between 1,500 and 2,000 nuns over two-and-a-half centuries. Another study concluded that in thirteenth-century England, there were more than 600 Augustinian and Benedictine houses for about 14,000 men, but convents for only 3,000 women, a little more than Power's estimate. Earlier, however, it was estimated that between 1130 and 1165, in only 35 years, at least 85 new communities had been founded, most by the women themselves.[2]

While many of the monasteries for men had incredible wealth, the women's convents were generally poor. The historian Jane Cartwright found that this was particularly true of those convents in Wales. In the early sixteenth century, the convents at Llanllugan, Llanllŷr, and Usk had net incomes from £22 to £57, roughly US$21,000 to US$55,000 in today's currency. Monasteries for monks had net incomes four times that amount. According to Power, the wealthiest women's convents or abbeys, Syon and Shaftesbury, had a gross annual income of £1,943 and £1,324, respectively.[3]

The food in convents depended on their wealth, and what they were able to produce on their own farms. Lenten fare was usually dried fish, pottage, almonds, raisins, and figs. Bread and ale was provided daily and there might be fresh fish, or meat.[4]

What purpose did the convents serve?

Sometime in the late seventh century, Aethelthyrth or Etheldreda (636–79) left her husband King Egfrith/Ecgfrith of Northumbria (645–85) to go back home to East Anglia (England). On her way, she rested at an island called Alftham where she founded a monastery. Like many of the stories of early nuns and convents, this may have been only legend. But according to the story, on her death, she was succeeded as abbess by her sister Sexburga (640–99), queen of Kent, then her niece Ermenhild, queen of Mercia, and later, great niece Werburg (?–700).[5]

Whether or not her story is historical, it raises the question of why Aethelthyrth left her husband in the first place, like so many of the women who ended up in convents or anchorholds in the middle of married life. An often-quoted passage from a medieval writer contrasts the peace and quiet of convent life to that of the married woman's lot:

> And how I ask ... how does the wife stand who when she comes in hears her child scream, sees the cat stalking food, and the hound at the hide? Her cake is burning on the stone hearth, her calf is sucking the milk, the earthen pot is overflowing onto the fire ... it ought maiden, to deter thee more strongly from marriage, for it does not seem easy to her who has tried it. Though happy maiden, who hast fully removed thyself out of that servitude as a free daughter of God and as His Son's spouse, needest not suffer anything of this kind.[6]

It was a fact that many women entered convents to escape marriage. Women, of course, entered convents to deepen their spirituality. Often, however, they were "dumping grounds" for wealthy unmarriageable women. Convents demanded extensive dowries and parents had to provide not only money but often furniture and clothing as well. The dowry, however, was less than for a well-placed marriage. It was said that a German duke sent all nine of his daughters to a convent to avoid the dowries that would be required if they were to marry.[7]

Widows and better-off wives could board in convents for short periods. Some convents offered small schools for upper-class children and for many women who wanted to obtain an education. The evidence suggests, however, that didn't always happen—as in the case of Juana de la Cruz.

Juana de la Cruz (1651–95), Juana Inés de Asbaje y Ramirez, a child prodigy from the village of San Miguel Nepantla, Mexico, died a diseased and broken woman partly because the church insisted that she write only rote declarations of religious piety. When she was very young, she had taught herself to read and begged her mother to allow her to wear boys' clothes so that she could attend university. She was sent to her grandfather's house instead, where there was an enormous library. By the age of eight, Juana was writing poetry. Five years later, she gave Latin lessons to neighboring children. She taught herself *nahuatl*, the indigenous language of the Mexican highlands. When she was 16, she was invited to join the Spanish viceregal court in Mexico City, where a panel of learned men tested her superior erudition.

Considered by some to be the greatest writer in the Spanish-speaking world, called the "Tenth Muse," Juana entered the Convent of San Jeronimo, where she wrote poems, plays, romances, and social manifestos, composed music, and kept her own laboratory. She had her own apartment and taught music and drama to girls. She supported women's rights. The archbishop of Mexico City, Francisco Aguiar y Seijas (1632–98), however, had problems with her writing, mostly because she was a woman, and in the convent, she had no patrons who would defend her as she had enjoyed earlier when she was growing up. Perhaps her poem "Foolish Men" (Hombres necios) was partly to blame:

> You foolish men who lay
> The guilt on women,
> Not seeing you're the cause
> Of the very thing you blame;
> If you invite their disdain
> With measureless desire
> Why wish they well behave
> If you incite to ill …[8]

In any case, Juana was forced to sell her library of 4,000 books, many of them inherited from her grandfather, her musical instruments, and her scientific equipment. Deprived of her passions, in her final years, she was left to look after the other nuns who were ill with the plague until she herself died from it at age 44. Her birthplace was named Nepantla de Sor Juana Inés de la Cruz in her honor and her image has been on the obverse side of the 200 peso bill issued by the Banco de México.

In her study of English convents, Eileen Power notes that there were no traces of women copying and illuminating manuscripts, and no nunnery produced a chronicle. "The whole trend of medieval thought was against learned women and even in Benedictine nunneries, for which a period of study was enjoined by the rule, it was evidently considered altogether outside the scope of women to concern themselves with writing," she claims. However, English scholar Josephine Koster Tarvers notes that Barking Abbey in London had a tradition of manuscript-making dating back to at least the tenth century and two nuns there, writer or copyist Matilda Hayle of Barking and Mary Hastings, owned a collection of devotional materials. There also appears to have been a woman scribe named Crane in the tenth century in the Benedictine Lyminster nunnery in West Sussex, where a different book was distributed to each nun every year for private reading. But in general, although Tarvers cites other examples, books appear to have been in relatively short supply in English convents.[9]

In contrast, from approximately 1300 to 1525 in Germany, 48 women's convents had *scriptoria* or book production centers and 306 women were acknowledged as scribes, identified by name, initials, or gendered endings. These women contributed in some way to 595 manuscripts that have survived to the present day. They produced or worked on books for liturgical services, contemplation, study, education, or reading at mealtimes. The convents with the highest number of female scribes were in Nuremberg (St. Maria Magdalena and St. Katharina) and Salzburg (Benedictine). Education appears to have had great importance in some areas of Europe for it has been calculated that by the fifteenth century, more than half of all the children in the cities of Bavaria had an elementary education.[10]

By the late seventeenth century, however, convent standards were being questioned on the continent. Madame de Sevigné (1626–96), noted for her numerous letters, wrote to her daughter about her granddaughter's considered admission to a convent: "Ah, my child, keep her with you. She will never get a good education in a convent, neither in religion (of which nuns know very little) nor in anything else.... At home she could read good books ... for her taste lies that way; you could discuss them with her. I am sure that would be much better than a convent."[11]

There were numerous rules for women in monasteries over the centuries. Some of the earliest were by Caesarius (c.470–542) and Aurelianus (523–51) of Arles, each archbishop of Arles in turn. Caesarius placed his sister Caesaria as head of the convent at Arles, and he wrote his rules for her and the other women there. The women were to sell all their personal possessions before they entered and donate the money to the monastery where all things were held in common. The abbess, the head of the larger monasteries for women, was in charge of distributing goods as necessary. Aurelianus and Caesarius demanded total enclosure for the women. None of the nuns was allowed to have her own private space. Even the elderly and the sick were to remain in one large sleeping room in separate beds.[12]

According to this rule, children under the age of six or seven were not to be received at all, especially to be educated, although the women themselves were to learn reading and writing. Singing was especially important, as were weaving and spinning, and taking turns cooking. No one, not even an abbess, was to have a maid, but if a nun needed assistance, then the younger nuns were to help out. In 506 at the synod of Agde in southern France, it was decreed that nuns should be 40 years old before being allowed to take the veil.[13]

While rules were different at certain times and in diverse communities, there were basic similarities. In Constantinople in the late thirteenth and early fourteenth centuries, a rule stipulated silence during meals and work, with two meals a day. Complaining about the food was not tolerated, and neither was eating or drinking in secret. Some of the wealthy nuns could receive special food, as did those who were ill. But the main rule was obedience. Nuns who did not attend to their duties, who were careless, or who spoke to other nuns inappropriately were disciplined by the abbess. This might take the form of genuflecting several times, or standing for long periods, or fasting more than usual.

Despite the rules, some medieval nuns sought to enliven their existence with stylish clothes, visitors, excursions, and even pets. Dogs were the favorite, but birds, monkeys, squirrels, and rabbits were also kept. In 1387 William of Wykeham, bishop of Winchester (1320–1404), threatened the nuns there with discipline if they continued to take birds, hounds, rabbits, and other "frivolous things" to church with them. After three warnings, the nuns would have to fast on bread and water one Saturday for each offense.[14]

The first set of monastic guidelines known to have been authored by a woman was by Chiara Offreduccio (1194–1253), better known as St. Clare of Assisi, an Italian who founded the Order of Poor Ladies. After her death, the Order was renamed the Order of St. Clare. Brought up in wealth, when she was 18, Chiara heard St. Francis of Assisi preach; she asked him how she might live his life. He arranged a meeting where her hair was cut and she garbed herself in a plain robe and veil. Her father tried to force her to return home, but the story is that she clung fiercely to a church altar, showed him her cropped hair, and he left her alone. Her sister Catarina (c.1197–1253), later called Agnes, joined her and they lived with Benedictine nuns until a small house was built for them next to the church of San Damiano in Assisi. Eventually other women joined the two sisters; they lived a life of poverty, austerity, and seclusion, according to a rule that Francis gave them. At first, the nuns went barefoot, slept on the ground, ate no meat, observed silence, prayed, and did manual labor. They were strictly enclosed. They were poor; Abbess Clare had insisted that they live entirely from the alms given by local people.

Often a woman built her own monastery, or her family did, and the woman automatically became the head. Glodesind of Metz (?–608) was widowed the day after she married, and refused to remarry. She fled to Metz where her parents eventually built a monastery for her, "Subterius," which held 100 nuns. She lived for only six more years. The historian Autumn Dolan notes that families were often opposed to their daughters' religious lives, but once they were an actuality, the family often became "as invested in their religious careers as the women themselves."[15]

Abbesses could be quite young. In southern Gaul, Rusticula (c.556–632) was selected as the abbess of the monastery of St. Jean in Arles when she was only 19 years old and remained abbess until she died around the age of 76. The abbess Liliola had rescued her after she was abducted at the age of five by a potential suitor who hoped to inherit her fortune.

Usually abbesses were ordained, just as abbots were when they became head of a monastic community. There were rites for this ceremony, such as the "Mozarabic Rite," also known as the "Visigothic Rite" or the "Hispanic Rite," which appears to have been first used in the seventh century. One rite began: "When an abbess is ordained, she is vested in the sacristy by one dedicated to God and the religious miter is placed on her head." At the end of the ceremony, the abbess received a staff from the bishop, as well as a copy of the rule of the order and a kiss of peace. One of the prayers in the ceremony referred to the Old Testament woman, Miriam, Moses' sister, and used only feminine endings; it had obviously been written for abbesses alone. If the abbess had been ordained outside the building of her order, she then processed back to it with a cross, holy water, incense, and the gospel.[16]

Abbesses heard their nuns' confessions, assigned penances, and reconciled them back to the community, the same functions that bishops or priests carried out in their communities. Sometimes, the abbess was even expected to undertake these duties in the wider community where the convent was located. The abbess was occasionally called upon to present the offering of bread and wine to the priest at Mass for the entire church, and often blessed the bread for pilgrims, giving them a drink of wine from the chalice. A twelfth-century communication noted that abbesses read the gospel in church.

The General Admonition of Charlemagne in 829 chastised abbesses for blessing lay people and consecrating nuns, as well as baptizing children and preaching, indicating that some abbesses were also fulfilling those functions.[17]

Abbesses were often deaconesses, or it may be that deaconesses became abbesses. Atto of Vercelli stated that the order of deaconess in the past had become the order of abbess. This was common from the ninth through to the twelfth centuries, and indeed the tasks of the deaconess and the abbess were much the same. They both read the gospel; they sometimes distributed communion; they taught young women and sometimes young men; they confessed their own nuns, gave penances, and absolved them from sin; and their ordination services were similar.[18]

Large abbeys might have extensive staff under the jurisdiction of the abbess: an obedientary in charge of the daily routine; perhaps a prioress and a sub-prioress and a treasurer; a chantress to look after church services; a sacrist who was in charge of vestments; a fortress in charge of furniture and other material goods; an almoness in charge of almsgiving; a chambress to look after bedding; a cellaress in charge of food and the farm; a kitcheness to do the cooking; an infirmaress to look after the sick; and a novice mistress who instructed the novices. There might be maids, a butler, a brewer, a baker, a dairy woman, a laundress, and even servants for individual nuns. Sometimes, aristocratic nuns had their own dishes cooked separately from all the others, despite rules and regulations.

Many of the abbesses became quite powerful. Anna von Stolberg (1504–74), an abbess at Quedlinburg Abbey, Germany, governed nine churches, two male monasteries, and a hospital. She made all "her" priests swear to Martin Luther's "Augsburg Confession," and turned the monastery into a school for girls and boys. At one point, the abbesses of both Quedlinburg and Gandersheim struck their own coinage. In 947, Emperor Otto I (912–73) had invested the abbess of Gandersheim with supreme authority so that she could rule her small autonomous kingdom without any interference from bishops. It was said that the abbey was built in the forest where mysterious lights thought to be from heaven had appeared. Some abbesses owned vast tracts of land and could summon their own armed knights and hold their own courts. When Matilda (955–99), aunt to King Otto III of Germany (980–1002), was abbess at Quedlinburg, she also served unofficially as regent. She led an army against invaders, but fortunately never had to use force.[19]

The abbesses of the ancient abbey of Notre-Dame-aux-Nonnains in Troyes installed new bishops in the local cathedral. The bishop-elect was required to travel to the abbey mounted on a palfrey that would later become the property of the abbess. The abbess led the bishop into the abbey, he knelt before her, and she vested him with **cope** and **miter**, placing a cross in his hands. He then swore to uphold the rights and privileges of the convent. The newly installed bishop spent the night in the abbey, but then was allowed to take the bed he had slept in and any other furnishings in the room back to his monastery.[20]

Often double monasteries with separate buildings for monks and nuns were administered by the abbess. Such was the case with the famous monastery of Fontevrault/Fontevraud in France. It housed 5,000 nuns by 1150, but turmoil over the years, various wars and the **Protestant Reformation**'s opposition to monasteries and convents, reduced it to the point where there were only 230 nuns and 60 monks by the end of the eighteenth century. In 1804, the abbey was used as a detention center for 15,000 prisoners. Founded by the itinerant preacher, Robert d'Arbrissel (1045–1116), around 1100, it was initially governed by an abbess, the first being the widow Petronilla of Chemillé (?–1149). The monks could not even receive a **postulant** without the permission of the abbess; later they rebelled against their subordinate position. The original rule for the monastery dealt with four major themes—silence, good works, food, and clothing—and mentioned that the abbess should be chosen from outside the monastery, although from the third abbess on, they were selected from among the nuns in the convent.[21]

Wimborne Minster was another impressive double monastery, a little inland from the seaside resort of Bournemouth on the south coast of England. Founded by Cuthburg (?–c.725) and her sister Cwenburga, sister of King Ine (?–728) and the wife of King Aldfrith (?–705), her early life is largely unknown. She had one son, Osred (c.697–716), but stories suggest her marriage was extremely unhappy. At some point, she went to Barking Abbey in Essex where she studied under Hildelith (?–c.725), the second abbess there. At Wimborne, the nuns and monks lived separate lives behind battlemented walls except when they met for daily Mass. Cuthburg administered the monastery until she died, when Cwenburga took over, and then later Tetta (probably a pet name), the sister of King Aethelheard, who reigned from 726 to 740. Under Tetta's direction, the abbey became a missionary center.

The English abbess of Tauberbischofsheim, Lioba/Leoba or Leofgyth (c.710–82), became an anchorite or recluse in her later life. Born to a noble family in Wessex, she entered the convent at Wimborne Minster. Her cousin, the famed missionary Boniface (675–754), repeatedly asked Lioba to go to Germany with him and in 748, she finally agreed. She had a dream that an older nun interpreted as meaning that Lioba was to accomplish her ministry among other people far away. Boniface established the convent at Tauberbischofsheim, appointed Lioba its abbess, and gave her his **cowl** when he traveled to indicate that she was in charge. She established other monasteries, was consulted by bishops, and was generally well thought of as a learned and wise administrator and missionary. When Boniface died, she lived as a recluse with a few friends.[22]

The canoness Hroswitha/Hrosvitha of Gandersheim (c.935–c.1002) was called the most remarkable woman of her time. Thought to be the earliest female German writer, she wrote poetry, prose, drama, sacred legends, and historical poems, many of them celebrating women. Well educated, she had studied Latin and Greek, scholastic philosophy, mathematics, astronomy, and music in the convent. At first she wrote secretly, then showed her work to her abbess who publicized it outside the convent. She claimed that she had the strength of a man in her heart, and in the prologue to her *Book of Legends* she wrote:

Scorn he should not render
At the writer's weaker gender
Who these small lines has sung
With a woman's untutored tongue
But rather should he praise
The Lord's celestial grace.[23]

As a canoness, Hroswitha could have servants, own property and possessions, and come and go as necessary. A plate and table runner were dedicated to her in Judy Chicago's celebrated feminist sculpture, *The Dinner Party*, created in the late 1970s.[24]

Many abbesses wrote extensively. Kassiani/Kassia (c.810–65), a Byzantine abbess, wrote poetry and gnomic verse (epigrams or aphorisms), such as,

"Today in the world/and tomorrow in the grave/the thought of death consumes life." Kassiani also composed music, but she is most famous for her hymns. Approximately 50 of her hymns are extant, and 23 remain in Orthodox liturgical books. Born into an aristocratic family, exceptionally beautiful and intelligent, she was courted by the Emperor Theophilos (813–42), but it is written that she "one-upped" him in conversation, and he married someone else. No one was allowed to "best" the emperor in dialogue. It is thought, however, that they both always harbored romantic feelings for each other. Kassia's best-known hymn is one for Holy Wednesday about the nameless woman who anointed Jesus while he was dining (Matthew 26:6–13; Mark 14:3–9; Luke 7:36–50):[25]

> Woe is me, for the love of adultery surrounded me with darkness: A lightless night of sin.
> Accept the springs of my tears,
> As you who disperse the waters of the sea from the clouds.
> Bow down to the sighs of my heart,
> As you bent the heavens, by your inapprehensible incarnation.[26]

The well-known Hild/a of Whitby (c.614–80), great-niece of King Edwin of Northumbria (c.586–633), may have been an anchorite or recluse before she became abbess of the abbey at Hartlepool, a town on the North Sea in England. She had been baptized at Easter in 627 when a timber structure was hastily erected to baptize the newly converted king and his entourage. Later, Hilda founded a double monastery at Whitby, the "Bay of the Lighthouse" or *Streaneshalch*, as the Anglo-Saxons called it, which became known for its educational work, training no fewer than five male bishops during her leadership from 660 to 680. She presided over a church Synod in 664 where the date for Easter was discussed, and although her personal preference was the Celtic rite for Easter, she agreed to adopt the Roman calendar for the sake of unity and peace. One of Hilda's most famous *protégés* was Caedmon, a simple herdsman whom she groomed to become a famous English poet and musician. The historian Bede (672–735) wrote that nobles, bishops, and learned men "did not merely ask her advice, but they followed it." Oswiu (612–70), a king in northern England, gave Hilda the charge of his one-year-old daughter Aelfflaed (654–713) along with a great deal of property. Aelfflaed succeeded Hilda as abbess.[27]

Although she became the prioress of the convent at Argenteuil and then abbess, Héloïse (1101–64) is known mostly for her love affair with her tutor, the theologian Abélard (1079–1142). As Abélard wrote: "We were united, first under one roof, then in heart; and so with our lessons as a pretext we abandoned ourselves entirely to love. Her studies allowed us to withdraw in private, as love desired, and with our books open before us, more words of love than of our reading passed between us, and more kissing than teaching."[28]

An extraordinarily intelligent young woman, Héloïse at first refused to marry Abélard because she felt that it would ruin his career. But after she became pregnant, they married secretly and then Héloïse entered a convent, not for "love of God," she wrote, but because Abélard commanded her. Héloïse's uncle Fulbert who had custody of Héloïse thought that Abélard had abandoned her, so her uncle and his friends took revenge on Abélard, forcefully castrating him. Héloïse wrote several letters to Abélard from the convent (although there have been scholars who believe she was not the author). In one of them she claims that she "preferred love to wedlock, freedom to a bond." She believed that most people married for property and money rather than love. She went into the monastery thinking that she had done nothing for God's sake, and therefore her religious life was worthless. Nevertheless, Héloïse set up a school of theology.

Hildegard of Bingen (1098–1179), "the Sybil of the Rhine," is probably the most widely known of all abbesses. Born in the Rhineland village of Böckelheim, the tenth child of well-to-do landowners, she was sent to the large convent at Disibodenberg when she was seven. As a child she saw strange lights, shimmering flames, and circling stars, now thought to be the aura that is part of migraine headaches. She was considered a sickly child, although she lived to be 81. The high-born anchorite, later an abbess, Jutta von Sponheim (1091–1136), taught her music, how to play the 10-string psaltery, Latin and the scriptures, and by age 14 Hildegard had become a nun. When she was 38, she succeeded Jutta as the abbess and began to record her visions. Her main work, *Scivias* (*Scito Vias Domini—Know the Ways of the Lord*), took 10 years to write, a compendium of science, theology, and philosophy. During that time, in 1147, she led 18 of her nuns to found a new convent 30 kilometers away at Rupertsberg near the ruins of the castle of the dukes of Bingen. Eventually there were 50 nuns in residence there.

Hildegard acquired a vast reputation as a sage and prophet, and even Pope Eugenius III (1088–1153) wrote in 1148: "We are filled with admiration, my daughter ... for the new miracles that God has shown you in our time, filling

FIGURE 4.1 Hildegard of Bingen (1098–1179) sketching on a wax tablet with her tutor and scribe, the monk Volmar (?–1173). Illumination from *Liber Scivias* printed c.1151, from the German Codex. Hildegard wrote of this event: "A fiery light, flashing intensely, came from the open vault of heaven and poured through my whole brain. Like a flame that is hot without burning it kindled all my heart and all my breast." Photo: Bridgeman Photos.

you with his spirit, so that you see, understand, and communicate many secret things. Reliable persons who have seen and heard you vouch to us for these facts. Guard and keep this grace which is in you."[29]

Eleanor of Aquitaine (1122–1204), queen consort of England and France, was enamored of Hildegard, although when she wrote the following they had never met:

> To Hildegarde, Tabernacle of the Divine Spirit …
> I salute you, gracious lady, noble abbess
> Mighty woman with the status of a feudal lord
> Though I have never seen you yet I think you
> A Sister who worships Mary's power
> I am told you dress in snow-white linen
> And in your hand the crozier of your rank
> A prophet, a healer, a mystic, a saint.[30]

Hildegard wrote prolifically—hymns, music, morality plays, commentaries on the Bible, books on medicine and natural history, in addition to the records of her visions—and corresponded around the known world with four popes, two emperors, several kings and queens, dukes, counts, abbesses, the masters of the University of Paris, and **prelates** including St. Bernard and Thomas à Becket, writing hundreds of letters. Her replies were often quite blunt when people asked for advice. For example, she warned the Holy Roman Emperor Frederick Barbarossa (1122–90), "Take care that the Highest King does not strike you down because of the blindness which prevents you from governing justly." But she retained a certain humility. "For my part," she confided to a monk, "I am always in fear and trembling because I have not any security as to what I am able to do." She preached on four extended tours believing that God commanded her, traveling widely to Cologne, Trier, Würzburg, Mainz, Frankfurt, Rothenburg, and into Flanders, often on horseback and sometimes accompanied by an armed guard because of the dangerous roads. She claimed that she was in great physical pain if she refused to obey God's order to travel and preach.[31]

Hildegard spent almost her entire life in the convent where she received many visions, and she is considered one of the great Christian mystics. She understood the world holistically, emphasizing the union of the spiritual and the physical. Many of her revelations were allegorical and she also interpreted those in her writings. Hildegard was also memorialized in Judy Chicago's *The Dinner Party* with a plate and a runner.[32]

The Garden of Delights, an interesting encyclopedic work written by Harrad (1130–95), the abbess or canoness of Hohenburg in Alsace, described in pictures and in words the history of the world from creation to the coming of the anti-Christ. The 47 nuns and 13 novices in the convent there wore colorful clothes similar to women outside the convent, according to the pictures in her book. Harrad founded houses for canonesses who read Mass in the women's chapel with the help of the bishop. Her massive work consisted of 324 parchment leaves of folio size, based on the Bible, but with digressions into philosophy and contemporary knowledge. There were several full-page illustrations along with a number of smaller ones. It is not known if Harrard drew and painted those as well. She left a motto in the work: "Despise the world, despise nothing, despise thyself, despise despising thyself—these are four things."[33]

As one might expect, some abbesses failed to live up to their high calling. Benedetta Carlini (1591–1661), the subject of the book *Immodest Acts*, from a middle-class family in Italy, was made abbess of the Mother of God convent in the early seventeenth century. Well educated and seemingly intensely religious, she grew up reciting five "Pater Nosters" and eight "Ave Marias" every day. When she was nine, her parents took her to the Santa Chiari convent at Pescia in central Italy. It would have cost them about 400 scudi or US$80. A laborer would have taken six to eight years to earn that much, but it was a great deal less than a marriage dowry of around 1500 scudi, or about US$300 at that time. By 1620, a new Mother of God convent under the protection of Catherine of Siena and fully enclosed was officially established with 30-year-old Benedetta at its helm.

She (Benedetta) received several visions, but the highlights of her spiritual life were a physical exchange of hearts with Christ which she reported (she claimed she lived for three days without any heart); receiving the **stigmata**; and a three-hour wedding with Christ as the bridegroom in which He was invisible and Benedetta vocalized all the parts. At one point, her visions became so terrifying that the convent assigned a young companion, Bartolomea Crivelli, to watch over her. For over two years, Benedetta discharged her duties as administrator of the convent and as a mystic, managing to fulfill both roles adequately. It was only during an investigation that it came to light that Benedetta had made the stigmata herself with a large needle. But what was more heinous to the ecclesiastic investigators was the fact that Benedetta had physically forced her companion Bartolomea into lesbian acts. Benedetta was sentenced to prison within the convent, and died at the age of 71 after spending 35 years confined to her cell. Homosexual acts were not acceptable, and since there were defined punishments, they must have occurred often.[34]

The Beguine Hadewijch (?–1248) recorded her series of visions, writing a lot about the love of Christ, and yet at least one of her letters to her sisters suggests that she, too, might have had a very close relationship with one of the other Beguines in her community:

> Greet Sara also in my behalf, whether I am anything to her or nothing. Could I be fully all that in my love I wish to be for her, I would gladly do so, and I shall do so fully, however she may treat me. She has very largely forgotten my affliction, but I do not wish to blame or reproach her, seeing that Love leaves her at rest…. Now that she has other occupations and can look on quietly and tolerate my heart's affliction, she lets me suffer.[35]

Several poems were found from a twelfth-century monastery, written by a woman poet to a woman beloved. One in particular is a very clear example of medieval lesbian literature:

> To G.; her singular rose
> From A. the bonds of precious love,
> What is my strength, that I may bear it,
> That I should have patience in your absence …
> Everything pleasant and delightful
> Without you seems like mud underfoot …
> When I recall the kisses you gave me …
> What can I, so wretched, do?[36]

There were penances for sexual acts in the monasteries, especially for male homosexuals, but also for women. The Archbishop of Canterbury Theodore of Tarsus (602–90) had decreed, "If a woman practices vice with a woman, she shall do penance for three years. And if she practices solitary vice, she shall do penance for the same time." The *Paenitentiale Ecgberhti* (*The Penitential of Egbert*), written around 740, increased the punishment to seven years for nuns who used "machines." The rule was based on the text in Romans 1:26, "Even their women exchanged natural sexual relations for unnatural ones."

It is to be expected that there would be infractions in the convents. Most nuns were dedicated to following a religious life, but many were placed in

FIGURE 4.2 A 1782 mezzotint satire of two nuns in low-cut dresses with their veils drawn back, about to embrace, sitting in a garden while a monk grins. Below the image are four lines of verse: "The Scene delightful Beauty here, what then!... We but dissemble for our Lusts prodigious." Photo: © The Trustees of the British Museum.

convents for expediency and were likely not terribly interested in following the rules. As John Milton had written, convents were "convenient stowage for withered daughters." In 1249, Archbishop Eudes of Rouen (1200–75) inspected the houses in his diocese in northern France and found numerous deficiencies both in the nuns themselves and in the buildings. For example, at one priory in Villarceaux where there were 23 nuns and three lay sisters, he found that silence was not well observed; that they ate meat for no good reason; they wore rabbit, fox, and hare fur which was forbidden; two of the nuns had become pregnant; some nuns let their hair grow to their chins which was also against the rules; and the prioress was drunk every night. But, he wrote, "they manage their own affairs as best they can."[37]

THE ANCHORITES

While nuns and abbesses pursued their spirituality in the convent, recluses or **anchorites**, *anker* or *ancresse*, had no such safety net; they often became quite prominent in their community, even though set apart in a cell. And anchorites were often not as solitary or as isolated as might be imagined.

The mother of the French Benedictine historian Guibert of Nogent (1055–1124) took two sons, both of her chaplains and her tutor with her into her anchorhold, and encouraged other household staff to enter the nearby abbey. She had been widowed after the birth of three sons, and when her youngest was about 12 and she was about 40, she entered a cell at the abbey church of St Germer-de-Fly in France to become an anchorite. She was often visited by friends. She changed her diet to plain food, slept on straw with only a sheet, and was apparently able to finance this new life herself in which she gradually became a prophetess, widely sought after.

The socialite Yvette of Huy (1158–1228), from a town in Belgium on the River Meuse, withdrew to a nearby leper colony and began living there in a rundown chapel outside the city walls. She had been widowed with three children when she was only 18, but as soon as her children were old enough to live by themselves, she, too, went off on her own. She did everything she could to become a leper herself, such as smearing infected blood on her body to do penance for her perceived sins, but she remained healthy. After about 10 years with the lepers, she took part in a ceremony of enclosure consisting of a Mass, the burial rite, and finally the enclosure itself. Her cell consisted of two floors, with another young recluse who received visitors in the floor below. There was also a nurse and a recluse-in-training living with them. They had access to the church from an opening in the cell. Yvette looked after a Beguine community as well; at one point there were at least 18 Beguine communities in Huy. Yvette may have lived more comfortably than many large families, for it seems that she at least had a room of her own.[38]

Lame Margaret of Magdeburg (c.1210–50), Germany, was enclosed when she was only 12. She had not been well accepted by her family because of her deformity. There was an old anonymous rhyme:

> Now earth to earth in convent walls,
> To earth in churchyard sod.
> I was not good enough for man,
> And so am given to God.[39]

Indeed, Margaret's mother agreed to have a cell made for her at St. Alban's Church in Magdeburg when Margaret expressed a desire for the anchorite life. However her confessor, a **Dominican** named John, felt that Margaret was not answering people's questions with orthodox theology, and he had her transferred to a Cistercian women's convent over her strong objections. While she fought being removed from her anchorhold, she finally found peace in a cell in the Newtown convent. Margaret believed that she had received her theological knowledge from the Virgin Mary.[40]

Bertke of Utrecht (1427–1514) in the Netherlands was a later anchoress, a heroine in her community although little known by the wider church. When she died at the age of 80 after being enclosed for 57 years, six guards had to be hired to control the crowds that came to pay their respects. She was a prolific hymn-writer and author of devotional and mystical articles; many of her hymns were sung outside her cell while she was alive. Some are still in existence. Her writings suggest that she had access to the local convent library.

The writer Anneke Mulder-Bakker notes that the anchorite often acted very much like a priest. She had to receive permission from a bishop to be enclosed, but she could sometimes keep her property—food and clothing—to fund her existence.

Cells might be uncomfortably small, or larger, like Yvette of Huy's two-story structure. A *Bavarian Rule* for anchorites directed that an anchorhold be of stone and 12 feet square. There were to be three windows, one to hear the choir in the church and to receive communion, one to receive food and to dispense slops, and one to provide light. The abbot Aelred of Rievaulx (1110–67) wrote a rule for his older sister, *De Institutis Inclusarum* (*Rule for a Recluse*) about 1158. She lived on her own property, confining herself to her own quarters. Aelred insisted that she earn her own living but at the same time that she remain silent and isolated, not the typical recluse "who perches at her window to soak up the scandal of … neighbourhood gossip, chattering about the local priest's manner, the young girls' frivolities, the self-justified widow, the cuckolding wife."[41]

The earliest cells were generally made of wood and much smaller than those from the fourteenth century on. Archeological evidence indicates that a cell in Leatherhead in Surrey was less than two-and-a-half meters square, and one in Compton even smaller but with a loft. The women who were enclosed were able to speak with authority to the local men and women and were much more acceptable than the Beguines or **tertiaries** who wandered about, upsetting the church because of their freedom. There were several rules for the anchoresses, possibly the first established by the monk Grimlaicus in the early ninth century. He wrote what might be considered common sense, although demanding incredibly high standards:

> Solitaries ought to be without offense, not imprudent, not bad-tempered, not wine-drinkers, not big eaters, not physically violent, not double-tongued, not neophytes, and not avaricious for filthy gain…. They should not be irritable and anxious, should not go to extremes or be obstinate, should not be jealous or overly suspicious…. They should be just, holy, and chaste. They should practice abstinence and hospitality and love good works. They should be modest, serious, patient, kindly, humble, charitable, and obedient…. Solitaries should live in such a way that those who disparage religion do not dare to disparage their life.[42]

After his rule, it was said that there were fewer eccentricities among the anchorites, but there were also fewer women who became recluses or anchorites in the ninth and tenth centuries; from the eleventh to the fifteenth centuries there were thousands. Three thousand names have been recovered in France alone. Technically, male and female recluses generally lived isolated in woods or forests and were free to roam. Anchorites lived in populated areas and were far more often women.[43]

One rule encouraged bathing in cold water. Anchorites were not to neglect personal hygiene. "Wash yourself as often as you please," the rule specified.

St. Bernard of Clairvaux Abbey (1090–1153) wrote, "I haue louyd pouerte [loved poverty] but y neuer louyd fylth."[44]

Gregory IX (1145–1241) also contributed a rule containing about 20 items. First, anchoresses had to request permission from their bishop to become an anchoress and then take a vow for life. They were to live in total seclusion, separated from the world by a black curtain at their window and only allowed to hold consulting hours once a week at a time set by the local priest. Perhaps some of the women obeyed these rules to the letter, but stories about others suggest that in reality their lives were somewhat less circumscribed. The current editor of the contemporary *Ancrene Wisse*, Robert Hasenfratz, discovered in his research that some anchorholds served as banks, post offices, school houses, shops, and even the local newspaper.[45]

The thirteenth-century *Ancren Riwle* or *Ancrene Wisse* (*Guide for Anchoresses*), written for three sisters of noble birth who lived near Wales and became anchorites, also required that the window open to the public be covered by a black cloth "more difficult to see through," and resistant to the wind. The later *Speculum Inclusorum* (*A Mirror for Recluses*) warned of the dangers of too much conversation with visitors. Some anchorholds, however, even had a courtyard and garden, and while the enclosing ceremony included bricking up the entrance to the anchorhold, there was often a door or some way out through the church or other structure that the cell abutted. Juliana, the anchoress at Worcester, had her anchorhold at the northwest corner of the church of St. Nicholas bounded by the main street and a side street. She asked to have her cell enlarged on three sides by seven, five, and four feet, respectively, which would result in a fairly large room. The king agreed after he was satisfied that this would not intrude on anyone else's territory. There was a pun at that time that the anchorites acted as a stabilizing "anchor" for the churches.[46]

The *Ancrene Wisse* forbade the self-torture practiced by many ascetics: "Wear no iron, nor haircloth, nor hedge-hog skins; and do not beat yourselves therewith, nor with a scourge of leather thongs, nor leaded; and do not with holly nor with briars cause yourselves to bleed without leave of your confessor; and do not at any one time, use too many flagellations." It also forbade fasting on bread and water without permission. Part Seven of the rule maintained that divine love, not pain and penance, was the highest goal of the anchorite life.[47]

Anchoresses spent several hours a day in contemplation and religious exercises, but they also prayed for the concerns of their community: the misery of the poor and the orphan, the needs of the widows and the pilgrims, the hardships of soldiers and travelers, and the anxieties of the church. Like the village priest, they listened to the sins and sorrows of the local men and women, and they wrote, illustrated books, sewed for the poor, and embroidered ecclesiastical hangings and other cloth for the church.

While there were many more anchorites in England than in continental Europe, Anneke Mulder Bakker reports that there were at least 19 anchorholds or anchoresses' cells in the city of Liège, Belgium, alone in the twelfth and thirteenth centuries, and many others in the Low Countries. Most of the anchorites there were women. The historian Rotha Mary Clay uncovered more than 750 cells throughout England, finding the names of over 650 hermits and anchorites. In her *Anchorites and Their Patrons in Medieval England*, Ann K. Warren discovered 780 recluses on 601 sites in all but four counties, twice as many women as men. At first, most of the anchorites were in the rural areas, but by the sixteenth century the anchorite was a fixture in most towns.[48]

Some early English anchoresses such as Keyne and Modwen may have been only legendary. There is no accurate information about them. Keyne Wyry (c.461–505), supposedly one of 24 daughters of King Brychan of Brycheiniog (c.419–?) in Wales, is said to have settled in what is now known as Keynsham in southwest England where she was able to turn all the poisonous snakes into stones through her prayers. It is also said that she cast a spell on the waters of a well in Cornwall, described thus in 1602: "The quality that man or wife whom chance or choice attains first of this sacred spring to drink thereby the mastery gains."[49]

Sometimes anchorites attracted such a large following of women that they found themselves head of a convent or monastery. Monegundis (?–570), a native of Chartres, France, married and bore children who all died. Her husband allowed her to leave the marriage and she lived in a room or cell in Chartres, later moving to the tomb of St. Martin at Tours. She was joined by so many women that she founded the convent of St. Pierre-le-Puellier at Tours, devising a rule for all of them.

There are other well-known anchorites, such as Christina of Markyate and Julian of Norwich, who were more celebrated and familiar.

Born Theodora in Huntingdon, England, into an affluent family, when quite young, Christina (c.1097–c.1161) would whip herself if she thought she had done something wrong. When she became a teenager, she was pledged by her parents against her will to marry a man called Burhred even though she had taken a vow of celibacy. There is a story that Bishop Ranulph Flambard (1060–1128) tried to rape her in her bedroom. Christina suggested that she lock the door before their sexual act, ran out, and locked the door from the outside. The bishop was so humiliated that he brokered a marriage in revenge. Christina married, but disguised as a man, she immediately fled to the anchoress Alfwen at Flamstead, lived with her for two years, and then with the hermit Roger (?–c.1121), possibly a former monk from St. Alban's. After her marriage was annulled, Christina returned to Markyate where she was invited to lead a community of nuns. She declined at first but formally became an anchorite in 1130. King Henry II (1133–89) granted her 50 shillings a year in support paid out of the exchequer "in corn which the king gives to Lady Christina of the Wood." Even though she was enclosed, she became an advisor to Geoffrey of Gorham (?–1146), abbot of St. Alban's, who appointed her the first prioress of Markyate.[50]

Christina's story involves many of the kinds of religious life open to women at that time. She was in turn a consecrated virgin, a recluse, an anchoress, a nun, and an abbess.

Like other communities, the priory at Markyate that developed in 1145 sometimes decided its own rules. When a bishop went there to advise the nuns of Pope Boniface VIII's rule of enclosure in 1300, that "on pain of excommunication, no nun or sister could go outside the bounds of the monastery," the nuns took the decree and threw it at the bishop as he left. They told him they were "not content in any way to observe such a statute." Over the centuries, reports kept being sent to various popes that nuns were still traveling, boarding outsiders, taking pilgrimages, and entertaining guests at convents in opposition to the various rules.[51]

About the same time that Christina was living in her anchorhold, Gudridur Thorbjarnadóttir of Iceland (950–1004) gave birth to Snorri, thought to be the first European child born in North America. Her husband, Thorfinn Karlsefni (980–?), led an expedition from Iceland in the early eleventh century to settle Vineland (or Wineland) and, while they were there, their son was born. After Thorfinn died, killed by Indigenous people in Greenland, Gudridur made a pilgrimage to Rome, and then returned to Iceland to live with her son, becoming a recluse.[52]

Julian of Norwich (c.1342–c.1416) was a mystic, anchoress of the church of St. Julian the Hospitaller from 1390, and author of what is thought to be the first book by a woman in English, *The Shewings or Revelations of Divine Love*. She was attached to a church dedicated to the patron saint of boatmen and travelers, close to the River Wensum, and many sought her counsel. She was always aware, though, that she was "only" a woman—"ignorant, weak and frail"; she was either socially conditioned to believe that, or politically astute enough to pretend she believed it. Several people left a bequest in their wills to Julian during her lifetime—20 per cent of all wills in her area at that time. She had two maidservants at different times: Sara and Alice.[53]

Julian's writings are full of mother imagery—Christ as Mother and God as Mother:

> We know that our mothers bear us for pain and death. But what is it that Jesus our true mother does? He who is all-love bears us for joy and eternal life.... This fair and lovely word "mother" is so sweet and gentle in itself that it cannot truly be said of anyone except of him and to him, who is the true mother of life and of all things. The properties of motherhood are: natural love, wisdom and knowledge. And this is God ... our heavenly mother, Jesus, can never allow us, his children to die; for he is all mighty, all wise and all love. (60–61)

The wealthy heiress Katherine of Ledbury (1272–c.1323), or Lady Audley, was another prominent anchoress. The daughter of the baron of Brimsfield in southwest England, widowed when she was 27, she entered an anchorhold at Ledbury around 1313, having arranged to receive £30 a year as a pension, about US$35,000 today, probably sufficient for her expenses of food, cloth for sewing clothes, a servant, and perhaps fuel for a fireplace. In fact, other sources suggest that she received £100 a year, which would certainly be adequate. Little is known of her later life except that at one point she had to fight to receive her inheritance and she was saddled with the responsibility of an orphaned grandson even though she was enclosed. Two British poets were inspired to write about her: John Masefield (1878–1967) and William Wordsworth (1770–1850). Wordsworth's 1835 sonnet tells the story of how Katherine wandered around England with her maid Mabel looking for a place to rest when she heard the church bells of Ledbury and decided to remain there:

> When human touch (as monkish books attest)
> Nor was applied, nor could be, Ledbury bells
> Broke forth in concert flung a down the dells,
> And upward, high as Malvern's cloudy crest:

Sweet tones, and caught by a noble Lady blest
To rapture! Mabel listened at the side
Of her loved mistress: soon music died.
And Catherine said, *Here I set up my rest*[54]

Whatever amount of money Katherine received yearly, it was more than many of the anchoresses collected, although before they could receive permission from the bishop to be enclosed, the women (and men) had to prove that they had access to sufficient funding so that they would not be a burden on the town or the church. However, it was evidently common to assist recluses and many received bequests from interested and supportive friends and family.

Alice Bernard of St. Leonard in Exeter was enclosed in a house in the cemetery in 1397. She received numerous bequests: a canon left her 40s. in his will, and the rector of Little Torrington willed her 20s. and a book of sermons in English. King Edward III (1312–77) gave alms to eight ancho-rites and three hermits around London and possibly others, and a Lord Scrope of a well-known Norman family bequeathed money to anchorites in 20 villages as well as some around London and York. King Henry III (1207–72) ordered three halfpence a day be given to Emma de Skepeye for life; she was enclosed by the church of St. Mary in Dover Castle in the early thirteenth century. Idonea de Boclaund near St. Peter's Church in London received a penny a day and a new robe every year on Henry III's orders. The historian Ann Warren, however, found that only 10 per cent of the wills she examined, calendared at the London court of Husting between 1351 and 1360, mentioned anchorites.[55]

Jeanne Le Ber (1662–1714) was a later anchorite, the first in North America. Withdrawn and introverted, Jeanne spent three years being educated by the Ursulines in Quebec, Canada, but when she was 15, she returned to her well-to-do family in Montreal, considered to be the most eligible young woman in French Canada. For a time she lived in a cell at the rear of a church, wearing a hair shirt and corn-husk shoes, remaining solitary and supposedly practicing flagellation. She even refused to leave the cell when her mother died. Jeanne took a vow of perpetual seclusion in 1685 when she was 23, but retained and looked after much of her inherited property and ate meat, contrary to the customary diet of a strict **religious**. She retained an attendant. Then 10 years later, she took the vows of a recluse or anchorite at a ceremony attended by many in the community, having had a three-story anchorhold built at the rear of a church. She embroidered altar cloths and church vestments, ordering silk, wool, and thread from France, spent six or seven hours a day in prayer, took communion several times a week and at night lay prostrate before the altar in the silent church. She had visitors, but remained in her "cell" as much as possible, not even attending her father's funeral. It was said, however, that her religious exercises were a burden to her.[56]

Religious communities of women exist not only in the Roman Catholic Church. There have been a number in the Anglican or Church of England denomination and in the Eastern Orthodox churches as well.

The Sisterhood of St. John the Divine, a community of nuns in the Anglican Church of Canada, was founded in 1884 in Toronto by Mother Hannah Grier Coome (1837–1921). A widow, Hannah taught decorative arts for a while, also embroidering church hangings, when she considered joining the Community of St. Mary the Virgin in Wantage, England. But friends and relatives begged her to help them organize a religious order in Canada and so she stayed. Hannah and a friend Amelia Elizabeth (Aimee) Hare who later became a novice in the organization, trained in New York City at the Peekskill Motherhouse, returning to Toronto to set up a new order, adopting a rule modeled on the Rule of St. Benedict. Their first task was establishing a hospital in Moose Jaw, Saskatchewan, to help with the wounded from the Northwest Rebellion in 1884. Since then they have set up other hospitals; cared for the elderly, people with disabilities, and the poor; run schools and orphanages; offered religious retreats; and made altar linens. By 1930, there were 500 sisters. After Hannah died, her niece Dora Grier (1874–1966) became Mother Superior. Today the Sisterhood of St. John the Divine operates in Toronto and Victoria, British Columbia.[57]

Most nuns decided on their vocation when they were young; the Greek Orthodox nun Gerontissa Gavrielia (1897–1992), or Avrilia Papayannis, was 60 when she became a religious with a wealth of education and experience behind her. Born in Constantinople to a wealthy Greek family, she was the second woman to be admitted to a Greek university. She held a degree in botany from a Swiss university, then earned a degree in philosophy from the Aristotle University of Thessaloniki, and after that, moved to England where she studied podiatry and physiotherapy. In 1954, she took a vow of poverty, gave away all her worldly possessions, and traveled to India to work with the poor and the lepers, providing free physiotherapy for four years. She eventually became a nun at the Bethany Community of the Resurrection of the Lord, east of Jerusalem. She was assigned to work in various countries: France, the United States, East Africa, and Germany, as well as

India. "Whoever lives in the past is as if dead," she wrote. "Whoever lives in the future in his fantasy … is naïve, because the future belongs only to God. The Joy of Christ is found only in the present, in the Eternal Present of God." When she was challenged in a country where she couldn't speak the language, she responded that she knew five languages: the smile, tears, touch, prayer, and love. With these five languages she said that she went "all around the World."[58]

FURTHER READING

PRIMARY

Amt, Emilie, ed. *Women's Lives in Medieval Europe: A Sourcebook*. New York: Routledge, 1993.

Luscombe, David, ed. *The Letter Collection of Peter Abelard and Heloise*. Oxford: Oxford University Press, 2013.

Spenser, M.A. "Rule for a Solitary in Aelred of Rievaulx: Treatises and Pastoral Prayers." Dubuque, IA: Cistercian Publications, 1971.

SECONDARY

Brown, Judith C. *Immodest Acts: The Life of a Lesbian Nun in Renaissance Italy*. Oxford: Oxford University Press, 1986.

Clay, Rotha Mary. *The Hermits and Anchorites of England*. London: Methuen & Co., 1914.

Gies, Frances, and Joseph Gies. *Women in the Middle Ages: The Lives of Real Women in a Vibrant Age of Transition*. New York: Barnes and Noble, 1980.

Hughes-Edwards, Mari. "Solitude and Sociability: The World of the Medieval Anchorite." Wiltshire, UK: Cathedral Communications, 2012.

Kidder, Annemarie S. *Women, Celibacy and the Church*. New York: Crossroad Publishing, 2003.

Mulder-Bakker, Anneke B. *Lives of the Anchoresses: The Rise of the Urban Recluse in Medieval Europe*. Philadelphia: University of Pennsylvania Press, 2005.

Power, Eileen. *Medieval English Nunneries, c.1275–1535*. Cambridge: Cambridge University Press, 1922.

Silvas, Anna M. "Kassia the Nun c.810–c.865: An Appreciation." In *Byzantine Women: Varieties of Experience 800–1200*, edited by Lynda Garland. London: Ashgate, 2006.

NOTES

1 King Henry VIII ordered monasteries closed, both to gain more wealth (some of the monasteries had incredible wealth) and to suppress political opposition. He had broken with the church in Rome. Monasteries followed suit in Europe later on for many of the same reasons after the Protestant Reformation. Male and female religious were generally pensioned off or relocated.

2 Fanous and Leyser, eds., *Christina of Markyate*, 6.

3 Cartwright, "The Desire to Corrupt: Convent and Community in Medieval Wales," 25; Power, *Medieval English Nunneries*, 2.

4 Power, *Medieval Women*, 94f.

5 Roffe, "St. Aethelthryth and the Monastery of Alftham," 1.

6 "Religious Nuns in Medieval Europe: Women of Action," 1.

7 "Religious Nuns in Medieval Europe: Women of Action," 4.

8 "Sor Juana Ines de la Cruz," Biography.com, https://www.biography.com/people/sor-juana-in%C3%A9s-de-la-cruz-38178; Chicago, *The Dinner Party*.

9 Tarvers, "'Thys ys my mystrys boke': English Women as Readers and Writers in Late Medieval England."

10 Cyrus, *The Scribes for Women's Convents in Late Medieval Germany*, Appendix B; Minnis and Voaden, eds., *Medieval Holy Women*, 315.

11 As quoted in "Religious Nuns in Medieval Europe: Women of Action," 4.

12 Cesarius of Arles, "Rule for Nuns (c.512–534)," in Amt, ed., *Women's Lives in Medieval Europe*, 221–31.

13 Eckenstein, "Woman under Monasticism," 99.

14 Power, *Medieval English Nunneries*, 305ff.

15 Williams, "From the Holy Land to the Cloister"; Dolan, "A Revival of Female Spirituality," 48.

16 Macy, "The Ministry of Ordained Women," 32.

17 Macy, "The Ministry of Ordained Women," 35.

18 Macy, "The Ministry of Ordained Women," 37f.

19 Kidder, *Women, Celibacy and the Church*, 204; Gies and Gies, *Women in the Middle Ages*, 65f; Dronke, *Women Writers of the Middle Ages*, 80.

20 Gies and Gies, *Women in the Middle Ages*, 89.

21 Webster, "Order and Abbey at Fontevrault"; Mulder-Bakker, *Lives of the Anchoresses*, 70ff.

22 King, "The Desert Mothers"; Mayeski, *Women at the Table*, 60.

23 Johnson, "Hrotsvit of Gandersheim: Tenth Century Poet and Playwright."

24 Chicago, *The Dinner Party*, 72f, 135.

25 Silvas, "Kassia the Nun," 23.

26 Wellesley and Toth, "Kassia: A Bold and Beautiful Byzantine Poet."

27 Hardesty, *Great Women of Faith*, 30.

28 Cahill, *Mysteries of the Middle Ages*.

29 Gies and Gies, *Women in the Middle Ages*, 83.

30 Chicago, *The Dinner Party*, 143.

31 Turpin, *Women in Church History*, 92f; Dronke, *Women Writers in the Middle Ages*, 165.

32 Chicago, *The Dinner Party*, 75f, 144.

33 Eckenstein, "Harrad and the Garden of Delights," 109ff.

34 Brown, *Immodest Acts*.

35 Matter, "My Sister, My Spouse," 85.

36 Matter, "My Sister, My Spouse," 82f.

37 Eudes of Rouen, "Visitations of Nunneries (13th c.)," in Amt, ed., *Women's Lives in Medieval Europe*, 248f; "Nuns, Spinsters, and Single Women in Early Modern Europe," *Radcliffe Centennial News*, January 1980, 7.

38 Mulder-Bakker, *Lives of the Anchoresses*, 70ff.

39 Power, *Medieval English Nunneries*, 31.

40 Mulder-Bakker, *Lives of the Anchoresses*, 8ff.

41 King, "The Desert Mothers"; Aelred of Rievaulx's *Rule for a Solitary*, Hermitary Resources and Reflections on Hermits and Solitude, https:// www.hermitary.com/articles/aelred. html.

42 Grimlaicus's *Rule for Solitaries*, Hermitary Resources and Reflections on Hermits and Solitude, https://www.hermitary.com/articles/grimlaicus.html.

43 King, "The Desert Mothers."

44 Clay, *The Hermits and Anchorites of England*.

45 Kasten, "Locked up Forever in the Wall of a Church."

46 Clay, *The Hermits and Anchorites of England*, 108.

47 Clay, *The Hermits and Anchorites of England*, 120.

48 Warren, *Anchorites and Their Patrons in Medieval England*.

49 Inscription on the plaque opposite the well.

50 King, "The Desert Mothers"; Clay, *The Hermits and Anchorites of England*, 23.

51 "Religious Nuns in Medieval Europe: Women of Action," 8.

52 "Helena, Egeria, Paula, Eustochium, Pega, Bridget, Guthrithyr, Margaret, Isolda, Birgitta, Catherine, Margery, Rose and Julia: The Bible and Women Pilgrims," http://www.umilta.net/egeria.html.

53 Deboick, "The Friendly Recluse"; "Extreme Hermits: The Anchorites," *City Desert: Desert Spirituality for the City*, n.d., n.p.; Johnston, "Marguerite Porete: A Post Mortem," 91.

54 McAvoy, "Uncovering the Saintly Anchoress."

55 Clay, *The Hermits and Anchorites of England*; Hughes-Edwards, "Solitude and Sociability," 2.

56 "Jeann Le Ber," *Dictionary of Canadian Biography*, http://www.biographi.ca/en/bio/le_ber_jeanne_2E.html.

57 Email conversation with Sister Elizabeth Rolph-Thomas, 6 September 2017.

58 Mother Gavrilia, *The Ascetic of Love*.

Chapter 5

LA PAPESSE AND LA PUCELLE

TWO YOUNG WOMEN, JOAN, *la papesse*, and Joan, *la pucelle* (c.1412–31), dressed in male attire in public space in the face of the prohibition in the Old Testament (Hebrew scriptures), Deuteronomy 22:5: "A woman shall not be clothed with manly apparel, nor shall a man make use of feminine apparel. For whoever does these things is abominable with God." This edict was repeated at a local synod in 340 in "The Canons of the Holy Fathers Assembled at Gangra," and later ratified by the Council of Chalcedon in 451 CE, the fourth **ecumenical** council of the Christian Church.

These two women lived centuries apart: Joan, *la pucelle*, also known as Joan of Arc, was cut down at a young age, probably at 19 or in her early 20s in the fifteenth century in what is today France, burned at the stake. Joan, *la papesse*, known as Pope Joan, lived in Mainz, Germany, born of English parents, then at age 12, traveled to Athens to get an education, and finally lived in Rome sometime between the ninth and eleventh centuries—or did she?

Historians, journalists, and church administrators have tried to prove either that she was a real person or only a legend. Her status is of concern to the Catholic Church in light of the tradition of male papal succession from the discipleship of St. Peter to today, and the church's justification for closing the priesthood to women.

The Dominican Martin Polonus or Martin of Poland (?–1278), an outstanding chronicler with a reputation for solid scholarship, archbishop of Gneisen had he lived longer, has left us the first extant detailed story of Pope Joan's purported existence in his 1265 *Chronicon Pontificum et Imperatum*, a history of popes and emperors based on resources that are no longer available:

> After the aforesaid Leo, Pope Leo IV (790–855), John, an Englishman by descent, who came from Mainz, held the see two years, five months and four days, and the pontificate was vacant one month. He died at Rome. He, it is asserted, was a woman. And having been in youth taken by her lover to Athens in man's clothes, she made such progress in various sciences that there was nobody equal to her. So that afterwards lecturing on the Trivium at Rome [generally the three subjects—arithmetic, geometry, and music, or grammar, logic, and rhetoric] she had great masters for her disciples and hearers. And for as much as she was in great esteem in the city, both for her life and her learning, she was unanimously elected pope. But when pope she became pregnant by the person with whom she was intimate. But not knowing the time of her delivery, while going from Saint Peter's to the Lateran, taken in labour, she brought forth a child between the Colosseum and Saint Clement's Church. And afterwards dying, she was, it is said, buried in that place. And because the Lord Pope always turns aside from that way, there are some who are fully persuaded that it is done in detestation of the fact. Nor is she put in the Catalogue of the Holy Popes, as well on account of her female sex as on account of the foul nature of the transaction.[1]

A later addendum to the Berlin manuscript of Martin's account, not integrated—the writer apparently made no attempt to hide his or her authorship—gives more details: that Joan's lover was a secretary-deacon, that the street where her baby was born was later called the *Vicus Papissa*, that after her disgrace she was sent to a convent, and that her son became the bishop of Ostia near Rome.[2]

An earlier reference from the Irish theologian Marianus Scotus, known as Máel Brigte (1028–82), who died in Mainz where Joan was allegedly from, mentions Joan specifically after Leo "died in the calends of August" in his *Historiographi*, although the first version we have of Scotus's work is from 1559.[3]

There are different endings to Joan's story. In the 1225 version of the French Dominican Jean de Mailly's *Chronica universalis*, he presents two details that are different from Martin of Poland's account. After the birth of her baby, according to de Mailly, "the Roman justices tied the feet [Joan's] to the tail

FIGURE 5.1 Woodcut of Pope Joan giving birth during a papal procession, from a German translation by Heinrich Steinhöwel (1412–82) of Giovanni Boccaccio's *De mulieribus claris* (1374) printed by Johann Zainer at Ulm. Photo: © The Trustees of the British Museum.

of the horse, but meanwhile the people stoned her for half a league. At the point where she died and was buried, it was written: *Petre, Pater Patrum, Papisse Prodito Patrum* [O Peter, father of fathers, betray the child-bearing of the woman pope.]"[4]

The Swiss theologian Frederick Spanheim (1632–1701), a professor of philosophy at the University of Leyden at the end of the seventeenth century, found 500 references to Joan's story, most of them now lost. He referred to the writings of Anastasius (c.810–c.878), the papal librarian and Joan's contemporary, and the Benedictine monk Rudolphus (?–c.865), writing five years later, among others, but this material cannot be found today.[5]

In his book *The Myth of Pope Joan*, Alain Boureau lists more than 300 works about Joan, from Jean de Mailly's history around 1260 to Peter Stanford's book in 1998, *The Legend of Pope Joan*, including histories, novels, dramas, articles, and other writings. In his *Colloquia Mensalia*, Martin Luther, the great mover and shaker behind the Protestant Reformation, wrote that he had seen, "in 1510, in Rome in a public square … a stone monument to commemorate the pope who was really a woman and gave birth to a child on that very spot. I have seen the stone myself," he wrote, "and find it astonishing the popes permit it to exist."[6]

There are several controversies or challenges in connection with the story of Joan, *la papesse*, the pope.

It was said that after Joan's *débâcle*, a special chair, *sedia stercoria*, with a hole in the seat, was devised which all designated popes had to sit in before they could be crowned; a junior deacon or other male church official would perform a genital examination to ensure that the pope-to-be was male. Hadrian VI (1459–1523) was supposed to have abolished this custom during his reign. The journalist and former editor of the *Catholic Herald*, Peter Stanford, who spent several months in Rome trying to verify the story of Joan, sat on this chair now stored in the Vatican Museum, and discovered that it could not be used as a commode as has been suggested by those who doubt Joan's existence. It has also been hypothesized by the Catholic Church that it was a "birthing" chair, or simply a way of symbolizing the pope's humanity when he sat on it before his coronation.

The Catholic Church has also responded to the naming of the street after a female pope by claiming that a woman named Mrs. Pape lived there, and the street had been named after her. Apparently, a carved bust of Joan entitled "Johannes VIII, Foemina de Anglia" was part of the parade of popes in the cathedral in Siena until the beginning of the seventeenth century when Clement VIII (1536–1605), elected to the papacy in 1592, ordered its destruction; however, the bust was turned into Pope Zachary so as not to waste the marble.

Over the main altar in St. Peter's in Rome, under repeated crests of the sculptor Gian Lorenzo Bernini (1598–c.1680), there are seven carved versions of a woman's contorted face; in the eighth, there is a sculpture of a baby. Various other details suggest a woman pope giving birth.

There is no legislation specifically forbidding a woman pope. In the early sixteenth century in his *Treatise on the Council*, Cardinal Domenico Giacobazzi (1444–1528) mulls over what would happen if a woman were to be elected:

> What would happen if the elect is accused and convicted of being a woman? I think that he [the pope-elect] could be deposed by a council, first, because the keys of the church cannot fall to a woman and [a woman] would not have the right to possess or conserve the pontificate; but also because she does not hold the right to judge, which is a male prerogative. Also because of the scandal [that would be] produced in the universal Church.[7]

But Domenico also feared that the "one who is elected by two-thirds of the cardinals cannot be rejected; he is accepted because no exception can be retained."

There were laws, however, concerning women in the priesthood, touching sacred vessels and altar cloths, and carrying incense around the altar. In the theologian Gratian's *Decretals*, written around 1140 (after Joan was presumed to have lived), all these acts of "pestilence" were prohibited. Because of the date, Joan would theoretically be clear on all counts although the church had listed those "evils" earlier.[8]

But perhaps the greatest problem with Joan as pope is the lack of source material close to her supposed papacy. Almost 400 years elapsed from the time she was to have been pope to the first reference extant. Joan's "detractors" point to this gap as proof that she didn't exist, that her story was later devised as a way to mock the Catholic Church, especially by Protestant Reformation leaders. Those reformers did use the story as an example of the corruption of the papacy at that time; however, a suggestion that the Protestants went about inserting Joan's story into the existing documents during the Reformation in thousands of libraries and museums throughout the known world just wouldn't be possible.

It seems more likely that the reverse would be true: that Joan's story could have been excised from documents or prohibited over the centuries until it was rediscovered by a few historians or scribes. Throughout the history of the Christian Church in denominations of every stripe, we can document several instances where stories of active women ecclesiastical leaders have been deliberately deleted, altered, distorted, or simply omitted to downplay women's roles and their achievements. Most church histories have been written as if women never existed. But it was not just women's activity that was subject to revision. Close to the time of Joan's possible existence, the monk and right-hand man to Charlemagne, Alcuin of York (735–804), admitted to destroying a report of Pope Leo III's (750–816) adultery and his corrupt administration of church offices. Alcuin probably had the church's best interests at heart. Hincmar (806–82), the archbishop of Reims, who lived in Joan's presumed time, also admitted to tampering with and suppressing information about the church, under orders from his superiors.[9]

The New York writer Donna Woolfolk Cross, who researched the story of Joan and her times intensively for seven years and recently wrote the historical fiction novel *Pope Joan*, argues that the clergy at the time were so appalled by Joan's trickery that they went to great lengths to avoid and eliminate any written report of it.[10]

Did Joan *la papesse* exist? The jury is still out; the jurors do not yet agree.

"Did this papacy truly exist? Certainly not," says Alain Boureau, the director of École des Hautes Études en Sciences Sociales in Paris and author of *The Myth of Pope Joan*. Perhaps it was a cautionary tale, he suggests.[11] Thomas F.X. Noble, professor emeritus at the University of Notre Dame, agrees. "This is a legend, nothing more," he writes. "There is no room for anyone—papa or papessa—between the death of Leo IV on 17 July 855, and the elevation of Benedict's three-year pontificate, moreover."[12]

However, the ninth century was a very confused time in Rome and the papacy. "The odd pope may have dropped out here and there," asserts the British historian and ex-Jesuit Michael Walsh. "The whole system was so corrupt." Even by the fourth century, a new bishop of Rome was "a prize to fight for" as numerous street battles can attest. "By the tenth century, gold might change hands and blood might flow when a pope died."[13]

The historian and ex-nun Mary Malone admits that "90 per cent of me thinks there was a Pope Joan." At that time, there were bawdy monks, scheming cardinals, cross-dressing saints, intrigue, melodrama, corruption, and violence in Rome and the Vatican, she points out. "Popes … killed each other off, hammered each other to death. There were 12-year-old popes … we have knowledge of a 5-year-old archbishop.… It was a very odd time in history," Malone agrees.[14]

Cross claims that "the historical evidence is there." She points out that it's the weight of evidence, "over 500 chronicle accounts of her existence." Where there's that much historical smoke, she notes, there must have been a fire. "Something happened," she suggests.[15]

After his stay in Rome looking for Pope Joan, Peter Stanford concludes, "Weighing all this evidence, I am convinced that Pope Joan was an historical figure, though perhaps not all the details about her that have been passed on down the centuries are true."

There are several suggestions as to how the story of Pope Joan began if indeed she were not real. One is from the sixteenth-century Italian historian Onofrio Panvinio (1529–68). He theorized that the tale may have begun with Pope John XII (937–64) who had several mistresses, one called Joan who was extremely influential in Rome. That Pope John was assassinated.[16]

The writer Brian Dunning thinks that Pope Joan may have lived later, perhaps in the eleventh century. There were a series of "antipopes" who were competing claimants at the same time. Joan may have been a minor pope among the anti-popes. And there was confusion over the numbering of the various popes called John; in the late tenth century there seems to have been a pope and an anti-pope both named John XIV.[17]

On the other hand, Joan of Arc's story is definitely fact. As with Pope Joan, there are myriad works about her life, but there are many more details that are known to be authentic. One of the first tributes to Joan was from the contemporary French court writer Christine de Pisan (1364–1430) in a lyrical ballad called "Song of Joan of Arc." Christine was so famous and talented that she was able to support herself financially through her writing:

> And you, blessed Maid, can we forget,
> Since God has honored you so much,
> Since you have sliced apart the rope
> That held us bound, with one sure touch?
> Could we praise you too much at all.
> When you have calmed our countryside,
> Once battered down by war's cruel blast,
> So that we may in peace reside?
> In a good hour you were born,
> Blessed be the one who made you so!
> His virgin, as He made you be,
> In whom the Holy Ghost does blow
> In great grace; for the Holy Spirit
> Such generous gifts will you afford,
> That he will deny you nil;
> Who else could grant a just reward?[18]

Joan, *la pucelle*, the maid, one of two girls and three boys in her family, had an ordinary upbringing in Domrémy, a small village in northeastern France on the River Meuse with fewer than 200 inhabitants. Baptized in the local church by the priest Jean Minet, she was taught the basic Catholic faith by her mother, Isabelle Romée (1377–1458); she could recite the Our Father, the creed, and the Hail Mary. A religious child, she confessed her sins at least every year. She learned to sew and spin, and helped out with the housework, but was illiterate. At times she played with the other children under the "fairy tree," an admission that her inquisitors later used to link her to the occult. Deciding to remain a virgin, she refused an offer of marriage arranged by her father, Jacques/Jacquot d'Arc/Tart (1380–1440), a farmer and minor village official.

When Joan was about 13—she was never quite sure of her age—she began to hear voices and see a great blinding light. The first time this happened was in the summer at noon in her father's garden. She was terrified. Joan kept hearing voices and seeing the light especially when church bells chimed.[19] She believed the voices came from God or an angel, later identifying her voices as those of St. Michael the Archangel, patron saint of France, who came with a band of angels, and two gentle virgins, the martyrs St. Catherine of Alexandria, who was much later "downgraded" in the Catholic Church as being apocryphal although maintained in the Orthodox tradition, and St. Margaret of Antioch, patroness of falsely accused people, who called her "Jehanne the Maid" or "Child of God." Joan never told her local priest about these visions, or at first, even her family. Finally, after about four years, the voices told her that she must raise the siege of the city of Orléans. The Hundred Years' War with England that had begun in 1337 was going badly for France. England's king claimed the French throne, and should Orléans fall, it was considered to be disastrous for the French because of the vast territory the English would then control.[20]

Joan's story is well known: she left home to save France because of her voices; she wore male dress suitable for travel and battle—including a suit of armor especially crafted, weighing about 60 pounds, a helmet, dagger, cutlass, lance, and a sword that she never used in battle; her personal banner as an identification in war; her cropped hair; the gift of a horse; she led an army of 1,000 or more French troops to victory time and time again against the English occupiers; and she eventually organized the coronation of the French king Charles VII (1403–61) at Reims on 16 July 1429. Joan fought in 13 engagements, being successful at Troyes, Lagny, Patay, Meung, Jargeau, Beaugency, Saint-Pierre-le-Moûtier, Montépilloy, and Orléans. Thirty cities surrendered without a fight. Once she was wounded by an arrow, but she kept on in battle and healed quickly.[21]

The theologian and biographer Donald Spoto points out that around that time, Joan was not the only woman to dress in armor and go into battle. Margaret of Jerusalem (c.1150–c.1215) took up arms in Jerusalem against the Saladin in 1187 when she was on a pilgrimage. "During this siege which lasted fifteen days," she wrote, "I wore a breastplate like a man; I came and went on the ramparts, with a cauldron on my head for a helmet. Though a woman, I seemed a warrior, I threw the weapon; though filled with fear ... I was taken prisoner, but on paying some guineas, I was set free." Eleanor of Aquitaine (1122–1204) took part in the Second Crusade in the twelfth century and in the fourteenth, Joanna, countess of Montfort (c.1295–1374), took up arms after her husband died, to protect the rights of her son the duke of Brittany. She led a "raid of knights" that successfully destroyed one of the enemy's camps. The Dominican theologian Johannes Nider (1380–1438) described a holy woman from Cologne who wore men's clothing and had a career as a war commander around this time, perhaps the same woman.[22]

On 23 May 1430, Joan and her army were attacking the Burgundian camp at Margny, north of Compiègne when she was ambushed and captured. The English bought her from the Burgundians for 10,000 *livres tournois* (over US$2,000,000 today); she was imprisoned and then tried for heresy. A 19-year-old illiterate French peasant girl, although obviously a clever one, was pitted against 131 theologians, university professors, canon lawyers, and politicians, more than 60 of them sitting in the room opposite her at any one time during many sessions of the five-month trial from 9 January 1431, until her burning on 30 May. This included various sittings such as a preparatory trial.[23]

Later, the trial would be declared invalid, but not before Joan was dead. Her accusers were largely concerned with her visions and her male dress. Trying to prove that Joan's visions were from the devil, that her voices were false, they challenged her over and over again about the appearance of the saints. She replied candidly but often in exasperation. "I saw them with the eyes of my body as well as I see you," Joan responded to the inquisition at one assembly. "And when they left me I wept, and I wished that they might have taken me with them." Once, the questioning went like this, with Joan skating on thin ice, for it was blasphemous to assert that one saw God or other religious personages in human form:

Did they have hair?
It is a comfort to know that they have.
Was Saint Michael naked?
Do you think God had nothing with which to clothe him?
Did Saint Margaret speak English?
Why would she speak English when she is not on the English side?[24]

At the end of the trials, the inquisitor summed up the charges against Joan in his counsel to the judges:

We charge you so that a certain woman commonly called Jeanne be by
you sentenced and declared to be a witch or sorceress, a diviner, a false
prophetess, a conjuror of demons, a committed practitioner of magic.
She thinks only evil of our Catholic faith, she is schismatic, sacrilegious,
idolatrous, apostate, evil speaking and evil doing, blasphemous, scandalous,
seditious, destroyer of peace, a warmonger who thirsts for human blood
and urges others to spill it. She has abandoned the decency of her sex, she
dresses unnaturally like a man-at-arms, she betrays human and divine law
and Church discipline, she seduces princes and people alike, she accepts
veneration and she has contempt for God.[25]

After Joan was burned, what was left of her was shown to the crowd so that
they could see that she was a woman and not the devil—or a man.

Joan wore male attire as a protection against rape and to facilitate her
movements in battle. While engaged in the war, she slept alongside soldiers
and although many of them respected and idolized her and left her alone,
there was always grave danger for a woman especially if she were wearing
a dress. Male battle attire gave her much greater security; her hosen, boots,
and tunic could be fastened together in one piece and would be difficult for
anyone to remove without a struggle. When she was in prison, several guards,
and at least once "a great English lord," tried to "take her" by force.[26]

In 1456, Pope Callixtus III (1378–1458) authorized an examination of the
trial, a rehabilitation trial with 115 witnesses, and proclaimed Joan innocent.
Her mother had asked the archbishop of Reims to "wipe out this mark of
infamy suffered wrongfully." She insisted that the trial and its resulting action
were "an insulting, outrageous and scornful action towards the rulers and
the people…. After having taken away all means of defending her [Joan's]
innocence … condemned her in a baneful and iniquitous way, flouting all the
rules of procedure, charging her falsely and untruthfully of many crimes …
provoking tears from all and heaping opprobrium, infamy and an irreparable
wrong on this Isabelle and her [family]."[27]

Joan had been denied a legal advisor as was her right. She was also denied
an appeal to the pope. She had asked to be transferred to a church prison
with women to guard her where she could safely wear a dress, rather than
in the dark tower cell where she was chained to the wall with an iron band
around her waist, her arms held by cuffs in the daytime, and additional
shackles at night with three male guards, but this was also denied her. Joan
had also been threatened with torture to obtain a confession sought by the

tribunal. Many of the trial records were falsified. The presiding judge, Pierre Cauchon (1371–1442), bishop of Beauvais, was determined to find Joan guilty and employed any means necessary; it was said that he and a nephew were in the employ of the English, Cauchon drawing a yearly salary of 1,000 *livres tournois* as a member of the (English) Royal Council along with wages for other services. Several of the jurors, who were opposed to the proceedings knowing they were illegal, either were forced to cooperate and say nothing, or hurriedly left town to save their life. In the end, only about half of them voted at all.[28] On 7 July 1456, a copy of the original trial was burned in the archbishop's palace, but no one was punished.

It was pointed out at this later trial that medieval cross-dressing was not always a crime. As stated in the *Summa Theologica* by the thirteenth-century theologian St. Thomas Aquinas (1225–74), it was to be evaluated in context: "Nevertheless, this (cross-dressing) may at times be done without sin due to some necessity, either for the purpose of concealing oneself from enemies, or due to a lack of any other clothing, or on account of some other thing of this sort."[29]

Joan was within her right to be disguised as a pageboy while traveling through enemy territory, to wear full armor in battle and afterwards to prevent molestation during the war and in prison. Most of the jurors would have been familiar with this ruling; the Thomas Aquinas statement was one of many such citations in canon law. The tribunal, however, used her male costume as a way to ensure that she was found guilty. After she had agreed to wear a woman's dress, it was mysteriously taken one night and she was left with only male clothes to wear, which she found beside her bed in a bag. Thus she was accused of a repeat offense, grounds for being charged with heresy.

Both Joans were guilty of appropriating male culture, of assuming the role of men. They went far beyond their "proper" place as women, which was to stay at home minding children and occupying themselves with "women's" activities. Pope Joan disguised herself as a man in order to be educated, a male prerogative, and then assumed male roles as various clergy, attaining in the end the ultimate male position of pope. Joan of Arc dressed in men's armor for protection and ease of battle, taking on the male vocation of soldier. She had her hair cropped, likely just so that it would fit under her helmet, but in the style of a male soldier. Pope Joan probably had her hair trimmed as well.

Both of them assumed equality with male clergy: in her papal role Pope Joan became superior to all; Joan of Arc evidently thought it unnecessary to consult the local priest about her voices, believing that she had a direct pipeline to God without the aid of the clergy. According to Roman Catholic tradition at the time, Joan should have sought permission from the Church before trusting in her voices and apparitions. As the trial judge stated in Article 62 against her, Joan took "upon herself the authority of God and the angels," and raised herself "above all ecclesiastical power to lead people into error," and later that "the Lord does not wish anyone to claim to be subject to God alone.... Instead he gave and entrusted to men of the Church the power and authority to know and judge the acts of the faithful ... and whoever hears them [men of the church] hears God."[30] Both Joans were punished for their "crimes." They received their just desserts in the eyes of the Church. Whether Pope Joan was real or only a cautionary tale, she was either stoned to death or condemned to do penance in a convent until pardoned by her son, the bishop. Joan of Arc was burned at the stake.

In 1920, Joan of Arc was canonized by the Church. Even more widely known than Pope Joan, there are hundreds of books about her in English, as well as at least a thousand histories in French along with novels, poems, songs, hymns, essays, operas, plays, films, paintings, engravings, and statues. Countless churches bear her name. "Pope Joan" lives in relative obscurity.

We need to note that not all writers or contemporary analysts of Joan of Arc believe her innocent of the charge of witchcraft. In her book *The Witch-Cult in Western Europe*, Professor Margaret Murray (1863–1963) suggested strongly that Joan was the head of a local "Dianic" cult, that she did indeed deliberately participate in rituals around the fairy tree, and that her angelic visitors were symbolic of the "Old Religion." She refused to say the Paternoster (the Our Father prayer), which witches were unable to recite, and there were other clues that led Murray to believe that Joan was an integral part of the local peasants' superstitions.[31]

FURTHER READING

PRIMARY

Hobbins, Daniel, ed. and trans. *The Trial of Joan of Arc*. Cambridge, MA: Harvard
    University Press, 2005.
Scott, W.S., ed. and trans. *The Trial of Joan of Arc*. Chatham, UK: The Folio Society, 1956.
Wirth, Robert, ed. *Primary Sources and Context Concerning Joan of Arc's Male Clothing*.
    Translated by Allen Williamson. Minneapolis: Historical Association for Joan
    of Arc Studies, 2006.

SECONDARY

Barstow, Anne Llewellyn. "Joan of Arc and Female Mysticism." *Journal of Feminist Studies in Religion* 1, no. 2 (Fall 1985): 29–42.

Boureau, Alain. *The Myth of Pope Joan*. Translated by Lydia G. Cochrane. Chicago: University of Chicago Press, 2001.

Harrison, Kathryn. *Joan of Arc: A Life Transfigured*. New York: Doubleday, 2014.

Noble, Thomas F.X. "The Legend of Pope Joan: In Search of the Truth." *The Catholic Historical Review*, October 1999.

Spoto, Donald. *Joan: The Mysterious Life of the Heretic Who Became a Saint*. San Francisco: Harper, 2007.

Stanford, Peter. *The Legend of Pope Joan*. New York: Henry Holt and Company, 1998.

Warner, Marina. *Joan of Arc: The Image of Female Heroism*. New York: Vintage Books, 1981.

NOTES

1 Stanford, *The Legend of Pope Joan*, 19.

2 Stanford, *The Legend of Pope Joan*, 19f.

3 Stanford, *The Legend of Pope Joan*, 24.

4 Stanford, *The Legend of Pope Joan*, 26f.

5 Stanford, *The Legend of Pope Joan*, 20f.

6 Charles River Editors, *Pope Joan*.

7 Boureau, *The Myth of Pope Joan*, 37.

8 Boureau, *The Myth of Pope Joan*, 37f.

9 Charles River Editors, *Pope Joan*, n.p.

10 Cross, *Pope Joan: A Novel*.

11 Boureau, *The Myth of Pope Joan*, 2.

12 Noble, "The Legend of Pope Joan."

13 As quoted in Stanford, *The Legend of Pope Joan*, 94; "New System Elects a Pope."

14 ABC News, "Looking for Pope Joan," 29 December 2005, https://abcnews.go.com/Primetime/pope-joan/story?id=1453197.

15 ABC News, "Looking for Pope Joan."

16 Knight, *Biography*.

17 Dunning, "Pope Joan," *Skeptoid Podcast* #353.

18 de Pisan, *Ditié de Jeanne d'Arc*, stanzas 21–22. The poem was written in 1429.

19 Curiously, church bells were rung to keep witches from flying over a village. Guiley, *The Encyclopedia of Witches and Witchcraft*, 23.

20 Spoto, *Joan*, 20f.

21 Spoto, *Joan*, 66ff.

22 Spoto, *Joan*, 73; Hobbins, ed. and trans., *The Trial of Joan of Arc*, 30; "Helena, Egeria, Paula, Eustochium, Pega, Bridget, Guthrithyr, Margaret, Isolda, Birgitta, Catherine, Margery, Rose and Julia: The Bible and Women Pilgrims," http://www. umilta.net/egeria.html.

23 Pernoud and Clin, *Jeanne d'Arc*, 182.

24 Trask, ed. and trans., *Joan of Arc: In Her Own Words*.

25 Spoto, *Joan*, 166.

26 Pernoud, "The Retrial of Joan of Arc," 236.

27 Harrison, *Joan of Arc*, 314f.

28 Spoto, *Joan*, 66ff; Robo, "The Holiness of Saint Joan of Arc"; Scott, ed. and trans., *The Trial of Joan of Arc*, 10.

29 St. Thomas Aquinas, "Secunda Secundae Partis, Q.169, Art. 2:Resp. Obj.3," in *Summa Theologica*.

30 Warner, *Joan of Arc*, 128; Hobbins, ed. and trans., *The Trial of Joan of Arc*, 152, 172.

31 Murray, *The Witch-Cult in Western Europe*.

Chapter 6

WOMAN AS WITCH

IN 1684, AT THE only witch trial held in Pennsylvania, the judge, Quaker William Penn, asked the accused woman, "Art thou a witch? Hast thou ridden through the air on a broomstick?" When she answered that she was, he replied that he knew of no law against it. She was charged with "the common fame of a witch," but not of being one, and was released on her husband's recognizance.[1]

The Dominican theologians Heinrich Krämer (c.1430–1505) and Jacob Sprenger (c.1436–95), co-authors of the *Malleus Maleficarum*, the 1487 manual for witch hunters, would not have agreed. In their eyes, being a witch—even being accused of being one—was the worst of Christian heresies, and grounds for severe punishment. Earlier, the French inquisitors Jean Veneti (?–1475) and Nicolas Jacquier (1410–72) had both argued in scholarly papers that witches were a new heretical sect. Margaret Murray (1863–1963), who wrote extensively on witchcraft, noted that there was no malice in the inquisitors' work; they sincerely believed that malevolent witch-craft existed and must be defeated. After all, it had been written in the Old Testament, in Exodus 22:18, "thou shalt not suffer a witch to live." Perhaps Murray had never heard of the inquisitor Pierre de Lancre (c.1553–c.1631), who played the flute at intervals in the proceedings at Labourd in 1609 and forced condemned witches to dance for him as entertainment. He believed that 3,000 people including clergy bore witches' marks.[2]

According to author and professor Herbert W. Richardson (1932–2013), 80 per cent of all accused witches in mediaeval Europe were female.³ Krämer and Sprenger might have put that figure even higher, for as they mention in their manual, "there are three things in nature, the Tongue, an Ecclesiastic, and a Woman, which know no moderation in goodness or vice": "When they [women] exceed the bounds of their condition they reach the greatest heights and the lowest depths of goodness or vice. When they are governed by a good spirit, they are most excellent in virtue; but when they are governed by an evil spirit, they indulge the worst possible vice."⁴

Krämer and Sprenger note that the experience and testimony of credible witnesses confirmed that most witches were of the "fragile feminine sex." They listed three reasons for this. The first was that there is "no wrath like the wrath of a woman." They would rather "dwell with a lion and a dragon than to keep house with a wicked woman": "What else is woman but a foe to friendship, an inescapable punishment, a necessary evil, a natural temptation, a desirable calamity, a domestic danger, a delectable detriment, an evil of nature, painted with fair colours!... When a woman thinks alone, she thinks evil."⁵ The second reason that more women were witches was that they were more "credulous" than men, and the third reason was that they had "slippery tongues, and are unable to conceal from the fellow-women [sic] those things which by evil arts they know; and since they are weak, they find an easy and secret manner of vindicating themselves by witchcraft." However, of all the wicked women they had come in contact with, they asserted that midwives "surpass all others in wickedness ... no one does more harm to the Catholic Church than midwives ... if a woman dare to cure without having studied she is a witch and must die." Women, of course, were generally not allowed to study. Jeffrey Russell points out that the accusation was understandable. As he says, the midwife is lonely and usually a widow. Babies die, and the death is fixed on the midwife. She must be a witch.⁶

But even before the *Malleus Maleficarum*, the Dominican Johannes Nider (c.1380–1438) had dealt with demonic baby-eaters—that is, witches—in the fifth book of his 1438 *Formicarius*, "Witches and Their Deceptions." He, too, had found that it was primarily women who were witches. As he explained: "The broom that the witch immerses in the water so that it should rain does not cause the rain, but a demon who sees this ... the witch gives a sign with the broom, but the demon acts, so that it rains through the action of the demon."⁷

He believed that women were particularly susceptible to demons because of their lust and their weakness, and therefore they were especially dangerous. It was also at this time that witches were depicted as women riding on broomsticks with special hats and long black cloaks, worshipping the devil, which was often shown as a goat. Witches were accused of subverting Christian symbols: for instance, drinking the blood of children they had supposedly murdered instead of the wine of the Eucharist, or eating sliced turnips instead of the Host, or trampling on a crucifix.[8]

Curiously, it was in the so-called **Dark Ages** that the Christian Church *forbade* a belief in witches. In the eighth century, the missionary St. Boniface (c.672–754) declared that believing in witches was unchristian. King Charlemagne (742–814) decreed the death penalty for anyone who burned "witches," because burning was a pagan custom. The archbishop of Lyon, St. Agobard (c.779–840), declared that witches did not make bad weather, and another church official declared that night-flying and other witch beliefs were hallucinations and views held only by pagans and infidels. King Coloman of Hungary (1070–1116) said that witches did not exist and John of Salisbury, bishop of Chartres (1120–80), agreed that the idea of a witches' *sabbat* was only a dream.[9]

By the end of the Middle Ages, however, the notion that witches existed was commonly held. The historian Jeffrey Russell posited that the persecution of witches by all Christian persuasions increased enormously in the sixteenth century because of the chaos of religious conflicts, popular movements, and wars engendered by social tensions. Plagues, famine, and the shift of men and women from rural areas to urban centers also led to social unrest. And as was noted in the chapter on the earlier church, a radical shift in the attitude toward women took place around the twelfth century.[10]

Richardson estimates that in the 400-year period of persecution of alleged witches, more than one million people were put to death. The author James Pennethorne Hughes puts the number even higher, at around nine million. Not every historian agrees. Estimates range dramatically from around 60,000 to several million.

The hounding of "witches" began in 1250, but between 1450 and 1650, an intense campaign took place to root out this most evil of evils, mostly on the European continent. In some towns, almost the entire population was wiped out; in one village, only one woman escaped—389 women were put to death. It is interesting and significant that at the same time, the phenomenon of "courtly love" was widespread in society: the art of worshipping women with a chaste, platonic, and ennobling love. As Richardson notes, the "shadow face" of the adoration of women was the condemnation of them as witches. He explains that if one mistreated women, then one compensated by treating them overly well—regarding women either as saints or as witches, holy Virgin Marys or penitent Mary Magdalenes.

In Germany, the persecution raged. Six hundred were burned by a single bishop in Bamberg; 900 were killed in a single year in the bishopric of Würzburg. In Nuremberg and other great cities, there were 100 to 200 burnings a year. Similar trials took place in Switzerland and France. A thousand people were put to death in one year around Como. The French lawyer and inquisitor Nicholas Rémy, called Remigius (1530–1616), is said to have boasted that he caused the burning of 900 people over 15 years, although it is thought that his total was twice that. In three months in Geneva in 1515, 500 were executed. Four hundred were killed at once in Toulouse, and there were 50 at Douai in one year. Two hundred were burned at Labout. In Scandinavia in 1669, 70 people were condemned to death at one time, including 15 children.[11]

And so it continued up to the late eighteenth century, except in England where very few were burned as witches and witchcraft was a civil not a religious crime. A British Member of Parliament, Reginald Scot (1538–99), wrote in his 1584 *Discoverie of Witchcraft* that there was no such thing as witchcraft. His reasoning was that the age of miracles was over, and since God no longer worked miracles himself, he would not allow the devil to do so either. There were, however, a small number of executions by hanging in that country: for example in 1633 in Lancaster County where 17 people were convicted; in 1645 at Bury St. Edmonds when 68 witches met their death on the gallows; and in the same year at Chelmsford when 38 people were condemned to die. There were a few lynchings: for instance, a poor couple in their 70s, Ruth and John Osborne, who were tied and thrown in a pond to drown. They were rescued but died soon after.[12]

In Scotland, witch trials went on longer than in England, with the last woman burned in Dornoch in 1722. The most famous witch trial in that country was in 1590 in North Berwick, where 70 people were accused of witchcraft or treason. The Scottish journalist Charles Mackay (1814–89), writing about the witch mania, suggested that:

We naturally expect that the Scotch ... a people renowned for their powers of imagination—should be more deeply imbued with this gloomy superstition than their neighbours of the south.... Ghosts, goblins, wraiths, kelpies and a whole host of spiritual beings were familiar to the dwellers by the misty glens of the highlands and the romantic streams of the lowlands.[13]

Witchcraft spread rapidly and widely; accused witches undergoing torture usually quickly confessed and named accomplices or colleagues to stop their own agony. Very few accused were silent in the face of such pain. There was a point at which it was simply humanly impossible to endure the torture to which the accused were subjected. The German burgomaster Johannes Junius (c.1573–1628) managed to smuggle a note from his prison cell to his daughter in July 1628:

Many hundred thousand good-nights, dearly beloved daughter Veronica. Innocent have I come to prison, innocent have I been tortured, innocent must I die. For whoever comes into the witch prison [at Bamberg], must become witch or be tortured until he invents something out of his head.... [The torturer] put the thumbscrews on me, so that the blood ran out at the nails and everywhere so that for four weeks I could not use my hands as you can see from the writing.... Then I thought Heaven and Earth were at an end; eight times did they draw me up and let me fall again.... The executioner said, "Sir, I beg you for God's sake, confess something ... for you cannot endure the torture you will be put to, and even if you bear it all, yet you will not escape."... Now dear child, here you have all my confessions, for which I must die. And they are sheer lies and made-up things ... for they never leave off with the torture until one confesses something.... I have taken several days to write this; my hands are both lame ... your father Johannes Junius will never see you more ... six have confessed against me ... and begged my forgiveness before they were executed.[14]

Thousands of "old ladies" and others had supposedly made pacts with the devil. Almost every night, they greased themselves with a lubricant often made out of the fat of murdered infants, slipped through cracks and keyholes, mounted on broomsticks or even flying goats, and soared off to their *sabbat* to meet the devil, who might appear as a toad or a goat or a big black bearded man. The witches kissed him, generally on his backside or "private parts," and then took part in a sexual orgy or a feast or both. When the witches weren't at their *sabbat*, they were reportedly destroying harvests, or causing their neighbors' pigs to fall ill, or starting tornadoes, or some such devastating event.

But it was not just old ladies who were accused of being witches. In 1294, the Irish, four-times-married, extremely wealthy Lady Alice Kyteler (1280–1324) was accused by her most recent husband of bewitching him, and the local bishop pursued the case. Lady Alice, her son William, her maid Petronilla de Meath (1300–24), and several others were accused of animal sacrifices and having sexual relations with the devil. Lady Alice managed to escape to England with Petronilla's child, but Petronilla was flogged and burned. It has been suggested that William was the child's father. In her feminist sculpture, Judy Chicago recognized the women who lost their lives in the witchcraft craze by honoring Petronilla with a plate and table runner.[15]

The witch craze had begun in the Alps and the Pyrenees, the mountainous regions where superstitions and folktales were most common. Coupled with the "heresies" of groups such as the Cathars and the Waldensians, it seemed to the church as if the whole area had become infected and out of control, at least out of the church's control, and must be "cleansed." Pope Innocent III (1161–1216) declared that heretics were "traitors to God," and Pope Innocent IV (1195–1254) described them as "thieves and murderers of souls." The historian Hugh Trevor-Roper (1914–2003) believed that the Dominicans themselves were responsible for creating the mythology of witchcraft. As it was written on the title page of the *Malleus Maleficarum*, "to disbelieve in witches is the greatest of heresies." The papacy backed the witch hunt and in 1484, Pope Innocent VIII (1432–92) decreed that the inquisitors were not to be molested or hindered in any way or the disturber would be excommunicated or given "even more terrible sentences." In 1468, Pope Paul II (1417–71) had declared witchcraft to be *crimen exeptum*, removing all legal limits on the use of torture, which Trevor-Roper suggests was largely responsible for spreading witchcraft so rapidly.[16]

There were, of course, voices of moderation, often with disastrous results. For example, the Dutch physician Johann Wier/Weyer (1515–88) argued in his treatise *On Magic* that most witches were only harmless old women suffering from mental delusions. But for his trouble, he himself was accused of being a witch. Dr. George Hahn, vice-chancellor of the diocese of Bamberg in Germany, who was in charge of the witch hunt there, was himself burned at

FIGURE 6.1 Witches flying, a section of a page from "Le champion des dames," 1451, a poem by Martin le Franc (1410–61), a defense of virtuous women, drawing possibly by Barthélemy Poignare. One woman is sitting astride a broom, the other on a stick. They are described as *vaudoises* or Waldensians. Manuscript: Bibliothèque nationale de France, MS Fr. 12476, fol. 105v.

the stake in 1628 along with his wife and daughter. Reginald Scot (c.1538–99), an English country gentleman, self-published a massive book, *The Discoverie of Witchcraft*, in 1584, in which he denounced the pope and the persecution of witches. Scot believed that there were some deluded witches but they derived no power from the devil. He abhorred the "extreme and intolerable tyranny" of the Inquisition. King James I (1566–1625) ordered copies of the book burned, but not, evidently, Scot. The German Jesuit Friedrich von Spee (1591–1635), confessor to condemned witches, published *Cautio Criminalis* (*Precautions for Prosecutors*) anonymously in 1631, writing: "Often I have thought that the only reason why we are not all wizards is due to the fact that we have not all been tortured.… She [a condemned woman] can never clear herself. The investigating committee would feel disgraced if it acquitted a woman once arrested and in chains, she has to be guilty by fair means or foul."[17] There were other dissenting voices. However, when the lawyers, judges, and clergy themselves were accused, widespread reason finally began to prevail.

By the middle of the seventeenth century, skepticism led to fewer trials and burnings, although the punishments continued into the eighteenth century.[18]

In the United States, there were only a few executions for witchcraft and the situation was somewhat different. Twenty people were killed as a result of the Salem witch trials, 14 of them women. Five others died in prison. However, there were other less well-known executions. In Hartford, Connecticut, Elsie (Alse) Young was hanged in 1647, and a healer with an "abrasive disposition," Margaret Jones of Charleston, Massachusetts, was convicted the next year. One historian has discovered that there were 344 people accused of witchcraft in New England between 1620 and 1725.[19]

The most famous cases, though, were in 1692 in Salem near Boston, Massachusetts, where young girls and some women began having fits. There was never any suggestion that the girls were play-acting, or just having fun because they were bored. It was thought that local witches were causing the girls' hysteria, local men and women named by the girls. The first three to be charged as witches were Tabitha, a black slave woman recently brought to the community; shrewish, slovenly Sarah Good, who begged from door to door; and Sarah Osborne, who had been "living in sin" and was lax in her church attendance. All three were obvious "social misfits." Another was Martha Cory, a rough countrywoman, outspoken and opinionated. From there, the witch craze spread as the girls thought of or heard other names, many of whom they didn't even know, men and women from neighboring towns and cities—Reading, Gloucester, Beverly, Lynn, Malden, Amesbury, Billerica, Marblehead, Boston, Charlestown, and Andover.

The inexperienced jurors at the witch trials based their decisions principally on three signs: "devil's marks," generally skin eruptions common in old age, which were discovered by stripping the accused in their prison cells; any mischief following anger between neighbors; and spectral evidence, that is the idea that the devil could assume the shape of witches, but not of innocent people, and anyone could say that the accused's "shape" or spectre had come to their room last night—and how could that be disproved?

There were skeptics in the community, many of whom were afraid to criticize too loudly lest they themselves be charged. As in Europe, it was only when some of the towns' gentle and more prominent men and women were accused that reason began to assert itself. First, spectral evidence was questioned, recognizing that the devil might assume the shape of an innocent person. (That the devil might not exist was never suggested.) Finally, the Puritan minister and president of Harvard University, Increase Mather

(1639–1723), publicly suggested that it was "better that ten suspected witches should escape than one innocent person should be condemned."[20]

In the fall of 1692, 24 brave citizens from Andover presented a paper denouncing the accusing girls as "distempered persons," and protesting their authority in court. "We know no one who can think himself safe if the accusations of children and others who are under diabolical influence shall be received as persons in good fame," they wrote. The brief had an impact.[21]

Three days later, Governor Sir William Phips (1651–95) of Massachusetts dismissed the court, but there were still more than 100 accused witches being kept in badly built, overcrowded jails. These included two eight-year-old children, and three other children aged 10, 11, and 13. There were numerous adults as well, most of them released by the governor to be placed in the charge of their families. Yet more were still being taken in. The courts sat again in November and December, but the judges agreed that they would not allow spectral evidence, which released most of the accused. All of those who were condemned were pardoned by Phips, as soon as they or some friend paid their prison fees (expenses), about two shillings and sixpence a week (or US$20 in today's currency), a hardship for many considering that many of the accused were held for months.

But the witchcraft craze was over. The last known execution was in 1775 in Germany.

FURTHER READING

PRIMARY

Krämer, Heinrich, and Jacob Sprenger. *Malleus Maleficarum*. Translated by Montague Summers. New York: Dover Publications, 1971.

SECONDARY

Deane, Jennifer Kolpacoff. *A History of Medieval Heresy and Inquisition*. Lanham, MD: Rowman and Littlefield, 2011.
Ehrenreich, Barbara, and Deirdre English. *Witches, Midwives and Nurses: A History of Women Healers*. Old Westbury, NY: The Feminist Press, 1973.
Guiley, Rosemary Ellen. *The Encyclopedia of Witches and Witchcraft*. New York: Facts on File, 1989.

Hughes, Pennethorne. *Witchcraft*. Middlesex, UK: Penguin Books, 1965.

Kirsch, Jonathan. *The Grand Inquisitor's Manual: A History of Terror in the Name of God*. New York: Harper Collins, 2008.

Russell, Jeffrey B. *A History of Witchcraft, Sorcerers, Heretics and Pagans*. London: Thames and Hudson, 1980.

Starkey, Marion L. *The Devil in Massachusetts*. Garden City, NY: Anchor Books, 1969.

Trevor-Roper, H.R. *The European Witch-Craze of the Sixteenth and Seventeenth Centuries and Other Essays*. New York: Harper & Row, 1969.

NOTES

1 Bacon, *Mothers of Feminism*, 29. Some sources recount the story with the woman's reply in the negative, that she said she was not a witch.

2 Deane, *A History of Medieval Heresy and Inquisition*, 207; Guiley, *The Encyclopedia of Witches and Witchcraft*, 194.

3 Herbert W. Richardson, lecture, Faculty of Religious Studies, McGill University, 1981; Monter, "The Pedestal and the Stake," 132f, analyzed witch trials and found that between 71 and 92 per cent of those tried were women, and from 34 to 55 per cent of the women tried were widows, mainly from Germany, Switzerland, Belgium, and England.

4 Krämer and Sprenger, *Malleus Maleficarum*, Part I, Question VI, "Concerning Witches who copulate with Devils. Why is it that Women are chiefly addicted to Evil superstitions?"

5 Krämer and Sprenger, *Malleus Maleficarum*, Part I, Question VI.

6 Ehrenreich and English, *Witches, Midwives and Nurses*, 17; Russell, *A History of Witchcraft*, 84.

7 As quoted in Deane, *A History of Medieval Heresy and Inquisition*, 207.

8 Deane, *A History of Medieval Heresy and Inquisition*, 208ff.

9 Trevor-Roper, *The European Witch-Craze*, 92f.

10 Russell, *A History of Witchcraft*, 82.

11 Guiley, *The Encyclopedia of Witches and Witchcraft*, 281.

12 Hughes, *Witchcraft*, 185f; Russell, *A History of Witchcraft*, 69, 96.

13 Hughes, *Witchcraft*, 191f; Guiley, *The Encyclopedia of Witches and Witchcraft*, 247.

14 Hughes, *Witchcraft*, 191ff.

15 Chicago, *The Dinner Party*, 76ff.

16 Guiley, *The Encyclopedia of Witches and Witchcraft*, 170ff.

17 Guiley, *The Encyclopedia of Witches and Witchcraft*, 322.

18   Russell, *A History of Witchcraft*, 85f; Guiley, *The Encyclopedia of Witches and Witchcraft*, 21.

19   Westerkamp, *Women and Religion in Early America, 1600–1850*, 62f.

20   Starkey, *The Devil in Massachusetts*, 214.

21   Starkey, *The Devil in Massachusetts*, 220f.

Chapter 7

THE MYSTICS

ACCORDING TO *THE CASSELL Encyclopaedia Dictionary* (1971 edition), a mystic is a person who, by self-surrender and spiritual apprehension attains to direct communion with and absorption in God or that truth may be apprehended directly by the soul without the intervention of the senses and intellect.

Over the centuries, many women have received visions, often unexpected. Indeed, many churches have been built and Christian denominations or orders begun because of visions. However, not all women who have received visions are thought of as mystics. The Anglo-Catholic writer and authority on mysticism, Evelyn Underhill (1875–1941), defined mysticism as a process by which the individual soul moves toward final and utterly ineffable union with the absolute.

The fourteenth century was the apogee of mysticism, although Underhill suggests that there were three ages of mysticism, all just after "great periods of artistic, material and intellectual activity": the thirteenth century, when the great Gothic cathedrals were built; the fourteenth century; and the sixteenth century, which produced the **Renaissance**. Many female mystics exercised a high degree of political power, counseling kings and popes. Considered feminine spirituality, their visions made it acceptable for them to have access to a spirituality unmediated by the ecclesiastics of the Catholic Church. They were thought to have received gifts of prophecy and clairvoyance, and while many women's writings were not accepted by the church, most of the mystics' literature was generally seen as inspired.

It should also be noted that many of these mystics were from noble or patristic families and would probably be better regarded and even more well-known than if they were from peasant stock. Jennifer Carpenter analyzed 33 female mystics whose social origins were known and found that only five were from humble but prosperous lower-class families, whereas 28, or almost 85 per cent, came from more privileged backgrounds.

Even before the thirteenth century, the German mystic Elisabeth of Schönau (c.1129–64) achieved wide renown. The abbot of Busendorf Abbey in Germany asked her if he was worthy enough to get a letter from her. She agreed, offering spiritual advice for him and his monks in one of the 22 letters she wrote that still exist. She strongly urged the monks not to get sidetracked by worldly affairs. She even advised men who hadn't asked for advice. For example, she warned the archbishop of Trier to "rise up in the spirit of humility and fear of the Lord your God," and chastised him for not passing on a divine message that she had received and conveyed to him earlier.[1]

At the age of 12, Elisabeth had been sent to the Benedictine convent at Trier, and when she was 23 she began to have visions, generally receiving them on Sundays and Holy Days, or after reading about the lives of the saints. The Virgin Mary or various saints or angels would appear and give her instructions. The visions depressed her because she was afraid of what people would think when they heard about them, but the Virgin Mary told her that they would not harm her. One of her visions was about Jesus, who appeared as a female virgin with long hair. Another pictured a woman lifted up to heaven being greeted by the Lord; the angel told Elisabeth that was Mary's assumption into heaven. Elisabeth's brother Egbert (?–1184) published three books of her visions under her name as well as *Liber viarum Dei*, a work similar to her friend Hildegard's *Scivias*, but with threats and admonitions to all kinds of ecclesiastics and groups, warnings she had received in her visions.

Elisabeth preached about both the avarice of the clergy and the exaggerated asceticism of the Cathars. Some historians note that Elisabeth never actually preached herself but sent her discourses to the various archbishops asking that they proclaim the content to the churches. She noted, "It is dangerous for me to keep silent about the mighty works of God, and I greatly fear that it is going to be more dangerous to speak out."[2] Abbess of the double monastery of Schönau where she had been educated, she became a strict ascetic herself and was advised by Hildegard of Bingen to be prudent in her ascetic life. She was very aware that men had more power in her society than women. However, she equated her situation with that in the Old Testament when "men were given over to sluggishness ... and holy women were filled with the spirit of God that they might prophesy."[3]

The mystic Bridget of Sweden (c.1303–73), Birgitta Birgersdotter, the mother of eight children, wrote a rule in the late 1300s for the double monastery she founded on her own estate at Vadstena, the Order of St. Savior or the Bridgettines, known for their simplicity, humility, and contemplative life. Bridget appointed her granddaughter Lady Ingegerd Knutsdotter (1356–1412) the first abbess in 1385. The order spread rapidly and by 1515 there were 27 houses. In England, the Bridgettine monastery of Syon Abbey in Middlesex, endowed by King Henry v (1387–1422), became one of the most influential religious communities in that country until it was dissolved by Henry VIII (1491–1547). In her rule for the monastery, Bridget wrote that the nuns could have as many books as they wished for study. Girls could become nuns at age 16.

The author of a book called *Revelations*, Bridget learned Latin with her sons and later, when she was widowed, studied theology and possibly Hebrew. When she was 70, she went on a pilgrimage to Bethlehem and Jerusalem, a trip she had wanted to undertake all her life. Respected as a visionary and prophet, Bridget became an advisor to kings and princes. She was aware that she had been given a special gift of love from God: "My daughter," she repeated God's words to her in her first book of *Revelations*, "I have chosen you for myself, love me with all your heart ... more than all that exists in the world." Like Elisabeth, Bridget rarely preached, using male "clerics to serve as her mouthpieces in church pulpits." But later in life she did address assemblies herself in Naples and on the island of Cyprus.[4]

Catherine of Siena (1347–80), Caterina di Giacomo di Benincasa, a Dominican tertiary, the 24th of 25 children, visited Pope Gregory XI (1329–78) in Avignon in 1376. She wanted him to move the papacy back to Rome, end his war with Florence, organize a crusade, and reform the Church: a heavy agenda for an uneducated woman. But she had a reputation for holiness and so he met with her and even paid her way back to Italy. So impressed was he with her, even though she preached, that he asked her to lead a mission the next year, and the year after that he sent her to Florence as a peacemaker. She wrote to the Florentine government: "I have spoken with the Holy Father. He graciously listened.... When I had talked a long time with him, at the conclusion of the words, he said that if what I had put before him about you was true, he was ready to receive you as his sons and do whatever seemed best to me."[5] The next pope, Urban VI (1318–89), sent her to Rome to support his claim to the papacy. But all this was too much for Catherine along with her ascetic practices, and she died soon after in 1380.

Catherine was political, but she was also a mystic. She stayed in a small room in her house for at least three years, fasting, praying, and keeping silence. She lived what she wrote: "A full belly does not make for a chaste spirit." Sometimes she sustained herself with a few glasses of water. As she told her confessor, "I feel so satisfied by the Lord when I receive His most adorable Sacrament that I could not possibly feel any desire for any other kind of food." She received the stigmata and performed cures. Like other ascetics then and earlier, she felt she should suffer as Christ had suffered on the cross, and in order to arrive at her spiritual goal she exercised strict self-control.

The American professor of medievalism Rudolph M. Bell studied the records of the lives of 261 women recognized as saints from the twelfth to the seventeenth centuries and concluded that more than 65 per cent of them suffered from the eating disorder anorexia. Bell engendered a lot of controversy with this theory. Whether or not he was correct in his analysis that these women suffered from this disorder, when one researches and reads the lives of female saints, their ascetic practices, including their constant fasting, stand out as a common element.

Bell uses the records of a few women to back up his thesis, one of them being Catherine of Siena who died at 33, likely from lack of sleep, lack of food, and constant traveling. The average age at death for women at that time was around 52. Catherine's friends and superiors often advised or even ordered her to eat, but food seemed to cause her to vomit. In a letter to "a Religious in Florence," she wrote: "You wrote to me saying in particular that I should pray God that I might eat.... I say it to you in the sight of God, that in every possible way I could I always forced myself once or twice a day to take food.... I beg you that you not be too quick to judge."[6] From the age of 16, Catherine had subsisted on bread, water, and raw vegetables. She gave up wearing a hair shirt in exchange for an iron chain bound so tightly around her hips that it inflamed her skin. She reduced her sleep to as little as 30 minutes every two days on a wooden board. She beat herself three times a day with an iron chain until she was too weak to continue. Each beating lasted one to one-and-a-half hours. In 1380, the year she died, she suffered a stroke and was paralyzed from the waist down.

But she was not a tender violet, traveling, preaching, and speaking out even though women were restricted from engaging in all those "male" activities. As the historian Karen Scott notes, a woman on the loose was considered a loose woman. Catherine's self-confidence came from her strong belief in Christ. If Pope Gregory should abandon her, she wrote to her confessor, "I will hide in the wounds of Christ crucified ... and I know that He will receive me." Catherine believed that God spoke to her, explaining that all the pain she experienced in her travels was her way of participating in Christ's suffering. When she was young, Christ had told her:[7] "You must know that in these days, pride has grown monstrously among men and chiefly among those who are learned and think they understand everything.... I have chosen unschooled women ... so that they may put vanity and pride to shame. If men will humbly receive the teaching I send them through the weaker sex, I will show them great mercy."[8]

Another example of extreme ascetic practice was that followed by the Florentine mystic Umiliana de' Cerchi (1219–46). She gave away many of her and her family's possessions or sold them to get money to help the poor until she was left with nothing. She fasted on bread and water for five 40-day cycles each year as well as every Monday, Wednesday, Friday, and Saturday. She flagellated herself until her blood ran and wore a hair shirt of goat skin with rough cords from horsehair. Her confessor ordered her to desist.[9]

Evelyn Underhill notes that asceticism connected with mysticism was "a problem." Perfect charity in life surrendered, she wrote, is an essential characteristic of the true mystic: "But when we come to the means by which it is to be attained, we enter the region of controversy.... Asceticism as identified ... with the idea of ... killing ... those impulses which deflect the soul from the true path to God." But, she remarks, when that end is attained, asceticism is generally thrown aside. Some ascetic practices, she notes, are merely repressed indulgences: "The true asceticism is a gymnastic, not of the body, but of the mind."[10]

Margery Kempe (1373–1438) is perhaps the most unusual well-known mystic. According to one critic, "God came down to her level; she did not rise up to God's." The highlights of Margery's life are contained in her detailed autobiography, *The Book of Margery Kempe*, possibly the first book in English. Her father was an important man locally, at one time representing their town of Lynn in the English Parliament, and was elected mayor five times. Margery married another local politician, John Kempe; during her first pregnancy she received her first visions, or perhaps more properly hallucinations, during which she had to be physically restrained. But it was also at that time that she was first visited by Christ, who sat on her bed in a purple silk robe, saying, "Daughter, why has thou forsaken Me and I forsook thee never?"

After bearing 14 children, Margery separated from her husband, but they had difficulty coming to that arrangement. Finally, John agreed to make her body "free to God," if she would give up fasting and join him in eating and drinking and pay off his debts.[11]

Margery donned white garments reserved for virgins, and set off on a pilgrimage to the Holy Land, but it was not easy for her. Often her fellow pilgrims refused to eat with her or even travel with her. In fact some of them expressed the wish that she were on the sea in a bottomless boat. As Elizabeth Alvilda Petroff writes, "The extent of Margery's martyrdom can be measured by the number of times she reports being told to shut up."[12] The problem was partly her constant attacks of raucous and strident crying, sometimes up to 14 times a day, usually during church services, when she would fall down and roll around on the floor, and her constant monologues about her spiritual experiences, in which she criticized others and compared them unfavorably to her own "saintly" behavior. For example, at one point she noted that "many neighbours came in to welcome her [back] for her perfection and her holiness." But Jesus was always supportive of her, saying "the more shame and more contempt that you endure for my love, the more joy shall you have with me in heaven." When Margery visited the Church of Father Jerome's tomb, he appeared to her telling her how blessed she was, for "in the weeping that thou weepest for the people's sins ... many shall be saved thereby."[13]

On several occasions, Margery was accused of being a heretical Lollard and narrowly escaped severe punishment; she was careful to include ecclesiastics in her planning and inform them of her visions so that they would affirm her orthodoxy. Her stated destination was sainthood, and she often checked in with others such as "Dame Jelyan" (Julian of Norwich) to find out how she was doing on the road to that goal. In fact, according to her story, God suggested to Margery that she was as saintly as Bridget of Sweden.[14]

Margery often had visions of Christ in which he spoke to her, generally approving of her behavior and guaranteeing her future: "You shall never come into hell nor into purgatory, but when you pass out of this world, within the twinkling of an eye, you shall have the bliss of heaven." Christ ordered her to call him Jesus, her love; to cast off her hair shirt; to refrain from eating meat; and to take communion every Sunday. He also ordered her not to say her beads (the rosary) so often: "Daughter, if thou wear the habergeon (coat of mail) or the hair (hairshirt), fasting [on] bread and water, and if thou saidest every day a thousand Pater Nosters, thou shalt not please Me so well as thou dost when thou art in silence, and suffereth me to speak in thy soul."[15]

Margery was not the only mystic afflicted with the "gift of tears." The thirteenth-century Beguine Marie d'Oignies also cried loudly and uncontrollably when she thought of Christ's Passion or saw images of the cross. Priests would order her to be quiet; once she soaked a priest's book and altar cloth with her tears.[16]

Angela of Foligno (1248–1309), an Italian **Franciscan** tertiary, had a problem similar to Margery's in that she would scream when anyone mentioned God. The first time a fit came over her, she was trying to sell a piece of property to give the money from the sale to the poor. People told her that she was sick and she was "deeply ashamed," and then thought that maybe she was indeed "sick and afflicted by a demon."[17] At the start of her visionary life, as is typical of mystics, Angela had an exaggerated perception of her sins and the need for public humiliation. "I did not blush to recite before the whole world all the sins that I ever committed," she wrote: "But I wanted to go through the squares and the towns naked, with fish and meat hanging about my neck, saying, 'Here is that disgusting woman, full of malice and deception, the sewer of all vices and evils.'"[18]

Born into a wealthy family, Angela had lived a worldly life as a well-to-do wife and mother up to the age of 40, but then suddenly she underwent a conversion. Since her family had all died, she devoted her life from then on to simplicity, poverty, and penitence, divesting herself of her possessions and keeping only one serving woman as a companion. She established a community of female tertiaries at Foligno where they devoted their lives to works of charity, not bound to enclosure. In her book *Instructions*, she emphasized the importance of prayer: "If you want faith, pray. If you want hope, pray. If you want charity, pray. If you want poverty, pray. If you want obedience, pray. If you want chastity, pray. If you want humility, pray. If you want meekness, pray."[19]

Many mystics showed an early desire for a life of piety. Evelyn Underhill described Catherine of Genoa (1447–1510) as "one of the deepest gazers into the secrets of Eternal Love that the history of Christian mysticism contains." Born into the Guelph family of Fiesca with connections to two previous popes, Catherine spent all her life in Genoa, one of five children. She had wanted to enter a convent when she was about 13, but the nuns felt she was too young. This disappointment gave her "great pain." She married a younger nobleman, but he turned out to be faithless, violent, a gambler, and ill-tempered, although was later converted to Christianity. When Catherine was about 26, she had her first mystical experience, an overpowering sense of

God's love, although she was best known for her later visions of purgatory, which she described in her works *Treatise on Purgatory* and *Spiritual Dialogue between the Soul, the Body, Self-Love, the Spirit, Humanity and the Lord God*. She wrote, "I received a wound in my heart of the immense love of God," and such a clear vision of her miseries and defects, and at the same time the goodness of God, that she almost fainted. She took daily communion, deliberately slept as little as possible on briars and thistles, wore a rough hair shirt and spent six hours every day in prayer. Still, Catherine worked tirelessly helping the sick in the large Genoa hospital Pammatone where she became the director; her husband later joined her there. During the plague of 1493, 80 per cent of Genoa's citizens died, and Catherine was put in charge of organizing the care of the sick in the hospitals. To handle the overflow of men and women who could find no room in the wards, Catherine set up rows of sailcloth tents on the hospital's grounds. She contracted the disease herself, surviving, but in a weakened state. She subsequently gave up the directorship, although she still volunteered and spent much of her time with a group of disciples, both men and women.[20]

The Spanish writer Teresa of Avila (1515–82), Teresa Sánchez de Cepeda y Ahumada, a sixteenth-century mystic, warned her disciples against fasting to extremes, yet she forced herself to vomit so she would have an empty stomach when she received the host. Like Jerome years earlier, she felt that eating and other bodily indulgences killed the spirit. And like the early ascetics whose sufferings were in sympathy with Jesus' agony on the cross, she regarded her own afflictions as a source of happiness. "When I am undergoing persecutions, my body suffers ... but my soul is completely mistress of itself," she wrote. Yet she also wrote that God prefers health and obedience to penances. "Get enough sleep and enough food," she advised. She also noted that there were other ways of controlling the body than by the infliction of pain, and that humility was better than fasts.[21]

Teresa was from the nobility with part-Jewish ancestry. When she was seven, she and her slightly older brother Rodrigo set out for the land of the Moors so that they could have their heads chopped off and see God. Since that didn't work out—an uncle intercepted them—they decided to become religious hermits and built a cave of pebbles, which immediately self-destructed. When she was 20, Teresa's father placed her in a convent in her town of Castile because her mother had died; he was distressed when she wanted to take vows. She eventually established 16 convents for women and 14 religious houses for men, reforming the Carmelite order, restoring its earlier purity. Her best-known writing was the *Interior Castle*, a guide for spiritual development through charity work and prayer. Teresa and Catherine of Siena were the first women to be awarded the papal honor of Doctor of the Church. A foremost writer of mental prayer, Teresa defined contemplative prayer as "nothing else than a close sharing between friends. It means taking time frequently to be alone with him who we know loves us."[22]

The youngest mystic may have been Rose of Viterbo (1233–51), who died when she was only 18. Two years earlier, she had applied to St. Mary of the Roses, a convent managed by the Poor Clares in Viterbo City, Italy, but her family couldn't afford the dowry, so she was turned down. That may have been true, or—as someone else has noted—she might have been turned away because she was an evangelical street preacher, a behavior not acceptable to the convent. In any case, she told the convent, "You will not have me now, but perhaps you will be more willing when I am dead."[23]

When she was three, Rose was supposed to have raised an aunt from the dead, and at seven she asked her parents to let her have her own space so that she could pray for sinners undisturbed. When she was 10, the Virgin Mary told her to join the Third Order of St. Francis; as a tertiary, she could still live at home. So she roamed the streets in a tunic with a cord tied around her waist, preaching and praising God. She publicly spoke out against Emperor Frederick II (1194–1250) and created miracles. Her father asked her to cease her preaching, but she replied, "If Jesus could be beaten for me, I could be beaten for Him. I do what He has told me to do and I must obey Him." Her family were all banished to Soriano nel Cimino. Rose continued to preach and prophesy, correctly predicting the emperor's death, and converting the local people. She died of a heart attack when she was 18; her remains were eventually buried at the convent that had earlier denied her admission.[24]

Jane Ward Lead/Leade (1624–1704), mystic, prophetess, and leader of the Philadelphian Society in London, wrote at least 15 books and articles, including her lengthy spiritual autobiography, *A Fountain of Gardens*. It was during Christmas in 1640 that she heard a voice saying, "Cease from this, I have another dance to lead thee in, for this is vanity." She was thrust into religious turmoil, and felt she must become "the bride of Christ." However, she married a cousin, the god-fearing William Lead. It was only on his death in 1670 that she received several visions of Sophia, goddess of wisdom who appeared as a woman in a bright cloud and who spoke to her: "Behold me as thy Mother ... I shall now cease to appear in a Visible Figure unto thee, but I will not fail to transfigure myself in thy mind; and there open the Spring of Wisdom and Understanding." Not long after, she met the Anglican priest John Pordage (1607–81), who introduced her to the writings of the German mystic and alchemist Jacob Böhme (1575–1624).

John and Jane lived together sharing their mystical experiences and, when he died, she took over his Behemist group, which was later known as the Philadelphian Society after the sixth of the churches mentioned in Revelation (1:4, 3:7) in the New Testament. Millennialists, the group believed that Christ's return was imminent. Followers named her their "Mother of Love." Some scholars today believe that many of the Philadelphians regarded Jane as a minor figure in their group; the Society apparently fell apart on her death.[25]

Another of the later and more famous mystics, Madame Jeanne-Marie Bouvier de la Motte-Guyon (1648–1717), became part of the Quietist movement, although she would not have used that term. Quietism emphasized the abandonment of the self to God, the annihilation of the will in union with God, pure love, and was considered a form of prayer. Even though she was a Roman Catholic, she provided a model for the sanctification sought by John Wesley and his Methodist followers, although Wesley faulted Mme. Guyon for placing experience above the Bible as a theological authority. This was also anathema to Roman Catholicism because it eliminated the mediation of priests. Guyon advocated inward prayer: "The only way to heaven is prayer," she wrote, "a prayer of the heart ... and not of reasonings which are the fruit of study." She even wrote a "how to" book that became popular, *Short and Easy Method of Prayer*, ranking prayer above "ecstasies and transports of visions."[26]

Born at Montargis, France, Guyon attended schools run by the Ursuline, Dominican, and Benedictine sisters, and by 15 years of age, she was married to a man much older. When he died, Guyon was left with three children and her family's business. She felt called to go to Switzerland, leaving her two oldest children, but taking her five-year-old daughter with her. She gave her money to a group of New Catholics (converted Huguenots) who later were part of the persecution against her, accusing her of fanatical mysticism and Quietism. As she had been doing, she continued to visit the sick, made ointments, dressed wounds, and shared her resources with the poor. At one point, she gave out more than 1,150 loaves of bread a week, hiring poor girls and boys to help in the distribution. Many people including ecclesiastics and nuns came to her to seek advice on how to develop a deeper spiritual life. But in spite of her popularity and her good works, or maybe because of this, she attracted a lot of vitriolic comments and dislike from bishops, her relatives, and others. The people opposed to her even counterfeited letters against her. She was arrested and jailed several times, finally placed in the infamous Bastille prison from 1698 to 1705. She died not long after she was released.[27]

FURTHER READING

PRIMARY

Guyon, Madame. *A Short and Easy Method of Prayer.* Translated by A.W. Marston. Createspace Independent Publisher, 2009.

Johnson, Jan, ed. *Madame Guyon.* Minneapolis: Bethany House Publishers, 1998.

Kempe, Margery. *The Book of Margery Kempe.* Translated by B.A Windeatt. London: Penguin Books, 1985.

Lead, Jane. "Signs of the Coming Kingdom of God's Love." *Theosophical Transactions,* April 1697.

Obbard, Elizabeth Ruth, ed. *Medieval Women Mystics, Selected Spiritual Writings.* New York: New City Press, 2002.

St. Catherine of Genoa. *Treatise on Purgatory.* Preface by Cardinal Manning. London: Burns & Oates, 1858.

SECONDARY

Bell, Rudolph M. *Holy Anorexia.* Epilogue by William N. Davis. Chicago: University of Chicago Press, 1985.

Corrington, Gail. "Anorexia, Asceticism, and Autonomy: Self-Control as Liberation and Transcendence." *Journal of Feminist Studies in Religion* 2, no. 2 (Fall 1986): 51–61.

Hirst, Julie. "Mother of Love: Spiritual Maternity in the Works of Jane Lead (1624–1704)." In *Women, Gender and Radical Religion in Early Modern Europe,* edited by Sylvia Brown, 161–88. Studies in Medieval and Reformation Traditions, Vol. 129. Leiden: Brill, 2007.

Scott, Karen. "St. Catherine of Siena, 'Apostola.'" *Church History* 61, no. 1 (March 1992).

Underhill, Evelyn. *The Essentials of Mysticism and Other Essays.* London: J.M. Dent & Sons, 1920.

Ward, John O., and Francesca C. Bussey, eds. *Worshipping Women, Misogyny and Mysticism in the Middle Ages.* Sydney, Australia: University of Sydney, 1997.

NOTES

1 Ferrente, *Epistolae: Medieval Women's Letters.*

2 Minnis and Voaden, eds., *Medieval Holy Women*, 53.

3 Johnston, "Marguerite Porete, A Post Mortem," 93.

4 Chicago, "Birgitta," in *The Dinner Party*, 145; Benedict XVI, "Saint Bridget of Sweden"; Minnis and Voaden, eds., *Medieval Holy Women*, 56.

5 Scott, "St. Catherine of Siena," 38.

6 Bell, *Holy Anorexia*, 23.

7 Scott, "St. Catherine of Siena," 41; Corrington, "Anorexia, Asceticism, and Autonomy," 51, 58.

8 Chicago, "Catherine of Siena," in *The Dinner Party*, 145.

9 Bell, *Holy Anorexia*, 92.

10 Underhill, *The Essentials of Mysticism*, 14f.

11 Bennett, *Six Medieval Men & Women*, 124–50.

12 Petroff, ed., *Medieval Women's Visionary Literature*, 302.

13 Several mystics received the "gift" of uncontrollable tears, such as Mary of Oignies, Dorothy of Montau (1347–94), Elizabeth of Hungary (1207–31), and Angela of Foligno (1248–1309); Kempe, *The Book of Margery Kempe*, 19, 20, 114, 225.

14 Kempe, *The Book of Margery Kempe*, 83.

15 Kempe, *The Book of Margery Kempe*, 354–490.

16 Atkinson, *Mystic and Pilgrim*, 31f.

17 Dronke, *Women Writers of the Middle Ages*, 216.

18 Petroff, ed., *Medieval Women's Visionary Literature*, 7.

19 McGinn, *The Flowering of Mysticism*, 143ff.

20 Turpin, *Women in Church History*, 119ff; Pope Benedict XVI, "On St Catherine of Genoa."

21 Corrington, "Anorexia, Asceticism, and Autonomy," 59; Bainton, *Women of the Reformation*, 49.

22 Bainton, *Women of the Reformation*, 48.

23 Damo-Santiago, "Saint Rose of Viterbo."

24 Fox, "St. Rose Died of Heart Attack, Analysis of Mummy Shows."

25 Hirst, "Mother of Love."

26 Stanley, *Holy Boldness*, 29ff.

27 Stanley, *Holy Boldness*, 29ff.

Chapter 8

WOMEN IN RELIGIOUS COMMUNITIES BEFORE THE PROTESTANT REFORMATION

THERE ARE COUNTLESS STORIES of women active in prominent roles in religious communities in virtually every century, most of whom have been left out of traditional church histories. However, those women who bypassed the clergy in the Roman Catholic Church or who disobeyed ecclesiastical rules and regulations "usurping" roles traditionally occupied by men often found themselves in a precarious situation.

The following two chapters highlight a few of these communities, from the tenth century to today, starting with the Bogomils, where women were welcomed and at least in the beginning were offered leadership roles. Chapter 8 gives examples of women's leadership in the church before the Protestant Reformation, although the church hierarchy summarily dismissed most of them; chapter 9 spans several centuries, documenting some women and groups in Protestantism. Although the Waldensians and Lollards were founded before the official beginning of the Protestant Reformation, they are considered forerunners of that tradition and appear in chapter 9.

It is interesting to note that although the key Protestant Reformers—for example, Martin Luther, John Knox, and Jean Calvin—regarded women as equal partners in marriage, they did not generally accept women as leaders in the church. The Methodist Church, however, and its offshoots often encouraged women in religious circles, sometimes reluctantly and sometimes enthusiastically. Because its influence has been so widespread, that denomination is described in a separate chapter.

THE CATHARS

Cathars walk about "with wan faces," the twelfth-century mystic Hildegard of Bingen wrote. They "seem saintly and filled with the Holy Spirit," but in fact they seduce devout Christians. They are "scorpions in their morals and snakes in their works," she declared.[1]

Not everyone described the Cathars in such negative language. When the Catholic knight Pons d'Adhémar de Rodelle was asked by Bishop Fulk (1150–1231), a key leader in the anti-Cathar crusade, why he did not expel the heretics (the Cathars) more efficiently, de Rodelle replied: "We have been reared in their midst. We have relatives among them and we see them living lives of perfection."[2]

No one knows for certain where or when Catharism began, but there were Cathars in the mid-twelfth century mainly in what is today France and northern Italy. They had some of the same religious beliefs as Bulgarian Bogomils; their dualist theology was also similar to early Christian Gnosticism. The Bogomils allowed women to preach in the vernacular and hear confessions, and according to one historian, advocated the "complete social liberation of women." *The Discourse against the Bogomils* (*Discours contre les Bogomiles*), written around 970 CE, pointed out that the Bogomils "included mere women who took it upon themselves to administer penance—that is to remit sins. What ... can be more contemptible?" The historian Paul Tice notes that a group of elders were chosen by lot to lead each Bogomil service, so any member, male or female, had the potential to lead worship. And in the 1143 Bogomil heresy trials in Cappadoce, two bishop-monks, Leonce and Clement, were accused of allowing women "to read the holy gospels and to serve mass together with Clement." The two bishops had already ordained women as deaconesses.[3]

An interesting early reference to Cathars is in the report from the Council of Constantinople, where 150 bishops gathered in 381 especially to deal with groups they considered heretical and those who were "being saved" from these groups. They mentioned the "Arians, Macedonians, Sabbatians, Novatians and those who call themselves Cathars and Aristae, Quartodeciman or Tetradites, Apollinarians—these we receive when they hand in statements and anathematize every heresy which is not of the same mind as the holy, catholic and apostolic church of God."[4]

The term Cathar might have been derogatory. It has been suggested that the name comes from the Latin *catus*, meaning "cat," referring to the rumor that Cathars kissed the hindquarters of a cat, the form in which the devil supposedly appeared to them. The word Cathar could also be related to the Greek *katharos*, meaning "pure." The Cathars themselves called each other Christians, especially Good Christians, Good Woman, Good Man, or Friends of God, as did many of the other men and women where they lived. Mark Gregory Pegg suggests that the term Cathar was first used in the middle of the twelfth century by a group of "heretics" from Cologne and that the inquisitors rarely used the term.[5]

Dualists, the Cathars believed in two Gods: a benevolent God who created the invisible spiritual world, and a malevolent God who created the visible and evil material world. Salvation was liberating the soul from its fleshly prison. Medievalist Jeffrey Burton Russell points out that Catharism would inevitably be associated with witchcraft in some people's minds; it would be a small leap in thinking that since Satan or the devil created the evil visible world, the Cathars could be involved in devil worship. Evidently, that was indeed what some people thought.

Around 1240, a Franciscan friar from Milan, James Capelli, wrote in the Cathars' defense:

> The rumor of the fornication that is said to prevail among them [the Cathars] is most false. For it is true that once a month, either by day or by night, in order to avoid gossip by the people, men and women meet together, not as some lyingly say, for purposes of fornication, but so they may hear preaching and make confession.... They are wrongfully wounded in popular rumour by many malicious charges of blasphemy from those who say that they commit many shameful and horrid acts of which they are innocent.[6]

There were two levels of Catharism: the "believers" who could marry and live ordinary lives, and the celibate clergy, male *parfaits* (perfects) and female *parfaites*. Only at approaching death would the believers receive the laying-on of hands from the clergy, the baptism or *consolamentum* (consolament) that was needed to enter the spiritual world, or the believers could receive it earlier if they wished to become a *parfait/e* before death.

After receiving the *consolamentum*, it was imperative to follow a strict life-style. One had to become mostly what today we call "vegan," giving up meat, fat, eggs, milk, butter, and cheese, although fish was allowed. Several periods of fasting were required during the year. *Parfait/es* tried to follow the New Testament teachings to the letter and lived lives of extreme honesty, kindness, chastity, celibacy, holiness, and simplicity, although it is highly unlikely that all of them were able to adhere to these strict demands consistently. They were not allowed to swear oaths as that was prohibited in Matthew 5:34. They wore black or dark blue. They preached and traveled around to administer the *consolamentum*, as well as to pray and teach, usually journeying in pairs, sometimes secretly, because the 1140 *Decretum Gratiani*, a body of church law, had banned women from preaching and instructing men.[7]

Manual labor was mandatory for all male and female clergy. They were shoemakers, tanners, hatters, saddlers, carpenters, weavers, spinners, and seamstresses. They took literally St. Paul's advice in the New Testament (Acts 18:1–4) that all evangelists and preachers were to have a trade to support themselves financially.

Cathar women set up charitable institutions—schools, boarding houses, hospitals, and workshops for poor women. They established hostels "of the type of nunneries"; in 1209, there were six of those in Montesquieu, and ten in Saint-Martin Lalande, others in Villeneuve-la-Comptal/Comtal, Cabaret, Mas-Saintes-Puelles, Laurac and Vitrac. The aristocracy sent their daughters to Cathar boarding schools. According to historian Georgi Vasilev, Cathars, especially the women, encouraged poetry and other arts; this ceased when the violent crusades began against them.

Not all the women who aspired to be a *parfaite* could tolerate the discipline. Dulcie Faure of Villeneuve-la-Comtal/Comptal in the Lauragais spent a year learning the rites of the Good Women. "I ate bread with them which they had blessed and adored them several times, genuflecting three times … and several times I heard them preach," she wrote. She stayed in a house run by mother superior Brunissende for another year where women also preached; but when questioned by the Inquisition, Dulcie avowed that she was not ordained because she could not "do what the heretics do or teach others to do." At that point, however, she was trying to save her life in the face of the Inquisition, so it may have been that she had indeed been planning to be ordained.[8]

Catharism was an attempt to return to the original simplicity of the early Christian Church, to counteract the corruption of the medieval church. The Cathar Pierre Maury testified at his trial that it was not surprising that the world hated Cathars: "For there are two churches," he told the Inquisition, "the one flees and forgives ... the other possesses and scourges." As Hildegard of Bingen wrote, it was the fault of complacent and corrupt priests that Cathars existed. "Because of the tedium brought on by your riches, avarice, and other vain pursuits, you do not properly teach your subordinates.... Wake up!" she admonished the mainstream clergy.[9]

The Cathars' exemplary lives, however, did not endear them to the church. For one thing, there were regions in France where the Cathar religion was much more popular than the Roman Catholic faith. The Cathars bypassed the mainstream clergy; their only sacrament was the *consolamentum* or laying-on of hands, adult baptism by their own male and female Cathar clergy. Female clergy had the same responsibilities as male clergy, preaching, visiting, and baptizing, although some historians suggest that female clergy could only perform the *consolamentum* if male clergy were unavailable. At his trial, the Cathar Arnaud Sicre of Ax testified that "Good Women have this power, and may console men and women upon their deathbeds—so long as there are no Good Men present; and those that are received into death by Good Women are saved as if they had been received by Good Men." Few names of active women Cathars are known but Arnaude de Lamothe, who was converted by missionary women and who recanted in prison; Bérengèa de Sègreville, the mother of Raimon Rasiere; and Stephana de Praudes, who believed that there was no salvation for anyone except those received in their sect, and one of the last to be burned alive, between 1307 and 1323, were three. Women preferred Good Women to Good Men as preachers. The Cathars usually preached in homes and did not harangue crowds in public.[10] They amassed funds, as believers and clergy often donated money on their deathbeds— money that could have been used to increase the already extensive Roman Catholic Church coffers. That Church decreed them "heretics."[11]

At first, the Catholic Church tried prolonged debates with some of the Cathar clergy to encourage them to return to the fold, but neither side would concede. The Cathars were quite learned in the scriptures and had the reputation of being excellent debaters. In fact, a *parfaite*, Esclarmonde de Foix (1151–1215), the widowed sister of the Count of Foix, took part in a public debate at Pamiers in 1207. The presence of an upper-class elderly lady with six children totally disarmed a Cistercian envoy. A Cathar abbess of a monastery at Pamiers, Esclarmonde was responsible for several conversions there. At one of the debates, a Dominican said to her: "Go tend your distaff, madam, it is no business of yours to discuss such matters."[12]

After the debates proved unproductive for the mainstream Church, geno-
cide was next. From 1143, and for 200 or 300 years, the Church ravaged
Cathar country, burning *parfaites* and *parfaits* at the stake and massacring
populations without discrimination, confiscating conquered lands. Even as
late as 1412, 15 Cathars were burned posthumously at Chiere.[13]

How many lives were lost?[14]

As John Foxe wrote in the introduction to chapter IV of his *Book of Martyrs*:
"We come now to a period when persecution under the guise of Christianity
committed more enormities than ever disgraced the annals of paganism.
Disregarding the maxims and the spirit of the Gospel the papal Church,
arming herself with the power of the sword, vexed the Church of God and
wasted it for several centuries, a period most appropriately termed in history,
the 'dark ages.'"[15] In 1143, several Cathars were burned at Cologne; in 1209
at least 9,000 were murdered at Béziers, although some historians suggest
it might have been as high as 20,000: the papal representative claimed that
his men "spared no one, irrespective of rank, sex or age, and put to the sword
almost twenty thousand people." In fact, the Catholics in that town were
allowed to leave before the violence began, but they opted to remain with
the Cathars. One of the Crusaders sent to do the job asked how they would
distinguish Cathars from Catholics. The Papal legate, Arnaud-Amaury, is
reputed to have uttered the notorious command, "Kill them all. God will
recognize his own."[16]

In 1210, male Cathars were blinded and mutilated at Bram; the same year,
140 or more were burned outside Minerve; the next year about 100 were
burned at Les Cassés. In 1213 at the battle of Muret at least 7,000 died; in 1219,
about 7,000 were killed at Marmande; in 1233, 200 Cathars and Waldensians
were burned in Verona; in 1239, 180 were burned at Champagne; 225 were
burned at Montségur and 80 at Agen in 1249; and in 1278, more than 200
parfait/es were burned in Verona.[17] The procedural manuals for the medieval
Inquisition had begun to help the inquisitors rid the earth of this "heretical"
blight. Few records of the Cathars exist today but most of those that do are
the painstakingly recorded proceedings of the inquisitorial trials.

For example, in 1320, Béatrice de Planissoles/Planisoles (c.1274–?), a
minor noble and a Catholic, the wife of the Châtelain at Montaillou, was
tried intermittently over a period of almost a month on the charge of Cathar
sympathy, blasphemy, witchcraft, and heresy. Her father had been convicted
of Catharism. And a young priest with whom she had been in a form of
"marriage" was also held in prison for a year. In fact the whole village was

eventually arrested. Witnesses were called against Béatrice, but none for her, as was the custom.

"Why have you hidden your views about priests and the mass for such a long time?" was one of the questions raised by the inquisitors when a villager claimed that Béatrice had wondered how God could allow himself to be eaten by priests in the "sacrament of the altar." Another villager stated that Béatrice did not go to church.[18]

The procedure was for the inquisitors to elicit names of anyone who might be a "heretic" or a sympathizer of "heretics," and after several days of intense questioning, it seemed that most of those charged, including Béatrice, would talk indiscriminately, sometimes to save their own life at the expense of others, and also because a serious Cathar should not tell a lie. Sometimes torture or the threat of torture was all that was needed. Any information was welcomed, even from years ago, and often those questioned admitted only to practicing the religion years ago. In the end, Béatrice was required to promise, at any future date, to reveal any other information she might remember about herself or anyone else. She escaped the stake, but was condemned to the "Wall" for more than a year: a prison known as "Hell" that few survived. Prisoners had to have friends or family who would "finance" their prison stay—give money to the guards and bring in food—but many people were reluctant to let it be known that they were friends with an accused heretic.

After her release, Béatrice had to wear a yellow cross on her clothing signifying that she had been charged with heresy by the Inquisition. It has been suggested that women of a higher social standing in their community were dealt with more leniently than others; an examination of a Cathar Amnesty in 1279 revealed that women with wealth were pardoned more often than ordinary women and men. However the punishment handed out to Béatrice was certainly severe enough.[19]

Another woman, Guirauda Vitalis, admitted that she was a Cathar *parfaite*, but only when she was a young girl; she said she had given up that faith 30 years earlier. Many of the accused talked freely believing that they would receive lenient penances if they confessed moderate guilt.

The *Martyrs Mirror* lists several martyrs over the centuries, naming the Cathars as Albigensians, often including them with the Waldensians and sometimes the Anabaptists.[20] The *Martyrs Mirror*'s records for the thirteenth century add, to the above figures, 50 Albigensians/Cathars burned at Chastelnau d'Ari in 1211, and more than 400 at Lavaur, undated but in the same century. Many of these executions were the result of the Albigensian

Crusade, a 20-year military campaign from 1209 to 1229 initiated by Pope Innocent III (1161–1216) to eliminate Catharism in the Languedoc area of France. "It seemed … as if the very furies of hell, so to speak, had broken loose, to destroy all believers, yea, almost the whole earth," the *Martyrs Mirror* wrote of the thirteenth century.[21]

It is estimated that one million Cathars and their supporters, women, men and children, were killed over the years, although that figure might be inflated.[22] The visible material world, however, must have seemed very evil, indeed.

Why was Catharism so attractive to women in the face of the penalties imposed by the Inquisition and the wholesale slaughter of men and women? In their analysis of the Cathar trials in Languedoc, Richard Abels and Ellen Harrison point out that somewhere between 31 and 51 per cent of the Cathars were women, many of them *parfaites*. This is within the same range as other historians have calculated. In one analysis of documents, it was found that the ratio of *parfaits* to *parfaites* was three men to one woman. At another heresy trial, 318 *parfaites* out of 719 men and women were questioned, or 45 per cent women. In the list of the 1279 Amnesty, when some men and women were given back their property which had been confiscated earlier, only 26 per cent of those listed were women. However, that list dealt only with "*hereditates*," surely a large percentage of women who had inherited property. This could mean that many of the Cathars who had been charged were well-to-do or from well-to-do backgrounds.[23]

It has been suggested by the Catholic Church that there were so many women Cathars since women were more susceptible than men to "heretical" teaching because of their temperament. However, it seems that the reverse is more likely to be true: that religious movements or churches were tagged "heretical" by the mainstream Catholic Church because, among other reasons, women were unusually active in them; women's leadership in the orthodox church was usually anathema. And persecution and martyrdom often bred followers—witness the early Christian Church.[24]

It has also been suggested that membership in a "heretical" movement was a form of women's social protest against exploitation and oppression. This may be true, but it is more likely that Catharism and other non-orthodox religious organizations that valued women's existence and recognized women's abilities would have been attractive to women for those very reasons. Catharism did not offer absolute gender equality in practice, but it did offer more freedom and a much greater role for women than the mainstream church, which continually berated its female members at that time.

The historical sociologist Lutz Kaelber points out that Catharism spread through a network of *parfait/es'* houses: the *parfait/es* took in young people, taught them artisanal skills such as weaving and processing leather and fur, and proselytized, teaching the tenets of their faith to the apprentices as well as the new skill. There were several of these houses. For example, around Toulouse, there were at least six in Saint-Marie-la-Montesquieu, and two in Issel.[25]

Many of the women and men had been born into the Cathar faith and remained within it to the end. But women and men also often chose the Cathar religion because of its ethical principles and theology, and many approached certain death with equanimity because of a firm belief that their martyrdom was a route to an immediate place in heaven. Of course, the persecutors thought that, too: those who took part in the Albigensian Crusade and other genocidal actions had been promised by the mainstream church that they would go straight to heaven if they were killed in the fighting, bypassing purgatory.

By the end of the thirteenth century, the church had virtually eliminated the Cathars.

THE BEGUINES

The Beguines fared somewhat better than the Cathars.

Called the first women's movement in Christian history, groups of single religious laywomen existed throughout Europe from the twelfth century and even minimally into the twentieth: women who took no permanent vows, followed their own separate house rule, supported themselves with manual labor, remained celibate, but interacted with the world. They were not enclosed in convents; they could have been married before they became part of the Beguine community or they could marry after, if they left.[26]

In France, Germany, and other European countries, there were more single laywomen than laymen at this time, the result of wars, crusades, and the many monastics and male clergy in existence. Not all women were marriageable, of course, or wanted to marry, and not all families could afford the dowry for convents, and neither did all religious women want to be enclosed. Hence some of the reasons for the popularity of the virtually autonomous Beguine communities that were springing up rapidly throughout Europe.

In his work *Cities of Ladies*, Walter Simons suggests another explanation for the proliferation of these groups: the widening gap between lay and clergy

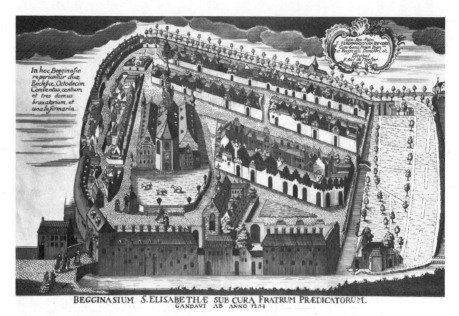

FIGURE 8.1 Plan of Beguinage Saint-Elisabeth, Ghent, and Sint-Amandsberg in 1234. Photo: Guido Van Poucke; Courtesy of Dr. Monika Triest.

in the eleventh and twelfth centuries and the resulting phenomenon of a "middle way of life" exemplified by the semi-religious living in the world along with anchoresses, recluses, and other groups devoted to the care of the sick and the poor. While some of these individuals and communities were supported by the church, the ecclesiastical hierarchy tried to ensure that they did not teach or preach in order to retain the separation of male clergy and laymen and women, and the privileges of the male clergy.[27]

The Beguine movement began in what is now Belgium around 1175. The first prominent Beguine was Marie d'Oignies (1177–1213) from Nivelles, where there were 2,000 Beguines in the mid-thirteenth century, although it has been speculated that a woman called Begga de Landen (613–98), who established a convent at Andenne in Belgium and served as the abbess, was the founder of the Beguines. The last known Beguine, Marcella Pattyn (1920–2013), died in Belgium, aged 92. The Beguines had lasted for almost 800 years.[28]

Some of the Beguines lived by themselves at home, some in small communities in ordinary houses, and many in larger *beguinages* in the center of a city. In the Great Beguinage at Ghent in the fourteenth century, there were walls, moats, two churches, over a hundred houses, a brewery, and an infirmary; the community reportedly housed at least 1,000 women. However, Walter Simons analyzed 74 Beguine communities from 1200 to 1565 in the Low Countries, and found the largest in Brussels with only 326 women, and in Herentals in what is today Belgium with 266 Beguines. A grand mistress and a council of other mistresses presided over each community, and in conversation with other Beguines, wrote and supervised their rules.[29]

The women lived modestly. Some of them were from poor backgrounds and needed to earn a living; some of the communities where they worked needed inexpensive labor. They worked in hospitals, especially leprosariums, and cared for the poor. They cleaned houses, did laundry, and looked after the bodies of the deceased before burial. They made lace, wove wool, and spun. They worked on farms and in gardens. They owned property and collected rents. They made loans and changed money. They founded orphanages. They translated the Bible into the vernacular and taught theology. They prayed, sometimes preached, taught children, and did works of charity such as visiting women in prison. They copied and illuminated books, and owned several: one sixteenth-century Beguine inherited 70 books. They wrote hymns, sermons, Bible commentaries, and biographies. They dressed in plain homespun wool—black or gray robes with a white headdress. According to the historian Sandy Bardsley, beguinages made up about 15 per cent of the population of Cologne, where the English chronicler Matthew Paris claimed there were 2,000 Beguines in 1243. Bardsley reports that Beguines made up 7 to 8 per cent of several late medieval northern cities.[30]

They were known by different names in various countries: *penitentia, bizzocha,* or *pinzochera* in Italy; *beata* in Spain; *beguines* or *mulières sanctae* (holy women) in France. They were also known as poor woman, poor sister, soul sister, virgin, or widow. Many of them became well-known mystics, spending much of their time in meditation and prayer.

The medievalist Herbert Grundmann suggests that this is a more ideal-istic picture than what actually took place. He asserts that the women often requested help from the *curia* because clergymen, monks, and laymen harassed and seduced them as they went about their work in the towns and cities. An order to allow only women over 40 to become Beguines was never enforced, and often the younger Beguines would fail to work, "wandering idly and frivolously about the towns," begging alms. How true this is cannot be determined; the church also complained that the women belonged to no "papally approved order" and refused to obey the local parish priests, with whom they would "neither confess nor receive the sacraments." The women were sometimes accused of spreading heresy about the Trinity, the nature of God, and the sacraments.[31]

The illiterate French Beguine mystic Marie d'Oignies was greatly admired by the French theologian, church canon, bishop, cardinal, and papal legate Jacques de Vitry (1180–1240). In fact, de Vitry had sought out Marie's advice on his career and as a result he was ordained a priest. De Vitry so admired Marie that after her death he carried one of her finger bones around with him as a relic.[32] Marie married at age 14 against her will, but convinced her husband that they should live chastely together. She gave up her great wealth, became an ascetic, worked at the leprosarium at Willambrouckon near Nivelles, gave up eating meat, and received the stigmata—that is, wounds that appear mysteriously, similar to those Jesus received on the cross. At one point, she accidentally cut out a piece of her flesh which she buried in the ground, but felt no pain. She had been remembering a time when she had eaten meat and drunk wine, and was feeling disgusted with herself. She ate bread that was so stale and hard it injured her gums, causing them to bleed. She had a large group of admirers, both male and female, and was noted for her emotional displays of tears and ecstasies. Marie's theology was traditional; like de Vitry, she approved of the Albigensian Crusade against the Cathars. She didn't preach but sang, sometimes for three days on end, praising God and giving thanks in a "high clear voice," in that fashion explaining the scriptures. Marie lived only to be 36.[33]

Although familiar with Latin, French, and Provençal, the Beguine Hadewijch of Antwerp (?–1248) was the first person to write in the vernacular in the area around Belgium and the Netherlands. She composed at least 31 letters and 61 poems, and had 14 visions. She was in charge of a group of young Beguines. "Since I was ten years old, I have been so possessed by a whole-hearted love for God that in the first two years when I began to love Him so, I should have died, had He not given me greater strength than most people have," she wrote in *Visions*. In her "Letter to a Young Beguine," she advised, "Do not believe that anything which you must do for Him whom you seek will be beyond your strength."[34]

Hadewijch was eventually exiled or imprisoned, but she refused to let it get her down. "Stand always ready to do God's bidding, never failing, never paying heed to others: let them mock, let them approve, let them rail, let them bless, let them do as they like," she wrote. Her love poems expressed her philosophy:[35]

He who wishes to follow Love's way
Must regard neither cost nor shame
Nor pain, he must stand to everything
Even her most terrible commands
And render perfect service in every manner
Alike in her coming and in her going.
Those who serve Love in faith and truth
Shall be made perfect lovers at last.[36]

Another Beguine, Mechthild of Magdeburg (c.1210–c.1282), is considered to be the first German mystic to write in the common language of her country, Middle Low German. In her work called *The Flowing Light of the Godhead* (*Das Fliessende Licht der Gottheit*), she wrote: "This book is to be joyfully welcomed, for God himself speaks in it.... Who has written this book? I in my weakness have written it, because I dared not hide the gift that is in it," but she claimed that God was the real author. Mechthild ran afoul of the Dominican friars. She called clerics whom she considered immoral "goats" and "Pharisees," and the Dominicans accused her of heresy—"unlearned, lay, and worst of all, a woman." She had written such disparaging statements as: "Alas! Crown of Holy Church, how tarnished you have become. Your precious stones have fallen from you because you are weak and you disgrace the holy Christian faith. Your gold is sullied in the filth of unchastity ... your purity is burned up in the ravenous fire of gluttony; your humility has sunk to the swamp of your flesh."[37]

Believing that God had given her the words to write, she stood firm at first against her detractors, but when she was 62 and becoming blind, she fled to safety in the Cistercian convent at Helfta. At that time, that community near Eisleben in Saxony was a remarkable community of women that would produce such names as Mechthild of Hackenborn (1240–98), the author of the *Book of Special Grace*, and the abbess Gertrude the Great.[38]

The well-educated German Beguine mystic from Hainault, Belgium, Marguerite Porete (1250–1310), was also indiscriminate in her criticism of the Catholic Church. The author of *Mirror of Simple Souls Who Are Annihilated and Who Only Remain in the Will and Desire for Love*, written in Old French, she intimated that the ecclesiastical authorities were not clever enough to understand her work, a form of mystical pantheism. "Theologians and other clerks, you won't understand this book," she wrote, "if you do not meet it humbly, and in this way Love and Faith make you surmount Reason." She didn't pretend to speak in God's voice but in her own, and traveled around preaching and handing out material she had written. Called before the Inquisition, she stubbornly refused to answer the inquisitors. She was pronounced a relapsed heretic because she had been warned many times to destroy her book; in fact at one point, it had been burned in front of her and all copies were ordered destroyed. "I was warned about this book," she wrote, "and was told by many people that if there were no wish to preserve it, then flames could consume it." Marguerite was burned at the stake in 1310.[39] As Thomas Aquinas had written in *Whether Heretics Should Be Tolerated*, "if he be found still stubborn, the Church gives up hope of his conversion and takes thought for the safety of others ... to be exterminated from the world by death."[40]

Sister Catherine, an anonymous Beguine in the fourteenth century, used the example of Mary Magdalen as a justification for women preaching: "She [Mary Magdalen] did everything the apostles did in a perfect life. She went into all the lands in which she could preach Christianity and reveal the truth. You must know that Mary Magdalen accomplished more in a shorter time than any of the apostles."[41]

Earlier, around 1236, the Beguine Aleydis of Schaerbeek (1204–c.1236) had been executed for heresy, accused of Amalrician beliefs or "Free Love." Between 1236 and 1239, the Dominicans had about 30 other people executed, but it is not clear if they were all Beguines. Another account notes that six Beguines had been burned by 1318 and altogether a hundred or so died at the stake; others were sent to prison. Another historian wrote that a Dominican sent many hundreds to the stake between 1335 and 1355, many of them Beguines. The burning in 1321 of Amegiardis, a 15-year-old girl, was particularly troubling to the Beguine community. Later, the beata Madre Cataline de Jésus (c.1565–1633), who preached, taught, prophesied, and wrote, was sentenced in 1627 to public penance and six years in seclusion.[42]

Other noted Beguine mystics were Beatrice of Nazareth (c.1200–68), a Cistercian nun who had been educated in the Beguine community, kept a diary and wrote theology; and Douceline of Digne (c.1215–74), who founded the Beguines of Marseilles and in other communities: an "effective" preacher who wept copiously when she received the Eucharist, and was seen to levitate or float in the air when at prayer. Treated with contempt, she replied, "Truly it is my honor and my glory, my joy and my crown that the world holds us in great scorn, and that everyone disdains us." After her death, an intense cult arose around her in Provence in the south of France.[43]

Francesca Bussa de Ponziani of Rome (1384–1440), of noble birth, opened her house to the sick and destitute when the hospitals were full. Chiara of Montefalco (1268–1308), Catherine of Siena (1347–80), Umiltà of Faenza (1226–1310), Margaret of Cortona (1247–97), and Angela of Foligno (1248–1309) were well-known Italian Beguines who preached and called for reform in the church and in people's lives.[44] Some in the Roman Catholic Church admired the Beguines. Jacques de Vitry wrote:

> Many holy maidens ... scorned the temptations of the flesh, despised the riches of the world for the love of the heavenly bridegroom in poverty and humility, earning a sparse meal with their own hands. Although their families were wealthy, they preferred to endure hardship and poverty, leaving behind their families and their father's home rather than to abound in riches.[45]

De Vitry persuaded both Pope Honorius III (1150–1227) and Pope Gregory IX (1145–1241) to offer recognition and some protection to the Beguines. De Vitry, however, did not respect all women: "Wanton woman" is not to be trusted, he preached. She is "slippery like a snake and mobile as an eel; so she can hardly be guarded or kept within bounds ... so it is with woman: roving and lecherous once she has been stirred by the devil's hoe."[46]

The Beguine lifestyle was puzzling to the Church. They fit into no known category. They were "not-wives" and "not-nuns." "There are among us women whom we have no idea what to call," the Franciscan Friar Gilbert of Tournai wrote in 1274, "because they live neither in the world nor out of it."[47] The Council of Vienne (1311–12) named Beguines heretical, and in 1318, the Bishop of Cologne called for the dissolution of all Beguine communities and their integration into approved church orders. "Their way of life is to be permanently forbidden," the Council decreed.[48]

It was unacceptable at that time for women to preach and travel around on their own. And as single women, they were considered "sexually and socially" dangerous to men, especially to male confessors. In 1318, Pope John XXII (1249–1334) declared that a "good" Beguine was one who stayed in her house and did not "dispute about the Trinity." The historian Abby Stoner notes that after 1320, "the beguine movement retained only the hollow shell of its former glory."[49]

Margaretha Sattler (?–1527) was one of the later Beguines. Sometime around 1523, she left the order to marry Michael Sattler (c.1490–1527), a former Benedictine monk and one of the early leaders of the Anabaptist movement. Michael was burned in 1527 as an "arch heretic"; Margaretha was drowned in the Neckar River. The countess of Hechingen, Ursula von Zollern, had offered her a position in her court if she gave up her faith, but Margaretha refused.

THE HUMILIATI

Until recently, it was thought that the medieval religious lay order the Humiliati consisted mainly of men, but the historian Sally Mayall Brasher has shown that the reverse is true: the Humiliati were predominantly female.

The earliest known reference to the Humiliati before their approval by Innocent III in 1201 is in a study by Jacques de Vitry, who discovered many of them living around Milan, Italy, in 1170. There was also a written reference to them around 1178 in the *Anonymous Universal Chronicle of Laon*:

> At that time, there were certain inhabitants of Lombard towns who lived
> at home with their families, who chose a particular form of religious life,
> refrained from lies, oaths and lawsuits, were satisfied with plain clothing
> and presented themselves as upholding the Catholic faith. They called
> themselves Humiliati, because they did not use coloured cloth for clothing
> but restricted themselves to plain dress.[50]

At the 1184 Council of Verona, the Humiliati were condemned as heretics by Lucius III, together with the Cathars, the Poor of Lyons (Waldensians), and other groups; however, by 1200, Innocent III had allowed the Humiliati of Tortona to build a hospital and oratory. In 1211, Gerardo da Sessa, cardinal bishop-elect of Albano, ordered all the clergy in his province "not to impede or disturb" the Humiliati, from whom "much good by the grace of God proceeds." In 1227, Gregory IX (1145–1241) allowed them to use mattresses and sheets normally forbidden by the order and released them from the observance of fasts and silence when necessary. Perhaps this suggests already a softening of their hard work or on the other hand, an exhausting life.[51]

The Humiliati flourished in the late thirteenth and early fourteenth centuries, mostly around Milan; they were suppressed in the 1570s. Women were allowed to be leaders of the various communities, although the historian Frances Andrews claims that in double orders, the women were subject to men.[52] Whether the women preached as the male members did and for which they were chastised is not known. There is no writing extant from the Humiliati themselves, so it is difficult to know precisely how they functioned; Brasher derives most of her information from notarial records.

In 1236, there is a reference to Humiliati women in a communication from Gregory IX to the archbishop of Milan, instructing the archbishop to allow the Humiliati to have priests administer the sacraments to the brothers and sisters, especially as it was not fitting for the women to go out into the streets for these reasons. And later that same year, Gregory instructs the patriarch of Aquileia to ensure that the Humiliati are not attacked by people who had previously "molested" them.[53]

The Humiliati were organized into three groups: sisters' houses, brothers' houses, and a family grouping, all of whom tried to follow the example of the early apostles, living a simple spiritual lifestyle while engaging in hard manual labor. Chastity was not a requirement. The women's group consisted more often of only women while the other two groups had both men and women. The groups were made up of people from all economic classes who donated their possessions and wealth to the cause—such as merchants, farmers, wealthy citizens, priests, widows, servants, and political refugees. For example, the community of the Gambara in Brescia began in a house donated by that family. In 1248, Ysabella, wife of Donadeus de Olcellis, sold nine "perches" of land (approximately 228 square meters) to the monastery of Sta. Maria in Biolo to enable her daughter to be accepted as a sister in the Humiliati, providing both clothing and food for her for the remainder of her life.[54]

The women's houses were often located in rural areas, where they devoted their time mainly to the cultivation or milling of crops; the men's, more often in urban settings, were usually involved in the wool and cotton industries. In an analysis of a group of 217 Humiliati houses in 1344, the brothers' houses contained 700 men and 582 women, whereas the sisters' houses had 788 women and 28 men in total. In another study, in all the cities with a population over 10,000, there were 301 brothers' houses and 216 sisters'. However, in the smaller cities, those under 10,000 in population, there were 317 brothers' houses and 838 sisters'. Women were assigned activities such as spinning, carding, and weaving in the textile industry, which could be done in rural houses, while the men's activity, such as marketing, had to take place in urban centers. The women involved in agricultural production were in the smaller areas as well. It appears that the grouping of houses into sisters' and brothers' was more a convenient administrative designation than a separation by gender.[55]

We know little about the men and women themselves. Lidosio of Domus Porto was given money for the order by her family, suggesting a fairly well-to-do household; Domina Alegrancia of Pignoli and Alasina of S. Agata Vercelli, both women of means, brought their inheritances with them when they joined. It is thought that the more well-to-do women became the leaders of the houses; however, all evidence suggests that after the men and women became part of the order, they became of one status.

The Humiliati were involved in several areas beside agriculture and the fabric industry. They worked in and endowed hospitals; for example, they were given the administration of a hospital in Bardonezza, and in 1249, a sister called Iacoba was given possession of the hospital in Rivarolio in the diocese of Genoa. There are references to the farming of wheat, and the tending of vineyards and orchards. They bought, sold, and leased land, likely much of it owned through the gifts or possessions that the members brought with them into the order. They also loaned money. By the fifteenth century they had become prosperous.

In the early twentieth century there were still five independent houses of Humiliati nuns in Italy.

FURTHER READING

PRIMARY

Bettenson, Henry, ed. *Documents of the Christian Church*. Oxford: Oxford University Press, 1963.

The Bloody Theater, or Martyrs Mirror of the Defenseless Christians who baptized only upon confession of faith, and who suffered and died for the testimony of Jesus, their Saviour, from the time of Christ to the year A.D. 1660. Translated by Daniel Rupp. Lampeter Square, PA: David Miller, 1837.

Duncan, Bonnie. "Marguerite Porète: The Mirror of Simple Souls, the Excerpted Text: Chapters 119–122." Millersville, PA: Millersville University, 1995.

Ehrman, Bart D., ed. *Lost Scriptures: Books That Did Not Make It into the New Testament*. Oxford: Oxford University Press, 2003.

Foxe, John. *Foxe's Book of Martyrs*. Nashville, TN: Thomas Nelson, 2000.

Gui, Bernard. *Inquisitor's Manual*. Translated by Daniel Burr, History Department, Virginia Tech, Blacksburg, VA. Accessed 18 September 2018, https://www2.kenyon.edu/projects/margin/inquisit.htm.

Petroff, Elizabeth A., ed. *Medieval Women's Visionary Literature*. New York: Oxford University Press, 1986.

"Source Documents: Béatrice de Planissolles, Testimony to the Inquisition." *Cathars and Cathar Beliefs in the Languedoc*. Translated by Nancy P. Stork, 1996. http://www.cathar.info/121213_fournier_beatrice.htm.

SECONDARY

Abels, Richard, and Ellen Harrison. "The Participation of Women in Languedocian Catharism." *Mediaeval Studies* 41 (1979): 215–51.

Andrews, Frances. *The Early Humiliati*. Cambridge: Cambridge University Press, 1999.

Brasher, Sally Mayall. *Women of the Humiliati: A Lay Religious Order in Medieval Civic Life*. New York: Routledge, 2003.

Deane, Jennifer Kolpacoff. *A History of Medieval Heresy and Inquisition*. Plymouth, UK: Bowman and Littlefield, 2011.

—. "'Beguines' Reconsidered: Historiographical Problems and New Directions." Commentaria #3461. *Monastic Matrix*. Accessed 19 September 2018, https://monasticmatrix.osu.edu/commentaria/beguines-reconsidered-historiographical-problems-and-new-directions.

Grundmann, Herbert. *Religious Movements in the Middle Ages*. Translated by Steven Rowan. Notre Dame, IN: University of Notre Dame Press, 1995.

"Inquisition against the Cathars of the Languedoc." *Cathars and Cathar Beliefs in the Languedoc*. Accessed 18 September 2018, http://www.cathar.info/cathar_inquisition.htm.

Kaelber, Lutz. "Weavers into Heretics? The Social Organization of Early-Thirteenth-Century Catharism in Comparative Perspective." *Social Science History* 21, no. 1 (1997): 111–37.

Knuth, Elizabeth T. "The Beguines" (December 1992). Accessed 18 September 2018, http://www.users.csbsju.edu/~eknuth/xpxx/beguines.html.

Martin, Sean. *The Cathars*. New York: Thunder's Mouth Press, 2004.

Mundy, John Hine. *The Repression of Catharism at Toulouse: The Royal Diploma of 1279*. Toronto: Pontifical Institute of Mediaeval Studies, 1985.

O'Shea, Stephen. *The Perfect Heresy: The Revolutionary Life and Death of the Medieval Cathars*. Madeira Park, BC: Douglas & McIntyre, 2000.

Oyer, John S., and Robert S. Kreider. *Mirror of the Martyrs*. Intercourse, PA: Good Books, 2003.

Roquebert, Michel. *Cathar Religion*. Toulouse, France: Editions Loubatières, 1991.

Simons, Walter. *Cities of Ladies: Beguine Communities in the Medieval Low Countries, 1200–1565.* Philadelphia: University of Pennsylvania Press, 2001.

Stoner, Abby. "Sisters Between: Gender and the Medieval Beguines." *Journal of the History Students at San Francisco State University* 5, no. 1 (1995). http://www.medievalists.net/2011/09/sisters-between-gender-and-the-medieval-beguines/.

Swan, Laura. *The Wisdom of the Beguines.* Katonack, NY: Sisters of Benedict, St. Placid Priory, 2014.

Vasilev/Vassilev, Georgi. "Bogomils, Cathars, Lollards and the High Social Position of Women during the Middle Ages." *Facta Universitatis Series Philosophy and Sociology* 2, no. 7 (2000): 325–36.

Woodard, Richard B. "A World Made by Women." *New York Times,* 13 July 2008.

NOTES

1 Deane, *A History of Medieval Heresy and Inquisition,* 1, 28.

2 Martin, *The Cathars,* 7.

3 Vasilev, "Bogomils, Cathars, and Lollards and the High Social Position of Women during the Middle Ages," 1; Tice, "The Bogomils."

4 The Council of Constantinople, Session 381, CE, #7, Papal Encyclicals Online, http://www.papalencyclicals.net/councils/ecum02.htm.

5 Pegg, "On Cathars, Albigenses, and Good Men of Languedoc," 191f.

6 Russell, *A History of Witchcraft, Sorcerers, Heretics and Pagans,* 127.

7 Brenon, "The Voice of the Good Women," 117. *Decretum Gratiani* was "The Law Book of Gratian." Gratian was a Benedictine monk who died pre-1159. The book contained 4,000 texts on all fields of church law.

8 Brenon, "The Voice of the Good Women," 125.

9 Deane, *A History of Medieval Heresy and Inquisition,* 1.

10 Guilhem Bélibaste, as quoted in Brenon, "The Voice of the Good Women," 114.

11 Brenon, "The Voice of Good Women," 114, 131.

12 Abels and Harrison, "The Participation of Women in Languedocian Catharism," 227, 229; J. Vaissète, *Histoire générale du Languedoc,* as reported in Gies, *Women in the Middle Ages,* 96.

13 Roquebert, *Cathar Religion,* 1; Martin, *The Cathars,* 178.

14 Martin, *The Cathars.*

15 Foxe, *Foxe's Book of Martyrs,* chap. 4, "Papal Persecutions."

16 Martin, *The Cathars,* 13.

17 Martin, *The Cathars,* 173–78; "Béziers Massacre."

18 "Source Documents: Beatrice de Planisolles, Testimony to the Inquisition."

19 "Source Documents: Beatrice de Planisolles, Testimony to the Inquisition";
    "Inquisition against the Cathars of the Languedoc," 1. John Hine Mundy studied
    the Amnesty of 1279 in connection with the return of the property seized from
    278 Cathars at Toulouse in *The Repression of Catharism at Toulouse*; see also Brenon,
    "The Voice of the Good Women," 127.

20 The Cathars were sometimes called Albigensians because the 1176 Church
    Council, which declared the Cathar doctrines heretical, was held near Albi,
    although Pegg, in "Albigenses in the Antipodes," 584, claims that there is no
    relationship with the town.

21 "Summary of Martyrs in the Thirteenth Century."

22 Several historians have calculated this figure, including Dimont, in *Jews, God and
    History*, 225.

23 Vasilev, "Bogomils, Cathars, and Lollards and the High Social Position of
    Women during the Middle Ages," 2. Pegg, "Albigenses in the Antipodes,"
    584, claims that the term "perfect" was never used by the "Cathars" or the
    Inquisition before 1300. See also Mundy, *The Repression of Catharism at
    Toulouse*, 61.

24 Abels and Harrison, "The Participation of Women in Languedocian
    Catharism," 215.

25 See Kaelber, "Weavers into Heretics?"

26 Bynum, *Holy Feast and Holy Fast*, 6, and as documented in Stoner, "Sisters
    Between: Gender and the Medieval Beguines," 1.

27 Simons, *Cities of Ladies*, 138ff.

28 S.C.S., "Who Were the Beguines?"; "Begga," in Chicago, *The Dinner Party*, 135.

29 Knuth, "The Beguines," 2.

30 Swan, *The Wisdom of the Beguines*, 141; "Jacques de Vitry," *Catholic Encyclopedia*;
    Gies, *Women in the Middle Ages*, 91.

31 Grundmann, *Religious Movements in the Middle Ages*, 142, 145.

32 Mundy, *The Repression of Catharism at Toulouse*, 23.

33 Stoner, "Sisters Between, Gender and the Medieval Beguines."

34 Petroff, ed., *Medieval Women's Visionary Literature*, 23.

35 Petroff, ed., *Medieval Women's Visionary Literature*, 191.

36 Hadewijch of Brabant, "Of Great Love in High Thoughts [No. 31]," quoted in
    Andreacchi, "Hadewijch of Brabant and the High Palace of Love," *Amazing Grace,
    a place for all things literary.* http://graceandreacchi.blogspot.com/2011.

37 Johnston, "Marguerite Porete, a Post Mortem," 92.

38 Petroff, ed., *Medieval Women's Visionary Literature*, 94; Chicago, *The Dinner Party*.

39 Stoner, "Sisters Between, Gender and the Medieval Beguines," 12; Johnston, "Marguerite Porete, A Post Mortem," 87.

40 St. Thomas Aquinas, "Summa Theologica," ii. Q. xi Article III, *Documents of the Christian Church*, 133f.

41 From the "Sister Catherine Treatise," 372f, as quoted in Jansen, *The Making of the Magdalen*, 274.

42 Swan, *The Wisdom of the Beguines*; Deane, *A History of Medieval Heresy and Inquisition*, 14; Simons, *Cities of Ladies*, 56ff.

43 Swan, *The Wisdom of the Beguines*, 34.

44 Swan, *The Wisdom of the Beguines*, 214.

45 Hoag, "Jacques de Vitry on the Women of the Beguine Movement"; Swan, *The Wisdom of the Beguines*, 22; Bardsley, *Women's Roles in the Middle Ages*, as reported in Mick, "A Bastion of Feminine Equality?" 41.

46 Alcuin Blamires as quoted in Stoner, "Sisters Between, Gender and the Medieval Beguines."

47 As documented in Stoner, "Sisters Between, Gender and the Medieval Beguines," 1.

48 Knuth, "The Beguines," 4.

49 Deane, "'Beguines' Reconsidered"; Stoner, "Sisters Between, Gender and the Medieval Beguines," 13.

50 Brasher, *Women of the Humiliati*, 3.

51 Andrews, *The Early Humiliati*, 254, 260ff.

52 Andrews, *The Early Humiliati*, 251.

53 Andrews, *The Early Humiliati*, 267.

54 Andrews, *The Early Humiliati*, 9, 200f.

55 Brasher, *Women of the Humiliati*, 74ff.

Chapter 9

WOMEN IN RELIGIOUS COMMUNITIES IN THE PROTESTANT TRADITION

THE WALDENSIANS

The Waldensians, Vaudois, or the Poor of Lyons, appeared as another movement amid the religious turmoil of the Middle Ages, although it seems unlikely that most ordinary laypeople would be able to keep them separate in their minds and distinct from other non-conforming religious groups.

Around 1173, a prosperous merchant and money lender of Lyon, Peter Waldo/Valdès (1140–1218), stricken by his conscience when he heard the story of the wealthy man who was told by Jesus to give up all his possessions (Matthew 19:16–30), did just that. He divested himself of his wealth, made provisions for the future of his wife, established his two daughters in the convent at Fontevrault/Fontevraud, and began a lifestyle as an itinerant preacher. He begged a copy of the New Testament in the vernacular from a local priest, and tried to obtain a license to preach, but was turned down. He did not intend to form a new church, but he attracted crowds of men and women including orthodox clergy who followed him, wandering in pairs around the country, barefoot or shod only in sandals. They were excommunicated, but kept on preaching. At first, many of the women followers preached; eventually they were silenced in public, partly because of cultural attitudes to women, but they kept on teaching and speaking about their faith in private homes.[1]

The inquisitor Bernard Gui (1261–1331) wrote about women Waldensian priests in the early fourteenth century. "They say," he wrote, "that the consecration of the body and blood of Christ may be made just by any person, although he be layman and not ... ordained by a Catholic bishop, provided he is a member of their sect. They even believe the same thing concerning women ... and so they say that every holy person is a priest."[2]

In the 1240s, Guilhelma Michaela of Auriac, a middle-aged woman who lived with the Waldensians at Castelnaudry for three years and at Limoux and Crestina for four more years, heard Waldensian women teaching, and "dressed, ate, drank and prayed with them," along with "other things." There was also mention of an "Old One," Zum Hirtze, who held a Waldensian school in her house and was knowledgeable about Waldensian doctrine.

After the 1240s, though, there was a severe decline in women preaching, possibly because of the intense persecution and the need to travel secretly and in disguise. The historian Peter Biller noted that in 1240, out of 175 cases he discovered of Waldensians preaching, only about "five or seven" were women. Even the inquisitor Gui mentioned that there were fewer women preaching, although he wrote of Sister Raimonda of Castres in that role. There is also some evidence that the Waldensians debated among themselves about the propriety of this practice, although the Waldensian congregations in Austria, where persecution was less intense, encouraged women to share in all the community tasks. However, it seems that the women were more likely to be involved as hostesses, recruiters, and oral storytellers, while the men were traveling preachers.[3]

Preaching has been described as a "work of authority," and it was apparently the act of preaching itself, not their particular theology, that led to the declaration of the Waldensians as "heretics." The French theologian Alan of Lille (c.1120–c.1202) wrote in his tract against the movement, *Contra Haereticos Valdenses, Iudaeos et paganos* (*Against the Waldensian Heretics, Jews and Pagans*): "They are called Waldensians after their heresiarch Waldo, who, led by his own spirit and not sent by God, contrived his own sect. Without the authority of the prelates, without divine inspiration, without understanding and without education, he presumed to preach."

In 1192, Bishop Otto of Toul ordered all Waldensians to be put in chains and delivered up to the ecclesiastical tribunal. Two years later, King Alfonso II of Aragon (1157–96) banished them from his dominion and forbade anyone to furnish them with shelter or food. A number of treatises were written in the twelfth and thirteenth centuries condemning the Waldensians and also referring to women preaching.[4]

At the Council of Verona (1184) the Waldensians were listed as schismatic and anathema. In *liber adversus Waldensium sectam*, Abbot Bernard of Fontcaude (?–c.1192) suggested how the group got its name: "new heretics suddenly raised their head who, choosing by chance a name with a forecast of the future, were called Waldensians, a name surely derived from 'dense Vale' (*volle dens*) inasmuch as they were enveloped in the deep, dense darkness of error." Fontcaude mentions two scriptural passages that the Waldensians used to justify women preaching: the prophetess Anna (Luke 2:36–38), and Titus (2:3–5), which mentions women teaching.[5]

Several other ecclesiastical writings mentioned the fact that Waldensian women preached. Of course most of these ecclesiastics attacked the practice: Italian theologian Joachim of Fiore (1135–1202), Dominican inquisitor Moneta da Cremona (1180–1238), biographer and abbot Geoffrey of Auxerre (c.1115–c.1194), and Pope Innocent II (?–1143) were among them. Moneta claims that "their women preach in church if their assembly should be called the church, which in truth it is not." He notes that they based their practice of allowing women to preach on the New Testament, where Mary Magdalene was sent to tell the disciples that she had seen Jesus after he rose from the dead. "Now whenever a woman is sent to announce something good to a church," Moneta writes, "should it be said that she preached?" In his *Super Apocalypsim*, Auxerre called women preachers "wretched little women, burdened with sins … curious and verbose, forward, shameless and impudent." The Dominican inquisitor and writer Stephen of Bourbon (1190–61) wrote that Waldo "drew to himself many men and women that they might do the same [renounce earthly possessions and preach the Gospel] … men and women alike stupid and uneducated, they wandered through the villages, entered homes, preached in the squares and even in the churches, and induced others to do likewise." He had watched a woman, who was later burned, preach atop a "box prepared like an altar." The Waldensians were also accused of allowing women to hear confessions and consecrate the body of Christ.[6]

Perhaps the most destructive writing against the Waldensians, however, was *The Arras Witch Treatises* of 1460, recently translated and published, used initially in the witch trials in Arras, France. Describing the rumored participation of the Waldensians in witchcraft, the treatises noted

> … when they (Waldensians) wished to go to the *vauderie* (assembly),
> from an ointment that the Devil had given to them, they anointed a yard's
> length of quite thin wood, and their palms and their hands, then put that
> branch between their legs, and soon they were flying themselves where they

FIGURE 9.1   Waldensian "heretics" were accused of gathering as "witches" in secret meetings where they made a pact with the devil, who often appeared in the form of a goat. Part of their ritual was supposed to be kissing the rear end of the animal. From the frontispiece of the French translation of the fifteenth-century *Tracts Contra Section Valdensium* by Johannes Tinctoris (1435–1511). Photo: Bibliothèque nationale de France, Cabinet des manuscrits, fonds français 961.

wanted to go over the cities, forest, and waters, and the Devil was taking them to the place where they were to have their assembly, and in this place they found each other. The tables were laden with wines and meats, and there they found a devil in the form of a goat, of a dog, of an ape, and sometimes of a man.

And they made oblations and paid homage to the Devil, and adored him, and most of them gave him their souls and almost all, or at least some, of their body; then they kissed the Devil in the form of a goat on his posterior, that is on the anus, with candles burning in their hands.[7]

The Waldensians had first been accused of being witches in 1435 in the Church's publication, *Errores Gazariorum* (*Errors of the Cathars*). In the famous work "Le champion des Dames" ("The Champion of Women") written in

1451 by the French poet Martin le Franc (c.1410–61), the Waldensians were also depicted as witches, a term often used for religious "heretics." The irony is that both the Cathars and the Waldensians ideally led plain and sober lives.

In May 1460 at Arras, five Waldensian women and two men were led onto a scaffold, each wearing a paper hat on which the image of the accused paying homage to the devil had been painted. They had been convicted of being witches. Most of them were burned at the stake, even though three of them protested their innocence. In the fall, six women and four men were brought to the same place; seven of them were executed.

The Waldensians preached against a corrupt clergy, advocated a simple lifestyle, and favored non-violence. They rejected prayers for the dead, the existence of purgatory, fast days, and other practices that could not be found in the New Testament. They were more interested in spirituality and ethics than in theology. Like the Cathars, they transmitted their faith often in small study groups—not in artisanal houses, but in schools. For example, 10 Waldensian schools reportedly existed in the parish of Kermatin in a small village with fewer than 2,000 inhabitants. It was in part these small support groups that made both Catharism and Waldensianism attractive to local men and women.[8] Also like the Cathars, whom the Waldensians opposed, they were hounded almost out of existence. As one wag put it:

If there are some who love and fear Jesus Christ,
Who wish not to malign others, nor to take oaths, nor to lie,
Nor commit adultery, nor kill, nor steal from another,
Nor seek vengeance on his enemies,
They say he is a Waldensian and worthy of punishment.[9]

Or as the English poet William Wordsworth wrote in his ecclesiastical sonnets: "then followed the Waldensian bands, whom Hate/In vain endeavours to exterminate."[10]

Because of similarities in their beliefs, in 1532 the Waldensians voted to join the Genevan (Protestant) Reformation. Some of the Protestants, though, were upset. They had heard the story of an Englishwoman in Tuscany, Miss Johnstone, who had gathered "converts" for the Lord's Supper, and "actually dispensed the bread and wine to them with her own hands." Initially the Protestants were opposed to women in ministerial positions. In 1531, after the merger, the Reformists even abolished an Order of Waldensian Sisters devoted to contemplation, prayer, and reading.[11]

The first Waldensian martyr is thought to have been a woman burned at Pinerolo in 1297; however, the *Martyrs Mirror* lists 24 Waldensians burned in Paris in 1210. In 1212, 100 were burned at Strasbourg, 39 at Bingen, and 18 at Mentz (Mainz). In 1560, Cardinal Ghislieri, later Pope Pius v (1504–72), attempted to exterminate them all. At Montalto, 88 men were taken one at a time to the town square where their throats were cut; their bodies were then hoisted on poles along the side of the road. In 11 days, 2,000 were executed with as many being held for the same fate. The women and children were sold as slaves.

Much later, in 1655, in spite of their non-violent beliefs, an army of 40 Waldensians facing 10,000 warriors was unable to prevent a massacre. Known as the Piedmont Easter, it is estimated that some 1,700 Waldensians were tortured and slaughtered. About 20 years later, another massacre took place at Piedmont; 2,000 Waldensians were killed and 8,000 were imprisoned, of which more than half died from deliberately imposed starvation.[12]

Over the years, the Inquisition interrogated individuals suspected of being Waldensians or Waldensian sympathizers. On 1 May 1320, Agnes Francou (c.1260–1320) and Raymond de la Côte (?–1320), an educated deacon, were burned as "heretics" after nine months of interrogation and imprisonment. Then on 2 August 1321, Huguette de la Côte (c.1291–1321) and her husband Jean de Vienne (?–1321) were also burned as Waldensians after two years of questioning and confinement. Agnes was a poor widow of about 60 who had been Raymond's wet nurse when he was a baby; Huguette was around 30, the daughter of a baker and the wife of a carpenter. She had joined the Waldensians when she was about 12.

The women's understanding of theology seemed severely limited. Both Agnes and Huguette believed that it was sinful to take an oath, however, and they told the inquisitor Jacques Fournier, who would later become Pope Benedict XII (1285–1342), that they would rather die. "I do not wish to take an oath at all, even to save my life," Agnes repeated. "Do you wish to take an oath?" the inquisitors asked over and over again. "Why did you refuse?" the inquisitors asked Agnes. "Because God has forbidden all swearing," was Agnes's answer. "For how long have you believed that taking an oath, even to tell the truth, is a mortal sin?" she was asked. "I have believed this for about 20 years," she replied. But the belief about taking oaths was a red flag to the inquisitors and enough to send her to the stake.[13]

Huguette's response was similar: "I swore the other time because I thought that I would be able to get out of this that way, but even then I believed that it was a sin, but I hoped that I could confess this sin and do penance for it. I did not believe that I would be dammed if I swore just once or twice to tell the truth."[14] The inquisitors persisted in questions to find out who had taught them this theology and whom they had talked to about swearing.

Agnes and Huguette were but two who met their fate in the fire. Some Waldensians escaped and hid in the mountains, some of them returned to the Catholic Church, and some emigrated to the United States. By 1989, there were about 45,000 Waldensian men and women around the world. In 2015, Pope Francis (b. 1936) asked Waldensian Christians for forgiveness for "un-Christian and even inhumane positions and actions."[15]

THE LOLLARDS

Lollardy has been described as a man's religion, but it attracted strong women as well.

In her study of Lollard communities in England, Shannon McSheffrey counted the number of men and women in a few of the heresy trial records still extant. Of 955 suspected Lollards, 271, or 28 per cent, were women. Half of the women were part of a married couple.[16]

The historian Georgi Vasilev found a similar split between Lollard men and women. In the Lichfield and Coventry trials of 1511–12, he calculated that one-third were women out of 45 men and women. During that same period in other locations, when 53 were interrogated, one was released, one abjured, that is changed their mind about their beliefs, five were sent to the stake, and the rest were given lighter sentences such as being confined to a certain area or wearing a badge signifying that they had been charged with heresy. Historian Jennifer Kolpacoff Deane estimated that between 1423 and 1522, there were 500 trials in England against the Lollards, from which only 30 people were burned, both men and women.[17]

It is estimated that 19 per cent of the Lollard men were literate, but only 3 per cent of the women. However, these figures may be low; the men and women on trial sometimes lied about their ability to read. It was dangerous to admit to being able to read the Bible, especially in the vernacular. The 1543 English "Act for the Advancement of True Religion" considered reading the Bible "seditious" even in private for women and lower-class men. Noble and gentlewomen were excepted.

☞ Seuen godly and conſtant Martyrs, ſuffering
at one fire together in Smithfield.

FIGURE 9.2 Preparing to burn religious "heretics" in Smithfield, London, a woodcut from John Foxe's *Book of Martyrs*, 1563, Part 6, 329. Entitled "Seven godly and constant Martyrs, suffering at one fire together in Smithfield," it depicts two or three women and four or five men, with only six labeled. The two women identified are Isabel (labeled Eliz.) Foster, wife, and Joan Warne, alias Lashford, maid. They were burned 27 January 1556.

According to inquisitorial documents, the Lollard beliefs included criticism of the authority of the priests, and the uselessness of images, pilgrimages, and saints' feasts. Lollards placed a great deal of emphasis on the Bible and believed that it should be available in the common language for everyone to read. Men and women often met separately in meetings that were called conventicles to discuss the Bible and theology, although it was only in the city of Coventry that women had their own conventicle. In the cities, women were able to get together with relative ease; they were not as able to travel on their own to various homes in the rural areas. The conventicles usually took place in homes.

In contrast to some of the other religious communities or movements recorded around this time, Lollards embraced life and marriage. It was unnatural to be chaste, they reasoned; people were supposed to bring forth "fruit" from their bodies. There is no evidence of Lollard asceticism, but neither of flagrant avarice, greed, corruption, or "high" living.

The Lollard movement began at Oxford University, inspired by the theologian John Wycliffe (1330–84), although historians are mixed as to how much influence Wycliffe had. He was never charged with heresy during his lifetime, but his corpse was dug up in 1428 and burned. Itinerant preachers spread Lollard ideas throughout southern and central England, running afoul of the church. In the 1401 *De Haeretico Comburendo* (*Of Burning a Heretic*), it was written that the Lollards "do wickedly instruct and inform people and … excite and stir them to sedition and insurrection … and commit other enormities horrible to be heard in subversion of the said Catholic faith."[18]

There is no doubt about the involvement of Lollard women. They were evangelists, studied the Bible, and disputed even with clerics.[19] The vicar at Eardisley was charged with allowing his servants, Agnes Knetchur and Isabel, to ring the bells and help him celebrate (Mass), "which is against the honour of the church."[20]

Alice Rowley (fl. 1511) from Coventry may have been the best-known female Lollard in that area. Charismatic, literate, and articulate, a book owner, a widow of a Catholic merchant who had been a mayor and land owner, of high social standing, she taught both women and men and attended and taught at men's meetings. She organized a conventicle of about 14 women in her home city. She gave to the poor rather than to the church. She preached against the host (the Eucharistic bread) being the real body of Christ: "How can the preiste [*sic*] make God?" she asked. As in other protest religious movements, Lollards disputed the theology that the bread and wine used at Mass or communion or the Eucharist became the real body and blood of Christ after priests' intervention and blessing, that is, the doctrine of transubstantiation. Margery Baxter also argued, "if that sacrament were God, the true body of Christ, there would be infinite gods, because a thousand priests and more every day make a thousand gods, and afterwards eat those gods, and once they are eaten discharge them through their hinder parts."[21]

Alice appeared before the court several times, and at last in 1512 she was punished but not burned. She had to walk in the procession with her friend Joan Warde and watch her burn. Alice was put on a fast of bread and water for several church feast days, but records suggest that she survived.

Joan Ward/e (?–1512) became a Lollard in about 1491 under Alice's tutelage, and married the Lollard shoemaker Thomas Washingbury. She passed around books, taught Lollard doctrine, and was brought before the bishop several times. Along with her husband, she was branded with the letter "h" on her jaw as a "heretic." She was eventually burned—but not before she was marched through the streets and made to carry the faggots that would burn her along with six others.

Margery Baxter (fl. 1429), a housewife in Martham, England, believed that every man and woman who shared her opinions was a "good priest." Lollard men held the view that women could be priests. At his trial in 1381, Walter Brut said that women could preach and had the power to grant absolution, because Mary Magdalen had preached. Sybil Godsell's husband, John, agreed. He stated at his trial: "I held and affirmed that every true man and woman being in charity is a priest." John received seven years' imprisonment.[22] Margery was charged with transporting books. She was flogged on successive Sundays in the parish church and also in the market square. In 1429, she was charged with proselytizing and heresy; an acquaintance testified against her. She, in turn, blackmailed a Carmelite friar who threatened to denounce her; she told him that she would charge him with sexual abuse if he spoke against her. In any case, she was let go, possibly because she denounced another Lollard. Margery seemed a bit confused or else very clever: when asked if she had ever confessed to a priest, she replied that she had "never sinned against a priest and therefore never wished to confess" to one.[23]

Hawise Mone (fl. 1428), a homemaker with several servants and the wife of a prosperous shoemaker, hosted many Lollards in her house in Loddon. Margery Baxter called her a "wise" woman. Hawise admitted that she "comforted Lollards, concealed them, maintained and favoured" them, "often hiding those at risk of severe punishment." Several priests were in her Lollard circle. She had a school or conventicle in her house and knew the Bible intimately. At her trial, she expounded on Lollard beliefs, stating that "the Pope of Rome is father Antichrist ... and has no power of God more than any other lewd man ... is no pope but a false extortion [sic] and a deceiver of the people ... and these that be called priests ... are lecherous and covetous men and false deceivers of the people." Hawise recanted, and signed a statement with a cross, signifying that she was illiterate in spite of the articulate speech she gave at her trial in Norwich. She was an example of a Lollard with high social standing in her community who was more likely to survive trials with only minimal punishment, although all punishments were designed to be humiliating.[24]

Joan Smythe was also a member of Coventry's social elite. Although she was declared illiterate, she exchanged books with several of her friends. She was exonerated at her trial, but as she was being taken home afterwards by a male official, he found English versions of the Lord's Prayer, the Ten Commandments and other religious writings hidden in her sleeve. She was taken back to the trial and subsequently burned. The Dominican friar Thomas Aquinas (1225–74) had stated that "if heretics who return are always taken back, so that they were kept in possession of life and other temporal goods, this might possibly be prejudicial to the salvation of others; for they would infect others … and if they escaped punishment others would feel more secure in lapsing into heresy." It was thought that fire purged the individual body and hence the whole community of infection.[25]

Christina More and her prominent husband kept a Lollard chaplain. When her husband died in 1412, Christina hosted Lollards and managed the estate.

Anna Palmer, an anchoress in Northampton, was summoned to a trial and accused of 15 charges of heresy in 1393 that she hosted Lollards secretly at night, although in a small anchorite, it is unlikely that many people were able to meet at one time. She refused to answer the charges and was sent to prison.

At age 60, Agnes Grebill of Tenterden was betrayed by members of her own family. Her husband had taught her Lollard beliefs, but he and a son testified against her at her trial. She was burned as a "heretic," lamenting that she had ever borne sons. Her crime was not so much being a Lollard, but stubbornly refusing to admit her connection—although apparently, she was only marginally involved in the group.[26]

The English professor Josephine Koster Tarvers also mentions other women Lollards who were questioned about their literate activities: Alice Dexter (c. 1389–?), who renounced her Lollard activities and was assigned penance; the nun Agnes Nowers, who was imprisoned after her trial; Agnes Tickhill, who, with her lawyer husband, boarded and protected Lollard preachers; Dame Anne Latimer (?–1402), widow of a Lollard knight; Dame Alice Sturry, Richard Sturry's (1330–95) widow; and the spinster Katherine Dertford. And there were a number of women Lollards who were teachers, supposedly literate.[27]

Alice Colyns/Colins was famous for being able to recite much of the Bible, and was often invited to recite at the men's conventicles. She is especially noted for reciting the Ten Commandments and the Epistles of Peter and James. Many of the women and men who could not read were able to memorize huge sections of the Bible and other books.

As Susan Groag Bell notes, most of the books owned or read by women at this time were religious or devotional. In her study of 242 laywomen who owned books before 1500, 75 per cent owned books of piety; 60 per cent owned books of piety in the vernacular, mainly the Gospels, Psalters (the Psalms), lives of the saints, and the devotional Book of Hours, daily readings for specific times of each day. Wycliffe's aim had been to have the Bible available in the common language so that everyone could read it, but as Bell points out this was generally opposed by the Roman Catholic Church, which claimed that untrained minds would misinterpret the Bible and damage Christian principles. No doubt the Church feared that its own authority would be undermined, she notes. Bell suggests that the Reformation was hastened by women reading books and by the spread of literacy as the public became more familiar with the teachings of the New Testament.[28]

Lollard communities and beliefs continued through the Protestant Reformation; it was deemed that they were a strong influence in furthering Protestantism.

THE ANABAPTISTS

In 1527, the widow Weynken, daughter of Claes of Monnickendam, was burned to death in The Hague. She was declared "obstinate" at her trial "which could not be passed by without punishment," and so she was sentenced to "be burnt to ashes, and all her property be confiscated." Weynken had been brought before the governor and the full council of Holland, answering their questions with arrogance and wit: "What do you hold concerning the sacrament?" they asked her. "I hold your sacrament to be bread and flour, and if you hold it as God, I say that is your devil," she answered. "What do you hold concerning the holy oil?" they asked. "Oil is good for salad, or to oil your shoes with," she replied. When two Dominican friars held up a cross, she told them, "This is a wooden god; throw him into the fire and warm yourselves."[29]

In 1544, the Dutch noblewoman Maria van Beckum (c.1510–44) and her sister-in-law Ursula van Beckum (?–1544) were also burned at the stake in Deventer in the Netherlands. Their story became the basis for a folk tale in which the charred stake that Maria was on burst into green foliage the next morning. Maria's mother had driven her from their home when Maria joined the Anabaptists, and being a devout Catholic, the mother set the police on her daughter's trail. Maria fled to her sister-in-law's house, but the two young women were both put to death.[30]

In 1571, in Amsterdam, the Anabaptist Anneken Hendriks, a housewife from Frisia, was tied to a ladder, her mouth was filled with gunpowder, and then she was thrown onto a bed of burning coals. Just moments earlier, she had publicly denounced the person who had betrayed her, and so her mouth was filled to keep her quiet. The officials considered her obstinate. Later, Dutch Mennonites would sing a hymn based on her story.[31]

In 1573, Maeyken Wens of Antwerp wrote a final letter to her 15-year-old son Adriaen, one of her nine children: "Love one another all the days of your life; take little Hans on your arm now and then for me. And if your father should be taken from you, care for one another … be not afraid of this suffering.… The Lord takes away all fear.… The Lord keep you one and all." Adriaen went to his mother's execution, taking his young brother Hans, but Adriaen fainted. After he revived, he scratched through the ashes, finding only the tongue screw that had kept Maeyken from speaking out at the last moment. Maeyken's letter is the sole surviving martyr's letter in the hands of Dutch Mennonites today.[32]

According to the short stories taken from the 1660 *Martyrs Mirror or The Bloody Theater or Martyrs Mirror of Defenseless Christians who baptized only upon confession of faith, and who suffered and died for the testimony of Jesus, their Saviour, from the time of Christ to the year A.D. 1660*, more Anabaptists died as martyrs in the sixteenth century than any other religious group. About one-third were women. Their main crime was rejecting infant baptism because children were "unknowing," and replacing it with adult baptism on confession of faith. Rebaptism and anti-clericalism had been declared a capital offense in 1529 at the Diet of Speyer, a Council of the Holy Roman Empire. Some Anabaptists also adhered to a literal interpretation of the Sermon on the Mount (Matthew 5–7), refusing to take oaths or take up arms. The Anabaptists came from various backgrounds with diverse beliefs, although they all appealed to the guidance of the Holy Spirit.

A large percentage of Anabaptists were women, especially when the sect first emerged. The historians Linda Huebert Hecht and Arnold Snyder point out that individuals were called to faith, not couples or groups. A woman needed to respond personally to the call. If her faith commitment was threatened by an "unbelieving" spouse, a woman was free to leave that relationship. The women were incredibly active in informal leadership, proselytizing, reading the Bible, teaching, preaching, and writing hymns. In looking at court records in the Tirol between 1527 and 1529, Hecht discovered that at least 60 per cent were women in the beginning, although later, between 1532 and 1536, only 29 per cent of those involved were women.[33]

Hecht divided these women into members, missioners, lay leaders, and martyrs. Two-thirds of the 268 women she analyzed were simply members;

10 women were missioners, those who actively sought out others and brought them into their church; seven were lay leaders, that is women who preached, baptized, organized, and hosted local meetings. One of the lay leaders had baptized 800 people. Forty-nine of the women who were studied were executed, about 18 per cent. Most of the women executed had been arrested at least twice. Whether they had a young family at home appeared not to deter women from placing themselves in a position where they might be arrested and killed.[34]

When the Swiss authorities tried to curtail the leaders in 1525, Margaret Hottinger was the only woman arrested. After six months in prison, she recanted, only to travel to a neighboring city where she continued to preach.

Sometimes those who spoke against accepted church theology were driven out of town; it was only if they dared to reappear that a more severe penalty was enforced. A teacher, Agnes Linck from Biel in Switzerland, was reported when she searched for a New Testament in a bookstore "without the Reformed preface" and pictures of saints, "no idols … or the heretical preface." She opposed both the Catholic theology of transubstantiation and the Protestant "Lord's Supper." She insisted that both were useless, and she insulted the saints by calling them "chimney sweeps."[35]

Agnes was driven out of Solothurn, to be punished appropriately if she ever returned. She was found in Basel, two-and-a-half years later, and thrown into prison. She recanted, however, and was released after four or five weeks on payment of the prison costs of £4 19s, 6d., approximately US$3,000 today.[36]

Anabaptist women were especially active in The Netherlands. They taught, preached, wrote hymns, and published hymnals. Around 1570, women became deaconesses and elders; they were appointed trustees of orphanages and old people's homes—although at no time in the early history of the Anabaptists were women treated completely equally with men. Women were also prominent in Strasbourg, where some of them held ministerial roles. Huebert Hecht claims, however, that women exercised considerable leadership in the early years of each of the different Ananaptist groups in Switzerland, Strasbourg, Augsburg, Northern Germany, and Holland.[37]

The communities of early Anabaptists were made up of men and women from all social strata. In 1528, a woman whose husband was out of town hosted a meeting in Augsburg on Easter Sunday in her home. Grocers and servants mixed with merchants and prosperous officials. The woman, Susanna, who owned the house, covered her windows with blankets, but the 200 celebrants were spotted and warned. Eighty-eight refused to leave and were arrested.

Despite a ban on meeting, there are records of other Anabaptist groups of 60 or more gathering secretly in homes in Augsburg, suggesting that there were large houses and therefore wealthy members. However, a study done by Claus-Peter Clasen of Anabaptists in that city found that 98 per cent were common people, and only 2 per cent were intellectuals or wealthy. Breaking that down even further, he found that 71 per cent were "low class" such as servants or laundresses; 16 per cent owned a medium-sized property; 11 per cent were well-to-do, and 2 per cent were at the upper end of the class scale. As with other non-orthodox groups, the wealthier members were more apt to be let go when arrested, and the lower classes penalized and tortured.[38]

The lives of three prominent Anabaptist women mystics, Ursula Jost (c.1499–c.1539), Elizabeth Dirks (?–1549), and Barbara Rebstock, were not typical, although there were at least eight women known among the Anabaptists in Strasbourg who experienced prophetic visions.

Ursula Jost and her husband, a butcher by trade, were both visionaries although illiterate; Ursula began having prophetic visions in late 1524. Seventy-seven of her visions were printed first and then an additional 29, but her name was left off the 40-page booklet describing them. Most of her visions were vivid in color and shape, emphasizing the biblical theme that the last shall be first, and that God was in control. Many of Barbara Rebstock's visions were less apocalyptic in tone, but also prophetic, counseling right behavior.

Raised in a monastery in East Friesland, Germany, where she learned to read Dutch and Latin, Elizabeth Dirks became a minister and possibly a deaconess. She had become disenchanted with monastic life and fled the monastery, helped by milkmaids. Known to have taught non-orthodox theology, she was taken into custody and tortured with thumb and leg screws. After five-and-a-half months in prison, she was tied in a bag and drowned at Leeuwarden in Holland. Earlier at her trial, she was asked what she believed concerning the Mass. "My lords, of your Mass I think nothing at all," she answered, "but I highly esteem all that accords with the Word of God." When they asked her what the Lord said when he gave his disciples the Lord's Supper, she asked them, "What did he give them, flesh or bread?" And when they answered "bread," she asked them other questions: "Didn't the Lord remain sitting there? How then could they eat the flesh of the Lord?"

One of the more unfortunate aspects of the history of the Anabaptists was the Münster rebellion: in 1534, Anabaptist fanatics took control of the North

German city, introducing communism and polygamy while they waited for Christ's second coming. All the inhabitants of the city were later executed.

Anabaptists continue today as Amish, Hutterites, and Mennonites, direct descendants of the early movement. There are records of deaconesses in the Mennonite tradition by the seventeenth century.

THE MORAVIANS

Persecution continued to dog many non-conforming Christians.

It has been suggested that a remnant from the Cathars/Albigensians and the Waldensians came together to form part of the Moravian Church, and probably some of those survivors also joined the Moravian settlement at Herrnhut on the southeastern border of present-day Germany when the news spread of its existence.[39] But the immediate origin of the Moravian Church is generally considered to be the Unity of the Brethren, or *Unitas Fratrum*, a forerunner of the Protestant Reformation, founded in 1457 in Bohemia by the followers of the Czech priest Jan Hus (1369–1415). A disciple of John Wycliffe, Hus incurred the wrath of the Roman Catholic Church for his call for ecclesiastical reform. He was burned at the stake with some of Wycliffe's manuscripts used as kindling for the fire.

The fifteenth-century Taborites, who met for worship on a hill called Mt. Tabor in Bohemia, are also part of the Moravian heritage. They were well educated theologically, and women in that group could discuss scripture "better than many trained theologians," much to the frustration of the Inquisition.[40] Also in the Taborite Church, women could be teachers and take a leading role in worship.

In the Unity of the Brethren, women were appointed as congregational judges, with the responsibilities of hearing confessions and helping congregational members "improve their behaviour and attitudes." Judges were trained to settle disputes, and to try to prevent disputes from happening in the first place.[41]

It was only in the eighteenth century that the Moravians received some measure of safety from the threat of persecution, when they were settled at Herrnhut in 1722 on land belonging to Count Nicholas Ludwig von Zinzendorf (1700–60). Moravian women received more than safety under the oversight of Zinzendorf: he appointed them to religious governing boards and they were ordained as acolytes, deaconesses, eldresses, and even

Priesterinnen, presbyters or ministers. An acolyte was someone undergoing preparation for religious service, and a deaconess helped the priest during worship, even assisting at communion. While women preached it was never in a public forum, according to historian Beverly Prior Smaby, except in one instance in Norway where the listeners "were exceedingly attentive." The date of that preaching is not known.[42]

Zinzendorf had been brought up by his very talented and strong-willed grandmother, Henrietta von Gersdorff (1648–1726). A religious poet, musician, and painter, an advocate for the translation of the Bible into the vernacular, a supporter of educating women, and a skilled administrator, Henrietta opened her house to religious refugees escaping persecution. She also insisted that everyone on her estate attend religious services every morning and evening, which she led.

Zinzendorf believed that men and women were different in religious temperament and should live separately. Hence there were separate buildings for men and women, for children (boys and girls separately), for married women and for married men, and for widows of each gender. They were segregated into groups called "choirs," with numerous religious services held regularly by each choir, with separate leaders. The result was untold opportunities for women.

In 1758, Zinzendorf even ordained three women as priests, Elisabeth Lairiz, Lenel Vieroth, and a daughter, Benigna Zinzendorf (1725–89). During the ceremony, he announced that 12 years earlier, he had ordained first two women and then 11, "about whom you will receive more information … who, however, are all involved with such important business that a public account of this honour would not be seemly.… The sisters like the brethren, also have a right to the priesthood." According to the records, he never did make the earlier names known or clarify their important business. After Zinzendorf's death, there were no more ordained female priests until 1967 in Dresden, Germany, and the number of deaconesses and female acolytes was severely reduced.[43]

Historian Katherine Faull suggests that Anna Johanna Seidel (1726–88), whose husband was ordained in 1758 and later became a bishop, was likely one of the women Zinzendorf had ordained earlier. Her life is an example of the interesting possibilities for Moravian women at that time. Before her marriage, she traveled to Moravian communities in Europe and North America with Zinzendorf. When she was only 19, she went to London where she learned English, and in 1752 when she was 26, she visited all the congregations in North America. She became head of the Single Sisters in the Moravian Church, then when she was 34, married Bishop Seidel and set out for the United States to look after the Moravian settlement in Bethlehem, Pennsylvania, with her new husband. "I was happy to go to America," she wrote, "but to enter into marriage! That cost me dear and there was much bitter pain until I was able to give up my will to the intention of the Saviour."[44] Later, however, after her husband's death, Anna recorded in her memoir that "we loved each other tenderly and shared joy and pain … because he was weak and frail for almost 10 years, it was a true blessing for me to serve him day and night." Moravians had to write memoirs of their lives, which were read to the entire congregation on their death.[45]

Anna Nitschmann (1715–60) was another prominent Moravian woman. When she was only 14 years old, her name was drawn by lot to become the chief "eldress" of all the women at Herrnhut. Zinzendorf advised her to refuse the appointment because she was so young, but she noted that it was really God's choice. She had already organized all the young women in the community for worship and ministry when she was 12. Anna traveled around the world to various Moravian missions and helped found the communities in the United States at Bethlehem and Nazareth, and among the First Peoples. Like many women, she wrote hymns for their German hymnal, at least 30. After Zinzendorf's first wife died, he and Anna were married when she was 42. Anna functioned almost as a bishop: along with Zinzendorf, she ordained women to the priesthood.[46]

Although it was not that common for Moravian women, Sarah van Fleck Grube (1727–93), a New York Moravian woman, had a vision when she was ill. Christ stood directly in front of her and showed her his hands with the wound marks. Sarah worked in several congregations in Pennsylvania, New Jersey, and Maryland.[47]

Anna Chase Hasse (1713–86) was sent with her husband as a missionary to Carmel, Jamaica, but it appears that she did not have a particularly happy life there. She and her husband were soon replaced in Jamaica; "hard and unpleasant external and internal circumstances," whatever they were, resulted in the change very soon after their arrival.[48]

Rebecca Freundlich Protten (c.1716–80), a freed slave in St. Thomas, married a Moravian missionary and became an evangelist for the Church. Their mixed marriage was not well received in the south, and Rebecca and her husband were both imprisoned, but Rebecca continued to preach from her prison cell. Zinzendorf was able to effect their release and they traveled to

Germany where Rebecca was ordained a deaconess. After her first husband's death, she returned to Africa and married a Moravian named Protten; they became missionaries there.

These are only a few of the women who played a major role in the Moravian Church and in its missionary settlements. Of the 270 known women who went to North America, 17 of those preached and 47 were ordained deaconesses, while others were eldresses, teachers of both men and women, overseers, and group leaders. They ran the choir houses, attended conferences and other meetings as full participants with men; they spoke, argued, and voted.

Women were likely attracted to the female imagery in Moravian theology. Zinzendorf believed that the Holy Spirit was the true mother of Jesus and "all of us." It can be no other way, he wrote: "that his [Christ's] Father must also be our father, and his mother also our mother." During the creation (of the world), the Spirit "hovered about the waters as the common Mother" and made all things living.[49] This sort of imagery permeated their hymnody, as for example in "The Church's Prayer to the Holy Spirit," written in 1759:

Thou, who from the Father hast
'Fore all Time proceeded,
Spirit, by whom the Virgin Blest
The Son here conceived!
Since the Lamb of God, so red,
Is his People's Brother,
And Christ's God their Father's made,
Thou art the Church's Mother.[50]

The idea of the Spirit as Mother was an important part of Moravian devotional life. The Church established a festival for the Holy Spirit called the *Mutter Fest* (Mother festival) observed annually from 1752 to 1770. Moravians held a very positive attitude toward the human body and reproduction, and Zinzendorf even proclaimed that women's bodies were holy, a revolutionary idea at the time.[51]

Jesus was often depicted as androgynous or female, and most early Moravians displayed sensual feelings toward him. Zinzendorf himself wrote in 1748: "Therefore by faith and love we must so enter the Saviour, that we can no longer see or hear anything else above or beyond him, that we and He remain inseparately together. He knows my danger and my security; in short I can be nowhere better than in His arms."[52]

In the late 1740s after one of their worship services, however, Anna Rosina Rosel Anders (1727–1803) described Jesus as male: "I cannot describe our feelings during this. Our eternal husband was unspeakably close to our choir. He especially allowed us to feel His proximity to us. His embrace and his feet. We all felt very happy inside." Other women called him their "blood bridegroom," an "eternal husband." The women were "chosen maids of the Lamb," "maidens very much in love," and "brides in his sidewound."[53]

After Zinzendorf's death in 1760, however, there was a noticeable shift in worship language: feminine themes and sensual language gradually disappeared.

THE BAPTISTS

The Baptists organized their first churches in Amsterdam in 1609, and in England in 1611–12. At first women made up more than half the original membership and they were allowed to be part of the leadership as deacons. Both John Smyth (c.1570–c.1612) and Thomas Helwys (c.1575–c.1616), considered the originators of the Baptist Church in these two countries, wrote in "A Pattern of True Prayer" that the church was to elect, approve, and ordain deacons, both men and women. Apparently, that didn't happen in most churches. Women served as deaconesses, not deacons, although they may have been considered the same, and in many Baptist Churches in the late 1600s there were widows who assisted male deacons in looking after the poor and relieving "the bodily infirmities of the Saints with cheerfulness."

As the "Somerset Confession" of 1656 stated, "The women in the church [are] to learn in silence, and in all subjection." In 1658 at a general meeting of the Abingdon Association of Baptists at Tetsworth in England, the matter of women's leadership was discussed again and the answer was that "in some cases they may speake [sic] in the church and in some cases againe [sic] may not." In Fleur de Lys Yard Church, Southwark, women were allowed to vote "being equally with the brethren members of the mystical body of Christ," but evidently not equal enough to pray, prophesy, preach, or give thanks.[54]

Many Baptist women, however, did speak in churches. In 1646, the Presbyterian preacher Thomas Edwards (1599–1647) published "A Catalogue and Discovery of Many of the Errors, Heresies, Blasphemies and pernicious Practices of the Sectaries of the time, vented and acted in England in these four last years." At the top of the list of "cankerous offences" among the disorderly Baptists and other dissenters "was permitting women-preachers" to "keep constant lectures, preaching weekly to many men and women." The Baptists were swarming with "illiterate mechanic preachers, yea of women and boy preachers," he said.[55]

Possibly the most notorious woman preacher in London, Mrs. Attaway (fl. 1645), known as the "lace woman" or "the mistress of all the she-preachers on Coleman Street," was a member of one of the most chaotic Baptist churches, the disorganized and "raucous" Bell-Alley Church of London led by Thomas Lambe (?–1686), a soap-boiler by trade. In 1645, Mrs. Attaway had begun holding Tuesday afternoon lectures that attracted around a thousand people, initially women, but later men as well. Soon the church became too small for the crowds, so they met in the Old Bailey. Mrs. Attaway would speak for about 45 minutes to an hour, and either closed with prayer or allowed other women to participate.

Described as a woman "tubber," a pejorative term for a preacher who pounded the pulpit called colloquially a "tub," Mrs. Attaway had divorced her husband and taken up with a married man. Their justification was that they were both married to "unbelievers." Both men and women objected to her preaching, but she claimed that she was just exercising her gifts as the Bible had instructed (1 Peter 4:10–11). She could not deny imparting those things that the Spirit had communicated to her, she said. It was written that she

> Did take a text and did descant
> The lawfulness to preach of a she-saint,
> Inform'd her auditory that there was
> More need to edify 'em than sell lace.[56]

About the same time, Dorothy Hazzard (?–1675) of Bristol was founding a Baptist church in that city. Widowed by her first husband, Anthony Kelly, Dorothy married Matthew Hazzard, an Anglican minister. Both husbands had **separatist** tendencies, even though Matthew remained the clergy in St. Ewen's Anglican Church. Dorothy and her first husband had been part of a group that supported women preachers.

Dorothy owned a grocer's shop in High Street, which she kept open on Christmas and other holy days when shops were supposed to be closed; she could be seen sewing or involved in other activities. She was renowned as a pious woman, and spoke against the superstitions of "invented times and feasts." Eventually Dorothy left St. Ewen's Church and found a house outside Bristol where she and several of her friends could gather for worship; they also used it as a house where women could deliver their babies and avoid the "**churching**" ceremonies that were often held after women had given birth. By 1640 they had constituted themselves as Broadmead Baptist Church and by 1643 there were 160 members. In the 1670s, her church appointed widows and deaconesses to visit the sick and "speak a word to their souls." Dorothy and Matthew remained married until death, to the surprise of their friends.

Many Baptists were uneasy about the full participation of women in the church even though women made up almost 60 per cent of the membership. Generally, women could make a profession of sin, say amen to prayers, sing psalms, accuse a "brother" of sin, or even defend themselves if accused, but to preach or even to prophesy was not acceptable.[57]

However, in 1641, an anonymous tract entitled "A Discoverie [*sic*] of Six Women Preachers" appeared, naming six women from Middlesex, Kent, Cambridgeshire, and Salisbury, all of whom are considered to have been Baptists. Two of the women, Mary Bilbrow, the wife of a bricklayer, and Anne Hempstall opened their homes to other Baptist preachers. Hempstall claimed that she had a vision about the biblical prophetess Anna (Luke 2: 36–38) that affirmed her own call to preach. The author of the pamphlet described Hempstall's preaching as "an astonishment" to the congregation: "long did she preach, and longer I dare avouch than some of the audience were willing." The author also suggested that the women preachers had been trained at Bedlam, an institution for the insane. The women, however, claimed that there was a deficiency of good men, and that they were simply filling their places.

A second pamphlet, *A Spirit Moving in the Women-Preachers*, claimed that the appearance of these "prophetesses" was due to a failure in the home. These women, it said, obviously wore the "breeches" in the family, leading their husbands around "by the nose."[58]

Baptists wrote of their visions and revelations; nine known Baptist women published several works. Five of them, Sarah Wight (1632–?), Anna Trapnel (1642–60), Jane Turner (?–1653), Katherine Sutton (1630–63), and Anne Wentworth (c.1629–c.1693), wrote in total over 100,000 pages. Often their pamphlets or tracts were so popular that they had to print multiple editions.

When Sarah Wight was 16, she wrote about her life beginning when she was 12, in a 186-page book, *The Exceeding Riches of Grace Advanced*, edited by a prominent Baptist minister. She had felt she had no future, and in 1647, after several failed suicide attempts, she began a 76-day fast. Drifting in and out of consciousness, and after receiving several visions, she finally heard a voice that told her to "rise and stand upon thy feet: for I have appeared to thee, for this purpose, to be a minister and a witness, both of the things thou hast seen, and in which I will appear unto thee."[59]

Anna Trapnel also received visions beginning about her twelfth year, but her writings were mainly political. Considered subversive, she was sent to Bridewell prison, where disorderly women were incarcerated. Ann Dutton Williams (1692–1765) wrote 25 printed volumes attacking Calvinist doctrine. Earlier she had published 61 hymns.

Elizabeth Poole (c. 1622–?), a Baptist prophetess, served as a spiritual advisor to the Council of Officers of the Army at Whitehall. She met with them twice in 1648 and 1649 while they were debating the fate of King Charles I. She recommended that they not execute the king, but they did not heed her advice on that occasion—even though, on being questioned, she told them that she believed she "had a command from God." Her gifts of prophecy were defended by a Baptist minister, John Pendarves (1622–56), who wrote: "I have heard many professors and professions, but to my knowledge I never heard one come so near the power."[60]

Baptist women were persecuted along with men. In 1664, 12 of the members of the Aylesbury congregation were arrested and condemned to death; two were women: Mary Jackman, a widow with six children, and Ann Turner, a spinster. Katherine Peck, "licenced for worship," who taught and preached in the Abingdon congregation for more than 30 years, was taken prisoner in 1684.[61]

In America

As in other denominations, theological training became a requirement for Baptist ministers, effectively halting the proliferation of women preaching; women were not allowed into the colleges. However, women preachers resurfaced in colonial America. Catherine Scott is thought to have been the first Baptist female preacher there in 1639 according to the *Encyclopedia of Women and Religion in North America*.[62] In the eighteenth century, around 1754, Martha Stearns Marshall (1726–54) often prayed and preached during worship services conducted by her husband Daniel Marshall (1706–84) or by her brother Shubael Stearns (1706–71). Described as a "lady of good sense, singular piety, and surprising elocution," Martha was thrown in jail in Virginia when she refused to stop preaching. In the 1750s, she and her husband founded a Separate Baptist church at Abbott's Creek in North Carolina. But there was often opposition there to her participation in church services.

In 1791, Mary Savage spent 12 months preaching in New Durham, New Hampshire. She was so well received that she was sometimes invited to speak at the quarterly or yearly meetings of the Freewill Baptist Church. It was thought that she was licensed to preach, but there is no evidence of a license. However, the Baptist Church lists her as being ordained in 1791.[63]

Abigail Roberts (1791–1841) was inspired to preach after hearing the Freewill Baptist preacher Nancy Grove Cram (1766–1815). Nancy was responsible for many revival meetings and organized a church. Abigail eventually joined the Christian Connexion, a loose fellowship of churches that had ordained women since it began in 1810. Abigail started four churches in her 12-year preaching ministry. Her son, Philetus Roberts, wrote that there was often "bitter opposition" to her from other denominations that did not approve of women preachers. In the 1840s Ruby Bixby (?–1877) and her husband were sent to minister in Iowa in Clayton County. Her church listed her as its minister from 1849 until her death in 1877, although her obituary listed her as an evangelist.[64]

Even in 1801, there were accounts of active Baptist women. In the notice of a meeting near Woodstock, Vermont, it read that there were "plenty of preachers, Male & Female," and female local preachers were said to be work-ing in the Kingsclear (New Brunswick, Canada), Prince William and Bear Island (Maine) meetings.

In her study of female preaching in America, between 1790 and 1845, Catherine Brekus found that there were at least 27 Freewill Baptist and 23 Christian Connexion women crossing the country preaching. These Baptist communities allowed women at that time to perform virtually the same duties as men: visiting, exhorting, preaching, presiding over funerals, and even voting. Sometimes, these were only stop-gap measures however, as there were not enough men to fill all the posts. For example in 1810, there were 100 Freewill Baptist congregations and 64 ministers for that denomination.

Elizabeth Godfrey Dolliver (c.1773–1856) was at the center of the Milton Calvinist Baptist Church in Maine in the early 1800s. The church met in her home and she would "give out the hymns, pitch the tunes, exhort and pray" in their meetings, which were heavily attended by women. When they acquired a male pastor, "Sister Dolliver did not occupy so conspicuous a place."[65]

Clarissa Danforth (1792–1855), a Freewill Baptist, born in Vermont, itinerant preacher and pastor, ordained in 1815, was considered "the preaching sensation of the decade" from 1810 to 1820 throughout the American Maritime states and Canadian Atlantic provinces. Among the many revivals she led was one that began in Rhode Island in 1819 and lasted 16 months, during which around 3,000 men and women from the "grey headed" to the "blooming youth" were converted. The New England preacher John Colby wrote that "it is generally allowed, that there never has been a preacher through these parts, that called out such multitudes, as went to hear her." It was difficult to find sufficiently large buildings, the crowds were so great. One of at least 27 Freewill preachers speaking across the States between 1759 and 1844, Clarissa traveled around Rhode Island as well as New Hampshire, Massachusetts, and Vermont, where most of the churches of several denominations were open to her.[66]

Generally described as "a young lady of respectable parentage, good education, extraordinary talents and undoubted piety," she was tall, "dignified in person, easy in manners," with her language "ready and flowing and her articulation so remarkably clear and full that she was distinctly heard in all parts of the largest house." It is no surprise that she also was invited to speak at yearly and quarterly Freewill Baptist meetings. It was said by one historian, though, that before her conversion, she was a "thoughtless and vain young lady."[67]

An interesting omission in the Freewill Baptist literature is the "oversight" of her name in a memoir published in 1846. A Freewill minister, David Marks, had written his memoirs in 1831, briefly mentioning Clarissa and another minister Susan Humes from Connecticut, who was disowned by her family but was nevertheless tremendously effective until her early death at age 24 from overwork. However, in the abridged version of his memoirs that his wife, Marilla, published a little later, there is no mention at all of Clarissa or Susan. The phrases containing their names were cleanly excised. As Jordan Fannin remarks in his study of Clarissa, it is important that these women be remembered, not just to fill in gaps in our history, but to articulate "a fuller vision" for the church and for all those "who have been impoverished by the loss."[68]

In his 1862 *History of the Freewill Baptists*, Samuel Agnew devoted only a page to the early women, noting that the Freewill Baptists "would be wanting in truthfulness, did it pass unnoticed those few women who labored in the cause with a spirit not akin to much of the retiring modesty of our day." He suggested that it had been woman's "right and duty to speak for her Saviour." He mentioned Clarissa Danforth and her sensational work, who preached only occasionally after she got married; "the melting power" of Mary Savage's exhortations; and the ejection of Sally Parsons from her family home when she became a "despised Baptist." At the New Durham yearly meeting in 1797, Sally had been given a horse, saddle, and bridle so that she could travel as an itinerant. Agnew also mentions that there was a "difference of opinion" in the denomination regarding women's preaching and that some members thought that women had truly been called by God. But this number, he wrote, "has greatly diminished in later years, so that now it constitutes a small minority."[69]

In 1868, a few years after Agnew's history, eight women and two men including Lucinda Williams (?–1931), organized a church and Sunday School in Dallas, Texas. They hired a minister for $1,000 a year, the equivalent of approximately US$20,000 today. There is some suggestion that Lucinda was the real power behind this church, but her role is not spelled out in detail.

In 1870, Pastor C.A. Stanton challenged Lucinda to organize the women in the church to build their own building, likely as fundraisers. "We went to work with a purpose to succeed," Lucinda wrote, and soon they acquired enough money to build the foundations for a building 35 by 65 feet. Eventually First Baptist Church covered six city blocks with seven major buildings. In the official 358-page church history written in 1968 by a male church history professor at Southwestern Baptist Theological Seminary, Lucinda is mentioned briefly in a few sentences, with the rhetorical question, "Who is to judge whether Will or Lou (Lucinda) Williams meant the most to First Baptist Church? From the records it appears a close race indeed, and perhaps should be declared a tie!" Given that women's contributions have been dreadfully understated or totally erased, that recommendation suggests that Lucinda's contribution was significant.[70]

Baptist congregations operated independently from each other, although there were different branches of the Baptist Church, some more liberal and more supportive of women's leadership than others. As in other denominations, however, as the churches became more regularized and respectable in the nineteenth century, women's contributions disappeared from the church's memory and records, often deliberately. An example of this is the case of Mary Narraway Bond (1779–1854), a minister for 30 years. In 1880, the historian Ingram Bill published the history of the Maritime Baptists without any mention of her career, even though he had been a speaker and pallbearer at her funeral. He had also written a 600-word obituary about her without mentioning her preaching. In 1820, she and her husband had organized their own religious meetings and built a meeting house known as "Mrs. Bond's Chapel." They had a mixed-race Sunday School, a Christmas Eve exhibition of scholars (a regular event when school children were questioned in public to display their learning), and Mary preached regularly there, as well as at other churches and on board harbor vessels. She studied the Bible continually and possessed the largest library in the area, "works of the greatest Divines, and other writers, from the sixteenth century to the present." As the historian D.G. Bell notes, Mary "must be accounted the most successful woman preacher in the entire history of the Maritimes."[71]

Nancy Towle (1796–1876) found resistance to women preaching as the churches became more formal and organized and more in tune with "women's proper place in society" from about the 1830s to the 1840s especially and even up to World War i. Born in New Hampshire to a well-to-do family—it has been suggested that her family home would be worth around US$6,000,000 today—well educated in a co-educational academy, Nancy began preaching in the Maritimes, both in Canada and the United States. During a visit to England and Ireland in 1829, she had great success among Wesleyan and Church of England congregations, long after the Methodist ban on women's preaching. But she couldn't stand the poverty she found there. "The cruel oppression and distress of this land, I could not endure," she wrote, even though English preachers begged her to stay on.[72]

Nancy usually traveled with a female companion by stagecoach, canal boats, railroad, and occasionally ocean-going vessels, although she described herself as "a solitary wanderer through the earth, a pilgrim who had been called to preach the gospel to a world lying in darkness."[73] She developed a network of at least 23 women preachers who supported each other: Clarissa Danforth, Susan Humes, Almira Bullock, Judith Prescott, Dolly Quinby, Martha Spaulding, Hannah Fogg, Sarah Thornton, and Betsey Stewart, as well as women from the Christian Connexion, from the Methodists, the Quakers, and Bible Christians. Initially Nancy was so confident of a positive reception around the country that she refused to carry letters of recommendation, as was customary. But by 1829, she found serious opposition. She noted that the Freewill Baptists, the Methodists, and the Christian Connexion especially began to withdraw their support of women preaching. Rachel Thompson, a Methodist preacher for nine years, was even excommunicated because she refused to stop preaching.

Nancy was threatened by a mob at one point, and her meetings were interrupted by guns, stones, and drums. Depressed, lonely, and broke, she wrote her autobiography, mentioning the discrimination she found against women preachers. Male evangelists always had their clothing, transportation and financial needs covered, she wrote. But women provided their own clothing, and had to help with the household chores where they were billeted. She was "unsalaried, dependent upon friends and limited publishing for support." Men, she wrote "were not left alone, destitute, no house, no home. No friend that dares to advocate their cause."[74] As a result of this pressure, Nancy became seriously ill in the spring of 1831 and returned home for a rest. Around that time, her father died, but before he passed away, he told Nancy that she should continue with her work: "I don't know, but that I am as willing, you should live as you do, as in any other way. I have never doubted that it was your duty so to do; and it is evident, the Lord has been with you; or you never would have prospered—as it is plain that you have done."[75]

Resistance, however, kept mounting. A Fredericton, New Brunswick, newspaper writer thought that female preachers "manifest disorder," and a Calvinist Baptist preacher was upset by women who "go boldly out to public observation, and seem to remove that veil of retirement which forms the graceful covering of the sex ... [who] invert the order of nature."[76]

Even the Freewill Baptists were struggling with women preaching. In 1830, the General Conference had ruled that women should be in subjection to male members, and the official newspaper, *The Morning Star*, noted the same year that "in *church meetings* for the transaction of the *business* of the church, women should be silent, they should learn in obedience—they should not be meddling with those affairs which are peculiarly designed for the transaction of men; at any rate, they should not usurp authority over men."[77]

There were a few exceptions. Harriet Livermore (1788–1868), a beautiful singer, the granddaughter of a United States senator, the daughter of a wealthy lawyer, decided in 1821 that she wanted to preach. Brought up a Congregationalist, she began preaching in Baptist churches—mainly the Christian Connexion and Freewill Baptist. She was also invited to speak in Congress in 1827, 1832, 1838, and 1843, each time to huge crowds—but she longed for a feminist millennium. "How long, O Lord," she wrote, "how long, ere women shall be clothed with the Sun, walk upon the moon, and be crowned with Apostolic glory." Harriet cut off her hair to be more comfortable traveling and refused to wear a cap in the pulpit.[78]

Nancy Towle decided that she would "stand up against injustice like her Revolutionary forebears." She would ally herself with some of the controversial suffragettes like Mary Wollstonecraft (1759–97), who championed women's rights, and continue her work. She vowed to "deliver up my life, a sacrifice … for remedying these evils: and seal my testimony, as with my blood, in vindication of the rights of women."[79]

Even with some opposition, however, before the nineteenth century was over several women had been ordained in the Baptist churches. In 1876, M.A. Brennan of the Bellevernon Baptist Church in Pennsylvania was ordained by the Freewill Baptists. Lura Maines was ordained by the same group of churches in 1877 and May C. Jones was ordained by a Northern Baptist church in Washington in 1882, now the American Baptist Churches USA, although her ordination caused some controversy. Francis E. Townsley was ordained in Nebraska in 1885, the same year that Experience (Perie) Fitz Randolph Burdick (1862–1905) was ordained by the Seventh Day Baptists, just after she received a Bachelor of Divinity degree from Alfred University. She was the first "white" woman ever invited to pastor a "black" church.[80] Edith Hill Booker was ordained in Kansas in 1894; in the next four years, she immersed (baptized) 170 men and women. It was not until 1964 that a woman was ordained by a Southern Baptist church—Addie Davis, and the next year, the first African-American, Druecillar Fordham. Since then hundreds of women have been ordained throughout the country, and in 2005, at least 505 Baptist women were pastors or co-pastors in American Baptist churches. However, the historian Pamela Durso claims that a significant number of women have left Baptist churches to find other denominations more receptive to women preaching.[81]

Baptists believe that only professing Christians should be baptized (as opposed to those who baptize children), but they do not acknowledge Anabaptists as their origin. Today there are Baptist churches on all continents, with about 40 million congregants in the United States, constituting about one-third of all Protestants in that country.

THE CHURCH OF THE BRETHREN

In 1708, three women and five men gathered at the Eder River in Schwarzenau, Germany, one person baptizing the others even though they had been baptized as infants. They started a new religious community simply called "brethren."

Because of persecution and economic hardship, members of this community began emigrating to North America in 1719. Their first congregation in the New World was at Germantown, Pennsylvania, in 1723, but soon they spread to the New England States and by the mid-1800s, they had churches all the way to the west coast.

Between 1881 and 1883, the new community divided into three groups. The progressive group became known as the Brethren Church; they were headquartered in Ashland, Ohio, and by 1890 had supported the right of women to be ordained. First the Michigan district conference, then the Indiana district conference, the Illiokota conference, and the Pennsylvania district all passed motions that gave women eligibility to the ministry. In a short 10 years after the fellowship was formed, the General Conference recognized that "there is neither male nor female, for ye are all one in Christ."[82]

Thirty-one-year-old Mary Malinda Sterling (1859–1933) from Masontown, Pennsylvania, a well-educated teacher and the first president of the Brethren Church's national women's auxiliary, was the first woman to be ordained—in 1890. She served as a pastor of a fixed congregation for a few years, and then as a traveling evangelist throughout Pennsylvania, New Jersey, and West Virginia. In 1894, she wrote that in 187 days, she had preached 207 sermons and held 13 **protracted meetings**, and that five years experience in the ministry had taught her "that prejudice against women's preaching is not as strong as one might suppose."[83]

In 1891, another teacher, Laura E.N. Grossnickle Hedrick (1858–1934), became the second woman ordained—at the Ohio district conference, because her home congregation in Indiana hesitated to ordain her. In spite of that, she was asked to preach a sermon at the 1892 National Conference held in Indiana, where the following motion was passed: "… this National Convention extends to the sisters all privileges which the brethren claim for themselves." Grossnickle, too, became a traveling worker, but this time as president of the "Sisters' Society for Christian Endeavour," a prestigious position in the church. Grossnickle also wrote a 16-page booklet, "Woman's Divine Right to Preach the Gospel."[84] The fact that she felt this necessary suggests that there must have been some prejudice against women in ministry in spite of the leadership of the church administrators. In 1895, however, Henry R. Holsinger, the editor of *The Brethren Evangelist*, the denominational magazine, wrote that he was glad that he had "never stood in the way of women preaching," and that he belonged "to a church that assists them in doing so."[85]

During the 1890s, nine women were ordained in the Brethren Church, 11 from 1901 to 1910, and five between 1911 and 1920. In the 1920s, however, only three women were ordained, two of those holding only brief **pastorates** and one serving as a missionary nurse in Africa for 35 years. Only one woman was ordained in the 1930s—again a missionary—and in the 1940s, one woman was ordained who took over her husband's pastorate when he enlisted for the war. On his return, they shared the ministry. In the 1950s, only one woman was ordained, to supplement her husband's pastoral work because of his ill health. After two years, both she and her husband withdrew from the denomination. The number of women in ministry had peaked in the 1910s, but there were never more than 15 working at any one time, representing only 10 per cent of the denomination's ministers.

For some time after 1957, no more women were ordained and it appears that the practice was forgotten, since in 1958, in Des Moines, Iowa, the Annual Conference passed a motion allowing the ordination of women. An explanation for this was given by a Brethren historian that suggested that the practice of ordaining women fell into disfavor with a better understanding of scripture. This, of course, made little sense. Another explanation was the increasing conservatism that crept into the church in the 1900s as a reaction against modern liberal theology, and in response to a fear that the Christian Church was becoming feminized. Items appeared in *The Brethren Evangelist* challenging men to assume leadership in the church. According to the historian J.R. Flora, the same phenomenon was found in the Baptist General Conference, the Church of God (Anderson, Indiana), the Church of the Nazarene, and the Evangelical Free Church.

While the Brethren's church membership grew after World War I, the number of congregations declined. Smaller congregations where women were serving either disappeared or joined larger churches where men tended to be the pastor.

In 2008, the Church of the Brethren General Board passed a resolution "on 50 years of women's ordination in the Church of the Brethren," celebrating the 1958 decision to ordain women, and to give thanks for the "nearly 400 women who ... served the church as ordained ministers over the last 50 years." Yet it had actually been 118 years since the first woman was ordained in 1890. The resolution also pointed to the "250" years that "women ministered without equal or official recognition from the wider church," noting that women had been spreading the gospel since the Church of the Brethren's "very inception."[86]

Today the Church of the Brethren operates mainly in United States and Puerto Rico, with groups in South America, Africa, and India.

THE CHURCH OF GOD (ANDERSON, INDIANA)

It was 1975. Johanna (Jennie) Kutcher (1921–2016) had experienced three restless nights. She would wake up in fear and wonder because each night she had clearly heard God asking her to pass on a message to her home congregation, the Church of God in Morden, Manitoba, Canada—a congregation affiliated with the Church of God (Anderson, Indiana). Finally, with trepidation, but now persuaded that she needed to listen to the persistent divine voice, she phoned her pastor and told him of her experience. Upon discerning that the message of reconciliation and healing that Jennie had received was indeed timely for the congregation, the pastor, Morris Vincent, agreed that she should speak to the congregation the next Sunday.[87]

It should have been no surprise that Jennie was welcomed as a speaker. Like other **Holiness movements**, the Church of God (Anderson, Indiana), founded in 1881, had ordained women as pastors, evangelists, missionaries, and teachers since it began. In fact, the first pastor of the First Church of God, in Germantown, Ohio, was a woman—Sarah B. Cox. The Germantown church was founded in 1926, after Sarah and Edwin Scott held a special prayer service that served as the catalyst for its formation.

In 1882, at the age of 61, Sarah Sauer Smith (1822–1908), known as Mother Smith, became part of an evangelistic team. After experiencing the Holy Spirit, Sarah exclaimed that she felt "such boldness" that all who knew her before were astonished that she was no longer timid. She had been born in Ohio, and her formal education amounted to three months after she was 12. She never learned to write, but always printed her letters. She attended the Lutheran Church, but they rejected her enthusiasm: clapping her hands and jumping up and down when she was praising God. The Evangelicals offered her a job, and the Methodist Episcopals wanted to give her a license to preach and a **circuit**, but she replied that she wanted to be free to go where God would send her. "They never got their yoke on me," she wrote. Eventually she became the leader of a small band of Holiness people and wanted to travel. "I am done with housework," she told her husband, and surprisingly he said that he had a cow to sell and then he would go with her. She preached and sang a high tenor throughout 10 states and in Canada from 1885 on. In 1892, there was a fierce fire in an oil field that the workers could not put out, as gale-force winds were blowing it across the countryside. Sarah rebuked the fire in the name of Jesus, and it miraculously went down immediately. Then Sarah prayed for rain, and before she had crossed a 10-acre field, the rain poured down.[88]

Jane Williams, another woman preacher, brought her black congregation into the Church of God in 1886, and by 1915, there were at least 63 black women leaders in the Church. Christina Janes is credited with beginning many of the Church of God congregations in Detroit. Amelia Valdez Vazquez, who taught at a Bible college in Mexico, was responsible for starting the Hispanic Church of God in Albuquerque, New Mexico. Esther Kirkpatrick Bauer (1905–98) was sent to Washington, DC, to rebuild a struggling congregation there.[89]

At the beginning, the women traveled in teams from one evangelistic campaign to another; women headed at least two teams—one by Mary Cole (1853–1934) and another by Lena Shoffner Matthesen (1869–1937), who advertised in the church newspaper, the *Gospel Trumpet*, for a woman to join her and two other women. Mary Cole and her husband began the Church of God ministry in Chicago, but many opposed her preaching. They threw eggs at her, put red pepper on the woodstove where she was preaching, and even shot bullets over her head. [90]

The seventh of 12 children, Mary was born on a farm in Iowa. When she was three, her family moved to Missouri. Often she was racked with convulsions and the doctors were unable to help, but even with this disability she felt called to preach. Finally through her faith, her body was healed, and she began preaching even though there was opposition.[91]

Lillie S. McCutcheon (1921–99), the pastor of the Church of God in Newton Falls, Ohio, mentored 28 other people who became ministers, in addition to nine missionaries or leaders in church agencies. Previously, Lillie had been mentored herself by two women pastors, Sarah B. Cox and Elizabeth Sowers. In her article, "God is an Equal Opportunity Employer," Lillie wrote, "preaching with authority is demanded by God; but the authority is in the Word—not in the preacher—be that preacher male or female." However, she also noted that the "potential reservoir of women in ministry has been only lightly tapped. Let's not rob the kingdom of dedicated ministries because of human traditions," she declared.[92]

Charles E. Brown, editor of the *Gospel Trumpet* in 1939, added: "... the prevalence of women preachers is a fair measure of the spirituality of a church, a country or an age. As the church grows more apostolic and more deeply spiritual, women preachers and workers abound in the church; as it grows more worldly and cold, the ministry of women is despised and gradually ceases altogether."[93] Dr. Joel Stanley of the Anderson University School of Theology supported this position. "Placing women as pastors is a matter of justice, a matter of fidelity to our holiness heritage, and a measure of the Church's willingness to be led by the Holy Spirit into growth and mission," he declared.[94] Another male Church of God supporter, F.G. Smith (1880–1947), pointed out that "a man is an evangelist because he has the gift of evangelizing. It is not because he is a man.... If a woman has a divine gift fitting her for a particular work in the church, that is the proof, and the only proof needed, [then] that is her place."[95]

The noted Methodist evangelist Phoebe Palmer insisted that everyone who experienced sanctification should testify in public; she herself conducted over 300 meetings with her husband Walter in Canada, the United States, and Great Britain without any ecclesiastical credentials. As Phoebe was aware, preaching was a short distance from testifying, and many women began preaching through that route. If a woman claimed that the Holy Spirit called her to preach, who could be opposed? The Church of God (Anderson, Indiana) relied on this authority and in 1891 and 1892, there were at least 88 women who served as evangelists throughout the country for the new denomination. By 1915, there were at least 63 women among the 232 leaders, many of them women of color.

However, as in the other Holiness groups that at first depended on women as well as men to develop their denominations, the Church became more institutionalized and organized with stable congregations, relying less on evangelistic campaigns and revivals. Women were pushed out of positions of authority to align more with woman's position in the surrounding culture. In 1925, there were 220 women preachers: 32 per cent of all the preachers. By 1992, however, that percentage had declined to 15.

To attempt to correct this, earlier in 1974, the Church of God had adopted a resolution stating in part: "... in light of statistics which document the diminishing use of women's abilities in the life and work of the church ... RESOLVED that more women be given opportunity and consideration for positions of leadership in the total program of the Church of God, locally, statewide, and nationally."[96] The resolution, however, had evidently not stemmed the decline in women pastors.

Today there are more than one million adherents, worldwide, in the Church of God, spread throughout about 90 countries.

FURTHER READING

PRIMARY

"Agnes Francou." *The Inquisition Record of Jacques Fournier Bishop of Pamiers 1318–1325.* Translated by Nancy P. Stork. San Jose State University. Accessed 17 September 2018. http://www.sjsu.edu/people/nancy.stork/courses/c4/s1/agnes_francou.

Agnew, Samuel. *The History of the Freewill Baptists, For Half a Century: With an Introductory Chapter.* Dover: Freewill Baptist Printing Establishment, 1862.

The Bloody Theater, or Martyrs Mirror of the Defenseless Christians who baptized only upon confession of faith, and who suffered and died for the testimony of Jesus, their Saviour, from the time of Christ to the year A.D. 1660. Translated by Daniel Rupp. Lampeter Square, PA: David Miller, 1837.

"Confession of Agnes, wife of the late Etienne Francou, a heretic or of the sect of the Poor of Lyons (diocese of Vienne)." Translated by Nancy Stork. San Jose State University. Accessed 17 September 2018. http://www.sjsu.edu/people/nancy.stork/courses/c4/s1/agnes_francou.

A Discoverie [sic] *of Six Women Preachers in Middlesex, Kent, Cambridgshire and Salisbury: With a relation of Their Names, Manners, Life, and Doctrine, Pleasant to be Read, but Horrid to Be Judged of: Their Names Are These, Anne Hempstall, Mary Bilbrow, Ioane Bauford, Susan May, Elizab. Bancroft, Arabella Thomas.* [London] 1641.

Dymok, Roger. "Against the Twelve Heresies." *English Historical Review* 22 (1907): 292–304.

Faull, Katherine M., ed. and trans. *Moravian Women's Memoirs, Their Related Lives, 1750–1820.* Syracuse, NY: Syracuse University Press, 1997.

"Lollardy Trials." *Literary Articles*, 12 September 2012.

"The Ordination of Edith Hill, Minutes of the meeting convened for the ordination of the pastor-elect—Miss Edith Hill." N.d.

"Source Documents: Interrogation of Huguette, Wife of Jean de Vienne." *Cathars and Cathar Beliefs in the Languedoc.* Translated by Dareth Pray. San Jose State University, 2006. Accessed 17 September 2018, http://www.cathar.info/121224_huguette_de_vienne.htm.

"Text of the Trial in Norwich of Hawisia Mone." N.d.

"The Trial of Weynken, a Widow, Daughter of Claes, of Monickendam, Burnt to Death in The Hague, the 20th November A.D. 1527." In *Martyrs Mirror of the Defenceless Christians*, 3rd ed. Translated by Thieleman J. Braght. Scottdale, PA: Herald Press, 1886.

SECONDARY

Anderson, Rebecca J. "The Waldensians." Accessed 17 September 2018, www.rj-anderson.com/docs/waldensians.html.

Aston, Margaret. *Lollards and Reformers.* London: Hambledon Press, 1984.

Bell, D.G. "Allowed Irregularities: Women Preachers in the Early 19th Century Maritimes." *Acadiensis: Journal of the History of the Atlantic Region* 30, no. 2 (2001).

Birch, Ian. "The Ministry of Women among Early Calvinistic Baptists." *Scottish Journal of Theology* 69, no. 4 (November 2016): 402–16.

Brekus, Catherine A. *Strangers and Pilgrims: Female Preaching in America, 1740–1845.* Chapel Hill: University of North Carolina Press, 1998.

Briggs, John. "She-Preachers, Widows and Other Women: The Feminine Dimension in Baptist Life since 1600." *The Baptist Quarterly* 31, no. 7 (1986): 337–52.

Curtis, Ken. "Anna Nitschmann Led Committed Women." *1701–1800 Church History Timeline*, n.d.

Durso, Pamela R. "She-Preachers, Bossy Women, and Children of the Devil: A History of Baptist Women Ministers and Ordination." *Journal of International Women's Studies* 5, no. 2 (March 2004).

Fannin, Jordan Rowan. "Historiography as Healing: Reassembling a Narrative of Clarissa H. Danforth, Freewill Baptist Female Preacher, 1815–1822." Young Scholars in the Baptist Academy 2011 Yearly Meeting, International Baptist Seminary in Prague, Czech Republic.

Flora, J.R. "Ordination of Women in the Brethren Church: A Case Study from the Anabaptist-Pietist Tradition." *Journal of the Evangelical Theological Society* 30, no. 4 (December 1987): 427–40.

Fogleman, Aaron Spencer. *Jesus Is Female: Moravians and Radical Religion in Early America.* Philadelphia, PA: University of Pennsylvania Press, 2007.

Freeman, Curtis W. "Visionary Women among Early Baptists," *Baptist Historical Society*, n.p., n.d.

Hamilton, Brian. "Waldensians, Women, and Preaching as a Political Act." *Political Theology Today*, September 2014.

Hecht, Linda Huebert. "Women and Religious Change: The Significance of Anabaptist Women in the Tirol 1527–1529." *Canadian Society of Church History Papers* (1991): 63–73.

—. "A Brief Moment in Time: Informal Leadership and Shared Authority among Sixteenth Century Anabaptist Women." *Journal of Mennonite Studies* 17 (1999).

Hoover, Peter. *Behold the Lamb: The Story of the Moravian Church.* N.p.: Crossreach Publications, 2016.

McSheffrey, Shannon. *Gender and Heresy: Women and Men in Lollard Communities, 1420–1530*. Philadelphia, PA: University of Pennsylvania Press, 1995.

Mick, Kenneth. "A Bastion of Feminine Equality? Women's Roles in the Waldensian Movement." University of Massachusetts Amherst, 2014.

Moravian Archives. "Women Leadership in the Moravian Church." 13 September 2011.

"Pope Francis Asks Waldensian Christians to Forgive the Church." *Catholic Herald*, 22 June 2015.

Shantz, Douglas. "Anabaptist Women as Martyrs, Models of Courage, and Tools of the Devil." Canadian Society of Church History Historical Papers, 2009.

Smaby, Beverly Prior. "Female Piety among Eighteenth-Century Moravians." Clarion, PA: Clarion University, n.d.

—. "Moravian Women during the Eighteenth Century." Comenius Foundation, 19 November 2011.

Snyder, C. Arnold, and Linda A. Huebert Hecht, eds. *Profiles of Anabaptist Women: Sixteenth-Century Reforming Pioneers*. Canadian Corporation for Studies in Religion/Corporation Canadienne des Sciences Religieuses, 1996.

"Waldensians, Women, and Preaching as a Political Act." *Political Theology Today*, 3 September 2014.

"Women Priests in the Moravian Church." *This Month in Moravian History* 31 (May 2008).

NOTES

1 Deane, *A History of Medieval Heresy and Inquisition*, 58f. Some historians question his background.

2 Aston, *Lollards and Reformers*, 67.

3 Lutz Kaelber as quoted in Mick, "A Bastion of Feminine Equality?" 10.

4 Alan of Lille, *Contra haereticos* II, chap. I, as quoted in Hamilton, "Waldensians, Women, and Preaching as a Political Act"; Kienzle, "The Prostitute-Preacher, Patterns of Polemic against Medieval Waldensian Women Preachers," 113.

5 Deane, *A History of Medieval Heresy and Inquisition*, 68.

6 Stephen of Bourbon on the Early Waldenses, as quoted in Mick, "A Bastion of Feminine Equality?" 18.

7 Gow, Desjardins, and Pageau, eds. and trans., *The Arras Witch Treatises*.

8 Kaelber, "Weavers into Heretics?" 124.

9 A. Monastier, *Histoires de l'Eglise Vaudoise* (Paris: Delay & Toulouse Tartanac, 1847), quoted in Audisio, *Preachers by Night*, 152.

10 Wordsworth, "The Waldenses," 339.

11 Kernohan, *An Alliance across the Alps, Britain and Italy's Waldensians*, 99; Mick, "A Bastion of Feminine Equality?" 35.

12 "A Waldensian Timeline," *The Reformation*, accessed 15 August 2018, http:// thereformation.info/waldensian_time_line.htm; "Summary of Martyrs in the Thirteenth Century," *The Bloody Theater or Martyrs Mirror*.

13 "Agnes Francou."

14 "Source Documents: Interrogation of Huguette, Wife of Jean de Vienne."

15 "Pope Francis Asks Waldensian Christians to Forgive the Church."

16 McSheffrey, *Gender and Heresy: Women and Men in Lollard Communities*, 151–66. In "Medieval Women Book Owners: Arbiters of Lay Piety and Ambassador of Culture," Susan Groag Bell finds that women in the fourteenth and fifteenth centuries owned a number of books, many inherited from their families instead of the land that was passed on to their brothers. In artwork from those centuries, women, especially the Virgin Mary, are depicted reading, often while Joseph looks after the baby Jesus! In a Flemish Book of Hours from 1475, the Virgin reads on a donkey, as Joseph walks carrying the baby, on their flight to Egypt.

17 Vasilev, "Bogomils, Cathars, and Lollards and the High Social Position of Women during the Middle Ages," III; Deane, *A History of Medieval Heresy and Inquisition*, 244.

18 "Henry IV, cap. 15": Statutes of the Realm, ii 125, in *Documents of the Christian Church*, ed. Bettenson, 180.

19 Aston, *Lollards and Reformers*, 49f.

20 A.T. Bannister, "Visitation Returns of the Diocese of Hereford in 1397," as quoted in Aston, *Lollards and Reformers*, 70.

21 Deane, *A History of Medieval Heresy and Inquisition*, 239, 244.

22 Aston, *Lollards and Reformers*, 60; Snyder and Hecht, eds., *Profiles of Anabaptist Women: Sixteenth-Century Reforming Pioneers*, 11.

23 McSheffrey, *Gender and Heresy, Women and Men in Lollard Communities*, 112f.

24 "Text of the Trial in Norwich of Hawisia Mone"; McSheffrey, *Gender and Heresy, Women and Men in Lollard Communities*, 124.

25 McSheffrey, *Gender and Heresy, Women and Men in Lollard Communities*, 123; St. Thomas Aquinas, "Summa Theologica," ii. Q. xi Article III, *Documents of the Christian Church*, 134.

26 McSheffrey, *Gender and Heresy, Women and Men in Lollard Communities*, 111f.

27 Tarvers, "English Women as Readers and Writers," 313f.

28 Bell, "Medieval Women Book Owners."

29 "The Trial of Weynken, a Widow, Daughter of Claes...."

30 Oyer and Kreider, *Mirror of the Martyrs*, 30f.

31 Oyer and Kreider, *Mirror of the Martyrs*, 24f.

32 Oyer and Kreider, *Mirror of the Martyrs*, 52f; "Maeyken Wens's Heritage."

33 Hecht, "Women and Religious Change," 64f.

34 Hecht, "Women and Religious Change," 65.

35 Snyder and Hecht, eds., *Profiles of Anabaptist Women*, 34f.

36 In 1515 in England, an archdeacon earned around £82 or US$40,000 in today's currency; a cardinal earned around £222 or US$171,000 in today's currency, although it appears that salaries varied from person to person.

37 Snyder and Hecht, eds., *Profiles of Anabaptist Women*, 247.

38 Umble, "Anabaptist Women in Augsburg," 121ff.

39 Hoover, *Behold the Lamb*.

40 Moravian Archives, "Women's Leadership in the Moravian Church," 13 September 2011. According to Moravian Church archivist Paul Peucker, the Church was never officially called the Moravian Church until the twentieth century, although Zinzendorf referred to the "Bohemian and Moravian Unity of the Brethren" (*Bohmische und Mährische Brüdergemeine*) in April 1728. Outsiders especially in England began referring to them as Moravians. (Interview with the archivist, 1 February 2017.)

41 Moravian Archives, "Women Leadership in the Moravian Church," Slide 5.

42 Smaby, "Female Piety among Eighteenth-Century Moravians."

43 Faull, ed. and trans., *Moravian Women's Memoirs, Their Related Lives*, xxvii.

44 Faull, ed. and trans., *Moravian Women's Memoirs, Their Related Lives*, xxviii.

45 Faull, ed. and trans., *Moravian Women's Memoirs, Their Related Lives*, 129.

46 Curtis, "Anna Nitschmann Led Committed Women."

47 Faull, ed. and trans., *Moravian Women's Memoirs, Their Related Lives*, 39.

48 Faull, ed. and trans., *Moravian Women's Memoirs, Their Related Lives*, 44.

49 Fogleman, *Jesus Is Female: Moravians and Radical Religion in Early America*, 75.

50 Smaby, "Moravian Women during the Eighteenth Century."

51 Moravian Archives, "Women Leadership in the Moravian Church," Slides 25, 26.

52 Fogleman, *Jesus Is Female, Moravians and Radical Religion in Early America*, 78.

53 Faull, ed. and trans., *Moravian Women's Memoirs*, 44; Smaby, "Female Piety among Eighteenth-Century Moravians."

54 "A Confession of the Faith of Several Churches of Christ," *The Reformed Reader*.

55 Freeman, "Visionary Women among Early Baptists."

56 Freeman, "Visionary Women among Early Baptists"; Hartley, *A Historical Dictionary of Women*.

57 Lloyd, *Women and the Shaping of British Methodism*, 21.

58 Freeman, "Visionary Women among Early Baptists."

59 Freeman, "Visionary Women among Early Baptists."

60 Durso, "She-Preachers, Sisters, and Messengers from the Lord: British Baptist Women, 1609–1700," 6; Birch, "The Ministry of Women among Early Calvinistic Baptists," 8.

61 Briggs, "She-Preachers, Widows and Other Women," 340.

62 Keller, Ruether, and Cantlon, eds., *Encyclopedia of Women and Religion in North America*.

63 "Baptist Women," Baptist Church PowerPoint Presentation, attended by author in 2006.

64 Durso, "She-Preachers, Bossy Women, and Children of the Devil," 3ff; "Abigail Roberts."

65 Bell, "Allowed Irregularities."

66 Billington, "Female Laborers in the Church," 384.

67 Fannin, "Historiography as Healing," 8; Livermore as quoted in Billington, "Female Laborers in the Church," 386; Loveless, "Clarissa H. Danforth Richmond."

68 Fannin, "Historiography as Healing," 22.

69 Agnew, *The History of the Freewill Baptists*, 150, 191f.

70 McBeth, *The First Baptist Church of Dallas*.

71 Bell, "Allowed Irregularities."

72 Billington, "Female Laborers in the Church," 374.

73 Brekus, *Strangers and Pilgrims*, 5.

74 Bailey, "Nancy Towle," 13.

75 Bailey, "Nancy Towle," 10.

76 Bell, "Allowed Irregularities."

77 As quoted in Billington, "'Female Laborers in the Church,'" 381.

78 Brekus, "Female Preaching in Early Nineteenth-Century America"; Harriet Livermore as quoted in Billington, "Female Laborers in the Church," 17.

79 Bailey, *Nancy Towle*, from Towle's autobiography.

80 Rogers, "Personality Profile: Rev. Elizabeth Fitz Randolph," 9.

81 Durso, "Learning from Baptist History."

82 Flora, "Ordination of Women in the Brethren Church," 431.

83 Flora, "Ordination of Women in the Brethren Church," 433.

84 Flora, "Ordination of Women in the Brethren Church," 434.

85 Flora, "Ordination of Women in the Brethren Church," 432.

86 Church of the Brethren General Board, "Resolution on 50 Years of Women's Ordination in the Church of the Brethren," 9 March 2008.

87 Conversation with John Kutcher (Jennie's son), Emmanuel College, University of Toronto, Canada, August 2017.

88 Byers, "Sarah Smith," 5, 6.

89 Stanley, "Doctrinal Dialogue."

90 Stanley, "Doctrinal Dialogue," 4.

91 Strege, *Foundations*.

92 McCutcheon, "God Is an Equal Opportunity Employer," 14f.

93 Brown, "Women Preachers."

94 Stanley, "Doctrinal Dialogue," 21.

95 Stanley, "The Promise Fulfilled."

96 Stanley, "The Promise Fulfilled," 9.

Chapter 10

METHODISM

PRIMITIVE METHODIST ELIZABETH RUSSELL (1805–36) was preaching at Milcheldever in the south of England when a young man dangled a row of bloody rats in front of her face. He'd strung them up on a stick and slit them open. Elizabeth closed her eyes and kept on preaching. Another time, a mob of men and boys were waiting to interrupt her with hand bells, sheep bells, horse bells, horns, and "wicked" songs, but she had been warned, and her supporters had stones and eggs ready in their pockets.[1]

The youngest of six children, Elizabeth "went into service" when she was 16. Her father had abandoned the family, enlisting on board a ship, leaving her mother struggling to care for the children. Soon Elizabeth set up her own dressmaking business but she didn't enjoy it. In 1825, when she was 20, she converted to Primitive Methodism and became a local preacher, and three years later, an itinerant preacher. She had such success that the fledgling denomination asked her to travel. Described as a good speaker, self-possessed and determined, she attracted crowds wherever she went. The 1830 Conference reported that she was "attentive to discipline; a general family visiter [*sic*]; very peaceable; her preaching generally acceptable; not addicted to long preaching; preaches a full, free and present salvation; is successful in the conversion of sinners; her general conduct good."

A zealous evangelist, Elizabeth felt compelled to travel throughout England to bring salvation to the unconverted. Methodist preachers often expressed their emotions in poetry and she was no exception. In 1837, she explained her motivation in "The Missionary's Prayer":

> But here our zeal cannot be ended,
> While parts of England desert lie;
> O, let thy arm be downward bended!
> Lord, send to Berks[hire] a rich supply.
> For Hampshire we as suppliants bow,
> Our humble cries besiege thy throne;
> Thy Spirit pour, O, pour it now,
> Answer our anguish'd earnest groan.[2]

Like most of the committed preachers, Elizabeth, and later her husband Thomas Russell (1806–89), endured extreme hardship for the cause. Their circuits were large, and they traveled on foot. They generally walked through a village singing a hymn and when people collected, preached the gospel. Elizabeth had to raise her own salary. When she began as an itinerant, she had asked what it was, and was told "Two guineas for the quarter" (worth a little more than US$300 in today's currency). "Oh," she replied, "I did not know that I was to have anything." One morning when Elizabeth felt so ill she could not eat, her husband offered to fill her appointment; it was 25 miles away.[3]

When Thomas was thrown in jail for preaching, Elizabeth prayed:

> Thanks be to God, the storm which distresses us helps us towards the shore;
> Though there are changes, it is but one journey and we soon shall be at the end.
> Though there are many conflicts, it is but one battle;
> And we shall soon shout VICTORY! through the blood of the Son of God![4]

Elizabeth was one of more than 100 female preachers in the Primitive Methodist movement in England from 1815 to the mid-century. Most of them were young. In Methodist historian Dorothy Graham's list of Primitive Methodist women who preached in Great Britain and abroad, most were in their early 20s when they were first listed on the Society's preaching plans, although some of the women began preaching in their teens, and a few in their 30s and 40s. In another study of 28 Primitive Methodist female preachers, their median age was 19½.[5]

It is thought that Mary Hawkesley and Sarah Kirkland Harrison Bembridge (c.1794–1880) were the first female traveling preachers for this new society.

Mary's husband was fighting in Spain; she was reduced to earning a little money by making lace. Her parents had thrown her out of their house because they could not stomach her newfound faith, a fate that befell a lot of these young female preachers.[6] Sarah had been put on a preachers' plan in 1813 as a local preacher, and became a traveling preacher in 1815. Her first convert had been a gypsy, and afterwards whenever she was speaking close by, he acted as her herald, announcing her presence. In her obituary in the *Primitive Methodist Magazine*, the author wrote, "Primitive Methodism has been vastly indebted to its daughters who have had the 'spirit of prophesy' ... our late sister Bembridge has excelled them all."[7]

By 1820, one-fifth of all the Primitive Methodist preachers were women. They were generally poor, and poorly paid. Many of them had been servants or farm laborers when they were converted. They were paid much less than their male colleagues: in 1820, a woman preacher received £8 a year, whereas an unmarried man earned £15 and a married man up to £37 14s, although they did the same work. The women were not allowed to speak at their annual conferences, and there is no evidence that they presided over communion.

The women often became ill, likely because of overexertion and hard working conditions. Each of the traveling preachers was expected to visit 30 families a week, exhorting, praying, and engaging in conversation in addition to their preaching. Elizabeth was 31 when she fell ill and died. Her 16-month-old daughter Julia had died from smallpox the month before. Local preacher Lucy Collison (1813–34) got wet going to an appointment, and died from a cold and scarlet fever at the age of 21. Matilda Archer (1815–51) died at age 36, also having caught a cold. Jane Aycliffe (1815–37) died from a "violent cold" when she was 22. The prison guard took pity on Suzanne Perry (Barber) when she was thrown in jail for preaching, and sent in two blankets to keep her warm, preventing her from getting chilled.

Some of the female preachers did live into their 60s and 70s, and one died at 81. Mary Porteous (1783–1861) lived to be 78, although she had a rigorous life, preaching from 1824 until she died. In one route, she traveled 682 miles, walking more than a third of them, 232 miles through wind, frost, and rain, resulting in "such rheumatic pains as I fear I shall never recover from." The average life expectancy for all women in Great Britain in the nineteenth century, however, was 50 years,[8] so even with their hard life, the average life expectancy of the Primitive Methodist female preachers—56—was above the norm.[9]

While there was hostility to women preaching, they were also well received. It was reported that after Elizabeth Smith died, her husband Thomas found a list of 13 stations where she had been asked to come and preach. He estimated that nearly 2,000 men and women attended her funeral, although that was possibly a hagiographical exaggeration.

Some male preachers supported the women. The eccentric Lorenzo Dow (1777–1839) recorded in his journal that he had heard one of them and was extremely "satisfied…. She stopped when she had done," he wrote, "whereas a great many men, instead of stopping when they have got through, must spin it out and add to it or have a repetition over and over again."[10] In 1821, the editor of *The Primitive Methodist Magazine* pointed out that the early Christian Church had set a precedent for women to preach. A number of biblical passages referred to women "prophesying" and in his opinion, prophesying included public prayer, preaching, exhortation, and speaking experience. In the same issue, the well-known Irish theologian and biblical scholar Dr. Adam Clarke came to the same conclusion, pointing out that many people have spent "much useless labour" trying to prove that women in the New Testament did not preach.[11]

While the Primitive Methodist Church was the largest offshoot of the main Methodist movement, the Bible Christians also provided women near equality in its earliest days and opportunities for those who believed they had received a "call."

On 9 October 1815, 20 women and men gathered together in a farm house in Devon, England, along with the renegade Methodist preacher William O'Bryan (1778–1868) and his wife Catherine Cowlin (?–1860), to form a new society. Johanna Neale Brooks (?–c.1858) may have been the first woman to preach in that group although she had to go to church three times before she had enough courage to stand up and speak in public. Her husband and a parish officer forced her to leave, but most of the congregation followed her outside and pressed her to continue. Catherine Cowlin O'Bryan and Mary Thorne (1807–83) began preaching in 1816, both married women with families. By 1819, all these women had received official sanction from the new church to preach.[12]

At their Conference that year, 14 women were listed as itinerant preachers out of a total of 29 men and women. Like the Primitive Methodist preachers, most of them were young. Patience Bickle was only 14 when she began working for the society. William and Catherine O'Bryan's daughter Mary (1807–83) began speaking in public at age 11.

O'Bryan had special instructions for the women:

> … our sisters who travel as helpers should keep their own place, be
> watchful, always neat, plain and clean, discreet, humble, grave as mothers

in Israel, diligent according to their sex as well as their brethren, being as much as they can their own servants and helps to families wherever they go and when they leave their room in the morning leave everything in its proper place … let all … take care of their heath; beware of taking too long journeys and of remaining with wet clothes and … going out after preaching at night and of sleeping in damp beds.[13]

Again, however, like the Primitive Methodist women, in spite of O'Bryan's instructions, they traveled in spite of ill health, grueling conditions, and opposition in communities where they were sent to open new societies. One year, Elizabeth Dart (1792–1857) traveled on a 20-mile circuit, preaching three times on Sunday and usually every evening except Saturday. Sometimes she felt that itinerating was "foolishness," but she believed her spiritual life would be "imperiled" if she refused to testify. She began teaching school to supplement her income, but she found teaching too exhausting.

The salary scale was again discriminatory. In 1837, a single Bible Christian male preacher received from £10 to £14/year with board and lodging. A single woman preacher earned £7 along with room and board. Married men were given a bonus; to encourage them to marry female preachers and try to keep their wives working, they received £30/year along with a furnished house and allowances for each child. A number of the women did itinerate while raising a family. Ann Vickery (1800–53) often carried her youngest child to church, handing it to a member of the congregation while she led the worship service.

At the first Conference, the question was raised as to whether or not women should be allowed to preach. Both supporters and opponents quoted biblical passages to bolster their arguments but in the end it was decided that "the Lord" had already used women "to turn many to righteousness … what but this is the end of all preaching?" They felt that it would be "insolent" to dictate whom God would use to preach. That year, a man and a woman were in every preaching place except one, where Elizabeth Gay was the only preacher.

The women did have some restrictions placed on them. Where they preached was under the direction of the General Superintendent; the men had more freedom. Catherine O'Bryan expressed her unhappiness with this male domination in a poem, "The Female Preachers' Plea":

By sweet experience now I know,
That those who knock shall enter in;

God doth his gifts and grace bestow,
On Women too, as well as men ...
The sacred fire doth burn within
The breasts of either sex the same;
The holy soul that's freed from sin,
Desires that all may catch the flame.
This only is the moving cause,
Induc'd us women to proclaim,
"The Lamb of God." For whose applause,
We bear contempt—and suffer pain.
If we had fear'd the frowns of men,
Or thought their observations just,
Long since we had believ'd in vain,
And hid our talents in the dust ...
While men with eloquence and fame,
The silver trumpet manly blow,
A plainer trump we humbly claim,
The saving power of God to show.[14]

At the second Conference, however, it was determined that if women were ill, they could continue to receive their salary, but only if they remained single or were married to a male preacher. No similar rule existed for men.

The women were popular, competent, and a curiosity, sometimes attracting hundreds or several thousands to their preaching. But they were often exhausted by the pace and the lack of good accommodation and food. Mary Ann Werrey (1801–25) was sent to the Scilly Islands off the southwest of England, the first missionary from the new Missionary Society founded in 1821. By 1824 she was worn out, and she died the next year. Like the Primitive Methodists, though, generally they lived long and active lives compared to the general population. Genealogist Jim Bowen's analysis of these women indicates that the median age of their death was 67 years. In the Scilly Islands, however, the conditions were worse than usual. The Scillonians were a lawless bunch, smugglers, drinkers, and poor. But in less than a month Mary Ann had a chapel built, and the converts were so numerous that she needed an assistant.[15]

By 1825, there were 68 Bible Christian itinerant preachers, 47 men and 21 women. In addition there were about 80 female and many more male local preachers. The *Conference Minutes* listed 60 women who itinerated for the denomination between 1819 and 1851. Gradually, however, the percentage of female to male preachers declined. By 1838, out of 95 preachers, only 11 were women. Even by 1832, in the society, so much resistance had developed to women preachers that O'Bryan published a vindication of women preaching in the *Arminian Magazine*. He suggested that it was totally inconsistent to allow women to pray, sing, and prophesy in public and not to preach. Nevertheless by the middle of the century, female preachers had virtually disappeared.

The same phenomenon was taking place in the Primitive Methodist Church. As membership increased owing to the effectiveness of their itinerant preachers, new chapels were built, headquarters were formalized, and publications appeared. The group evolved from a "cottage" religion to a mainstream denomination. Ministers became theologically educated, an option not open to women; men claimed the title of Reverend. Institutionalization was closing churches to women's participation. By 1853, only one woman remained on the list of Bible Christian preachers, but she had no posting. Not only were women no longer involved, but the denominations soon forgot that women had once been active and effective preachers. Generally, their official obituaries in the society's publications omitted any reference to their preaching.

Many of the women had dropped out during their itinerancy well before this "forced" retirement. By 1831, in the early days of Primitive Methodism, 19 per cent of the women and 5.5 per cent of the men had quit. But by 1837, 52.6 per cent of the women and 11 per cent of the men had given up the itinerancy. Much of this was because of ill health and their virtually impossible work schedule; also the women often married other itinerants and stayed home to look after children. As well, the Primitive Methodist Church had a rule that "no married female shall be allowed to labour as a travelling preacher in any circuit, except that in which her husband resides." So if a woman had married "out of her circuit," she would also have had to retire.[16]

While these two Methodist offshoots, the Bible Christians and the Primitive Methodists, offered the most opportunities for women who felt called to a public ministry, in its early days, mainstream Wesleyan Methodism in Great Britain also accommodated several women in prominent leadership positions.

The Anglican minister John Wesley (1703–91), the unintentional founder of the Methodist Church as a separate entity from the Church of England, only gradually accepted women preachers. At the heart of his organization were small bands and larger class meetings, both segregated by gender if possible. Set up to check on the morality and spiritual progress of their members, the bands and the classes required leaders, thus thrusting women into leadership roles immediately. The bands were limited to about four people, but the classes, although supposedly for six or seven members, often grew to the point where the leader was put into the position of a public speaker. The fact that there were more women than men among the Methodists also helped the women's cause. It has been estimated that in the early nineteenth century, 60 per cent of Methodists were women, compared with 52.3 per cent of the adult population in England as a whole.[17]

Wesley insisted that talents be used. "I fear you are too idle," he wrote Elizabeth Bennis (1725–1802) in 1773. "Up and be doing," he challenged. "See that your talents rust not." The next year he wrote again with a similar rebuke: "You are not sent to Waterford to be useless. Stir up the gift of God which is in you; gather together those that have been scattered abroad, and make up a band, if not a class or two."[18]

By this time, Wesley was even encouraging women beyond the sphere of groups confined to women. In response to a Miss Furly, he agreed that she could certainly meet with a class of men if the members desired it. This would not assume authority over men, he explained, but would be an "act of friendship and brotherly love." She would be acting as an equal, not a superior. In fact, Wesley could hardly oppose women leaders as he had preached in a sermon on bigotry that "the conversion of sinners is the work of God, and whoever is the instrument of doing this work is the servant of God. And we must not forbid such a one."[19]

The women themselves were concerned about speaking publicly. In correspondence with Sarah Crosby (1729–1804), who eventually became one of the most outstanding Methodist preachers, Wesley advised that she should read notes or sermons, and just tell the people what was in her heart "as other women have done long ago." She should never take a biblical text, he advised, and never speak in "continued discourse" without four- or five-minute breaks. By 1771, however, he had sanctioned her to preach. He believed she had an extraordinary call. Methodism, he noted, was an extraordinary "dispensation" from God, and extraordinary things were bound to happen.

Six years later, Wesley gave Sarah Mallet Boyce (c.1761–1843/6), a poor tailor, advice on how to speak effectively. "Never scream," he wrote; "never speak above the natural pitch of your voice." At first, Sarah could preach only in a trance, "speaking clear and loud although she was utterly senseless," but by 1786, she was preaching without having "fits." Sarah admits that "in time past, [she had been] no friend to women's preaching. [She] therefore resolved never to do such thing," but she could not disobey her "call" from God. In 1787, the Manchester Conference issued her a written license to preach. It read: "We give the right hand of fellowship to Sarah Mallet, and have no objection to her being a preacher in our connexion, as long as she preaches the Methodist doctrines and attends to our discipline." After Sarah's husband's death, she and the wealthy Martha Gregson (c.1774–1839) lived and traveled the country together preaching in Methodist chapels, Sarah up to at least 1841, long after the ban on women preaching. It was common for never-married and widowed female preachers to share living quarters, possibly because of financial need, mutual support, or a deep emotional attachment.[20]

Wesley encouraged Miss Newman to preach, and Ann Gilbert (?–1790) to "do all the good" she could, and she preached to crowds estimated up to 1,400 people. Alice Cambridge (1762–1829) was given Wesley's blessing in 1791. When God commanded her to speak, she was not permitted to be silent, he wrote. "If you want books or anything," he offered, "let me know; I have your happiness much at heart."[21]

Diaries, letters, and journals reveal the remarkable careers of many Wesleyan Methodist women who were preaching and speaking publicly in the latter part of the eighteenth and early nineteenth centuries in Great Britain. Mary Bosanquet Fletcher (1739–1815) often had crowds of up to 3,000 men and women, and male ministers, in her congregations. Considered to be one of the most eminent female Methodists of her generation, Mary was acknowledged by Wesley as a minister, "entitled to preach from a biblical text." She directed an orphanage and boarding school, bringing "sickly, filthy, ignorant, vermin-infested children" into her home to clean and clothe them, giving them both instruction and recreation; she managed a large inheritance, administered a farm as well as preached in partnership with her husband. She was still preaching five times a week when she was 75. And yet, when she was young, she had been alienated from her family because they thought she was "righteous over much."[22]

In one year, Sarah Crosby (1729–1804) walked or rode 960 miles, spoke at 220 public meetings, and led 600 classes and bands along with her other ministerial duties. Most days of the week, she rose at 4:00 a.m., conducted a service an hour later, and often held others in the afternoons and evenings. Alice Cambridge (1762–1829) did most of her work in Ireland, even preaching to soldiers in their barracks.

Elizabeth Tomlinson Evans (c.1776–1849) stayed up until 2:00 a.m. or later, mending lace to earn enough money to travel as an itinerant. She is memorialized in George Eliot's novel, *Adam Bede*, as Dinah Morris. Mary Barritt Taft (1772–1851) probably traveled the most of all the women itinerating. She preached in barns, town halls, dye-houses, and malt-kilns. One Conference meeting even requested that she preach at it.

Most of the women preached because they could not help it. At the heart of Methodist doctrine was the experiential knowledge of the forgiveness of sin. When men and women felt the removal of the burden of their guilt, sin and fear, they were filled with a happiness that could not be contained and had to be shared. In this sense, every Methodist was an evangelist. "It is good to conceal the secrets of a king," Wesley wrote, "but it is good to tell the loving-kindness of the Lord."

The women approved by Wesley had to meet the three Methodist tests for preachers: their theology had to be correct, they had to have obvious talent, and their lives had to indicate that they had been "well and truly converted."

Many of the women showed organizational ability. Selina Shirley Hastings, Countess of Huntingdon (1707–91), has been called the first "Methodist bishop." She built chapels, appointed preachers to their circuits, and expelled those who were unfaithful. She established a theological college to train "her" preachers. The Methodist mystic Hannah Ball (1733/4–92), encouraged by Wesley, started a Sunday School in 1769 in High Wycombe, years before Robert Raikes began his experiment, although it is Raikes who receives credit for beginning the Sunday School movement. Hannah wrote about her first students, children from the local coaching inns, "They are a wild little company but seem willing to be instructed, I labour among them earnestly desiring to promote the interest of the Church of Christ!" At a wreath-laying ceremony at her grave in 1933, her bicentenary, those attending sang a special hymn:

> We thank thee for our Sunday School today,
> The first of Schools, whose foundress led the way
> And gathered little ones around her knee.[23]

Grace Norman Murray Bennet (1715/8–1803), a woman Wesley had hoped to marry at one time, became one of his chief administrators. She was appointed matron of the Orphan-House, the Methodist Centre in Newcastle-upon-Tyne. Wesley put her in charge of all the women's classes in England and Ireland. She traveled by horseback, allowing no man to assist her into the saddle. She trained her horse to kneel down when she touched its shoulder so she could mount by herself.

Although many of the women who preached had been poor and uneducated, Wesley required all Methodists to be as well-read as possible. He set up book rooms where books could be purchased inexpensively. His mother Susanna Annesley Wesley (1669–1742) had insisted that girls be taught to read, well before they learned housekeeping, and Wesley encouraged women to be as literate as men. He suggested a reading list for a "Miss L.," recommending that she study four to five hours a day. The list included books on poetry, grammar, arithmetic, geography, logic, ethics, natural philosophy, history, metaphysics, and divinity, a course he suggested should take her three to five years. He expected his preachers to read Sallust, Caesar, Cicero, Castellio, Terence, Virgil, Horace, Vida, Buchanan, Plato, Epictetus, Ignatius, Homer, Arndt, Boehme, Pascal, and other authors. Methodist followers were required to keep diaries, and itinerants had to submit regular reports and journals. Wesley's educational expectations were certainly much greater than was usual for English women—and even for men—at that time.

Nevertheless, in spite of the women's success, and perhaps because of it, opposition began to mount against them. Mary Bosanquet Fletcher announced meetings rather than preaching services because she felt it gave less offense. Wesley advised Alice Cambridge never to speak close to where a man was preaching "lest you draw away his hearers." Ann (Nancy) Cutler (1759–94), or "Praying Nanny" as she was affectionately known, an ascetic and a mystic, was responsible for several revivals even though she spoke simply of God, sin, and salvation. Yet she offended some by the "loudness" of her voice. Male preachers confessed that they were extremely jealous of her success. Wherever she went, the evangelist William Bramwell wrote, "there was an amazing power of God attending her work. . . . This was a very great trial to many of us to see the Lord make use of such simple means, and our usefulness comparatively small."[24]

Mary Barritt attracted such crowds to her services that the Connexion chairman ordered her to stop preaching, even though it was reported that "not one minister in five hundred could produce so many seals [sic] to their ministry," and that "of those who had been brought to Christ through her labours, over two hundred entered the ministry."[25] Mary continued preaching with the support of her husband—preacher Zechariah Taft (1772–1848), who later recorded the immense activity of these women. Indeed, supporters sent numerous poems to Zechariah affirming his work. One of them read in part:

Hail noble worthies, ministers of grace,
You holy females fir'd with zeal for God;

Call'd to endure the scandal, shame, disgrace,
To tread the thorny path your master trod.
… Let grave divines, and learned doctors, too

Dispute your call, forbid you to aspire,
Say you invade their priestly rights, and vow
To keep you silent and to quench your fire …
Your names shall live, shall from oblivion rise,
Transmitted down to ages yet unborn:
A TAFT is found commission'd from the skies,
To tell the world you rise above its scorn.
Go on brave veteran, servant of the Lord,
'Tis nobly done, and heaven approves the deed;
Be thine the task their virtues to record;
And smiling heaven will say, be thine the meed.[26]

In spite of the popular support, Mary's refusal to stop preaching precipi-
tated a nation-wide controversy in the denomination, resulting in an almost
total ban on women preaching. In 1802 and 1803, the Methodist Conferences
in Ireland and England passed legislation making it almost impossible for
women to preach except on occasional circumstances where they could speak
only to women. John Wesley had died in 1791, no longer around to support
and encourage these women.

Yet the women persisted, often as part of a clergy couple. Most of the
women preachers were still received enthusiastically by ordinary men and
women. In fact the legislation designed to stop women preaching barely
passed. For example, a local preacher and farmer, William Moon from North
Yorkshire wrote in his diary "I am thankful to God that I have always been
preserved from the error of those who disapprove of the way of God in calling
and qualifying women to be messengers of the gospel.… [W]hen a sister has
… preached the word of eternal life, my soul has been abundantly blessed."[27]

The official Methodist magazines refused to print their stories. Richard
Collett submitted a biographical obituary of his mother, Elizabeth Tonkin
Collett (1762–1820), which had been written by a male minister. The editor
returned it saying that "it might set a precedent to young females." The mother
of 11 children, Elizabeth had founded seven societies and seven chapels, set
up numerous classes, and led at least one revival. Zechariah Taft agreed that
women's "public labours" in ministry were either suppressed, or passed over

in silence "as if they never existed." The majority "of Biographers and Editors of Magazines are enemies to female preaching," he wrote, "so that we have very little concerning their labours."[28]

IN THE NEW WORLD

Gradually, women either ceased their work or joined other emerging denominations. Some joined the Quakers; many emigrated to North America with their families.

In 1833, Elizabeth Dart and her new husband, John Hicks Eynon (1801–c.1888), arrived in Canada after a frightening 42-day ocean voyage where they "were tossed up and down upon the raging sea." Methodism was poorly regarded in Upper Canada (later called Ontario) where they began their ministry; the Church of England was almost, but not quite, the established church, but it was privileged over other denominations. Yet Elizabeth and John labored for years with other Bible Christian preachers who had also emigrated. Conditions had been harsh in England where they had itinerated, yet in Canada they found the "Misquitos," the heat of summer, and the deep cold of winter almost unbearable. "I have scarcely known what to do," John wrote. He pleaded for a horse to get around the bush and on the bad or non-existent roads of his large circuit.[29]

The Bible Christians settled in Prince Edward Island and Upper Canada, where some of the women met resistance to their preaching in Canada's social and political conservatism. Ann Vickery's husband, Paul Robins (1804–90), noted in 1847 that the Society in Peterborough, Ontario, would not tolerate a woman in the pulpit even though they desperately needed more preachers. There were a few exceptions: Elizabeth Trueman Hoskin (1807–82) who preached for several years "as long as her health held out," was held in such high esteem that she was known as "Rev. Mrs. Hoskin." Elizabeth Dart was considered to be the best preacher the Bible Christians had.

Martha Jago Sabine (1807–75) began work as a domestic servant when she immigrated to Prince Edward Island and immediately on her twenty-third birthday in 1829 began preaching in Charlottetown. The press named her "the marvel of the week," even though they also described her as an "ordinary looking personage." She spoke with "an astonishing volubility of utterance and with considerable energy and effect." Martha drained neighboring churches when she spoke, and once the floor of a meeting house collapsed from the weight of so many attending the meeting, precipitating "a great number into the cellar." But her preaching also began debates in the press about the propriety of women preaching. Martha and her husband opened their home for religious services, but she became known as an "exemplary, useful Christian," rather than as a preacher. There was no mention of her preaching in her obituary.[30]

Ann Copp Gordon (1837–1931) was probably the last Bible Christian woman to preach in Canada. Unlike many of the other women, Ann was from a well-to-do home in England, but her father, a staunch member of the Church of England, banished her when she converted at age 16. She became an itinerant, but exhausted, sailed for Canada four years later to visit her brother and recuperate. She soon married another Bible Christian itinerant and together they "caused a bit of a flurry among other established Methodist bodies," preaching in the streets in Canadian cities. After her husband Andrew Cory died, Ann was still asked to preach, but only on special occasions such as church anniversaries. Her last appointments were in the 1870s.[31]

Some Primitive Methodists also came to Canada, more to the United States, but both the Canadian and American societies received little support from the parent body in England. While the English body was excited at the possibility of sending out evangelists, they had not calculated realistically how much it would cost. The first two single women to serve as missionaries in the New World, Ruth Watkins (c.1802–?) and Anne Wearing, found it very expensive, especially in New York City, where Ruth had to live in a cellar "in the back part of the city." Ruth had been in tears the day in 1829 they had sailed from Liverpool.[32]

Possibly the most popular couple in Canada were Jane Woodill (1824–93) and Isaac Wilson. Jane had been born in that country to immigrants. When she was 18, her name appeared on the Primitive Methodist Etobicoke Circuit plan; seven years later she married a first cousin. Jane thought nothing of riding 30 miles and preaching two or three times on Sunday in addition to raising a family and looking after sick people in her home community north of Toronto. Jane and her husband were reasonably well off financially, even offering $500 to a neighboring Wesleyan church to help repair their roof. As was apparently happening to all the female Methodist preachers in the late nineteenth century, however, Jane was eventually invited to speak only on special occasions rather than as a regular preacher on a scheduled plan.

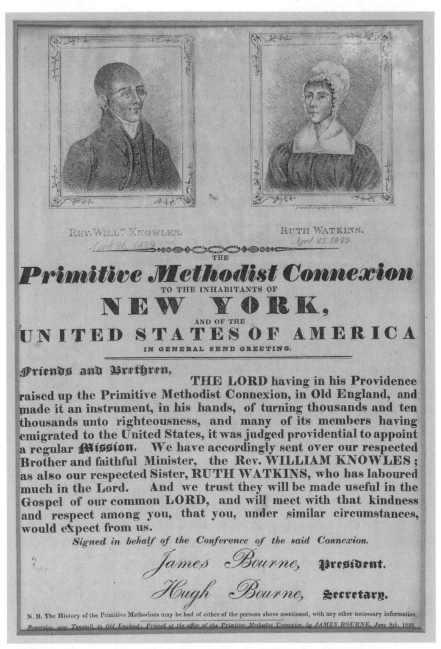

FIGURE 10.1 The first Primitive Methodist missionaries sail from England for the United States. Ruth Watkins and William Knowles were appointed in 1829 to minister to the Primitive Methodist emigrants in the United States and convert others. Photo: Reproduced with permission by The University of Manchester and the Trustees for Methodist Church Purposes, England.

Eventually both the Bible Christians and Primitive Methodists in Canada united with other Methodist movements to form the Methodist Church of Canada, one of the founding denominations of the United Church of Canada, the largest Protestant denomination in that country. It was some time before the Methodist Church and later the United Church of Canada ordained women—in 1936. In Australia, five Methodist denominations joined together in 1902 to found the Methodist Church of Australasia, which then became part of the Uniting Church in Australia in 1977. A Methodist woman was ordained there in 1969.

Methodist women fared better in the United States than in Canada. The historian John Wigger notes that women in the States formed the backbone of the Methodist movement and were clearly in the majority. Between 1786 and 1801 in New York, Baltimore, and Philadelphia women made up between 57 and 66 per cent of the total membership, although by 1795, generally women were no longer even class leaders in those cities. Still a few preached and many were able to exhort, that is speak in church of their personal experiences. Perhaps the best known was Fanny Butterfield Newell (1793–1824) who spoke after her husband Ebenezer preached. Often her young children were with her. Lacking a male minister, Sarah Roszel (1751–1830) organized the services in and around her hometown in Virginia, sometimes reading one of Wesley's sermons, then exhorting, and afterwards leading a class meeting. Methodist women might not be able to preach, admitted a male itinerant, but "they could read and sing and shout ... talk in class and **love-feast**, encourage mourners, and pray as if they would bring heaven and earth together."[33]

Researching female preaching in America between 1740 and 1845, the historian Catherine Brekus could find only nine female preachers out of 100 women belonging to the more conservative Methodist Episcopal Church. Perhaps the strangest event, however, was the proposal by the Methodist Episcopal Church in Philadelphia to invite Jemima Wilkinson, the Universal Friend (described in a later chapter), into its pulpit.[34]

There was a "trial" and later excommunication of the popular Sally Thompson in 1830 in New York State. A mild woman with "good manners" and "plain good sense" who had been preaching with great success for about nine years, Sally was suddenly seen as being too masculine, and out of her place. At a Methodist quarterly meeting, she was accused of evil speaking, immorality, and insubordination to the church, even though she had never gone where she had not been invited. At a public trial where she was told to be silent, she was defended by several men and women and pronounced not guilty. This was appealed by a male minister and the result was excommunication on the grounds of insubordination.[35]

Eventually, however, women were ordained in some of the Methodist branches, although in the beginning, ordination was confusing and somewhat "unstable." In 1861, Mary A. Will was ordained in the Wesleyan Methodist Connection (later the Wesleyan Church, part of the Holiness movement) by the Illinois Conference. Mary had been licensed as a minister the year before. But at the 1864 General Conference, neither a motion to disapprove of women in the ministry nor one to provide for licensing and ordination received a majority vote, so Mary's licensing and ordination were revoked. She tried to appeal that decision but the 1875 Conference refused to hear an appeal. Four years later, the Conference voted to license women, but that decision was also repealed two years later.[36]

A minister from the Wesleyan Church preached the ordination sermon for the first woman to be ordained in the United States, Antoinette Brown Blackwell (1825–1921), in 1853, eight years before Mary Will. In his sermon, Luther Lee (1800–89) quoted the Bible passage: "There is neither Jew nor Gentile, neither slave nor free, nor is there male and female, for you are all one in Christ Jesus" (Galatians 3:28). "I cannot see how the text can be explained so as to exclude females from any right, office, work, privilege or immunity which males enjoy, hold or perform," he noted. Antoinette received so little support from women that she left the Church the next year and became a Unitarian.[37]

Recent research on ordained women in the Wesleyan Church shows that the most active periods were from 1920 to 1959; around 200 women were serving in each decade of that period. It is interesting to note, however, a significant drop in the 1960s, whether that was because more women were going into the job market and not into church ministry, or perhaps because of a backlash against feminism.[38]

Helenor M. Davison (1823–76) of the Methodist Protestant Church was also subject to reversals in her preaching career. From Pennsylvania, "with deep blue eyes and raven hair," Helenor was the first of 18 children, divided among three wives of the Rev. John Alter. When her mother died, 14-year-old Helenor became responsible for a home and seven siblings; when her father and the rest of the family were ill with typhoid fever she had to care for them and also operate their sawmill, eventually becoming seriously ill herself. At age 19, Helenor married John Draper, and it was around this time that she became an itinerant, along with her father, for the Methodist Protestant

Church. They rode through open prairie, tall grass, ponds, and sloughs, also organizing a church that appears to have operated in the open air.

In 1863, it was moved and approved to recommend Helenor to the Annual Conference "to preach the gospel or at least a small work," although a "small work" was not defined. She was ordained a deacon at the annual meeting held in her father's home in 1866 for the North Indiana Conference. One year later, however, an objection was made. A motion was put forward by two male ministers: "Resolved that the election of females to orders is incompatible with the teachings of the Holy Scriptures, and not in accordance with our book of discipline." The matter was referred to the next General Conference. In 1867, at the Conference in August, H.M. Davison was listed as scheduled to "write, preach or lecture" on foreign missions. In 1868, she was listed among the ministerial members.

In 1871, a study committee was formed and after the reports were brought forward, a majority supported "female ordination," but a vocal minority opposed "the ordination of ladies." Somehow the minority opinion was approved by a vote of 46 to 17. Next, a motion was made that each Annual Conference should have the power to authorize females to preach the Gospel in the Methodist Church. The minutes of that meeting do not indicate whether the motion was adopted or not, but in 1874, Helenor's name appeared in the Register of the Grand Prairie Circuit. She continued to work for the church as her health permitted until her death in 1876.[39]

Anna Snowden Oliver (1849–92) and Anna Howard Shaw (1847–1919), Methodist seminary graduates, tried to become ordained in the Methodist Episcopal Church in 1880. Both were denied. The Conference even decided to revoke all local preachers' licenses that had been issued to women since 1869; Shaw had been given one earlier. Shaw left that Methodist Church, turned to the Methodist Protestant Church and was ordained there in 1880 in a special service the day after the male candidates were ordained. However, embittered, she turned her efforts to the suffragette and temperance movements. Still, she kept in touch with women in ministry, for she wrote an article in 1898 listing the various women who had been ordained in the United States in other denominations. She also conducted marriage services, but would not perform a ceremony that contained the word "obey." Oliver remained in the Methodist Episcopal Church and continued applying for ordination but her health was broken and she soon died. Earlier, she had been invited to preach at a Methodist Preachers' meeting in 1877, but she was uninvited after a male minister opposed her on the grounds that if she were to preach it would look as if the Methodists supported women preachers.[40]

Perhaps the most well-known early Methodist preacher in the United States was Maggie Newton Van Cott (1830–1914). Maggie's parents were Episcopalian, but her grandfather introduced her to Methodism. Her mother forbade her to attend that church, but Maggie went secretly, hiding in an inconspicuous place, and eventually converted, joining the Methodist Episcopals. She became sought after as a traveling evangelist, and in 1869, was given an exhorter's license to speak after the preacher finished his sermon. That same year, she was handed a preacher's license, although she didn't apply for it. This threw the "cat among the pigeons." Her supporters praised her feminine qualities; her detractors felt she had lost those qualities. In spite of the ensuing discussions and debates, it is estimated that Maggie traveled 143,417 miles and held 9,933 revival meetings, preached 4,294 sermons—all before her fiftieth birthday.[41]

There were several women preaching in the African Methodist Episcopal Church (AME), although as with other women, a traveling female evangelist was more acceptable than a female preacher. In 1819, Jarena Lee (1783–1864) was authorized to preach by Richard Allen (1760–1831), the founder of the African Methodist Episcopal Church, but only eight years after she had first requested it. She had heard a voice clearly tell her to "Preach the Gospel; I will put words in your mouth, and you will turn your enemies to become your friends." At first Allen agreed that Jarena could be an exhorter or hold a prayer meeting, but preaching was something else. Finally he gave her permission, and she traveled thousands of miles around the country by foot, usually by invitation, to camp-meetings, meeting-houses, churches, private homes and in the open air, to black, white or mixed groups. She calculated that in one year alone, she traveled 3,325 miles, walking much of it, and preached 178 sermons. Describing one of those sessions, she wrote, "we had a most melting, sin-killing, and soul-reviving time." Yet she faced hostility because she was black and a woman. In the *Religious Experience and Journal of Mrs. Jarena Lee*, she argues, "If the man may preach, because the Savior died for him, why not the woman, seeing he died for her also? Is he not a whole Savior, instead of a half one? As those who hold it wrong for a woman to preach, would seem to make it appear?"[42]

Julia Foote (1823–1901) preached in the Methodist Episcopal Church, although her mother told her she would rather hear of her daughter's death than her exposure in the pulpit. Her husband threatened to commit her to an insane asylum, but eventually he just drifted out of her life. Receiving no support from her denomination, she became an independent itinerant traveling around the United States and Canada, teaching the doctrine of sanctification, the controversial belief that one could be totally freed from sin and lead a life of spiritual perfection. "My business is with the Lord," she told anyone who opposed her, "and wherever I found a door opened I intended to go in and work for my Master." In 1894, she was the first woman in the African Methodist Episcopal Church to be ordained a deacon, and in 1900, the second woman to become an elder.[43]

Many preachers wrote their autobiographies; another AME preacher, the freed slave Amanda Berry Smith (1837–1915), was one of them. Usually excluded from official histories, these women's writings show the extent of their activity. In her work *An Autobiography: The Story of the Lord's Dealings with Mrs. Amanda Smith the Colored Evangelist: Containing an Account of Her Life, Work of Faith, and Her Travels in America, England, Ireland, Scotland, India and Africa as an Independent Missionary*, she writes of how her beautiful singing voice was often her *entrée* to several congregations where she then preached.[44] She had begun her career after she heard a voice telling her to "Go Preach." In addition to preaching, Amanda opened a home for black orphans and wrote a monthly newspaper, *The Helper.*

Methodism was not the only denomination that accepted women's ordination one year and found it anathema the next. The Cumberland Presbyterian Church ordained Louisa Mariah Layman Woosley (1862–1952) in 1889, and not until 1956 was there another woman ordained in a Presbyterian church to "word and sacrament"—Margaret Towner (1925–?) in the American Presbyterian Church. But in between there was controversy. Nolin Presbytery ordained Louisa but almost immediately, the Kentucky Synod ordered Nolin Presbytery to remove Louisa from its rolls. The Nolin Presbytery "lettered her out," which meant that she could be a minister in another presbytery, which was not the intention of the Synod. Ironically, in 1938, she served as a moderator in the Kentucky Synod. She also wrote a book, *Women Shall Preach*, in 1891, shortly after her aborted ordination. While she continued to minister in Presbyterian churches, Louisa ended her ministry as a teacher of a Bible class in a Methodist Church.[45]

While female evangelists may have been better received than female preachers, newspapers in the very early 1900s took pains to mention that the American Presbyterian evangelist Edith Livingston Peake (c.1850–1934) was formerly an actress; actresses were then not considered to be at the top, morally and spiritually, in many people's minds. Edith had been appointed an evangelist in 1893.[46]

There was something threatening to male ministers especially, about a woman preaching. Richard Lyle Tucker (1827–75), a Canadian Primitive Methodist minister, expressed a concern that female preachers often lacked "meekness, charity and domestic qualities," although he pointed out that this was not the case with his mother-in-law, the successful Primitive Methodist preacher Mary Ann Lyle (1797–1862). Another ministerial son-in-law, William Clarke, agreed that Mary Ann was "modest and retiring," and "only a sense of duty ... could have overcome her natural diffidence and nerved her for this work."[47]

However, women did want to preach; they felt called or compelled to preach. The American Frances Willard (1839–98), who became president of the Women's Christian Temperance Union (WCTU) in 1879, confessed to wanting to be a minister in the church. She wrote in *Women in the Pulpit*: "The deepest thought and desire of my life would have been met, if my dear old Mother Church had permitted me to be a minister.... Let me as a loyal daughter of the church, urge upon younger women who feel a call, as I once did, to preach the unsearchable riches of Christ."[48] A "maternal feminist," influenced by the "cult of true womanhood," Frances presented an unusual argument for women's inclusion in ministerial ranks. She believed that the work of an evangelist was quite unsuited to women, as evangelists had no home—they were "tossed from place to place." Whereas pastoral work, or being ordained to be a minister, is "motherly work.... The mother has her work, the pastor the flock," she wrote. "As a mother spreads her table with food suited to the individual needs of her family, so the pastor feeds the flock."[49]

Frances, of course, was putting forth an argument that would support women as pastors, for in the nineteenth century, women's authority in the home was not only accepted but normative. Women had been pushed into the domestic sphere, and if "pastoring" could be equated with mothering in the home, then it followed logically that women could and should be pastors.

Phoebe Palmer (1807–74), the influential Methodist Episcopal evangelist who traveled throughout the United States, Canada, the United Kingdom, and Europe, believed a church would decline if women were denied their ministry. Those women who feel they have been "filled with the Pentecostal flame" must speak out, she insisted. "If these women are rebuked or silenced, the Holy Spirit is grieved and the church will suffer," she wrote in *Promise of the Father*.[50] However, as one writer noted in 1967, the clergy was the "one profession" that was most resistant to change, "which has not only been defined as masculine but as 'sacredly' masculine. The father figure, a prominent feature of Christianity, is also a predominant ingredient in the image of the clergy. Sacred tradition has therefore helped maintain the boundaries of the clerical profession."[51]

Women had more opportunities in Methodist churches than preaching, although whether or not a woman was allowed to preach was a good test of gender equality. However, many women found they could exercise leadership, hone their skills and learn new ones in the vast mission fields. Isabella Thoburn (1840–1901), a missionary to North India for the Women's Foreign Missionary Society of the Methodist Episcopal Church, wrote:

> We have found sickness and poverty to relieve, widows to protect, advice to be given in every possible difficulty or emergency, teachers and Bible women to be trained, houses to be built, horses and cattle to be bought, gardens to be planted, and accounts to be kept and rendered. We have found use for every faculty, natural and acquired, that we possessed, and have coveted all that we lacked.[52]

Isabella was one of thousands of women who found travel to foreign fields stimulating, challenging, and exciting. In the beginning, the women were expected to convert foreigners by preaching or to engage in the work to support their missionary husbands. Later missions gradually focused more on social activism. The missionary impulse will be examined in chapter 14.

FURTHER READING

PRIMARY

"An Account of S[arah] Mallitt [*sic*]." *Arminian Magazine* XI. London: The Wesleyan Methodist Church, 1788.

Lee, Jarena. *Religious Experience and Journal of Mrs. Jarena Lee, Giving an Account of her Call to Preach the Gospel*. Philadelphia: Jarena Lee, 1849.

Smith, Amanda. *An Autobiography: The Story of the Lord's Dealings with Mrs. Amanda Smith the Colored Evangelist: Containing an Account of her Life Work of Faith, and Her Travels in America, England, Ireland, Scotland, India and Africa as an Independent Missionary*. Chicago: Meyer & Brother Publishers, 1893.

Taft, Z. *Biographical Sketches of the Lives and Public Ministry of Various Holy Women: Whose eminent usefulness and successful labours in the Church of Christ, have entitled them to be enrolled among the great benefactors of mankind: in which are included several letters from the Rev. J. Wesley never before published.* London: Kershaw H. Cullingworth, 1825–28.

Woosley, Louisa. *Women Shall Preach.* Edited by Matthew H. Gore and Susan Knight Gore. Memphis, TN: Historical Foundation of the Cumberland Presbyterian Church and the Cumberland Presbyterian Church in America, 2014.

SECONDARY

Bowen, Jim. "The Bible Christian Connexion and Their Female Itinerant Preachers." Ontario Genealogical Society, Durham Region Branch, 6 October 2015.

Graham, Dorothy. "Chosen by God: The Female Itinerants of Early Primitive Methodism." PhD diss., University of Birmingham, 2013. http://etheses.bham.ac.uk/4557/1/Graham86PhD.pdf.

James, Janet Wilson, ed. *Women in American Religion.* Philadelphia: University of Pennsylvania Press, 1980.

Keller, Rosemary Skinner, Louise L. Queen, and Hilah F. Thomas, eds. *Women in New Worlds.* Vol. 2. Nashville, TN: Abingdon, 1982.

Lloyd, Jennifer. *Women and the Shaping of British Methodism: Persistent Preachers 1807–1907.* Manchester: Manchester University Press, 2009.

Mack, Phyllis. *Heart Religion in the British Enlightenment: Gender and Emotion in Early Methodism.* Cambridge: Cambridge University Press, 2008.

Muir, Elizabeth Gillan. *Petticoats in the Pulpit: The Story of Nineteenth-Century Methodist Women Preachers in Upper Canada.* Toronto: The United Church Publishing House, 1991.

Muir, Elizabeth Gillan, and Marilyn Färdig Whiteley, eds. *Changing Roles of Women within the Christian Church in Canada.* Toronto: University of Toronto Press, 1995.

Shoemaker, Christopher M. "A Small Work: The Story of Helenor Alter Davisson, Methodism's First Ordered Woman." *Methodist History* 41, no. 2 (January 2003): 3–11.

Thomas, Hilah F., and Rosemary Skinner Keller, eds. *Women in New Worlds.* Vol. 1. Nashville, TN: Abingdon Press, 1981.

"Through the Front Doors: Methodist Women's Journey toward Ordination." Pitts Theological Library, Emory University, Atlanta, Georgia, c.2006.

Wigger, John H. *Taking Heaven by Storm: Methodism and the Rise of Popular Christianity in America.* Champaign, IL: University of Illinois Press, 2001.

NOTES

1 Muir, *Petticoats in the Pulpit*, 36ff. Unless otherwise noted, information on women in Methodism is found in Muir, *Petticoats in the Pulpit*.

2 Muir, *Petticoats in the Pulpit*, 39.

3 Graham, "Chosen by God," 152.

4 Price, "Praying through the Storm," *The Primitive Methodist Movement Blog*, accessed 15 August 2018, http://daves-little-blog.blogspot.com/2010/10/praying-through-storm.html.

5 An analysis of Dorothy Graham, "Primitive Methodist Women," http://www.myprimitivemethodists.org.uk/page_id__591.aspx; Valenze as quoted in Muir, *Petticoats in the Pulpit*, 38.

6 Graham, "Chosen by God."

7 "G.W.," 478.

8 Lambert, "A Brief History of Life Expectancy in Britain."

9 Graham, "Chosen by God," 148.

10 Muir, *Petticoats in the Pulpit*, 37.

11 Muir, *Petticoats in the Pulpit*, 37.

12 Muir, *Petticoats in the Pulpit*, 41ff.

13 *Bible Christian Minutes*, 1820, as quoted in Colin C. Short, "Portraits of Some Female Bible Christian Ministers."

14 As quoted in Muir, *Petticoats in the Pulpit*, 45.

15 Bowen, "The Bible Christian Connexion and Their Female Itinerant Preachers"; Short, "Portraits of Some Female Bible Christian Ministers."

16 Graham, "Chosen by God," 172.

17 Lloyd, *Women and the Shaping of British Methodism*, 21.

18 Muir, *Petticoats in the Pulpit*, 14.

19 Taft, preface to *Biographical Sketches of the Lives and Public Ministry of Various Holy Women*, ii.

20 "An Account of S[arah] Mallitt [*sic*]"; East, "'Lightly Esteemed by Men.'" Phyllis Mack, in *Heart Religion*, has done a comprehensive study of many of these relationships.

21 Muir, *Petticoats in the Pulpit*, 16ff.

22 Mack, *Heart Religion in the British Enlightenment*, 168, 305.

23 Atkins, "Hannah Ball, Friend of John Wesley and Founder of the First Sunday School."

24 Muir, *Petticoats in the Pulpit*, 23f.

25 As reported in Mrs. Booth, "Female Ministry or Woman's Right to Preach the Gospel," in Dayton, ed., *The Higher Christian Life*, 21.

26 Taft, preface, xvi.

27 McKenzie, "An Early Tribute to Women Preachers," 2.

28 Taft, preface, i. Today there is approximately a 3:2 ratio of male to female ministers in the Methodist Church in the United Kingdom.

29 Muir, *Petticoats in the Pulpit*, 61ff.

30 Muir, *Petticoats in the Pulpit*, 75f; Bell, "Allowed Irregularities."

31 Muir, *Petticoats in the Pulpit*, 77ff.

32 Graham, "Chosen by God," 119.

33 Wigger, *Taking Heaven by Storm*, 151ff.

34 Brekus, *Strangers and Pilgrims*, 81f.

35 Brekus, *Strangers and Pilgrims*, 267ff.

36 Haines, "Women in Ministry."

37 Dayton, ed., *The Higher Christian Life*, 5.

38 Haines, "Women in Ministry."

39 Shoemaker, "A Small Work."

40 Brereton and Klein, "American Women in Ministry," 180; *The New York Times*, 27 February 1877, 8; *Chautauquan*, v. 27, August 1898; "Through the Front Doors."

41 Everhart, "Maggie Newton Van Cott," 300ff. In 1851, at the quarterly meeting of the United Brethren Illinois Conference, Lydia Sexton was licensed as a preacher long before Maggie Newton Van Cott. Lydia worked as a tailor to support herself, noting that she was paid three dollars for a coat while a male tailor at the time earned seven dollars a coat. Hardesty, *Great Women of Faith*, 79.

42 Lee, *Religious Experience and Journal of Mrs. Jarena Lee*.

43 MacLean, "Julia Foote."

44 Smith, *An Autobiography*.

45 Woosley, *Women Shall Preach*.

46 "Woman Speaks of Scriptures"; "United Presbyterian Church."

47 Muir, *Petticoats in the Pulpit*, 99.

48 Hardesty, "Minister as Prophet? Or as Mother?" 89.

49 Hardesty, "Minister as Prophet? Or as Mother?" 97.

50 Hardesty, "Minister as Prophet? Or as Mother?" 95f.

51 E. Wilbur Bock as quoted in Joel Tibbetts, "Women Who Were Called," 43.

52 Brereton and Klein, "American Women," 177.

Chapter 11

WOMEN WHO FOUNDED CHURCHES UNDER THE ROMAN CATHOLIC CHURCH

SCORES OF WOMEN FOUNDED or co-founded abbeys, nuns' orders, churches, denominations, and religious movements, most of them with male as well as female followers. Many of the early groups were considered "heretical" by the Catholic Church and forced out of existence. The Protestant Reformation and the later social ills of the Industrial Age triggered a variety of religious expressions and new churches, often as a result of the study of the scriptures in the vernacular and a desire on the part of women to find a spiritual home that permitted major roles for them. In this chapter and in the following two chapters there are stories of religious orders and churches initiated by women from the thirteenth century on. There are many others. This chapter describes women who operated within the Roman Catholic Church, although they were not necessarily well received by that Church; chapters 12 and 13 tell mainly of women in Protestantism.

THE GUGLIELMITES

Little is known about Guglielma (c.1210–c.1281), a woman who arrived in Milan, Italy, around 1260. It was thought that she came originally from Bohemia and was related to the king, possibly sister to the Abbess Agnes of Prague (1211–82). The name Guglielma translates as Vilemina in a Bohemian dialect, and since Queen Constance of Hungary (c.1180–1240) and King Přemysl Ottakar I (1155–1230) of Bohemia had a daughter called Vilemina Blanchena, Guglielma was likely of royal blood. It was later rumored "that the archangel Raphael announced to Queen Constance ... the incarnation of the said Guglielma" just as Mary the mother of Jesus received the announcement of his conception and birth from the angel Gabriel.[1]

A widow with a son, Guglielma was around 50 when she arrived in Italy. She lived simply in the convent of Santa Caterina di Brassona like a Beguine/*pinzochera*, wearing a plain brown tunic, attracting both men and women as disciples. She was renowned as a counselor, comforter, alms-giver, miracle-worker, and healer, especially curing headaches. It was thought that the stigmata appeared on her body, although she took pains to hide them. When she died, she was buried in the Cistercian monastery at Chiaravalle; she had lived in one of the monks' houses there earlier, and she had bequeathed her property to them.[2]

After her death, a cult sprang up around her. During her lifetime, it had been rumored that she was the embodiment of the Holy Spirit because she had been born on Pentecost, the day the early disciples received the Holy Spirit, but whether she had started this idea herself, it is not known. One of her disciples, Andrea Saramita (?–1300), who was attached to the monastery, reported that she had told him of her divinity, that she had come down from heaven to begin a new age in which the whole world would be saved including the Jews and Saracens. Earlier, Saramita had bought a house for Guglielma in Porta Nuova. Another close follower, Manfreda/Maifreda Visconti da Pirovano (?–1300), an abbess in the lay Humiliati Order nearby, and a cousin of the lord of Milan, insisted that indeed Guglielma was the Holy Spirit, and that she had refused to take the Eucharist because she viewed it as her own body. Others in the group of followers, however, claimed that Guglielma strongly denied that she was the Holy Spirit. When asked to perform healings, she would say, "Go away. I am not God." Or, "You are fools! What you say and believe about me is not so. I was born of a man and a woman."[3]

In any case, the Guglielmites claimed that, in a new age to come, some or all of the church administrators would be women, Maifreda as Guglielma's vicar, the pope-designate. A female cardinal had already been chosen, a poor unmarried seamstress named Taria Benedetti.

Acting the part of pope or papesse after Guglielma's death, Maifreda conducted services in the chapel built on top of Guglielma's tomb, and allowed followers to kiss her hands and feet. She officiated at Mass, preached, taught, wrote hymns, epistles, and liturgies. She kept a vial of the water she had used to wash Guglielma's body after her death, and she anointed those who were ill with the water. Maifreda claimed that Guglielma often appeared to her in visions, telling Maifreda what to say on various occasions. Her followers said that "Maifreda herself, or Saint Guglielma, had greater grace and virtue and authority on earth than blessed Peter the apostle ever had."[4]

Men could have a role, too, in this future church; Saramita read the words of consecration while Maifreda conducted the services. He was the group's theologian and evangelist, but she had the power. A special service was held on Pentecost, for that was Guglielma's birthday; her followers expected that she would appear then.[5] Two other memorial services took place: 24 August to commemorate Guglielma's death, and in October on the day she was buried.

Needless to say, the Inquisition became interested in what was happening in that part of Italy, even though the sect was fairly private and secreted in a remote area. In 1296 and again in 1300, they questioned members of the group. Evidently two previous members, one a recently ordained priest, and the other a male H/Umiliati, had informed on the rest. At first, all the Guglielmites escaped punishment, but in the end, Maifreda, another nun, Giacoma dei Bassani da Nova, and Saramita were burned as "heretics." Guglielma's body was dug up and her bones also were burned. Other followers were fined or forced to wear the penitential cross signifying that they had been charged with heresy. Guglielma's tomb and the group's writings were destroyed.

That, however, was not the end of Guglielma. Around 1425, a full-length story of her life was written, although it bore little similarity to her real life in Milan. A Florentine playwright, Antonia Tanini Pulci (c.1452–1501), also produced a drama about her, and a fifteenth-century Tarot card, a Visconti-Sforza card, depicted Maifreda as a papesse. Sitting on a throne, holding a scepter in her right hand and a closed book in her left, the triple tiara of the papacy on her head, a nun thought to be Maifreda sits regally in a plain brown habit with a white veil and rope belt, similar to what the Guglielmites wore. Even later on in 1685, a report states that there were three altars in the Church of San Andrea, one dedicated to St. Guglielma.[6]

On the north wall of a church in Brunate, there is a painting from around 1450 of Guglielma: a framed fresco supposedly contracted by Bianca Visconti-Sforza, the same woman who commissioned the Tarot cards. The identity of two other figures in the painting, who are receiving a blessing from Guglielma, has been disputed, but different historians believe them to be Maifreda and Saramita.[7] In a letter written in 1842 in response to an enquiry, the parish priest at Brunate, Pietro Monti stated: "There is a fresco of Santa Guglielma that seems to me to date from around 1450. In 1826, workmen demolished the wall adjoining ... and there I saw many other figures previously covered with paint ... that formed a series with the picture that still exists and recorded the story of Guglielma."[8] In the fresco painting, Guglielma is dressed in purple damask with ermine hangings behind her, suggesting a royal origin; she wears three golden rings, probably representing her purported relationship to the Trinity.

In 1912, the bishop of Como published an indulgence prayer that begins:

> O glorious Santa Guglielma, in these times of great moral laxity and weakness of character, we appeal with confidence to your intercession to obtain strength and purity from the Divine Heart of Jesus and his Immaculate Mother. At the school of Jesus and Mary, O Guglielma, you studied Christian dignity and learned to respect it in such a way that neither riches, nor honours, nor promises, nor threats, nor privations, nor slander, nor persecution, nor exile could ever make you unfaithful.[9]

Guglielma's feast is still celebrated each year in Brunate on the fourth Sunday of April. In her study *From Virile Woman to WomanChrist*, the feminist writer Barbara Newman suggests that the worship of Guglielma was understandably part of the unconscious desire through the ages for a more utopian Christian church and society: "In spite or indeed because of the Church's official androcentrism, the womanChrist paradigm remained firmly lodged in the unconscious of Christendom ... here, it was activated ... by a new ideal of gender complementarity rooted in the changing relationships of holy women and their devotees."[10]

THE URSULINES

After years of preparation, in 1535 when she was over 60, Angela Merici (1474–1540), along with 28 other women, established the Company of St. Ursula in Brescia, Italy, a religious group set apart from society, but not cloistered, later known as the Ursulines. The women wore ordinary clothes and like the Beguines, did not take public vows. Angela wrote a rule of life specifying celibacy, poverty, and obedience; the women's purpose was to foster Christian values in the family and society.

Orphaned when she was 15, Angela had joined the Third Order of St. Francis: men and women living in the world, often married, who visited the sick, taught children, and prayed. She was considered very pretty, so she dyed her hair with soot to avoid attracting attention, especially from men. She wore a hair shirt, rarely ate meat or fish, fasted often, and some days ate nothing at all. As with most women who founded churches or orders, she reportedly had a vision; in her case, the vision foretold that she was to begin an association of women who would devote their lives to the religious training of young girls. She was noted for opposing the common use of physical punishment in schools.

After Angela's death, the Ursulines concentrated on teaching and caring for girls. By that time, they had 150 followers, but they were soon forced to become a cloistered community wearing traditional nuns' habits. By 1700, the Ursulines had over 350 convents throughout France that boarded up to 12,000 girls and educated other poor students.

The first Ursuline convent in France was formed in 1592 by Françoise de Bermond (1572–1628) and 24 women in Avignon. Like the Italian Ursulines, they were not cloistered at first. This led to a strange reception in parts of the country, as sometimes the women were mistaken for repentant prostitutes.

In France their teaching was not restricted to their schools; they were known to teach Christian doctrine and catechism in churches, much to the horror of the male clergy. The difference between teaching and preaching was not clearly defined and at times the Ursuline nuns were seen as usurping the role of male priests. Mère Perrette de Bermond, pehaps related to Françoise, started a congregation in Moulins in 1616. The Ursulines sang Vespers in the choir, taught Christian doctrine, and gave catechism on Sundays in the chapel to crowds of welcoming citizens. But after seven years, in 1623, their male superiors forbade them to teach any longer. However, not only did the sisters keep on teaching in religious spaces, but they were known to teach in places such as barns and poultry yards to large mixed audiences.[11]

In the seventeenth century in France, pastoral care by the clergy was often nonexistent; for the most part, the priests were not well educated. The Ursulines, then, felt justified in taking on the roles that the clergy were neglecting. Indeed the women were often teaching the priests how to teach catechism, and instructing the monks in prayer.[12]

Even when their French convents became enclosed, some of the Ursuline nuns managed to continue teaching the public. In Avignon, Marthe de la

Visitation defied the enclosure and taught publicly in the convent's church, and Paule de la Mère de Dieu in Montélimar attracted such crowds that they couldn't fit into the church. Louise de Saint Paul taught at the choir grille.

Suzanne Marie des Anges's Sunday catechisms were so well attended that the crowds were flowing out of the convent, and Claude Anne de S. Benoît taught young girls in front of several men and women. Dauphine Lanfreze made her sickbed into a "preacher's pulpit." The women who came to hear the catechisms given by Elizabeth des Nots in the parlor of the Paris convent said that she was no different from other good preachers; the catechisms of Anne de Beaumont were compared to the preaching of St. Paul. Antoinette Micolon preached to about 50 or 60 peasants in a large poultry yard, women who had come to the town to hear holy Mass first and then flock to Antoinette's teaching. The Ursuline *Paris Rules* warned that the sisters should instruct visitors without "seeming" to preach. Indeed they believed strongly that they were simply following the life that the Son of God had led, similar to his mother Mary and the apostles.[13]

In 1609, *The Constitutions of the Bordeaux Ursulines* was drawn up by the Catholic Church, ordering the Ursulines to adhere strictly to the catechism and not to aspire to teach things "they did not know." By then, there were 29 communities in France and a hundred years later, by 1700, there were more than 300, housing some 10,000 nuns.

The historian Heidi Keller-Lapp has analyzed four overseas Ursuline missions during the seventeenth and eighteenth centuries: Quebec, Canada in 1639; Martinique in 1681; New Orleans in the southern United States in 1727; and Pondicherry, India in 1738. Keller-Lapp claims that they circumvented the rule of strict enclosure in these foreign institutions by claiming that they were *femmes fortes* (heroic women).

The Ursuline Marie Guyart, *dite* Marie de L'Incarnation (1599–1672), a widow with a young son who later became a Benedictine superior-general, was sent from Tours in 1639 to lead their first mission to New France (Quebec), with the charge of helping French Jesuits convert young "Amerindian" girls to Christianity. A mystic with a strong business sense, Marie was a sensible choice for the backwoods of Canada. In France, she had often acted as a "preacher's mouthpiece" by telling her family what she had heard in sermons, developing her own skills of speaking and persuasion. For her overseas mission, she chose nuns from various convents in France in the hope of unifying all the Ursulines on the continent. She called her cohort of nuns in Quebec

Canadoises, missionaries who were "physically strong, healthy, young, tenacious, self-sacrificing and brave." They needed to be vigorous and resourceful for their three-month ocean voyage and their temporary quarters in Quebec City until the erection of their convent in 1642. While they were waiting for their impressive three-story stone home to be built, they had to sleep in serge-lined chests in the winter to keep warm.[14]

In the hundreds of letters sent back from Quebec, the various Mothers Superior recounted the challenges they endured: fires that gutted their convent in 1650 and again in 1686; a threat from the English trying to conquer French Canada; several epidemics; and bitter winter weather. A bombardment in Quebec in 1759 during the Seven Years' War destroyed part of their convent and they had to rebuild—again. Marie de L'Incarnation operated a farm and cultivated a garden that the Iroquois destroyed, along with killing servants and friends.[15]

In her letters back to France, and especially to her son, Marie de L'Incarnation recounts their trials, but always with thanksgiving. Reminiscent of early ascetics, Marie wrote in 1640 to "a lady of rank," "We rejoice when we are given nothing so we can be poor in all things. In consequence, Madame, are we not the happiest and most fortunate of the earth?" And in the same year to Mother Marie-Gillette Roland, she emphasized, "this is an earthly paradise where crosses and thorns grow so lovingly that the more one is pricked by them, the more filled with tenderness is the heart."[16]

Their mission to Christianize the Indigenous children was not successful, though, despite the fact that Mother Marie studied Indigenous languages, wrote French-Algonkin, Algonkin-French, and Iroquois dictionaries and a catechism in Iroqouis. In one of her several letters, she admitted: "It is however a very difficult thing, if not an impossible one, to adapt the Indians to French customs or to civilize them. We have had more experience with it than anyone else, and we have observed that of a hundred girls who have passed through our hands, we have scarcely civilized one."[17]

The boarding school where they taught reading, writing, drawing, needlework, and domestic arts began with about 20 French girls who paid 120 livres per year each. Since a skilled laborer such as a stone mason earned only about 900 livres a year in 1650 in Quebec, this would be out of reach for a large middle-class family. It is not surprising that the school records for the year 1646 show receipts of "3½ cords of firewood," "one pot of butter," and one "fat pig," along with "one barrel of peas" and "one barrel of salted eel" for payment of the students' board.[18] Mother Marie noted that too much freedom was allowed young girls in Canada. In one year, the nuns had to teach them to read, write, count, "and everything that a girl should know."

In Martinique, their main mission was not to Christianize the Indigenous people, but to educate the daughters of colonists to become good French Catholic mothers. Boatloads of marriageable French girls and indentured servants were arriving on nearly every ship. At the same time, the nuns were inadvertently forced to live in poverty in that mission, and many found the tropical climate too fatiguing.

In Louisiana, the Ursulines continued as a teaching institution but were prevailed upon to nurse in the military hospital as well. However, it took six years to build them a suitable convent close to the hospital, and the nuns initially reneged on their promise to nurse. Mother Marie Tranchepain (c.1680–1733), a young convert from Protestantism known as Sister St. Augustine, did not particularly want her nuns to become involved in nursing, so she used the lack of a suitable convent as a bargaining chip: "The Company [The French Company of the Indies] has promised to build us [a convent] next to the [hospital]. When it will have kept its word, we shall think of carrying out ours. For it is not fitting that every day we should walk from one end of the city to the other. Our duty does not oblige us to that."[19]

Twelve nuns were the first Ursulines to arrive in New Orleans in 1727 after a harrowing five-month ocean voyage and an even more difficult journey from the Gulf of Mexico to New Orleans, a distance of only "thirty leagues," a little over a hundred miles. The New Orleans community was as amazed to see them as they were relieved to finally arrive; they had been given up as lost at sea. In the new land they established a school for girls, thought to be the first girls' school in the United States. They taught European, African, and Indigenous girls, both slave and free, wealthy and poor, even including a Quaker girl, in spite of the prevailing New Orleans attitude that "all women should be prohibited from learning to write and even read." As one local administrator who was opposed to education for women explained, "this (ignorance) would preserve them from loose thoughts, confining them to useful tasks about the house, instilling in them respect for the first sex." The Ursuline sisters even encouraged women to educate their slaves. The French monarch, Louis XV (1710–74), had decreed that all slaves in the province of New Orleans be instructed and baptized in the Catholic religion.[20]

The nuns established not only a school but also an orphanage and a home for abused and widowed women. At one point the convent accepted 30 girls orphaned by an "Indian" attack in 1729 on a French fort north of New Orleans.

FIGURE 11.1 The first Ursuline sisters arrive in New Orleans. A charcoal sketch of the landing of the Ursulines by one of the sisters, Marie Madeleine Hachard, c.1727. Photo: Courtesy of the Office of Archives and Records, Archdiocese of New Orleans, United States.

The Ursulines' educational program raised the women's literacy rate in New Orleans to one of the highest in America at that time. In 1750 it was 71 per cent for women, higher than for men, whereas in the New England States at the same time, it was half for women what it was for men.[21]

The calendar for the boarding students was divided between academic lessons and religious devotion. The day began early at about six in the morning, and ended when they retired to bed around eight o'clock at night. The children learned reading, writing, spelling, figuring with the aid of counting beads, and needlework in addition to **catechism** and other religious studies.

Sickness was pervasive. Of the 18 nuns who emigrated to New Orleans between 1727 and 1736, four died, four went back to France, and four left religious life, leaving a heavy burden on the remainder. In 1731, there were only six nuns in the convent.[22]

One of the nuns, Marie Madelaine Hachard, called St. Stanislaus (1704–60), wrote home often of their life in New Orleans, noting the high cost of food and materials. Nevertheless, they ate well: several kinds of local fresh fruit such as peaches, melons, figs, oranges, and blackberries; a variety of vegetables and nuts; as well as wild beef, goat, goose, wild turkey, rabbit, chicken, duck, pheasant, partridge, and quail; fish such as salmon, "monstrous" catfish; and

a lot of chocolate. The local inhabitants, feeling indebted for their daughters' free education, donated animals and poultry to fill an enclosure at the
Ursulines' convent.[23]

France had established Louisiana as a colony in 1699, resulting in a strip
of land from Quebec down the Mississippi Valley to the Gulf of Mexico, a
barrier between the English to the east and the Spanish to the west. In the
1720s, however, the state of Louisiana was miserably poor, the climate hot
and humid. The land was infested with stinging insects, snakes, and alligators.
Yet the Ursulines adapted. In 1734, they purchased a plantation worth 2,500
livres, about US$630,000 today. They participated in real estate development
and agriculture and still taught, in addition to holding slaves, eventually
operating the hospital and sheltering orphans. They functioned well beyond
the stereotype for women in their day in New Orleans.[24]

The fourth mission in India failed to get off the ground because of political conflict.

There were two unusual and unfortunate events in the history of the
Ursulines, the first in 1834 in Charlestown, Massachusetts, where their
convent was burned down by a Protestant mob; and the other in France
where a prank perpetrated by a group of young nuns got out of hand, resulting in torture and death.

When the State of Massachusetts was founded, its charter enshrined
tolerance for Protestant groups, but excluded political benefits for Roman
Catholics. In 1820, the Ursulines set up a school next to their convent in
Charlestown, now an old section of Boston; the school accommodated about
100 girls. This was moved in 1827 to larger quarters, but because of its location, the enlarged school enrolled mostly upper-class Protestants. By 1834,
there were only 47 students, of whom just six were Catholic.

That year, the anti-Catholic atmosphere already strong in the city of Boston
was inflamed by a young Episcopalian (Anglican) student who decided to
become an Ursuline nun. She left the convent after six months and published
a story called "Six Months in a Convent," in which she accused the Ursuline
nuns of trying to force her to become a Roman Catholic. It was even rumored
that she was being tortured. Placards were put up throughout Boston urging
the "gentlemen" of Boston to have this affair "investigated immediately" or
the "truckmen of Boston" would demolish the "Nunnery."[25]

In fact that is what happened, even though the citizenry were assured by
the city administrators that all was in order. The night of Monday, 11 August, a
mob of angry men, assumed to be Protestants, set fire to the Ursuline convent

leaving it in ruins. Several men were arrested, but all were exonerated, even the self-confessed ringleader. Eventually the Boston Ursulines were disbanded in 1840–41 and the nuns moved either to Quebec or New Orleans.

The second extraordinary occurrence was in France, and became the subject of one of Aldous Huxley's novels, *The Devils of Loudun*, published in 1952.

In 1617, a wealthy, handsome, and well-educated priest, Urban Grandier (1590–1634), was appointed to the parish of Loudun, France. He was notorious as a "ladies man," alienating much of the town: fathers and husbands who feared for their daughters and their wives, administrators, and even other clergy. The young 15-year-old Mother Superior at the Ursuline convent, Jeanne des Anges (1602–65), became obsessed with Grandier, but also annoyed at him because he ignored her. Along with several disaffected townspeople, Jeanne and the other young Ursuline nuns in the convent plotted to punish him. The nuns pretended to be demon-possessed, blaming Grandier whom they claimed was in league with the devil. As a result, exorcists were called in, and Grandier was charged with witchcraft.

In spite of the fact that his doctor claimed there was no evidence of witchcraft—there were no "witch marks" on his body—Grandier was sentenced to be burned at the stake. Alarmed and contrite, Jeanne des Anges confessed to the plot, but the sentence was still carried out. Perhaps it was an imitation of a similar case at a French convent in Aix-en-Provence in 1611 when another priest, Louis Gaufridi, was accused by two nuns, Madeleine Demandoix de la Palud and Louise Capel, of bewitching them. That priest was also burned as a witch even though the nuns involved had a reputation for instability, and there was no reason to accuse the priest. The nuns were dismissed from the convent. Two years later, in 1613, in nearby Lille, three nuns accused Sister Marie de Sains of bewitching them, and in 1647 there was a similar case at the convent in Louviers.[26]

Today, the term Ursuline refers to several women's religious institutes of the Catholic Church, the best known being the group founded in 1535 at Brescia by Angela Merici.

MARY WARD AND THE ENGLISH LADIES

Mary Ward (1585–1645) did not found a church but schools for girls and a new religious order. As part of the Roman Catholic Counter-Reformation,

Mary's plan was to strengthen the Catholic faith in women especially in England, and through training young girls similar to the Ursulines, to influence the wives and mothers of future generations.

In 1609, Mary opened her first free school for English girls and local French girls in Saint-Omer, France, and then several more in Europe. Because of religious persecution and the civil war in England, it was not until 1686 that she could open one in that country. Altogether, she set up 13 schools and houses throughout Europe.

Mary also created a new order, the Institute of the Blessed Virgin Mary, which was non-monastic and non-cloistered. The women dressed in ordinary plain clothes, generally black, worked with the poor and taught. Mary based her order on the lifestyle and rules of the Jesuits, who in turn wanted nothing to do with her. "When all is done," they said, "they are but women" and bound to fail. Indeed, Mary's order was so revolutionary that she even encouraged women to act in plays at a time when actresses were considered to be no better than prostitutes, and young men played female roles on the stage. In England, the women became known as "chattering hussies," "galloping girls," or "wandering nuns." The Jesuit canonist Francisco Suarez (1548–1617) described them thus: "They go up and down the land with little of the decorum of the feminine sex and to the ignominy of the Catholic religion, practising great liberty with young people."[27]

Mary believed that women were mentally, physically, and morally equal to men. She questioned the treatment women received, and the Jesuits' assessment: "wherein are we so inferior to other creatures, that they should term us but women ... as if we were in all things inferior to some other creature which I suppose to be man, which I dare be bold to say is a lie, and with respect ... may say it is an error."[28] In instructions to her sisters, she claimed that the will to do well was not a matter of gender or nature. "There is no such difference between men and women," she wrote.[29]

Like many other spiritual women, Mary's career path was shaped by a voice she heard, in her case when she was recovering from an illness: "Take the same of the Society." By this, she understood "that we were to take the same both in matter and manner (of the Jesuits), the only excepted which God by diversity of sex hath prohibited," she wrote. "These few words gave so great light in the particular institute, comfort and strength and changed so the whole soul, as that [it was] impossible for me to doubt that they came from him whose words are works," she added.[30]

Mary Ward had been born Joan Ward in Ripon in the northeast of England to a staunch Roman Catholic family, but later took the name of Mary. Some of her relatives had been involved in the treasonable "Gunpowder Plot" to blow up the Houses of Parliament in 1605. It was said that her first word, and all the words she "spooke [*sic*] of many Months after" was "Jesus."

Well educated and determined to remain celibate, Mary practiced self-mortification in many ways. For example, although very neat and tidy herself, she deliberately lay in bed "with one of the Maides that had the Itch, and got it." She wore a "most sharpe hairecloath, which by continuance did eate into her flesh." She "put on Servants and meane Womens cloathes," ate one meal a day, and lay on "Straw-bedds only." She had a "burning desire to be a martyr." She decided to join the Poor Clares when she was 15, but soon felt that God had another purpose for her. It was a few years later that she heard the voice that determined her future.[31]

When she was 46 in 1631, with one pair of shoes that did not fit, Mary walked more than 1,500 miles from Belgium to Rome to speak to Pope Urban VIII (1568–1644) to gain approval for her order and the schools she had opened. Instead, he threw her in jail in Munich as a "heretic, schismatic and rebel to Holy Church" and issued a papal bull to suppress her movement, naming her sisters, the English Ladies, "poisonous growths in the Church of God [which] must be torn up from the roots lest they spread themselves further." Twenty-three of Mary's notes written in prison on wrapping paper with lemon juice to hide their messages, and later smuggled out of jail, still exist today.

Mary had already submitted three plans to the pope for her order, one in 1612, another in 1616, and a third in 1621. In this last one, she described herself and her followers as "soldiers of God" wishing to serve "beneath the banner of the cross." They envisioned their mission as being worldwide and under a Mother Superior General who would be obedient only to the pope, bypassing other male ecclesiastical administrators.

The plan was received with both ridicule and fear. The women's mission was condemned as insignificant and only the feeble attempt of weak women. But it was also seen as being unfeminine, usurping roles that were rightfully male. "Up to now, it has never been known that women undertake apostolic work," the shocked Catholic Church administrators wrote. "They are not capable of it." The women were seen as meddling with the conversion of England, a male preserve; the women's ideas were unbecoming to their sex. Traveling at will and living an ordinary manner of life and dressing in secular fashion was "not only a scorn but a great scandal to many pious people." The women were guilty of both "arrogant contumacy" and "great temerity."[32]

Mary argued that she had been chosen by God; she saw herself as a vessel of the divine will and God's humble instrument on earth. "I have never undermined the authority of the Holy Church," she wrote from her prison cell: "On the contrary, for 26 years, with great respect to both His Holiness and the Holy Church, and in the most honourable way possible, I have put my frail efforts and my industry to their service, and this, I hope, by the mercy of God and His benignity, will account for at the right time and place."[33]

It is ironic that Mary's only motivation was to restore the Catholic Church in England, but instead she was accused of being subversive. She believed, and rightly so, that the survival of her church would depend to a large degree on the ability of women to pass on their faith within the home, but she was incredibly naïve about how the Church would receive this idea.

After Mary was released from jail, she retired to England where she continued to work with the recusant Catholic community. Her first companions, the "English Ladies," those who were still living, all reputed to be of noble birth— Mary Poyntz (c.1593–1667), Winifred Wigmore (1585–1658), Johanna Brown, Susanna Rookwood, Catherine Smith, Barbara Babthorpe (1592–1654), and Mary's sister Barbara Ward (1592–1623), who died from smallpox—were allowed to continue teaching as long as they no longer claimed to be a religious order.

Some years later, Pope Pius XII (1876–1958) praised Mary as an "incomparable woman," recognizing the value of her work and the harsh treatment she had received. Today, Mary Ward's order has about 4,000 sisters in two branches in every continent—the Institute of the Blessed Virgin or Loretto Sisters and the Congregation of Jesus.

THE COMPANY OF THE DAUGHTERS OF CHARITY

The Catholic priest at Châtillon-les-Dombes, Vincent de Paul (1581–1660), was a driving force behind the development of the Daughters of Charity, but it was a French widow, Louise de Marillac (1591–1660), who actually organized the community in 1633.

Born into a noble family, although illegitimate, Louise was well educated in the royal Dominican monastery at Poissy, France, and later placed in a boarding house for young girls, where she learned domestic tasks. She was turned down as a religious by the Capuchins because of delicate health.

Married at 21 and widowed 12 years later, she bore one son. Struggling to survive after her husband died, Louise met a neighbor, Vincent de Paul, who suggested that she volunteer with the Confraternity of Charity, a group of wealthy women who were trying to help the poor by distributing food and clothes, but the arrangement often resulted in tension—beautifully gowned women offering care to those in rags or country garments. Or the women would send their servants to tend to the poor and the sick because they simply didn't know how to cook or look after sick people themselves. (Later these women would be helpful as fundraisers for the Daughters of Charity, who were women of "lesser birth" and therefore had fewer wealthy contacts.)

Louise had a vision while at prayer in which she saw herself serving the poor and living in a religious community. Agreeing to work for Vincent, she conducted spot checks to ensure quality of service and reviewed the financial accounts: both good preparation for administering her new community. She was a talented organizer, and especially frugal, later demanding extreme thrift of the young women in the new community, the Daughters of Charity.

Marguerite Naseau (1594–1633), the daughter of a peasant family in the Pouy village, was also helping with the poor, and Vincent introduced the two women. Marguerite became the first woman to volunteer with the new community. Marguerite had taught herself to read by asking people she met along the road, and in turn she helped teach young girls in her village in improvised outdoor schools.

Similar to the Beguines, the Daughters of Charity lived together in small communities where they could be independent and provide for themselves. They looked after the poor in their own homes, worked in hospitals, educated abandoned children, and tended to the war-wounded and galley convicts where they found them. *The Fronde*, civil wars in France between 1648 and 1653, resulted in widespread poverty, sickness, and violence, and the Daughters of Charity went from village to village to help. Vincent de Paul wrote at that time that they were sheltering "from 800 to 900 women; they distribute soup every day to 1,300 bashful poor. In St. Paul's parish, they aid 5,000 poor and altogether 1,400 persons have for the last six months depended on them for their means of subsistence."[34]

The new company refused to be cloistered, officially remaining a secular confraternity, not a "religious" order, and therefore the community was accepted by the Catholic Church hierarchy; in 1668, it received approval from Pope Clement IX (1600–69). The community vowed obedience to the Superior General of the Congregation of the Daughters of Charity; unlike Mary Ward and her Ladies, they did not attempt to bypass the male ecclesiastics. It was also quite apparent to the church hierarchy that the women could not treat the sick unless they had the freedom to travel about.

As Vincent wrote:

> They do not belong to a religious order, that state not being compatible with the duties of their vocation, yet ... they are much more exposed to the world than nuns; their monastery being generally no other than the abode of the sick; their cell, a hired room; their chapel, the parish church; their cloister, the streets or wards of hospitals; their enclosure, obedience; their grate, the fear of God and their veil holy modesty.[35]

The Daughters of Charity took annual, not perpetual vows, promising to serve the poor, to remain chaste, to be obedient, and to espouse poverty. They dressed in the costume of country women at the time they were founded: a gray habit with wide sleeves, a long apron, and a headdress of white linen. They negotiated their own contracts with the hospitals' governing boards where they worked, charging for housing, clothing, travel expenses, hospital equipment, and other expenses. By 1640, they had begun to assume complete control of hospitals; by the end of the seventeenth century, there was a waiting list for their services, and by the 1720s, they were turning away requests, the needs were so great. Similar to the Ursulines in New Orleans, they became skilled in business, operating beyond the bounds of women's usual sphere. The male leaders were so relieved to rid their streets and villages of the poor, the sick, and the disabled that they accepted the women. The Catholic Church was also aware that their educational programs were teaching Catholicism and strengthening the faith of women and children, in some instances bringing Protestant Huguenots back to the fold—although the women had to be very careful not to impinge on Catholic priests' territory of doctrinal instruction.[36]

Generally the women's days were long; they rose in the morning at four, then meditated and attended church services. At noon, there was an "examination of conscience," with readings and meditation in the afternoon. They could be excused, however, if their work demanded them elsewhere. There was a three-month probation period, then training over six months. After a trial of five years, the women took annual vows of poverty, chastity, obedience, and the service of the poor.

The company grew rapidly. In 1660, there were approximately 100 houses. By 1711, there were 250. In Poland, the country where they first worked beyond France, the women became known as "Angels of the Battlefield," as they actually appeared on the field of battle. By the late eighteenth century, they had spread throughout France, into Switzerland, Italy, and Spain. They survived the secularization of the French Revolution (1789–99), although seven Daughters, four of them teachers and social workers, were executed. By the nineteenth century they had engaged in a variety of work around the world. In Great Britain in the early twentieth century, there were more than 600 sisters looking after 23 orphanages, 7 industrial schools, 24 public elementary schools, 1 normal school, 7 training homes, 2 homes for working girls, 1 home for women ex-convicts, 1 asylum for insane women, 8 hospitals, and 35 houses where they had soup kitchens, their base when they went out to help the poor.

In the United States, the New Yorker Elizabeth Ann Bayley Seton (1774–1821) converted from the Episcopal Church to Roman Catholicism after she spent time in Italy, where it was hopeful that the warm weather would cure her husband's tuberculosis, but he died in 1803. Two years later, she joined the Catholic Church. Shunned by many friends and relatives because of her conversion, she moved to Maryland, where she set up a school for Catholic girls, one of the first such schools in the United States, and a religious community to care for poor children. In 1810, this community adopted the rule of the Daughters of Charity, beginning their involvement in America.

In France today, the Daughters of Charity are known as the Grey Sisters because of their bluish gray dress (not the Grey Nuns). In the United States, several communities who follow a modified rule are called the Black Cap Sisters because of their black dress. However, like other companies and orders, vocations declined in the mid-twentieth century. In the early 1950s, there were more than 40,000 Daughters of Charity; today there are about 21,500, ministering in 94 countries around the world, focusing on globalization, immigration, and ecology, although they still serve the poorest of the poor. Their mandate includes education to youth and children; ministry with the homeless, the elderly, persons with disabilities, prisoners, those addicted, and migrants; as well as working with communities to accomplish systemic change.[37]

FURTHER READING

PRIMARY

Clark, Emily, ed. *Voices from an Early American Convent: Marie Hachard Madeleine and the New Orleans Ursulines*. Baton Rouge: Louisiana State University Press, 2007.

Glimpses of the Monastery—A Brief Sketch of the History of the Ursulines of Quebec from 1672–1739. Quebec City: C. Darveau, 1875.

Kenworthy-Browne, Christina, ed. *Mary Ward 1585–1645.* Suffolk: The Boydell Press, 2008.

Marshall, Joyce, ed. and trans. *The Selected Letters of Marie de L'Incarnation.* Toronto: Oxford University Press, 1967.

SECONDARY

Caraman, Philip. *Saint Angela: The Life of Angela Merici Foundress of the Ursulines (1474–1540).* London: Longmans, 1963.

Clark, Emily. *Masterless Mistresses: New Orleans Ursulines and the Development of the New World Society, 1727–1834.* Chapel Hill: University of North Carolina Press, 2007.

Dinan, Susan E. *Women and Poor Relief in Seventeenth-Century France: The Early History of the Daughters of Charity.* Hampshire, UK: Ashgate, 2006.

Keller-Lapp, Heidi. "Floating Cloisters and Heroic Women: French Ursuline Missionaries, 1639–1744." *World History Connected.* Accessed 20 September 2018, http://worldhistoryconnected.press.uillinois.edu/4.3/lapp.html.

Lux-Strerritt, Laurence. "An Analysis of the Controversy Caused by Mary Ward's Institute in the 1620s." *Recusant History* 25, no. 4 (2001): 636–47.

—. *Redefining Female Religious Life: French Ursulines and English Ladies in Seventeenth-Century Catholicism.* Aldershot, UK: Ashgate, 2005.

Newman, Barbara. *From Virile Woman to WomanChrist: Studies in Medieval Religion and Literature.* Philadelphia: University of Pennsylvania Press, 1990.

—. "The Heretic Saint: Guglielma of Bohemia, Milan, and Brunate." *Church History* 74, no. 1 (March 2005): 1–38.

Peterson, Janine Larmon. "Social Roles, Gender Inversion, and the Heretical Sect: The Case of the Guglielmites." *Viator* 35 (2004): 203–19.

NOTES

1   Peterson, "Social Roles, Gender Inversion, and the Heretical Sect," 203. Guglielma would be related to Elizabeth of Hungary (1207–31), Agnes of Bohemia (1211–82), and Margaret of Hungary (1242–71), three Roman Catholic saints.

2   Shahar, *Women in a Medieval Heretical Sect,* 28f; Franklin, "Typhon." It is suggested that Guglielma must have been an oblate of the Cistercians, see Newman, *From Virile Woman to WomanChrist,* 181.

3 Newman, "The Heretic Saint," 12.

4 Peterson, "Social Roles, Gender Inversion, and the Heretical Sect," 209.

5 Shahar, *Women in a Medieval Heretical Sect*, 29f.

6 Newman, "The Heretic Saint," 29, 32.

7 Newman, "The Heretic Saint"; Franklin, "Typhon."

8 Newman, "The Heretic Saint," 32.

9 Newman, "The Heretic Saint," 37.

10 Newman, *From Virile Woman to WomanChrist*, 184f.

11 Lierheimer, "Preaching or Teaching?" 212.

12 Lierheimer, "Preaching or Teaching?" 212ff.

13 Lierheimer, "Preaching or Teaching?" 216, 219; Lux-Sterritt, *Redefining Female Religious Life*, 38.

14 Lierheimer, "Preaching or Teaching?" 217.

15 *Glimpses of the Monastery.*

16 Marshall, ed. and trans., *The Selected Letters of Marie de l'Incarnation.*

17 Chabot, "Guyart Marie, *dite* Marie de L'Incarnation."

18 Chabot, "Guyart Marie, *dite* Marie de L'Incarnation."

19 Keller-Lapp, "Floating Cloisters and Heroic Women," 5.

20 Jacobs and Kaslow, *The Spiritual Churches of New Orleans*, 22.

21 Clark, *Masterless Mistresses.*

22 Clark, *Masterless Mistresses*, 64.

23 Clark, ed., *Voices from an Early American Convent*, 39, 79.

24 Clark, *Masterless Mistresses*, 35ff.

25 Prioli, "The Ursuline Outrage," 101–5; "The Outrage."

26 Guiley, *Encyclopedia of Witches and Witchcraft*, 7.

27 Lux-Sterritt, *Redefining Female Religious Life*, 36.

28 Simmonds, "Mary Ward: Then and Now."

29 Simmonds, "Mary Ward: Then and Now."

30 "Mary Ward," *Internet Shakespeare Editions*, accessed 20 September 2018, http://internetshakespeare.uvic.ca/Library/SLT/literature/women%20writers/ward.html.

31 Kenworthy-Browne, ed., *Mary Ward*, 3, 8.

32 Lux-Sterritt, "An Analysis of the Controversy Caused by Mary Ward's Institute in the 1620s," 6; Kenworthy-Browne, ed., *Mary Ward*, xix.

33 Lux-Sterritt, "An Analysis of the Controversy Caused by Mary Ward's Institute in the 1620's," 6.

34 "Origin of the Company" and "Sisters of Charity of St. Vincent de Paul," *Daughters of Charity of Saint Vincent de Paul*, accessed 20 September 2018, https://www.daughtersofcharity.org.au/.

35 Dinan, *Women and Poor Relief in Seventeenth-Century France*, 46.

36 Clark, *Masterless Mistresses*, 27ff.

37 "Company of the Daughters of Charity," *Vincentiana*, July–August 2006, accessed 20 September 2018, https://cmglobal.org/vincentiana-novus-en/files/downloads/2006_4/vt_2006_04_06_en.pdf.

Chapter 12

OTHER WOMEN WHO FOUNDED CHURCHES, PART I

THE QUAKERS

Quaker minister Elizabeth Collins (1755–1831) was ill in bed weeks or months of almost every year, yet she traveled around the Eastern Seaboard of the United States, visiting hundreds of Friends in their homes and attending their yearly meetings; "the invisible arm of divine love and mercy, was near" for her "preservation … from utter ruin," she wrote. Even with her "weakness," which she never fully explained in her autobiography, Elizabeth survived two husbands, several friends, children and grandchildren, dying in her seventy-seventh year, although life expectancy for women at that time in the United States was well under 50 years.[1]

Elizabeth had become an "apprentice" minister when she was 15. Like many of the Quaker women preachers, she resisted the call at first, feeling unworthy or incompetent or not wanting to be ridiculed. Some women even resisted joining the Quakers in case they would be "called on" by God to preach. Yet Elizabeth heard a voice spoken to her inward ear, "If thou art not more faithful, thy gift shall be taken from thee."

Thinking back on her life, Elizabeth could remember only one bad thing she had ever done: that was staying out late until almost midnight at a wedding, "spending the time in lightness and vanity," when she had promised to be home early.

Elizabeth was only one of several hundred female Quaker ministers traveling in Great Britain, the United States, and other countries around the world from the seventeenth century on, preaching in meeting houses, town halls, courthouses, and other public spaces. Twelve of the first 66 Quaker preachers were women, and of the 300 men and women identified as preachers in England between 1649 and 1660, 220 were women.[2] Hundreds more Quaker women were elders, overseeing the pastoral care of their home meetings. By the nineteenth century, Quakers, especially Quaker women, would spearhead movements for women's suffrage, the abolition of slavery, prison reform, peace, and be fully engaged in other areas of social action.

Perhaps the most famous reformer was the well-to-do Quaker preacher Elizabeth Gurney Fry (1780–1845), noted for advocating shelters for the homeless, prison reform, and upgrading the training of nurses. She was a major influence in the 1821 prison reform bill in England, and was also instrumental in instituting prison reform in Scotland, Australia, France, Germany, and Holland. Another Quaker not as well known but responsible for changing attitudes in society was Elizabeth Heyrick (1769–1831), who campaigned against the slave trade, demanding immediate emancipation instead of a gradual end to the practice. Between 1815 and 1830, she wrote over 20 pamphlets on various social, economic, and political subjects. "We must not talk of gradually abolishing murder, licentiousness, cruelty, tyranny," she wrote, "why then would we not immediately end slavery at once," she asked. "Righteousness demands no compromise with evil," she exclaimed. Elizabeth also advocated a boycott of slave-grown sugar.[3]

The Society of Friends, or the Quakers as they were soon called, began in England in the late 1640s when George Fox (1624–91), a shoemaker's apprentice, received a new revelation of Christianity. He came to understand that each person possessed an Inward Teacher or Light: "Christ was the true Light which lighteth every person who came into the world" (John 1:9). Fox rejected most of the rituals, traditions, and doctrines of the Protestant churches at that time, including the Lord's Supper/Holy Communion/the Eucharist, baptism, paid ministry, and hymn singing. He believed that such "external forms were hollow exercises."[4] Quaker worship was often silent until someone felt called to speak. At business meetings, the members operated by consensus.

Margaret Askew Fell Fox (1614–1702), who became George's wife in 1669, is credited with being the co-founder of the Quakers. Both George and Margaret were firm in their belief and support of women as Quaker ministers. George's tract, "Concerning Sons and Daughters, and Prophetesses Speaking and Prophesying in the Law and the Gospel," and Margaret's small pamphlet written while she was in prison, "Womens [*sic*] Speaking Justified, Proved and Allowed of by the Scriptures," were quite clear about where they stood. As Margaret wrote: "… and though we be looked upon as the weaker vessels, yet strong and powerful is God, whose strength is made perfect in weakness, he can make us good and bold, and valiant Souldiers [*sic*] of Jesus Christ, if he arms us with his Armour of Light…."⁵

According to George, "the light is the same in the male and female, which cometh from Christ." He believed that by the power of the Spirit, women had the same capacity as men to voice the Word of God. He was horrified by some of the attitudes that he found in England—that "women have no souls … no more than a goose."⁶

Margaret Fell was converted by George one weekend when her well-to-do first husband Thomas (1598–1658) was away on his magisterial duties, and although Thomas never became a Quaker, he was always very supportive. Margaret never traveled extensively, but was able to offer assistance to other Quakers, both financial and as a powerful advocate. She came from a wealthy family. On his death, her father had left her £6,000, the equivalent of almost $1,500,000 in today's United States currency.⁷ As well, Thomas left her their substantial residence, Swarthmoor Hall, where Quakers gathered; through her connections, she was often able to lessen or negate prison sentences, although she was sometimes in jail herself. She wrote prolifically, mostly pamphlets and letters, took care of the large staff and grounds of her property, and her eight children.

During the Civil War in England (1642–51) and the Interregnum period between the kings Charles I (1600–49) and Charles II (1630–85), England was in turmoil, questioning old institutions and beliefs. During this period, many new religious groups were formed, including what was later known as the Quakers. At first, the men and women in this new sect called themselves "Children of the Light" or "Friends in the Truth." The tradition is that they became known as "Quakers" when George Fox told an English magistrate to "tremble at the Word of the Lord"; the judge then called them, pejoratively, the "Quakers."

While there were Quakers from every level of society, an analysis of a small area in the north of Essex in England, a stronghold of this new religion, indicates that most members in the seventeenth century were from the middle class. Almost half the people were engaged in the cloth industry—such

FIGURE 12.1 A satirical etching by Marcel Lauron in Dutch, English, and Latin, c.1678, "Fronti Nulla Fides—The Quakers Meeting" depicts a Quaker woman preaching on a "tub," a popular name for a pulpit, but in this case a washtub or barrel. In the background, a couple fondles one another and a dog in the foreground urinates on a woman's skirt. The English reads: "Woman in Public Speaks not, St. Paul said, Yielding respective silence to her Head: She on the Barrels head raised yet Nulls this Right; Raves darkly and cries Ah Friends, Mind the Light; In the meanwhile look where a female stands As Modesty herself, with unseen hands Silent consenting to all as true; Gives the next he-saint a Fellow feeling too." Photo: © The Trustees of the British Museum.

as weavers, drapers, fullers, glovers, and merchants. Other craftsmen and agricultural workers made up the balance.[8]

The first female Quaker preacher, the teacher Elizabeth Hooton (1600–72), was thrown into prison at Derby in 1651 as a disturber of the peace after she began preaching Quaker theology. She had been "speaking to one of the priests there, who so resented her Reproof that he applied to the Magistrate to punish her. For it is common with Men who most deserve Reprehension, to be most offended with those who administer it," her biographer, Emily Manners, wrote. Formerly a Baptist from Nottingham, Elizabeth was the "first of her sex who attempted to imitate Men and Preach," when she was 50, "pretty far advanced in years," Emily noted.[9]

Not long afterwards, Elizabeth traveled to Massachusetts, where the more rigid, patriarchal, and intolerant Puritans stripped both her and a pregnant companion to the waist, whipped them as they traveled from town to town tied to a cart, finally abandoning them in a forest that was a two days' journey from civilization. "There they left us towards the night amongst the great rivers and many wild beasts ... we lay in the woods without any victualls, but a few biskets y' we brought with us which we soaked in the water," she reported in her journal. They survived by following a track made in the snow by wolves, and eventually returned to England. Elizabeth's third missionary voyage across the Atlantic was to Barbados, where she died when she was 72.

In 1662, Elizabeth had written about how she had confronted the king: "My goeing to London hath not beene for my owne ends, but in obedience to the will of God, for it was layed before me when I were on the sea, and in great danger of my life, that I should goe before the King, to witness for God, whether he would hear or noe, and to lay downe my life as I did at Boston if it bee required." She followed the king around in London and cried out to him, "I wait for justice of thee, O King, for in the country I have had no justice among the magistrates, nor sheriffs, nor bailiffs, for they have taken away my goods, contrary to the law." She wrote that she "waited upon the King which way soever he went. I met him in the park and gave him two letters which he took at my hand but the people murmured because I did not kneel; but I went along by the King and spoke as I went."

Elizabeth could get no answer, so she appeared the next day in sackcloth and ashes at Whitehall and "both great men and women was strucken into silence. The witness of god was raised in many, and a fine time I had among them, till a soldier pulled me away and said I should not preach there; but I was moved to speak all the way I went up to Westminster Hall."[10]

It was some years before Massachusetts accepted Quakers. When two female preachers, Anne Austin (?–1665) and Mary Fisher (c.1623–98), who had been a housemaid, arrived in Boston on board *The Swallow*, they were immediately examined for "witch marks" on their bodies and then thrown in jail. With both men and women present, the male officials "stript them stark naked, not missing head nor feet, searching betwixt their toes, and amongst their hair ... and abusing their bodies more than modesty can mention, in so much that Anne who was a married woman, and had born 5 children said, That she had not suffered so much in the birth of them all, as she had done under their barbarous and cruel hands."[11]

At their trial, the 1656 Council held at Boston, Anne and Mary were found to be "transgressors of the former Laws, do hold very Dangerous, Heretical and Blasphemous Opinions." Also, their "Books, wherein are contained many most Corrupt, Heretical, and Blasphemous doctrines contrary to the Truth of the Gospel" professed by the Puritans, were ordered burned.[12]

The Puritans in Boston had already dealt with Anne Hutchinson (1591–1643) in 1638, not a Quaker but a preacher and midwife whom they banished from the colony and who eventually founded the state of Rhode Island. Anne was told at her sentencing, "You have rather been a husband than a wife, and a preacher than a hearer; and a magistrate than a subject…."[13] There was a proper place for women and preaching or traveling freely was not a part of it. They were alarmed at the possibility of Quakers living among them.

Legislation had been passed during the reign of Charles II prohibiting "secret" meetings for worship and demanding oaths of allegiance which the Quakers refused to take, although the Puritans were hostile to most religions except their own. It is estimated that between 1660 and 1680, in only 20 years, 12,000 Quakers were imprisoned and 366 died during imprisonment in England.[14]

Quaker women spoke to clergymen, kings, magistrates, in churches, on street corners, before Parliament. They were more literate than the average woman. In an analysis of Quakers in Essex county in England, it was found that almost 66 per cent of Quaker women were literate compared to 29 per cent of other women. They wrote speeches, memoirs, tracts, and pamphlets. They interpreted scripture and composed theology. As the itinerant preacher and writer Quaker Hester (Ester) Biddle (c.1629–97) noted, "We are not like the World, who must have a Priest to interpret the scriptures to them … the Lord doth not speak to us in an unknown Tongue, but in our own Language do we hear him perfectly."[15] It has been estimated that published works by female Quakers consisted of up to 20 per cent of all seventeenth-century women's publications.

The women also traveled around the world. According to historian Mary Maples Dunn, women constituted 36 per cent of Quakers who visited the United States from England as traveling missionaries between 1656 and 1701; and later between 1702 and 1760, the percentage dropped only slightly to 33 per cent. It is estimated that there were about 1,500 Quaker women preachers traveling in England and across the ocean in the latter part of the eighteenth century. The historian, Rebecca Larson, analyzed less than a third of Quaker women's monthly meeting records in the United States between 1700 and 1775, and found 302 women ministers active there during those years.[16]

Many Quaker women married later than the average woman at that time. In the 1700s in Ireland and in New England, women usually married in their late teens, while the average age for Quaker women was almost 23 in New England and just over 24 in Ireland. In England, the average age for all women was about 26. Many Quaker women never married at all. In the eastern United States, of daughters born to Quakers before 1786, almost 10 per cent never married, and after 1786, that figure rose to almost 24 per cent. In Philadelphia in the late 1800s, 40 per cent of all Quaker women were single, although that may have been an anomaly. Generally, Quaker women had fewer children to care for, although young children in the home did not prevent the women from traveling. For example, Charity Cook (c.1745–1822) from North Carolina began traveling in 1776 at age 31. She left seven children with her husband Isaac, the youngest a baby of three months and the oldest a boy of 12.[17]

Travel was not easy. The celebrated preacher Rachel Wilson (1720–75) sailed to the United States in 1768 on the Quaker-owned *Pennsylvania Packet*, but before she embarked, she waited to receive spiritual confirmation that she should be on that boat. When she did decide to travel on it, she had to take with her enough food for a possible three-month voyage. Her provisions included:

> 30 Fowles, 12 Ducks, 4 hams, 2 doz. Madeira wine, 2 bottles Jamaica Spirit, Keg W.I. Rum, 4 bottles of brandy, 2 do. Vinegar, 6 lbs. Rusks, 2 lbs. Maple biscuits, 3 do. Ginger bread, 8 do. Raisins, ½ lb. Single Tea, 2 lbs. ground coffee, 2 do. Chocolate, 1 Loaf D refined sugar, 14 lbs. Musco sugar, 1 Pack cranberries, 2 qts. Oatmeal, 6 lbs. rice, 5 bushlls. Indian corn, 100 Eggs.[18]

Often a ship's diet was supplemented by fresh seafood. On board the *Pennsylvania Packet*, Rachel dined on two dolphins caught at sea: "… as I had never seen anye Before," she wrote, "it was Very agreeable to Me & I Eat it with a pretty good gust & found no Bad Effects from it."[19]

In 1752, Margaret Ellis (?–1765) and Margaret Lewis (1712–89) encountered a near mutiny on board as they sailed from Pennsylvania to Great Britain. After having prayed for guidance, Ellis distributed some of her cakes, cheese, and liquor to the sailors who were squabbling and gave them a short sermon. This appeared to have stopped the trouble. Susanna Morris (1682–1755) from Pennsylvania was shipwrecked three times, once in Chesapeake Bay, once off the coast of Great Britain, and once in the Irish Sea, but she survived.[20]

In 1760, during the Seven Years' War, a Maryland preacher, Ann Moore (1710–83), was put ashore in Spain when the French captured the ship on which she was traveling to Great Britain. She had already endured six weeks of seasickness, a storm so violent "that it seemed as though we should unavoidably be swallowed up in the waves," and nine days being becalmed. She had to remain in Spain for several months before a ship came by that would take her home to England.[21]

Katherine Evans (1618–92) and Sarah Cheevers (1608–64), Quaker missionaries, were imprisoned in Malta by the Spanish Inquisition for four-and-a-half years from 1658 to 1663 for their beliefs. They were often hungry and hallucinating, thinking they would die. "We did eat but little in two months and then they did bring us whatever we did speak for, for eight to 10 days. And afterwards we were so straitened for want of food, it did us more hurt than our fast," one of them wrote from prison.[22]

Travel on land could be almost as demanding. In a letter to her husband in 1752, Mary Weston (1712–66) wrote that she and her companion had "rid (ridden) about 1800 miles" during her 1750–52 American tour and that she "took above a hundred meetings in 4 months … finding my Concern to Lead me to back Settlements, where no English fr[ien]d has Ever been before … in New England." The next year, Catherine Payton (1726–94) traveled in the Carolina backwoods "in a very thinly inhabited country through unbeaten paths in the woods, dangerous creeks and swamps with wild and venomous creatures around us." She traveled more than 8,750 miles over three years in North America, mostly by horseback. Mary Peisley (1718–57) rode 5,000 miles throughout England in less than three years before traveling to the United States with Catherine Payton. Mary Fisher walked by herself 500 miles to visit the ruler of the Ottoman Empire, Sultan Mehmed IV, in Turkey and was well received by him. She had crossed Macedonia and Thrace from the coast of Greece, and afterwards made her way to Constantinople and then back to England.[23]

In the snowy winter woods, Rachel Wilson fell off her horse which then "crushed" her leg, but she got up and rode 15 miles to an inn where she held a meeting. She had traveled 2,000 miles in the New England States. Her last year in America in 1769, 51 Princeton University students had asked her to preach to them, and the meeting was so crowded many had to stand.[24]

Catherine Payton had preached to the students at Oxford while she was in England and reports about her preaching style varied. One male admirer described her thus:

Free, solemn and distinct her Doctrine flowd
Charmd every Ear, and every Bosom glowd

No empty Period, all was sterling sense
Tinctured with love and pure Benevolence

Other men noted that she lacked "that feminine softness, which to our sex is so generally attractive."[25]

While Quakers respected all people, they bowed before no one. Quakers were taught that everyone was equal; the divine light was available to all to the same degree. Men kept their hats on even in the presence of the king, although they removed them during prayers in church worship, bowing before God. They refused to address people with exalted titles, such as "Your Excellency" and kept to the simple "plain" terms of "thee" and "thou." Women refused to curtsey.

At that time preaching women were considered by many people to be simple-minded or mentally unstable. Priscilla Cotton and Mary Cole, two Quaker women imprisoned in 1655 in Exeter for preaching, responded to the church hierarchy that "silly men and women may see more into the mystery of Jesus Christ, than you." While they were in prison they wrote the impassioned pamphlet explaining why women should be allowed to preach, "To the Priests and People of England."[26]

At first, some of the early Quakers did go beyond the bounds of good behavior, believing the Light of God gave them permission to speak out at any occasion. They interrupted church services of other faiths. In 1677, a Quaker woman led by two others entered Boston's South Church in sackcloth and ashes with her hair disheveled and her face as "black as ink." Another woman walked naked through a Massachusetts town, and another entered a Puritan church service, also naked.[27] Elizabeth Adams (c.1747–1823) stood before Parliament for two days with a large earthenware pot upside down on her head. On 3 May 1655, Sarah Goldsmith "with her hair hanging down her, and without any other clothes upon her, excepting shoes on her feet," stood in a public street until the tumult grew so violent that someone forced her into a shop.[28]

It was inevitable that Quakers would be seen as mad and dangerous. As a result, Fox established rules that any man or woman who felt called to preach or to travel had to be approved at a Friends' regular meeting and receive a signed certificate, although the Quaker George Keith defended women by noting, "If [women] speak, they are not to do it by permission, but by commandment ... if the Spirit of the Lord Command or move a godly and Spiritually Learned Woman to speak ... she is to speak...." Writings had to be accepted by a Friends' meeting before being published.[29]

Not all women who hoped to become part of the Quaker faith were accredited. The outspoken Dorothy Ripley (1767–1831) made repeated bids to become a Quaker but was rejected because of rumors of licentious behavior, which was most unlikely. Some Quakers supported her financially. One writer claimed that she "had an unerring, sober knack for zeroing in on others' faults, often alienating the very people whose favor she sought to curry." Described by the *Christian Advocate* as the most extraordinary woman in the world, she crossed the Atlantic between England and the United States about 19 times, 11 of those trips between 1825 and her death in Virginia in 1831. She is one of very few women to be mentioned in Harmon's *Methodist Encyclopedia*.[30] Brought up as a Wesleyan Methodist in Whitby, England, she reportedly helped out in the Primitive Methodist community. Her father, a close friend of John Wesley, the founder of Methodism, had encouraged her to become a preacher, but Ripley left the Methodists because of opposition to women preachers.[31]

In the States, she visited prisons, berated slave owners including the president of the country, and preached to the Oneida "Indians" where the crowds were so great, she had to stand up in a cart in the blazing sun to be seen, and spoke out against capital punishment. In one six-week period alone in the States, she filled 46 preaching appointments in various denominations.

Thomas Jefferson invited her to address the United States Congress in 1806 and she spoke to the legislature of Maryland. But even with all those credentials, the Quakers did not open their arms to her. They were not impressed by such accomplishments. The eccentric Methodist preacher, Lorenzo Dow, was aware of opposition to her. Those who tried to block her were nothing but "religious bigots," he wrote, "of narrow contracted minds for little minds are only capable of little things."[32]

Like the Methodist women preachers in the late 1700s and early 1800s, Quaker women gained experience and self-confidence in women's only meetings. While not universal for Quaker women, there were quarterly and yearly Friends' meetings and "Box" meetings to look after charity, where the women gained a great deal of practical skills. They received and replied to letters from Quakers around the world, they collected and dispensed charity, and they prepared reports. They took minutes and honed their public-speaking ability. They shared their own experiences and counseled each other. One observer wrote that their authority "produces in them thought, and foresight, and judgment.... It elevates their ideas. It raises in them a sense of their own dignity and importance as human beings … their pursuits are rational, useful and dignified."[33]

The prominent Quaker, William Penn (1644–1718), founder of the State of Pennsylvania, insisted that women and men should meet apart, "women whose bashfulness will not permit them to say or do much, as to church affairs before men, when by themselves, may exercise their gift of wisdom and understanding, in a direct care of their own sex.…"[34]

Quakers who were certified to travel could receive financial assistance not only for themselves but for the family they had to leave behind. When the women married, they did not promise to obey their husbands; it was understood that they were equal. Their spiritual obligations took preference over family responsibilities, even if it meant being away from their families for a few years. Indeed, sometimes when a traveling female Quaker returned from a long missionary journey, she found a child or husband had died in the interval.

The Society of Friends offered virtual equality between men and women, especially compared to other religions and organizations at the time. One area where women did not experience equality, however, was in the school-room. Quakers established schools for their children, partly to keep them from associating with children who might spend too much time in secular amusements such as dancing. In New England, both women ("mistresses") and men were hired as teachers after 1699 with "mistresses" generally hired for the summer as well as the winter. But there appears to have been a wide discrepancy in the earnings of men and women. Salaries, though, were not straightforward. Reports indicate that some teachers were paid a fixed amount while others were paid according to the subjects they taught and the number of pupils in their classes, although it appears that they each had to teach a few "poor" students free of charge.

In 1700 in Philadelphia, the Welsh Quaker, John Cadwalader (1676–1742), was paid £20 for half a year, but found it not enough to support his family; consequently this was raised to £50 per year. At the same time, Olive Songhurst's salary was increased "five or ten pounds," but there is no base salary given in the school reports for her. In 1757, the male teacher Elisha Pickering received £150, which was one of the top salaries then. In 1784, the classicist, historian and writer of some renown, the Englishman Robert Proud (1728–1813), was paid a fixed salary of £250 per annum; that rate was comparatively excessive. He also had an assistant, an "usher," who was paid £80. That same year, Mary Harry taught 15 or 16 children, earning about

£40 for the year, and Mary McDonnell taught 15 children at £14 per quarter or £44 per annum.

The school subjects in the various schools differed, although most were fairly basic. In 1779, John Todd taught reading, English, writing, arithmetic, and mathematics, while Ann Rakestraw taught spelling and reading in another school, and Sarah Lancaster taught the younger female children "the rudiments of learning and other branches suitable to girls." There were Latin schools, English schools, girls' schools, mixed schools, boys' schools, and Negro schools; education was not uniform. Committees of both men and women were named to supervise the schools although the majority of committee reports list only men.[35]

The first Quaker school in Canada, set up in 1841, was looked after by two American Quakers, Mary V. Hoag and Joseph H. Haines. They were required "to perform the same description of duties," which included supervision at meal times. Mary was paid £50 per annum to "take charge of the female department," while Joseph received £100 "to take charge of the male department for the same amount of time.[36]

Today, there are approximately 377,000 Quakers around the world, more than 146,000 living in Kenya, almost twice the number of those in the United States.

THE SHAKERS

Jane Wardley received a message from God that the end of the world was at hand; Christ was returning to earth, this time in the form of a woman. Members of the Society of Friends or Quakers preached and taught this good news in Bolton-on-the-Moors in the south of England where they lived; around 1747, followers formed the Wardley Society around them. They worshipped together in the Wardley's home, beginning quietly, but the worshippers generally erupted into dancing, shaking, and shouting, believing that they were possessed by the spirit of God. They also thought that the shaking and trembling were caused by the Holy Spirit expunging sin in their bodies. Sometimes the meetings were so loud that neighbors called the police; the few members of what was then known as the United Society of the Society of Believers in Christ's Second Appearing were often thrown in jail for disturbing the peace.

One of those members was Ann Lee (1736–84), a young illiterate woman from Manchester, the second oldest child of eight whose parents were too poor to send their children to school. Described as short, rather stout, with penetrating blue eyes, a fair complexion, and brown hair, Ann joined the "Shaking Quakers" in 1758 when she was 22. She had wanted to remain single and celibate but her father forced her to marry in 1761. She had four children, all of whom died in early childhood. Ann claimed to have received several visions from God with the main message that celibacy and confession of sin were the only ways to salvation.

Once when Ann was in jail for breaking the Sabbath Day by making loud noise during worship, she reported that Jesus visited her, uniting with her in body and spirit. She became the female Christ that the Wardleys had preached about and the leader of the new Society. "I am the first Elder in the Church—I have seen God, and spoke with him face to face, as we speak to one another," she reportedly told another member. "My soul is married to him;—he is my husband; it is not I that speak; it is Christ who dwells in me." The story was also told of the time when Ann was in jail a member of the group fed her a mixture of wine and milk through the keyhole, keeping her alive while the jailers had hoped to starve her to death.[37]

Ann preached of the sins of the flesh to anyone who would listen, and disrupted church services. Even the *Manchester Mercury* (20 July 1773) reported on Ann and her colleagues' behavior:

> Saturday last ended the Quarter sessions, when John Townley, John Jackson, Betty Lees, and Ann Lees [*sic*], for going into Christ Church, in Manchester, and there willfully and contemptuously, in the time of Divine service, disturbing the congregation then assembled at morning prayers in the said church, were severally fined twenty pounds each.[38]

Ann and her friends were so annoying that at one point people in the village threw stones at them, but only one of them was slightly hurt. It was also claimed that once, when she was about to have her tongue bored through with a hot iron as a penalty for blasphemy, Ann began speaking in tongues in 72 different languages, and she was left alone.[39]

In the summer of 1774, after a turbulent 79-day voyage across the Atlantic, the ship *Mariah* sailed into New York harbor with a crew, cargo, and nine passengers who had been charged a reduced fare because the ship had been condemned. The passengers were Ann Lee and eight followers, but not the Wardleys who were by then too old and too poor to travel. Ann believed that God had asked her to form a new church in America. She would begin what has been described as "the most successful experiment in Protestant Christian communitarian living."[40]

For a few years, the members of the group went their own way, but they joined together in 1776 in Watervliet, near Albany, New York State, where they began to organize farms and build houses. Religious revivals sweeping the country around that time provided fertile ground for new members for their society. Ann Lee, now called Mother Ann, and some of the other members traveled around preaching and gaining converts, and by the time of Ann's death in 1784, Shakerism had spread through several states—New York, Connecticut, Massachusetts, New Hampshire, and Maine.

Success was not without its problems. Because they were pacifists, during the Revolutionary War (1775–83) the Shakers were seen as traitors or spies, although they helped soldiers on both sides who were wounded and hungry. Mother Lee was considered to be a witch and, because of the Shakers' strict practice of celibacy, also a family destroyer. As one anti-Shaker tract explained: "If the Mother or any other woman call herself a prophetess and set herself up for teacher and leader, usurping authority over men, and deceive, debauch, and mislead people, she comes full into the character of a Jezebel, and is a seducer."[41]

Ann was repeatedly threatened, harassed, and even beaten by mobs on a tour of New England. At one point, in 1781 in Massachusetts, a group grabbed her and tore her clothes to find out if she was really a woman, all this in spite of the fact that her very muscular brother, William, acted as her bodyguard. In 1780, Ann was jailed in Albany for several months and charged with subversion, but she preached from her prison cell.

The Shakers were communist in their organization. They worked long hours; everyone was involved in production, both for their own community needs and to create goods to sell for profit. There was men's work and women's work, and it was impossible to share with the other gender as this would create a situation where a man and a woman would need to work too closely with each other. However, all the work was considered equal in value and importance.

In 1850, of the 34 men in one community, 14 worked outside gardening, farming, and caring for livestock. The other men were engaged mostly as mechanics, cabinetmakers, shoemakers, and stone masons. They were inventors, and the men often created equipment that would make the women's life easier, such as a steam engine that could wash, dry, and iron. They invented the flat broom, the standard clothespin, an apple peeler and corer, the first packaged garden seeds, water-repellent cloth, wrinkle-free fabric, and many other useful innovations.

Most of the 54 women in that same community worked with clothing as seamstresses, "tayloresses," weavers, spinners, taking care of the men's and children's garments as well as their own. Ten of the women manufactured goods for sale such as baskets, chair cushions, brushes, bonnets, medicinal herbs, pickles, cheese and jellies, always with the reputation of high quality. There were two female physicians, two "wash-house deaconesses," one cook, and one dairy woman. The men had their own male physician.[42]

A male teacher taught a small school of boys, and a female teacher taught the girls, instructing them in the basic subjects of reading, grammar, and mathematics. Sometimes whole families were converted to the Shaker Church resulting in children becoming part of their communities.

As in other faiths where women and men were separated, there were opportunities for women that did not exist in other religions. For each group or "family" of about 50 to 100 women, two eldresses and two deaconesses were appointed. Elders and deacons had oversight of the men. The eldresses heard confessions from the women, and deaconesses worked in business and finance with the women. Both had opportunities for travel to other Shaker communities. Aurelia Mace, a Maine Shaker, claimed that "in the Shaker Community, woman has taken her place as an equal with man, by intellectual, if not by physical strength … a Deaconess (is) … considered equal in … powers of government."[43]

One arena where men and women did come together, though without physical touching, was in worship. Initially there was freedom to "do one's own thing"—dancing, hopping, swinging, groaning, shouting, clapping, and singing without words. Even though Mother Ann insisted on celibacy, this physical emphasis was the focus of their worship. Later, after Mother Ann's death, under the leadership of James Whittaker (1751–87), a relative of hers and one of the original nine who traveled to New York, worship became much more formal, although with many of the same components. It was sometimes open to the public, only to watch. Sermons, when they were included, were given by males. This trend toward more formal worship continued under ex-Baptist minister Joseph Meacham's (1742–96) leadership.

Joseph Meacham claimed that he had received a new "Holy Order" of dancing from God and that it was to be handed down through generations. Called the "square order shuffle," it required men and women to form themselves into ranks, men on one side, and women on the other, where they stepped and shuffled in unison with an erect and loose-jointed posture. Meacham also made singing with words a standard element of their worship.[44]

Women's leadership continued under Meacham, and the Shakers became known again as the United Society of Believers in Christ's Second Appearance. Lucy Wright (1760–1821), a married woman from Massachusetts, joined the Shakers, and as was compulsory, lived apart from her husband. He became a Shaker itinerant preacher. Meacham brought Lucy into a leadership role, and when he died, she became the new leader. She introduced marching into their worship.

Early on, there were many strange rumors about the Shakers that they danced and ran naked through the woods, burned religious books, and drank to excess. Mother Lee was said to be physically and verbally abusive, often striking and whipping her followers, but what actually happened and what was simply animosity toward an unusual woman and sect is difficult to tell.

By 1830, Shakerism was well accepted by neighboring communities. Their goods were eagerly sought after. Shakers were considered to be honest, reliable, neat, sober, and industrious. There were communities from Maine to Kentucky and, by 1845, there were around 6,000 members, but by then Shakerism was beginning to decline. The prohibition of procreation worked against the continuation of the society, and it was beginning to appear old-fashioned. As Shaker women were spinning and weaving and sewing their own garments, many secular women and women in other religions were buying their clothes ready-made.

But as the Eldresses Anna White (1831–1910) and Leila S. Taylor wrote in answer to the question, "What would become of the world if all were to become Shakers?":

> In view of the condition of a good part of the people in it, the thought has
> sometimes suggested itself that it might not be a bad idea to let the world
> run out. But there is not the least danger of the world's population failing
> from religious motives, nor is there any fear that all mankind will become
> Shakers in this life. The greater part could not, for they are not on the plane
> to hear the call of the Spirit....

Lucy Wright was the last single female leader. After 1821, an elder and an eldress, Ruth Landon and Asenath Clark, were in charge and, from 1890 to 1947, the communities were led by Eldress Frances Hall, Eldress Emma

King, Eldress Gertrude Soule (1894–1988), and Eldress Bertha Lindsay (c.1897–1990). In 1957, the Shaker Covenant, the document all new Shakers signed when they joined, came to an end. As of 2017, only two Shakers remained.

Although Shaker women had been mainly confined to their communities, some of them did become involved in local and even national issues. Eldress Anna White was appointed a vice-president of the Alliance of Women for Peace, a member of the National American Suffrage Association, and a vice-president of the National Council of Women of the United States, and spoke at public conferences on behalf of these organizations. She wrote songs and Shaker history and, in 1904, co-authored the book *Shakerism: Its Meaning and Message*.

While the Shakers flourished, women had access to leadership roles, and an understanding of God as both male and female. As observed by Eldress Antoinette Doolittle (1810–86), editor of the paper *Shaker and Shakeress*, "As long as we have all male Gods in the heavens, we shall have all male rulers on earth." The Shakers had a male and female god, and male and female leaders on earth. Paulina Bates from the Canterbury New Hampshire community wrote in 1849 of the dual role of male and female in nurturing children: "… ye who think to be born and reared by the exertions of my Beloved Son, exclusive of the aid of my beloved Daughter, the Bride, the Lamb's wife, know ye your hope is vain; for this can never be."[45]

During their history, the Shakers attracted approximately 16,500 followers.[46]

THE SOCIETY OF UNIVERSAL FRIENDS

Jemima Wilkinson (1752–1819) was brought up as a Quaker in Rhode Island, the eighth of 12 children. Her mother died when Jemima was 14. After a severe six-day illness—probably typhoid—when she was 18, Jemima announced that she herself had died and a genderless spirit had taken over her physical body. Her carnal life had ended. She claimed that she was a holy vessel of God and Jesus Christ. Jesus had been God's first messenger; Jemima was the second. She was a prophet sent by God. During her illness, she had visions, and God had inspired her to preach. She became known as the Publick [*sic*] Universal Friend, and afterwards refused to answer to the name Jemima. Some of her friends at that time considered that she was not in her right mind.[47]

A strong preacher with a "harmonious voice" and "persuasive manner," Jemima developed a following of friends who accompanied her throughout Rhode Island, Pennsylvania, and Connecticut.

Rejected by her fellow Quakers, however, because of her zealousness, she set up her own community focusing on strict abstinence and friendship, with a mixture of fairly bland Quaker, Shaker, and New Light Baptist evangelical theology, although one of her hearers reported that "she do preach up terror alarmingly." She was opposed to slavery and war. She favored celibacy over marriage; however, records indicate that members of her community did marry. On at least one occasion, she demanded that her followers fast for 30 days on bread and water; "most of them strictly obeyed."

Jemima adopted a dramatic style, rode a white horse with a white-leather-and-blue-velvet saddle and silver stirrups, and dressed in a long formless black gown, petticoats peeking out at the hem, with a white cravat at her neck, although the colors sometimes varied, her hair swept back off her face. A fashion plate since childhood, she wore a white Quaker-styled beaver hat. When she rode to meetings, she led a procession of followers—usually 12 suggestive of the 12 disciples—riding behind, two by two. Wilkinson always ate by herself in her room with a closed door, and was excessively clean. She had her own pewter dishes and table service marked with the initials U.F. She bathed daily, including washing her hair, unusual for the time, insisting on fresh, clean clothes.[48]

It was said that there were "sittings" for Sunday worship because of the numbers of people in her community. The men and women "would wait for an hour or more, then rise and shake hands." A similar silence took place during their worship on Saturday afternoons. Obviously influenced by Quaker tradition, they would sit quietly until someone rose up to speak. Generally this would be Wilkinson, and after her, a follower and her primary inheritor, Rachel Malin.[49]

In 1787, the *Connecticut Magazine* published this description of her:

She is about the middle size of a woman, not genteel in her person, rather awkward in her carriage; her complexion good, her eyes remarkably black and brilliant, her hair black and waving with beautiful ringlets upon her neck and shoulders.... She wears her neck cloth like a man; her chemise is buttoned around the neck and wrists. Her outside garment is a robe, under which it is said, she wears an expensive dress, the fashion of which is said to correspond with neither that of man or woman. Her understanding is not deficient, except touching upon her religious fanaticism. Her memory is very great. Her preaching has very little connection and is very lengthy, at times cold and languid, but occasionally lively, zealous and animated.[50]

Other physical descriptions of her vary, describing her as tall, but her choice of clothing might have made her look taller than she actually was.

In 1790, when she was 32, Wilkinson and her followers began a long trek through the backwoods of Pennsylvania in the wintertime to the north end of Keuka Lake, "where (they) might live in peace and plenty," naming the township where they were to settle Jerusalem, but today it is known as Penn Yan, New York. Some of her disciples were well-off and they were "liberal in supplying her wants." They built houses for 260 women and men along with a two-story house with nine fireplaces for Wilkinson, erected a grist mill at present-day Dresden, a blacksmith shop, and a public house. Eventually a three-story house was built for Wilkinson, with 12 windows on the south side and nine on the east, with a staircase landing where she could preach. The building housed needy members as well as Wilkinson.

One of her staunchest followers, Ruth Pritchard (1761–c.1816), had been operating a school in Wallingford, Connecticut, when she fell under Wilkinson's influence. Ruth had traveled seven miles to hear Wilkinson preach: "… blessed be the day I went," she wrote. "It was the voice that spake as never man spake," Ruth noted. "It is that which if obey'd will bring light, life, & love unto the soul…."

In 1797, Ruth married a man 13 years her junior, and continued teaching school in the new community. Ruth's diary tells the story of their journey to Jerusalem: enchanted by Wilkinson, Ruth and the others put up with apparent discomfort as Wilkinson and her special friend Sarah Richards (?–1794/5), whom Wilkinson called the "Prophet Daniel," rode in somewhat more "luxury," but there is no indication of the place Sarah's daughter, Eliza, was assigned. When they were traveling on the Susquehanna River, "The Friend & Sarah slept in the carriage in the boat all night, and this day stayd in the boat…. For my part I had a comfortable lodging on a muddy floar [*sic*]." On 31 March, they "Landed at Sugarbottom. No shelter till the dear Friend came out of the boat & erected for us a tent, very comfortable. How could anyone think it tedious to lay out(side) when such a hand spread the tent!"[51]

Perhaps Wilkinson's most illustrious follower was Judge William Potter (c.1722–1814), a wealthy Rhode Island judge who had 13 children, 11 slaves, and a household of 27. He converted in 1779, began freeing his slaves and rode beside Wilkinson when she traveled to meetings. He also built a 14-room addition onto his mansion for Wilkinson and her followers.[52]

The members of the new community, including three sisters and one of Wilkinson's brothers, worked the fields and cut firewood, gradually expanding their arable land. One man admits that he helped out when he was a boy, but that "it seemed strange" to him to see "the movements of so large a company of men, all ordered by a woman." Wilkinson's family remembers that her followers "gratuitously planted and hoed her corn, sowed and reaped her wheat, cut and gathered her hay, always careful to cause the Friend no trouble or expense." Another man noted that "there is not to be found, perhaps, in the annals of human society, any instance of such strict, uniform and preserving fidelity and devotion to any leader, as was shown by these people, to Jemima." Members would claim the honor of doing the farm work, but it was always done under her direction. It was reported that even when she was young, she was "averse to anything like labor," and persuaded her elder sisters to "take responsibility for her assigned tasks."[53]

Herbert Wisbey, though, whose parents were part of her society, writes that Wilkinson "would not hesitate ... to take hold of one end of a cross-cut saw and help work up a log into firewood. She would also assist in plucking live geese, pick berries, hoe and weed her garden...."[54]

Initially the community prospered. It was literally a land of milk and honey. The members' flocks increased and their teams and horses were first-rate. Visitors arrived from France and England as well as the southern United States and were welcomed to the community. Outsiders called the members "Jemimakins."

Eventually, however, the community died out after Wilkinson, at age 61, "Left Time," as she expressed it. The community had been focused on Wilkinson, and when she grew old and died, the reason for the community's existence disappeared. Also, the members had been forbidden to multiply, although a "few persons transgressed." There were a number of law suits over land, and many followers became disillusioned and left. At one point, Wilkinson was put on trial for "blasphemy" (1800), but the court ruled that the American courts could not try blasphemy cases due to the separation of church and state. The last survivor of the group died in 1874. In her will, Wilkinson had insisted that all the poor people in her society be provided for by her inheritors receiving "such assistance, comfort and support during their natural life as they may need," or else her descendants would forfeit any benefits from her estate.[55]

A lot of stories circulated about Wilkinson. One of the most popular, with several versions, concerns walking on water. In one of the versions, a crowd insists that she walk on water. "Do you have faith that this is possible?" Wilkinson asked. When someone in the crowd jeered, she looked straight at that person and said, "Without thy faith, I cannot do it."[56]

It has been suggested that Wilkinson was either a lesbian, a transvestite, or a "transgendered evangelist." However, she believed that she was a soul or a spirit in a genderless body and that she had gone beyond gender. Numerous comments were made, however, that she appeared more masculine than feminine because of her clothes and her hairstyle.

The mansion built for Wilkinson still exists, and museums in New York State contain many artifacts from her life.

THE SEVENTH-DAY ADVENTIST CHURCH

An unfortunate accident when Ellen Gould Harmon White (1827–1915) was nine years old kept her out of school. Another schoolgirl had thrown a rock that hit Ellen on her head, causing her to fall unconscious for three weeks. Ever afterward, she had headaches when she tried to read or write. Yet, later in life, she was the author of many books. Of that early time, she wrote:

> For two years, I could not breathe through my nose…. It seemed impossible for me to study and retain what I learned…. My nervous system was prostrated, and my hand trembled so that I made but little progress in writing … the letters on the page would run together … and a faintness and dizziness would seize me. I had a bad cough, my whole system seemed debilitated.[57]

Raised on a farm, later helping her father manufacture hats, she became a devout Methodist at the age of 12. However, Ellen and the rest of her family were thrown out of that denomination about 1843, when they became followers of the Baptist preacher William Miller (1782–1849) and accepted the "Millerite" prophecy that Christ was returning to earth in 1844.

When that didn't happen in "The Great Disappointment," Ellen rejoined the Methodists, attended prayer meetings, and, during one session, received the first of several thousand visions she had during her life, visions that lasted from less than a minute to nearly four hours. She described them in a later book, *A Sketch of the Christian Experience and Views of Ellen G. White*; they became foundational for her new church, although later some of her followers would dispute the validity of her visions. She began itinerating and preaching that Christ had indeed returned—not to earth, but to a heavenly sanctuary that he cleansed to prepare for his later appearance. After her visions when God commanded her to write down what she had seen, a shaking that had developed in her hand ceased.[58]

In 1846, she married the minister James S. White, and together they began the periodical *The Present Truth*, known as the *Advent Review and Sabbath Herald* by 1850. Ellen's theology focused on the Bible, and, convinced that Saturday was the true Sabbath, kept it as the day of worship.

In 1855, Ellen and her husband moved to Battle Creek, Michigan, where they developed a new church based on her visions, and there she wrote her seminal work, *The Great Controversy between Christ and His Angels and Satan and His Angels*, the battle between good and evil. In all, with the help of several literary assistants, Ellen wrote more than 40 books and about 5,000 periodical articles, thousands of manuscript pages translated into more than 140 languages. Her grandson (and biographer) claims that she is the most translated female non-fiction writer in the history of literature. Her writings cover religion, social relationships, prophecy, publishing, nutrition, creationism, agriculture, theology, education, health, Christian lifestyle, and evangelism.[59]

Ellen worked with the Quakers to establish Battle Creek as a part of the Underground Railroad system; she was opposed to slavery and urged her followers to disobey the American Fugitive Slave Law of 1850, commonly known as the "Bloodhound Law" as dogs were often used to track down escaped slaves who were then returned to their masters. She collaborated with the American ex-slave Isabella "Bell" Baumfree/Hardenburgh/van Wagenen, known as Sojourner Truth (c.1797–1883), the famous Methodist abolitionist, women's rights activist, and speaker. "The black man's name is written in the book of life beside the white man's," Ellen wrote. "All are one in Christ." In the 1890s, one of her four sons built a Mississippi River steamboat using it for about a decade as a floating mission for people of color in Mississippi and Tennessee. Ellen also helped build a school in Hunstville, Alabama, to educate African-Americans.[60]

Ellen was in favor of a good diet, convinced that coffee, tea, drugs, and meats were harmful, and advocated fresh air, sunshine, pure water, and exercise. In 1864, when she promoted eating nutritious food, the average life expectancy in the United States was around 45 years of age; meals contained lots of "suicidal" fried foods, rich gravies, pastries, and sugars.

Ellen's followers believed that she could heal through prayer, and she was responsible for some miracles, but she felt that a doctor would be necessary in many instances. She spoke out for temperance, and founded a Health Reform Institute, which later became the well-known Battle Creek Sanitarium. In 1874, she founded Battle Creek College open to children of all social and economic backgrounds; her husband became the principal. Ellen had firm ideas about education. "It is more than merely having knowledge of books," she wrote. Children need to be taught "how to think, act and decide for themselves ... develop their own judgment and have an opinion of their own...." God never designed that "one human mind should be under the complete control of another human mind," she explained.[61]

She wrote about the use of music, which she believed "when not abused, is a great blessing." Singing, she wrote, "is as much an act of worship as is prayer. Indeed many a song is prayer...."[62]

Ellen traveled around the United States, to Europe and Australia, promoting the Seventh-Day Adventist approach, attracting great crowds and, by the end of the twentieth century, Seventh-Day Adventism had spread around the world. Her book, *Steps to Christ*, has been published in several languages. The *Smithsonian* magazine, acknowledging her influence on religion, named Ellen among the "100 Most Significant Americans."

There have been critics of Ellen's philosophy and her writings. She has been accused of plagiarism, especially concerning her revelations about health and spirituality. She was charged with taking those ideas from other health reformers at the time. Another minister she treated as a son claimed that her visions were the result of diseases or various mental conditions such as epilepsy, catalepsy, hallucination, and ecstasy. However, a Roman Catholic lawyer with no vested interest in Seventh-Day Adventism, and later, several doctors, undertook a detailed study of Ellen's writings, concluding that they were "conclusively unplagiarized."[63]

Today there are approximately 20,000,000 baptized members and 25,000,000 adherents in the Church, the twelfth largest religious body in the world. Membership has been increasing recently every year.

THE SALVATION ARMY

Catherine Mumford Booth (1829–90) is considered to be one of the most extraordinary women of the nineteenth century. Co-founder of The Salvation

Army with her husband William Booth (1829–1912), it is said that she "turned an energetic, rather vulgar, but simple minded dyspeptic into one of the great religious leaders of the world," referring to William.[64]

Born in England to Methodist parents, Catherine spent her young years at home, often in bed with spinal pain. Her mother kept her out of school most of the time to protect her from the bad habits of other children, such as reading novels. She did read a lot, not popular literature but the Bible and theology and history books; she taught Sunday School and was secretary of a Juvenile Temperance Society. Even as a young child, she developed strong ideas on a lot of subjects: the benefit of social work for the poor; the dangers of alcohol; the absolute need to raise the legal age of consent for young girls; the value of vegetarianism; the humane treatment of animals; and the ideology that women must have full equality with men in the Christian ministry. She even engaged in her own trade embargo: she gave up sugar in protest against apartheid in South Africa. Quaker women had been advocating this action for some time.

Catherine and William met at a friend's house, and were married in 1855 in a very simple service in the Congregational Church, although that year, William became a Methodist New Connexion minister with a salary of £100 a year (approximately US$18,000 today). During their honeymoon, William preached and spoke at various meetings, with Catherine's blessing.

Even before they were married, Catherine had quizzed William on his attitude to women in ministry. He answered that he "would not stop a woman preaching on any account," but neither would he encourage one to begin. He told her that she should preach if she felt moved to do so, "although, I should not like it," he said. "I am for the world's salvation," he added. "I will quarrel with no means that promises help." Later he would admit, "Some of my best men are women." However, he also admitted that he believed "women have a fibre more in their hearts, and a cell less in their brains" than men.[65]

Later in 1859, with William's support, Catherine published "Female Ministry: Woman's Right to Preach the Gospel," a powerful response to criticism that the great American evangelist Phoebe Palmer (1807–74), the "Mother of the Holiness Movement," had received from an independent minister who objected to women preaching. Phoebe and Walter Palmer were just finishing a four-year evangelistic tour in Great Britain, and although Catherine never met her, she was impressed by Phoebe's ability. Generally, Phoebe received a much more positive response; she explained that she only exhorted after her husband rather than preached. Earlier when she was touring the Maritime provinces in North America, the *Provincial Wesleyan*'s Woodstock (New Brunswick) correspondent noted, "Mrs. Palmer has a pleasing manner in her style of address, and cannot offend by her simple, ladylike manners." But she did believe that the church had lapsed from scriptural truth by silencing women and used strong language in her writing: "The church in many ways is a sort of potter's field, where the gifts of women as so many strangers, are buried. How long, O Lord, how long before man shall roll away the stone that we may see a resurrection?"[66]

In her pamphlet, Catherine claimed that women were not morally or naturally inferior to men, that there was no biblical reason to deny women the right to preach, and indeed that the Holy Spirit had ordained this right. But it was not just in ministry that she sought this equality, but at home as well:

> How can it be expected that a being trained in absolute subjection to the will of another, and taught to consider that subjection her glory, as well as an imbecile dependence on the judgment of others, should at once be able to throw off the trammels of prejudice and sound judgment which are indispensable to the proper discharge of maternal duties? … Never until she is valued and educated as man's equal will (marital) unions be perfect and their consequences blissful.[67]

The next year, following the birth of her fourth child, Catherine gained enough courage to announce at a meeting where William was preaching that she wanted to speak. Afterward, when she began preaching, one of her sons remarked, "She reminded me again and again of counsel pleading with judge and jury for the life of the prisoner." Another man said, "If ever I am charged with a crime, don't bother to get any of the great lawyers to defend me; get that woman."[68]

Catherine became much in demand as a speaker, and sometimes when William was ill, she was the sole breadwinner. Once she took over his pastoral duties as well as her own and, at the same time, looked after four children with whooping cough. Many times, however, Catherine relied on her mother for help with her eight children. Catherine found that she enjoyed preaching and it helped them financially. The first time she spoke, she told her mother afterward that she felt quite at home "on the *platform*—far more than I do in the *kitchen*." But she told William that she "must try to possess (her) soul in patience and do *all* in the kitchen as well as in the Pulpit…." (The italics are Catherine's.)[69]

In 1865, Catherine and William began a Christian Mission in destitute areas of London. Catherine generally made all the decisions regarding William's career, and it was her desire initially that they should begin a ministry to the poor, although William gradually realized that he was being called to minister in East London. William preached in the "unsavoury" areas, while Catherine preached to the rich in the West End, asking for funds for their social programs.

In 1878, their Mission evolved into The Salvation Army. William was the General and Catherine the "Mother." She designed their flag and the bonnets for the women as well as influencing their policies. She organized "Food for the Million" shops where people could buy inexpensive meals, and established rescue homes for prostitutes and other "wayward" young women. Her shy daughter-in-law Florence Soper Booth (1861–1957) was put in charge of this program. Despite her youth and retiring nature, the Women's Social Services grew from one rescue home to 117 houses in Britain and around the world in 30 years. Florence claimed that unmarried mothers were the class she most liked to help. It was difficult for an unmarried woman to support herself and a child, and figures show that those women happily went to The Salvation Army for help. More than 26 per cent of all referrals to homes were made by the women themselves. There were also soup kitchens and hostels and practical assistance for recently released prisoners. The Salvation Army also organized farm colonies, but those required too much supervision and had to be closed.[70]

One of the Army policies was that there was to be no difference between men and women as to rank, authority, and duties: "Women shall have the right to an equal share with men in the work of publishing salvation." Nurses received $8 a week, captains the same; all the army officers received between $7 and $10 a week, with $4.50 of this to be returned for room and board. Clothing, food, accommodation, and "necessities" along with postage for personal letters were provided. At first when a husband and wife ministered together as a couple, the husband received the paycheck; the historian Andrew Mark Eason claims that in some areas, single men received 15 to 40 per cent more in pay than single women.[71]

Some historians state that female officers never equaled male officers in numbers. In 1906, of 47 leaders worldwide, only seven were women, or 14.9 per cent. This percentage fell even lower as The Salvation Army spread around the world. It is reported that by 1930 *The Salvation Army Year Books* indicated that there were only four senior female leaders compared to 83 men. However, when the East London mission was first organized, 41 of 91 officers were women, almost half. And the historian Susie Stanley notes that, in 1896, The Salvation Army had over 1,000 women officers out of a total of 1,854 in the United States; at the turn of the last century, Stanley claims that women still comprised most of the 24,779 ordained officers. A count in the 2015 *Salvation Army Handbook* of all active officers with the rank of lieutenant colonel and above shows that there are slightly more women than men, although many of the women are part of a married couple. There have been three female generals responsible for the Army throughout the world: Evangeline Booth from 1934 to 39; Eva Burrows from 1986 to 1993; and Linda Bond from 2011 to 2013.[72]

Young women called the "Hallelujah Lasses" or the "shock troops" were an integral and important part of the new Army, such as 18-year-olds Rose Clapham and Jenny Smith, uneducated factory workers, who in 1878 convinced 700 men in the poorer district of London to come to a meeting in a local theater where 140 of them made a decision to become members of the new church. The young women "Lasses" preached, gave communion, and handled all the spiritual and practical demands of a corps. They often marched through streets in uniform, singing religious songs and playing musical instruments, usually in the most depressed areas, but attracting both men and women to Army meetings. Generally, they wore black woolen capes over plain black dresses and Quaker-like bonnets. Often crowds pelted them with rotting vegetables and, using filthy language, told them to go home, considering the women to be utterly disreputable. But the women were courageous and fearless and traveled around the world to open new ministries. For example, from 1882 to 1900, either alone or with another woman, they opened 124 new churches in the central and eastern provinces of Canada, whereas men were responsible for 69 corps, although in the roster of openings, the men or women in 139 places were not identified as to gender because initials only were used instead of first names. They might have been men or women. Still, the women's work was prodigious.[73]

There were several songs about the women. In one, the singer related that he joined the Army because he fell in love with two of the girls:

They call one Happy Eliza, and one Converted Jane
They've been most wicked in their time, but will ne'er do so again;
They said pray come and join us and I was just in the mood
They're Hallelujah Sisters and they're bound to do me good.[74]

Referring to the use of parades and marching bands and other dramatic and startling effects, The Salvation Army explained:

> Many of our methods are very different to the religious usages and social tastes of respectable and refined people, which may make those measures appear vulgar, that is, in bad taste, to them: but this does not make them wrong in the sight of God.... And if it can be proved from the results that these methods lay hold of the ignorant and godless multitudes ... we think they are thereby proved to be both lawful and expedient.[75]

Catherine Booth died when she was 61; her funeral was an impressive event. At first her body lay in state while more than 50,000 mourners filed past her casket over five days. Then the funeral itself was attended by 36,000 in a hall where the Barnum Circus had recently filled the place with 12,000. The funeral procession was limited to 3,000 to avoid an unseemly crowd pushing and shoving. Catherine was indeed a beloved figure.[76]

The Salvation Army spread quickly around the world. In 1879, Lieutenant Eliza Shirley (1862–1932) emigrated to the United States and meetings began there. The next year, the first meeting was held in Australia, and the next, Catherine (Katie) Booth Clibborn (1858–1955), the most precocious of Catherine's daughters took the mission to France. By 1884, there were 1,644 officers and 637 mission stations or corps in Britain and overseas. By 1887, on its tenth anniversary, there were 7,107 officers, 2,587 corps and 653 outposts in 33 countries. Ten years later, the first Salvation Army hospital was set up in India.

The eloquent and adventurous Evangeline Booth (1865–1950), the seventh of eight children, was sent to the Klondike during the Gold Rush (1896–99) as Commissioner of The Salvation Army in Canada in 1898. However, the Gold Rush was over the next year so her work there was limited. In 1904, she headed The Salvation Army in all of the United States. Two other Booth daughters became active in the mission field. Emma Booth-Tucker (1860–1903) had conducted children's services in her family home when she was only 13, and at 17 years of age, she preached to adults, even shouting down the "roughs" who kept interrupting the services. She was sent abroad.

The work of The Salvation Army became so respected and admired that William Booth was invited to Edward vii's (1841–1910) coronation in 1902, and President Theodore Roosevelt (1858–1919) received him in the United States the next year.

FIGURE 12.2 Cadets from Rwanda and Burundi take part in a march, from the 2015 *Salvation Army Handbook*. Photo: Courtesy of The Salvation Army. ©Copyright 2017 The General of The Salvation Army. Reproduced by permission.

Today The Salvation Army operates in approximately 126 countries around the world, with almost 109,000 employees, around 14,000 corps, and 27,000 offices, with 1,500,000 members in Sunday Schools, and more than 2,000,000 beneficiaries of community development programs designed to meet the immediate needs of children, adults, and seniors.

CHRISTIAN SCIENCE

Mary Morse Baker Eddy (1821–1910) was 58 when she founded the Church of Christ Scientist in Boston, Massachusetts. Among the high tributes to her was this assessment in 1907 from the American writer and humorist Mark Twain (1835–1910):

> In several ways, she is the most interesting woman that ever lived and the most extraordinary.... She started from nothing.... Christian Science is "humanity's boon." Mother Eddy deserves a place in the Trinity as much

as any other member of it. She has organized and made available a healing principle that for two thousand years has never been employed, except as the merest kind of guesswork. She is the benefactor of the age….[77]

Born in New Hampshire, the youngest of six children, Mary had digestive problems as a child, although whether or not she also had hysterical fits at that time is controversial. When she was young, she ate little besides bread and vegetables and drank only water. "Thus we passed most of our early years, as many can attest, in hunger, pain, weakness and starvation," she wrote.[78]

When she was about eight, she kept hearing a voice, "calling me distinctly by name, three times and in ascending scale" time after time, until at last, prompted by her mother, she answered, "Speak, Lord, for Thy servant heareth," but she never again heard the voice.[79]

Mary's father kept her out of school because "her brain was too large" for her body, but she read widely, mostly natural philosophy, logic, and moral science, and her brother tutored her in Hebrew, Greek, and Latin. A church minister also helped her, and pronounced her an intellectual and spiritual genius, "bright, good, and pure, aye brilliant." Later, she attended a secondary school, an academy in Plymouth, and became a substitute teacher at the same institution, the New Hampshire Conference Seminary and Female College.

Tall, chestnut-haired, and hazel-eyed, Mary was considered the village beauty. She married in 1843 when she was 22, but her husband died in a few months, as did a fiancé six years later. She was left with a young son who was sent away to be looked after; single women were not considered to be adequate mothers. The family who cared for him told him that his mother had died. Mary never saw her son again until he was 30 and their relationship was unpleasant. She married again when she was 32, but later divorced because of her husband's adultery. Then again in 1877 she remarried, but this new husband soon died.

When she was 45, Mary fell on ice, and while convalescing from what she believed was a life-threatening injury, she read her Bible, noting especially the story of the man sick with palsy who was healed by Jesus (Matthew 9:2). On the third day, she got up, dressed and felt great, the suggestion, conscious or unconscious, that she was resurrected like Christ in three days.

For the next three years, Mary withdrew from society, as she wrote, "to ponder my mission, to search the Scriptures, to find the Science of Mind that should take the things of God and show them to the creature, and reveal the great curative Principal—Deity." She became convinced that illness could be healed through an awakened thought brought about by a clearer perception of God, believing that health was everyone's natural birthright and that God is not the cause of evil in any form. She rejected drugs and medicine.[80] "It is plain that God does not employ drugs or hygiene, nor provide them for human use," she wrote.

Mary also believed in God as Mother and Father: "I believe in God as the Supreme Being. I know not what the person of omnipotence and omnipresence is, or what the infinite includes; therefore I worship that of which I can conceive, first as a loving Father and Mother; then a thought ascends the scale of being to diviner consciousness…. 'God is Love'…."[81]

In 1881, Mary founded the Massachusetts Metaphysical College where she taught her theology and her developing principles of healing to over 700 students between the years 1882 and 1889, charging $300 each for tuition, almost $7,000 in today's American currency. Some of her students actually took 30 lessons for $800, equivalent to almost US$18,000 today. More than 70 per cent of all her pupils were women. Her students were not allowed to take notes; one wonders if this was to prevent them from competing with her professionally as some did. She also disliked interruptions in her class, especially coughing. "Anyone with the least understanding of God does not cough," she is quoted as saying.[82]

Mary believed unequivocally that Christian Science, if not she herself, represented the Second Coming of Christ. She believed that a careful analysis of Christian history revealed great gaps and serious errors in the church's understanding of its ministry. She felt that she filled the gaps, corrected the errors, and for the first time made Christianity understandable. One of her followers asserted that she personally interpreted the femininity or Motherhood of God, as Jesus Christ interpreted the masculinity.[83]

Mary published several journals and magazines, including the *Christian Science Monitor* which she founded when she was 87, a newspaper still widely read with a first-class reputation, winning several Pulitzer prizes over the years. Her major book, *Science and Health with Key to the Scriptures*, first published in 1875 was selected as one of the "75 Books by Women Whose Words Have Changed the World" by the Women's National Book Association established in 1917. The book went through 438 separate printings and six major revisions and made money both for Mary and for the Christian Science Church. "I was a scribe under orders (from God)," she explained, noting that it was God's book, "and who can refrain from transcribing what God indites, and ought not one to take the cup, drink all of it, and give thanks?"[84]

While Mary's accomplishments were substantial, her ride through life was rocky. At one point, she believed in "animal magnetism" and that people could use it maliciously, that is use their mental power to destroy other people's health. She called this one of the greatest crimes, and suggested that people should be put to death for using that power.

Before she established her church, she had a difficult time earning money, although she wrote articles and did substitute teaching. She could afford only to stay with friends, usually disputing so much with each one that she soon had to move on. She was accused of plagiarism, stealing her ideas of Christian Science healing from Phineas Parkhurst Quimby (1802–66), a healer from Maine, who had helped her earlier when she was mentally depressed.

In her latter years, she was sued by both her son and an adopted son for a greater share of her wealth than she had already given them, but both lost their court cases. There was also an unsuccessful lawsuit against her called the "Next Friends Suit" in 1907 that the *New York World* newspaper orchestrated, questioning her mental competence.

During her lifetime Mary was called, among other pejorative expressions, a shameless swindler, shallow, egotistic, incapable of love, paranoiac, mad, mercenary, tyrannical, illiterate, the modern witch of Concord, an enchantress, a pope in petticoats, greedy. "What's Christian Science?" asked Mr. Hennessy. "'Tis wan way iv gettin' the money," said Mr. Dooley.[85]

Both doctors and male clergy were alarmed at the speed with which so many men and women accepted Mary's teaching. Doctors claimed that she was depriving them of "millions of our good paying and intelligent patrons." Clergy feared that "thousands of bright men and women [had] been deceived into accepting the (Christian Science) faith." Doctors envisioned the loss of substantial potential income, clergy their parishioners. "Whenever the devil undertakes to do anything unusually diabolical he performs it through the agency of a woman," a male minister claimed. Mary, he said, had "first coiled herself around the Christian system, breaking all the doctrinal bones of Christianity," and had then "slimed it over" so that it would "all go down easy."[86]

Yet both men and women who followed her teaching—senators, congressmen, mayors, judges, lawyers, professors, writers, and people from almost every profession and occupation—testified to the release they found from various difficulties such as heart, kidney and stomach troubles, malignant growths and alcoholism when they followed Christian Science. Childbirth was made "markedly easier and quicker." And converts felt that the Bible and Jesus' life and works were at last understandable and made sense.[87] As one converted clergyman wrote:

> Like every minister of the gospel, I had the usual prejudice against Christian Science … without a careful investigation … my ten years' ministry were filled with good work, and yet … [now] I serve Him (God) more fully and consistently. His omnipotence, omniscience, and omnipresence are a reality to me now, instead of a vague, impractical theory.[88]

In their early years, female Christian Science practitioners outnumbered men five to one and the offices of reader and teacher were open to women as well as men. The retired professor of religion, Mary Farrell Bednarowski, believes that Christian Science has had a strong appeal to women because it stresses self-help rather than helplessness, and reduces dependence on doctors and clergy. Mary, she notes, stressed that God is non-anthropomorphic, but incorporates the feminine as well as the masculine. God is not the creator of the material world—that is the work of the mortal mind.[89]

Today, the Christian Science Church has a membership of around 85,000 in 1,000 congregations around the world. At its zenith, there were about 270,000 members and 1,800 churches.

FURTHER READING

PRIMARY

Brown, Elisabeth Potts, and Susan Mosher Stuard, eds. *Witnesses for Change: Quaker Women over Three Centuries*. New Brunswick, NJ: Rutgers University Press, 1989.

Collins, Elizabeth. *Memoirs of Elizabeth Collins of Upper Evansham, New Jersey*. Philadelphia: Friends Book Store, 1873.

Otten, Charlotte F., ed. *English Women's Voices: 1540–1700*. Miami: Florida University Press, 1992.

Pritchard, Ruth. *Manuscript Diary of a Journey into the Wilderness with the Public Universal Friend*. N.p. 1790.

Stirredge, Elizabeth. *Strength in Weakness Manifest in the Life, Various Trials, and Christian Testimony, of the faithful Servant and Handmaid of the Lord, Elizabeth*

Stirredge, Who departed this Life, at her House in Hempstead, in Hertfordshire, in the 72nd Year of her Age. London: James Phillips, 1795.

Wilkinson, Israel. "Jemima Wilkinson." *Memoirs of the Wilkinson Family in America*, Biography No. xii. Jacksonville, IL: Davis & Penniman, Printers, 1869.

Wisbey, Herbert A. "Recollections of Jemima Wilkinson, as Related in 1890 by Mrs. Huldah Barnes Davis." *The Crooked Lake Review*, October 1992.

SECONDARY

Bacon, Margaret Hope. *Mothers of Feminism: The Story of Quaker Women in America.* San Francisco: Harper & Row, 1986.

Baker, Caroline. "An Exploration of Quaker Women's Writing between 1650 and 1700." *Journal of International Women's Studies* 5, no. 2 (2004): 8–20.

Betcher, Sharon V. "The Second Descent of the Spirit of Life from God: The Assumption of Jemima Wilkinson." *The Journal of Millennium Studies* (Summer 1999).

Brown, Sylvia, ed. *Women, Gender and Radical Religion in Early Modern Europe.* Leiden: Brill, 2007.

Clemmons, Theresa Mackle. "Friends and Families: A Study of the Quakers of the Earls Colne Area, 1655–1750." MA thesis, Oklahoma State University, 1980.

Eason, Andrew Mark. *Women in God's Army, Gender and Equality in God's Army.* Waterloo, ON: Wilfrid Laurier University Press, 2003.

Everson, Elisa Ann. "A Little Labour of Love: The Extraordinary Career of Dorothy Ripley, Female Evangelist in Early America." PhD diss., Georgia State University, 2007.

Gill, Gillian. *Mary Baker Eddy.* Reading, MA: Perseus Books, 1998.

Hattersley, Roy. *Blood and Fire: The Story of William and Catherine Booth and the Salvation Army.* London: Abacus, 2000.

Larbi, Ohenewaa. "The Shakers." Northampton Silk Project, Smith College, Northampton, MA, 2003. Accessed 20 September 2018, https://www.smith.edu/hsc/silk/papers/larbi.html.

Larson, Rebecca. *Daughters of Light, Quaker Women, Preaching and Prophesying in the Colonies and Abroad, 1700–1775.* Chapel Hill: University of North Carolina Press, 1999.

Moyles, R.G. "Chronological List of Corps Openings in Canada to 1900." In *The Blood and Fire in Canada: A History of the Salvation Army in the Dominion 1882–1976.* Fredericton, NB: Acadiensis Press, 1994.

Murdoch, Norman H. "The Army Mother." *Christian History* 26 (1990).

Procter-Smith, Marjorie. *Women in Shaker Community and Worship: A Feminist Analysis of the Uses of Religious Symbolism*. Lewiston, NY: Edwin Mellen Press, 1985.

"Shaker Village of Pleasant Hill," The Shaker Society. N.d.

Wergland, Glendyne R. *Sisters in the Faith—Shaker Women and Equality of the Sexes*. Boston: University of Massachusetts Press, 2011.

Wisbey, Herbert A. *Pioneer Prophetess: Jemima Wilkinson the Publick Universal Friend*. Ithaca, NY: Cornell University Press, 1964.

Woody, Thomas. *Early Quaker Education in Pennsylvania*. New York: Teachers College, Columbia University, 1920.

NOTES

1 Collins, *Memoirs*, 18. The average age for women in seventeenth-century England was 35 to 40, whereas the average age for Quakers in the Essex area was just over 55: Clemmons, "Friends and Families," 52.

2 Larson, *Daughters of Light, Quaker Women*, 26.

3 Corfield, "Elizabeth Heyrick: Radical Quaker," 41ff.

4 Larson, *Daughter of Light, Quaker Women*, 17f.

5 Fell, "Women's Speaking Justified."

6 Fell, "A Seventeenth-Century Quaker Women's Declaration," as quoted in *Witnesses for Change*, ed. Brown and Stuard, 15; Larson, *Daughter of Light, Quaker Women*, 16f.

7 "An abstract of the Life of Margaret Fell," Gwynedd Friends Meeting Historical Notes, based on Crosfield, *Margaret Fox of Swarthmoor Hall*.

8 Clemmons, "Friends and Families," 41f.

9 Manners, *Elizabeth Hooton, First Quaker Woman Preacher*, 1, 6.

10 Hooton, "In Pursuit of the King," 111.

11 Humphrey Norton as quoted in Levenduski, *Peculiar Power*, 19.

12 "An Order of the Council at Boston, for burning the Books brought by Mary Fisher and Anne Austin, and for keeping them closed Prisoners.... At a Council held at Boston the 11th of July 1656," from *An Abstract of the Sufferings of the People Called Quakers, For the Testimony of a Good Conscience, from the Time of Their being first distinguished by the NAME Taken from Original Records, and other Authentick Accounts*.

13 Bacon, *Mothers of Feminism*, 25.

14 Larson, *Daughters of Light, Quaker Women*, 28. The Toleration Act passed in 1689, benefiting the Quakers and other sects.

15 Biddle, *The Trumpet of the Lord Sounded Forth unto These Three Nations*; Clemmons, "Friends and Families," 45.

16 Larson, *Daughters of Light, Quaker Women*, 320–33.

17 Dunn, "Latest Light on Women of Light," 73; Larson, *Daughters of Light, Quaker Women*, 63; Bacon, *Mothers of Feminism*, 36, 59.

18 Larson, *Daughters of Light, Quaker Women*, 104.

19 Larson, *Daughters of Light, Quaker Women*, 104.

20 Larson, *Daughters of Light, Quaker Women*, 105f; Bacon, *Mothers of Feminism*, 37.

21 Larson, *Daughters of Light, Quaker Women*, 107f.

22 Baker, "An Exploration of Quaker Women's Writing," 11.

23 As reported in *Quaker Faith and Practice*.

24 Larson, *Daughters of Light, Quaker Women*, 114f, 175; Braithwaite, "An Account of Rachel Wilson's religious visit to Friends in America...."

25 Mack, "In a Female Voice," as quoted in *Women Preachers and Prophets*, ed. Kienzle and Walker, 250.

26 Freeman, "Visionary Women among Early Baptists," 7; Baker, "An Exploration of Quaker Women's Writing between 1650 and 1700," 14f.

27 Levenduskie, *Peculiar Power*, 26.

28 Baker, "An Exploration of Quaker Women's Writing between 1650 and 1700," 9.

29 George Keith, "The Woman Preacher of Samaria" (London: 1674), as found in Baker, "An Exploration of Quaker Women's Writing between 1650 and 1700," 14.

30 Harmon, *Encyclopedia of World Methodism*.

31 Everson, "A Little Labour of Love."

32 As quoted in Muir, *Petticoats in the Pulpit*, 140ff.

33 Mack, "In a Female Voice," as quoted in *Women Preachers and Prophets*, ed. Kienzle and Walker, 250.

34 Bacon, *Mothers of Feminism*, 50.

35 Woody, *Early Quaker Education in Pennsylvania*, 54, 71ff, 212.

36 Dorland, *The Quakers in Canada*, 280.

37 Procter-Smith, *Women in Shaker Community and Worship*, 13, 17; Tibbetts, "Women Who Were Called," 327.

38 Tibbetts, "Women Who Were Called," 67.

39 Tibbetts, "Women Who Were Called," 68.

40 Procter-Smith, *Women in Shaker Community and Worship*, 1; it appears that the Wardleys went into an alms-house where they soon died (9).

41 Procter-Smith, *Women in Shaker Community and Worship*, 19. Part of a letter to the chief elder of the Shakers in 1785.

42 Procter-Smith, *Women in Shaker Community and Worship*, 59f.

43 Bednarowski, "Outside the Mainstream."

44 Procter-Smith, *Women in Shaker Community and Worship*, 119ff; Bednarowski, "Outside the Mainstream."

45 Procter-Smith, *Women in Shaker Community and Worship*, 221.

46 Bednarowski, "Outside the Mainstream."

47 Tibbetts, "Women Who Were Called," 93.

48 Martin, "Saints, Sinners and Reformers."

49 Wilkinson, "Jemima Wilkinson."

50 Wilkinson, "Jemima Wilkinson."

51 Pritchard, *Manuscript Diary of a Journey into the Wilderness with the Public Universal Friend.*

52 Martin, "Saints, Sinners and Reformers," 3.

53 Wilkinson, "Jemima Wilkinson"; Tibbetts, "Women Who Were Called," 91.

54 Wisbey, "Recollections of Jemima Wilkinson."

55 Wilkinson, "Jemima Wilkinson."

56 Martin, "Saints, Sinners and Reformers."

57 Levterov, *The Development of the Seventh-day Adventist Understanding of Ellen G. White's Prophetic Gift, 1844–1889*, 25.

58 Hartley, "White, Ellen Gould (1827–1915)."

59 Hartley, "White, Ellen Gould (1827–1915)"; White, "Proper Education," 7.

60 Ramik, *The Ramik Report Memorandum of Law Literary Property Rights 1790–1915.*

61 Hartley, "White, Ellen Gould (1827–1915)."

62 White, *Testimonies*, vol. 1, 497.

63 Hodder, "Visions or Partial-Complex Seizures?" 35; Couperus, "The Significance of Ellen White's Head Injury," 31; Numbers, *Prophetess of Health.*

64 Murdoch, "The Army Mother."

65 "Catherine Booth"; Eason, *Women in God's Army*, 40, 55; Pederson, *The Lost Apostle*, 126.

66 Bell, "Allowed Irregularities"; Laird, *Ordained Women in the Church of the Nazarene*, 36.

67 Catherine Booth as quoted in Diniejko, "Catherine Mumford Booth."

68 "Catherine Booth."

69 Walker, "A Chaste and Fervid Eloquence," 294.

70 Higginbotham, "Respectable Sinners," 217ff.

71 Eason, *Women in God's Army*, 52; "Women in the Pentecostal Movement," Fuller Studio.

72 Eason, *Women in God's Army*, 147; Higginbotham, "Respectable Sinners," 216ff.

73 Moyles, "Chronological List of Corps Openings in Canada to 1900," 272ff.

74 Walker, "A Chaste and Fervid Eloquence," 297.

75 Eason, *Women in God's Army*, 2.

76 Hattersley, *Blood and Fire*, 340f.

77 Twain, *Christian Science*, 102f.

78 Baker Eddy, *Science and Health*, 189f.

79 Baker Eddy, *Retrospection and Introspection*.

80 Baker Eddy, *Retrospection and Introspection*, 24f.

81 Gill, *Mary Baker Eddy*, 323.

82 Tibbetts, "Women Who Were Called," 158.

83 Tibbetts, "Women Who Were Called," 269, 382.

84 Tibbetts, "Women Who Were Called," 145.

85 Gill, *Mary Baker Eddy*, 101. From an article in *Harper's Weekly*, 1901.

86 Gill, *Mary Baker Eddy*, 94ff.

87 Gill, *Mary Baker Eddy*, 108ff.

88 Gill, *Mary Baker Eddy*, 110.

89 Bednarowski, "Outside the Mainstream," 218.

Chapter 13

OTHER WOMEN WHO FOUNDED CHURCHES, PART II

THE CHURCH OF THE NAZARENE

Mary Lee Wasson Cagle's (1864–1955) family opposed her desire to preach, but eventually she became a well-known Holiness preacher and the co-founder of the Church of the Nazarene.

Born in Alabama to farmers, Mary Lee was brought up a Methodist. At first she thought she would become a missionary, the only church occupation generally open to women, and then she felt called to preach, but her family was opposed to both of her dreams in spite of the fact that her father had been a member of the Cumberland Presbyterians, who were sympathetic to women in ministry, ordaining Louisa Woosley (1862–1952) in 1889. Mary Lee's mother stated that she would rather see her daughter dead than a foreign missionary. A brother-in-law declared that if she became a preacher, his children would never again acknowledge her as their aunt. So she became a school teacher, noting that her "outward life was consistent and I kept up the form of religion but without power."[1]

She married a traveling minister in the Methodist Episcopal Church, Robert Lee Harris, who left that denomination in 1894 and founded a new church, the New Testament Church of Christ (NTCC). When the NTCC composed its "Government and Doctrines" statement in 1903, a line simply said, "We believe that women have the same right to preach the gospel as men have."[2]

Historian Stan Ingersol believes that Mary Lee hoped that she would find peace by supporting her husband's ministry. Unfortunately he took ill, propped up in his ministry at the end by two women preachers, Susie Sherman (?–1895) and Emma Woodcock (?–1902), who shared the services. Other sources note that the preacher Grace George helped, too. Sherman had been preaching to the poor on the streets of St. Louis, and both Sherman and Woodcock had been members of the Vanguard Mission and the American Pentecost Bands, which were made up of women, similar to The Salvation Army's Hallelujah Lasses. Mary Lee's husband died a few months later, leaving Mary Lee, a new congregation, and a church book of discipline.[3]

It was some time, however, before Mary Lee became confident and determined enough to carry on her husband's ministry. It was not until a **camp meeting** that she completely overcame her timidity, experiencing "a full deliverance" from the "man-fearing" spirit. "What a struggle I had," she wrote. "On my face before God, with tears, I would plead to be released. I knew to go out in this country as a woman preacher would mean to face bitter opposition, prejudice, slanderous tongues, my name cast out as evil, my motives misconstrued and to be looked upon with suspicion." She had even bargained with God—that if he would heal her husband, she would go out and preach—but she realized the absurdity of trying to coerce the divinity.[4]

Mary Lee was also aware of her educational shortcomings and her lack of knowledge of parts of her country outside Alabama. Even though it was embarrassing to her family, with two other women, Donie Dee Adams Mitchum (1860–1952) and Elliott J. Doboe Sheeks (1817–1946) (known as E.J., but whom Mary Lee was wont to call "My dear old Sheeksie), and Donie's husband, Mary Lee organized new churches in Tennessee, Arkansas, and Texas. Donie generally "pastored" the established churches while the others organized or "planted" new churches. Elliott's husband had bought her tents where she could hold **revival** meetings. Both Mary Lee and Elliott were ordained in 1899.

Mary Lee also worked later with the music evangelist and lay preacher, widow Fanny McDowell Hunter (c.1860–1935), and other women.[5] Fanny was the granddaughter of a Methodist circuit rider, and had been converted when she was 12. At 19, she married W.W. Hunter, but he died after a few years, leaving Fanny with a daughter and a stepson. She kept preaching and by 1903, she, too, had been ordained. Fanny and Mary Lee preached in

Arkansas at a revival and to prison inmates, Fanny explaining to Mary Lee "the perils of an unmarried woman in gospel ministry."6

In 1900, Mary Lee married a cowhand who became a preacher under her direction, and together they conducted many revivals. Mary Lee organized at least 28 congregations on her own. Four years later, she brought her church into union with the Independent Holiness Church and, in 1908, with several Holiness denominations, formed the Church of the Nazarene, now the largest Wesleyan-Holiness denomination in the world.

Wearing plain dress and eschewing anything "worldly," Mary Lee stopped putting on make-up and curling her hair. Like the other women preachers, she avoided anything that might make it seem as if she didn't put God first in her life. Very rigid theologically at first, as she became more comfortable in her preaching, she also became more flexible in her theology.7

Known as "the Mother of Holiness in the West," Mary Lee continued her ministry for about 40 years, even preaching on her 90th birthday. Mostly she led revivals in the summer and remained in the pastorate in the winter. Her female colleagues were important: they banded together in a sisterhood, supporting one another. They wrote extensively, including a book called *Women Preachers*. While half of that work was an apologetic for women preachers written by such noted people as Phoebe Palmer and Catherine Booth, the rest of the book consisted of nine "**call**" narratives written by Mary Lee, Donie, Elliott, and four other women, as well as two men who were strong supporters of the women. The book was dedicated to "my beloved sisters, who are anointed by the Holy Spirit and commissioned, like Mary of old, to tell the sorrowing of the risen Lord, and who as they go on their blessed mission for the Master, often meet the opposition and scorn of their opponents."8

In the Holiness Church of Christ in 1908, 23 of the denomination's 156 ordained clergy were women. When the church merged with the Church of the Nazarene that year, women made up 17 per cent of the ordained ministry and 21 per cent of licensed ministers. A photograph of women preachers in the Church of the Nazarene at the Seventh General Assembly in 1928 shows about 90. As one of the Nazarene ministers allegedly said, "some of our best men are women"—a phrase others had used earlier!

While Mary Lee Cagle was the most famous of the female Nazarene pastors, there were many others who made their mark, such as Agnes White Diffee (c.1889–1970), the pastor of Little Rock First Church of the Nazarene, which grew to be the largest Nazarene congregation in the United States while she shepherded it. Because of her radio broadcasts, she was so well known that

FIGURE 13.1 Nazarene women preachers photographed at the Church of the Nazarene General Assembly in Columbus, Ohio, June 1928. Photo: Courtesy of the Church of the Nazarene Archives.

Arkansans referred to the Nazarenes as "Sister Diffee's Church." Charlotte Graham from Barbados ministered in Trinidad for most of her career.

Lucía Carmen García de Costa (1903–84) was the primary Nazarene Church "planter" in Argentina. She began more than a third of the Nazarene congregations there—around 30—during her 60 years as a minister in that country. Not only was she a pastor, but she translated Wesleyan material into Spanish, earned a PhD from the University of Buenos Aires, edited and published a newsletter, and taught in the Nazarene Bible School there.[9]

Mary Lee Cagle founded at least 18 new congregations and assisted with dozens of others. She was involved in an enormous amount of work; for example, in 1927, she reported that she had held 13 revival meetings, preached 175 times and traveled about 10,000 miles by car as well as other trips by train. She became so tired that she had to take three weeks off the next year, and during those weeks, preached only twice.

Mary Lee preached in black churches against the wishes of her family, who had eventually become supportive of her ministry; she worked with prostitutes and unwed mothers and in the slums. She often held meetings in what she called "the little neglected places." She was subject to vicious rumors. She said that if one hundredth of what was said about her was true, she would have been in the penitentiary instead of the pulpit. In Texas, it was said that she had robbed the United States mail, run a house of ill repute, and given away her four children—even though she never had any.

One of Mary Lee's colleagues, Mary Cole (1853–?), was said to be one of the James Boys, the famous outlaws, disguised as a woman. One story about Mary Cole tells of a camp meeting, where all the preachers sat on the platform and whoever wanted to preach would stand up and walk to the pulpit. Cole preached that day because she literally raced across the platform, beating a male pastor to the pulpit. She was not normally aggressive; on the contrary, she had responded to what she believed was God's call to preach with the reply that she was not talented and had "a stammering tongue."[10]

Mary Lee was an early proponent of using inclusive language. She refused to complete a standard clergy form because it consistently used male pronouns in reference to clergy. But it was not until 1975 that her church adopted an inclusive language policy. The male pronouns in the form that Mary Lee found so offensive have since been removed.[11]

Deaconesses were an integral part of the Church of the Nazarene from the beginning. Elders were ordained, but deaconesses were consecrated and worked under the supervision of a pastor. Nellie Barrett who engaged in a ministry to prisoners noted that "no service is too small for a deaconess to do." Mrs. M.E. Gasaway reported in March 1919 that in Plantersville, Mississippi where she worked, that year, she had already "prayed in 125 homes, held three meetings, helped forty souls get saved … held two street meetings." But by the mid-1920s, the deaconess program was declining. In 1914, there was a deaconess in almost every congregation. Twenty years later there was a deaconess for every six churches.[12]

In an analysis of pastors and evangelists in the Nazarene Church, Richard Houseal shows how women in those professions declined over the years both in numbers and as a percentage of the total. In 1908, female pastors made up 8.5 per cent of the pastors and 43.4 per cent of evangelists. By 1925, women pastors were 12.2 per cent of the total. But by 1970, women pastors consisted of only 2.6 per cent of all the pastors in the denomination. Female evangelists did not fare much better. While they peaked in 1955, by 1985, women made up only 6.14 per cent of all evangelists, 19 women out of 299. In an effort to find out why women were less accepted than at the beginning of the denomination, Houseal surveyed the denomination's members in 1995 and found that roughly the same number of men and women stated in various degrees that they would be happy with a female pastor, but perhaps not surprisingly, members in the larger pastorates were less accepting of females in the pulpit than they were in the country or smaller churches. It appears that the women's movement of the late twentieth century had the effect of creating less rather than more acceptance of women in ecclesiastical roles in this denomination.[13]

Today, the Church of the Nazarene has about 2,500,000 members world-wide in 162 "world areas," representing more than 30,000 churches, with more than 500,000 members in the United States. In Brazil, the church has an average Sunday worship attendance of more than 88 per cent of its more than 8,000 members. The church operates 52 educational institutions in 35 countries, with its largest university in Korea. Many of the church's pastors are still women: in 2010, the Bangladesh District ordained 30 women out of 193 men and women. One woman, Dr. Nina Gunter (1940–?), was elected General Superintendent in 2005, the highest church office.

THE FOURSQUARE GOSPEL CHURCH

Young Aimee Elizabeth Kennedy (1890–1944) was being teased at school, the only "Salvationist" there. So she made a drum from a round wooden cheese box, used a ruler for a drumstick, and with a "Blood and Fire" banner created from a red tablecloth, led the other young children in a march around the room, playing "Army." They all thought that was great fun and decided that Aimee was okay.

Aimee's mother was a Junior Sergeant-Major in The Salvation Army, which meant looking after the Sunday School. Often she'd put Aimee on the handlebars of her bicycle and pedal the five miles over hills and dusty roads to work. At home, Aimee played Salvation Army herself, lining up chairs for imaginary children, and conducting her own worship services. "Now the Sergeant-Major will sing a solo," or "Now, the Sergeant-Major will lead in prayer," she would tell her fantasy friends. At five years old, she could recite whole chapters of the Old and New Testaments. Her mother believed that Aimee was the reincarnation of The Salvation Army's co-founder, Catherine Booth, and would become a great evangelist.[14]

When Aimee was 17, one day praying alone in her room, she believed that she heard the Lord speak the words from Jeremiah 1:4–9 very clearly to her: "Before I formed thee … I sanctified thee and I ordained thee a prophet unto the nations. Then said I, Ah! Lord God! Behold I cannot speak; for I am a child. But the Lord said unto me, Say not, I am a child; for thou shalt go to all that I shall send thee and whatsoever I command thee thou shalt speak."[15] Aimee was determined to obey.

Fortuitously, not long after, at a revival meeting led by an Irish Pentecostal missionary, Robert Semple, she and Robert fell in love, and after a short courtship they were married in 1908; both were ordained the next year and almost immediately set off to China as missionaries. There, Robert died from malaria, leaving Aimee a 19-year-old widow with a small baby. Penniless and distraught, Aimee managed to get home, and in 1912, married an accountant, Harold Stewart McPherson. She had a second child. Aimee felt called to participate in revival meetings but Harold wanted a more stable life. They divorced and Aimee married a third time—an actor and musician—but this marriage was short lived, too.

In her autobiography, *This Is That*, Aimee tells the story of her broken foot and how it was healed in a service of prayer. She had tripped running down the stairs, and according to the doctor she had torn and severed four of the ligaments that move the toes so that her foot was turned around and backward. Two doctors straightened her foot, but told her that the ligaments would never heal. She would always limp. The doctors put on a plaster cast, but almost immediately, Aimee felt that her foot had been cured through prayer at a healing service with friends. "Many of the on-lookers who knew not the healing power, doubted that the ankle had ever been broken.... [M]any of the public [who] knew it was broken would not believe it was healed," she wrote. The experience, however, was central to the healing services she herself would later conduct as part of her Pentecostal ministry.

Aimee became one of the best-known women preachers in the **Pentecostal** movement, leading revival services throughout the United States and even into Australia. Her services became so popular that people lined up hours ahead of time to try to get a seat. At first she used tents, then auditoriums. Sometimes hundreds were turned away, unable to get in because the crowds were so great. "One moment I am all a-weeping for the multitudes shut outside the crowded doors, and for the thousands we could never reach, though we toiled day and night," Aimee wrote. "And the next, my face is smiling, mine eyes are made to shine a-through the tears, in remembrance of the thousands who went away skipping, with singing in their hearts."[16]

In St. Louis, Missouri, there was standing room only in the Coliseum that seated up to 16,000, while hundreds remained outside. The president of the Board of Trustees of Texas Presbyterian University wrote of that time: "For three weeks this city of St. Louis has been in the grip of probably the most remarkable series of religious meetings in the history of the city."[17]

Thirty thousand who crowded into a facility set up in Balboa Park in San Diego belted out a rousing chorus at the beginning of a revival there:

It's the old time religion,
And it's good enough for me,
It was good for our fathers,
It was good for our mothers,
It is good for San Diego,
And it's good enough for me.[18]

Male ministers from various denominations would sit together on platforms to help with the services—Methodist, Baptist, Episcopal, Evangelical, Presbyterian, Salvation Army, Pentecostal, and Nazarene. The sick and disabled were brought in on stretchers and in wheelchairs; they left thousands of testimonials of healing both of the mind and of the body. Dozens of volunteers from the surrounding churches acted as guides and ushers. "Awake! Thou that sleepest, arise from the dead! The Lord still lives today," Aimee preached. "His power has never abated.... The things He did in Bible days, He still lives to do today."[19]

Often, Aimee and her workers had no food or not enough money to pay to rent a facility in a city where they had just arrived. Then they'd pray and miraculously, the correct amount of money or supplies would arrive—neither more nor less. In her first foray into Florida, she and her workers had no money and no food the night before her meetings. "Oh Lord," she prayed, "if you want us to fast and pray until the meeting opens tomorrow—Amen. But if you want me to have something to set before these people [working with her], please supply the food." And then almost immediately, she wrote, a wagon driven by a supporter appeared with a "box full of tins of corn, peas, salmon, a box of crackers, rolled oats, sugar, condensed milk."[20]

Aimee worked day after day and night after night, traveling miles between cities where she believed God wanted her to go, driving her 1912 Packard touring car covered with religious slogans. She was often exhausted. "My strength has been holding out in a remarkable way, through this strenuous winter," she wrote one year in the middle of winter storms during a series of revival tent meetings, but at present I am very weak in body.... All around are thousands of hungry souls. The harvest is great, the laborers few. I am alone, playing [the piano], leading, singing, preaching and praying at the altar ... it is only the power of God that can sustain me.... [T]he Lord helped me while left alone ... to drive stakes, the heavy guy ropes, and battle to keep the tent up, amidst wind and rain, sometimes preaching all day and sitting up the greater portion of the night to watch the tents and keep driving the stakes in with the big sledge hammer, as fast as the wind pulled them out.[21]

Eventually Aimee achieved her dream of finding a permanent facility: the Angelus Temple in Los Angeles opened 1 January 1923, with hundreds of colorfully clad Roma in the audience; they had named her their queen. With a dome rising 125 feet from the main floor, the church was designed to seat 5,300 people. The construction had cost over $250,000 at the time, the equivalent of well over US$3,500,000 today, even with donations of time and materials from her followers. Within the first seven years, the Temple received 40 million visitors. A commissary and dining hall were attached to the building. Over one 11-month period during the Great Depression, the commissary gave out free groceries to more than 40,000 people. Aimee never forgot her childhood years when The Salvation Army provided soup kitchens, free clinics, and other relief, and this was always part of her ministry.[22]

One of the great stained glass windows in the Temple contains an anachronism. In the depiction of the second coming, Aimee is standing along with the biblical apostles, the only woman in the scene, and the only non-biblical figure.[23]

Aimee's church eventually evolved into its own denomination, The International Church of the Foursquare Gospel. She wrote that the four phases of the Foursquare Gospel are Jesus Christ the Savior; Jesus Christ the Baptizer with the Holy Spirit; Jesus Christ the Great Physician; and Jesus Christ the Coming King.

She began broadcasting by radio, and became the first woman to preach a sermon over the "wireless telephone." When airplanes were in their infancy, she soared above San Diego, scattering 15,000 pamphlets; she used all means possible to get her message across. As the writer Joel Tibbetts notes, Aimee and all the women who founded churches were "products of their environment," but also "transcended their environment," illustrating what a woman could do in the face of cultural prejudices and taboos. Aimee became more than a household name; she was a folk hero and a civic institution.[24]

While there is no evidence that Aimee was hampered because of her gender, she is quoted in *The New York Times* as being aware of gender "imbalance." She stated that she had learned from experience that "the male has no monopoly on intelligence. In fact, I have been led to believe at times that stupidity is an outstanding male characteristic. I do not mean that men are stupid or even that men are more stupid than women, but I do maintain that they are no more intelligent."[25]

While Aimee's career did not seem to be obstructed because she was a woman, Elaine Lawless, who studied the Pentecostal religion, claims that the Pentecostal folk community is a male hierarchy. According to her, "God [is] at the top, followed by men, followed by women, followed by children." Even though women participate freely and openly in parts of the religious services, she notes, "the Pentecostal religious service is male dominated."[26]

In many ways, life was not always rosy for Aimee. For years, her mother was her business manager and helped look after the children. Eventually she and her mother became estranged and never re-established a close relationship. Aimee also ended up alienated from her daughter Roberta, whom she charged with refusing to help out at Angelus Temple, and from her associate minister, a well-known evangelist, Rheba Crawford (1899–1966), who sued Aimee for libel for over $1,000,000. Male colleagues were not always kind; Robert Shuler (1926–2015) often wrote critical articles about her:

> I am going to name a lady with a record long and shady,
> One who in this world has caused a lot of strife!
> Now I know you're laughing hearty—but I do not mean that party!
> For the one I have in mind is the devil's wife![27]

Toward the end of her life, a news service counted 45 lawsuits that had been brought against Aimee within a few years, all demanding money; two-thirds of these were settled out of court. Of all her close friends, Aimee's son alone remained faithful. Aimee died in a hotel room when she was not quite 54, having taken too many barbiturates; the coroner ruled it accidental.[28]

Not long before her death, Aimee disappeared for a few weeks, then resurfaced, claiming that she had been kidnapped from a beach in California. It was suggested, however, that she and a married engineer at a Christian radio station had gone off together for a holiday. While many people considered this scandalous, her followers took it in their stride, and she became even more popular.

On Aimee's death in 1944, 45,000 people waited in line to file past her body, which lay in state at the Angelus Temple. People sent $50,000 worth of flowers; 11 trucks were needed to transport them to the cemetery. Today the Foursquare Gospel Church claims a membership of almost eight million worldwide in nearly 30,000 churches.[29]

Aimee was not the only woman to found a Pentecostal church, although she may have been the most famous.

In 1924, Ida B. Bell Robinson (1891–1946) received a number of visions, believing that God wanted her to found a church that would "loose the women." While fasting and praying in a church for 10 days, she heard a voice: "Come out to Mount Sinai." She immediately obtained a charter for a new church, the Mount Sinai Holy Church of America in Philadelphia. She appointed nine officials, six of them women, and she herself was consecrated bishop in 1925. When she died the denomination consisted of 84 churches, more than 160 ordained clergy of whom 125 were women, a school in Philadelphia, mission work in Cuba and Guyana, and a farm and retreat in South Jersey for church members.

Maria Buelah Woodworth-Etter (1844–1924), another well-known Pentecostal preacher, once argued, "It is high time for women to let their lights shine; to bring out their talents that have been hidden away rusting, and use them for the glory of God."[30] Born in Ohio, Maria became an itinerant minister for the Holiness movement when she was 35 with spectacular success. She and her first husband ran a "traveling Holiness revival," but her husband's heart wasn't in it and they divorced when Maria was 47. Maria also conducted a healing ministry, but she was charged with hypnotizing people. On 1 September 1890, the *Boston Daily Globe* was headlined: "Steals Men's Wits Away. Male and Female Bipeds in Frenzied Prayer. Evangelist Charged with Hypnotizing her Hearers." During some of her meetings, young men threw rocks and eggs and dumped buckets of water on stage.[31]

Maria started several churches and appointed ministers. In 1918, she founded what is today the Assemblies of God, which has had up to 19 per cent female ministers. Maria had been ordained in the Indiana Church of God, but that was revoked after male elders protested, calling her a "regular Jezebel," meaning a "shameless woman" after an Old Testament princess.[32]

Mary Magdalena Lewis Tate (1871–1930) founded the Church of the Living God, the Pillar and Ground of the Truth in 1903, with headquarters in Nashville, Tennessee. She ordained ministers and presided as bishop as the denomination expanded into 20 states. During the church's first 100 years, several women served as evangelists, ministers, and bishops.

Florence Crawford (1872–1936) was working at the Azusa Street Church in the correspondence office when the famous Pentecostal revival took place there. She became a minister and published a church paper, *The Apostolic Faith*. Healed of spinal meningitis through prayer as an adult, Florence went on to found her own church in Portland, Oregon, in 1906: the Apostolic Faith Mission. The Azusa Street phenomenon of glossolalia, or **speaking in tongues**, that took place in her church that year was widely known. The *Los Angeles Evening News* published a front-page story about it, ridiculing the mission for violating Paul's injunction to keep women silent in church.[33]

Historian Cheryl Sanders notes that the ordination of women was accepted virtually throughout the Holiness movement and Pentecostalism in the United States. In 1996, women in five Wesleyan-Holiness denominations—Church of God (Anderson, Indiana), Church of the Nazarene, Free Methodist Church, The Salvation Army, and the Wesleyan Church—constituted 25 per cent of the clergy, whereas women constituted only 7 per cent of the clergy in 39 other denominations that ordained women. However, various churches had restrictions. For example, even though the Assemblies of God ordained women to preach from 1922 on, it did not permit them to serve as senior pastors except in an emergency, and the Church of God (Cleveland) defeated a motion in 2000 to allow women to serve as bishops. Over the course of the twentieth century, women's leadership dramatically declined in both Pentecostal and Holiness churches. Sanders quotes a study that shows that the proportion of women clergy in the Church of the Nazarene declined from 20 per cent of all clergy in 1908 to 1 per cent in the late 1990s; in the Church of God (Anderson, Indiana), it went from 32 per cent in 1925 to 15 per cent in the late 1990s.[34] As churches lost their first flush of enthusiasm and became more orderly and regimented, the acceptance of women as leaders dropped substantially. As the General Overseer of the Church of God, A.J. Tomlinson wrote, "let the good sisters feel at perfect liberty to preach the gospel, pray for the sick or well, testify, exhort etc., but humbly hold themselves aloof from taking charge of the governmental affairs." Women were generally not wanted by male church hierarchies as pastors of local churches, either.[35]

Pentecostalism is an American-born phenomenon from around the turn of the twentieth century, but it goes back to the revivals and tent meetings of the first heady days of the early Methodist churches. In 1900, a group of theological students in Topeka, Kansas, sought to replicate the tongue-speaking or glossolalia that occurred at Pentecost in the biblical Upper Room. They were successful and their Pentecostal message spread to the surrounding countryside.

Others claim that the 1906 revival at the black Methodist Azusa Church in Los Angeles was the origin of modern Pentecostalism, where Jennie Evans Moore (1874–1936) was the first woman to speak in tongues and is supposed to have then played "In the Spirit" on the piano without any training. Others look to the glossalalia that happened in Topeka, Kansas, in 1901, where Agnes Ozman (1870–1937) was the first to speak in tongues, or another similar happening in Cherokee County in North Carolina in 1896, as the beginning of the Pentecostal Church.[36]

Speaking in tongues was the outward evidence that one had received the Holy Ghost or Holy Spirit, and Pentecostal preachers preached what they called the "full gospel," a combination of biblical teachings with a renewed emphasis on the baptism of the Holy Spirit and healing "miracles." For those who were touched, the experience was dramatic and life-changing.[37]

Pentecostalism is the fastest growing family of churches in Christianity today, increasing membership at the rate of about 35,000 a day, or 13 million a year. There are around half a billion adherents in about 11,000 denominations around the world. This brand of Christianity is especially strong in Latin America. It has been calculated that at the turn of the twenty-first century, more than 30 per cent of the total population of Latin America called themselves Pentecostals. In Brazil, Pentecostals number 43 million and gain about 600,000 adherents a year; in some urban centers, Pentecostal places of worship can outnumber Catholic ones by seven to one. Two Pentecostal churches in Buenos Aires attract together 150,000 worshippers each week. Thirty-eight per cent of Guatemalans are Pentecostal, as have been two of their presidents since the mid-1980s. In Quetzaltenango, Guatemala, a new 2,000-member Pentecostal Church originated from a women's prayer circle.

In a study of Pentecostalism and women in Latin America, Carol Ann Drogus reports that Pentecostal communities offer a sense of belonging: they teach life skills and basic management to women, primarily to run their churches, but these skills can be applied to other areas of life as well. In contrast to Elaine Lawless's assessment, Drogus reports that the churches also promote women to positions of responsibility; women are often called to teach and preach with authority equal to men. Fundamentalist groups often place a low priority on education, allowing more women to become leaders than might otherwise be the case.[38]

The largest Pentecostal church, however, is in Korea: the Yoido Full Gospel Church founded in 1958, where 240,000 parishioners attend weekly. It was a female missionary, Mary C. Rumsey (c.1885–?), or *Om Seh* in Korean, who took Pentecostalism to Korea in 1928, but she was forced out of the country by the Japanese around 1938.

Born in New York State, Rumsey, a nurse and Methodist "chanter,"[39] heard a voice at a revival meeting in Los Angeles: "Go to Korea." She studied at the Rochester Bible School in New York, which had been founded in 1906 by missionary, minister, and faith healer Elisabeth Baker (1849–1915), and four sisters. Then, financed by a wealthy Methodist, Rumsey went to Korea as a missionary, becoming loosely affiliated with the Pentecostal American Assemblies of God. Rumsey, two single women from Australia, and Mildred M. Bassey from England were criticized for working independently as missionaries in Korea, instead of in unison. But by 1938 when they were forced to leave the country, there were six Pentecostal congregations with 173 members.

THE MITA CONGREGATION

The Pentecostal preacher Juanita Garcia Peraza (1897–1970) and 11 other Puerto Ricans left the Roman Catholic Church in 1940 to found their own church in Arecibo, later moving to Hato Rey, a suburb of San Juan. Juanita became known as *la diosa Mita* (goddess Mita). The movement spread rapidly, especially among the poor, not only in Puerto Rico, but into the Dominican Republic and elsewhere.

Juanita had been born into a wealthy family who had immigrated from the Canary Islands. During a severe illness, she promised that if she were cured, she would always serve God. She became a leader in the Catholic Church and preached the gospel, but for this was told she had to leave, although another source claims that it was the Pentecostal Church from which she was expelled.[40] She claimed that the Holy Spirit gave her the new name of Mita; she became the body or living incarnation of the Spirit. She believed that the Holy Spirit spoke to her: "My servant, Lend me your body. I need you to do great work. Those who hear you hear me; those who join you, join me." A star descended from the sky in a circular motion and struck her on the forehead, "confirming her ministry."[41]

Mita's followers gave all their money and possessions to her; she invested the money to benefit everyone. Soon the movement owned all sorts of businesses—such as laundries, apartment buildings, bakeries, carpentry shops—which in turn employed their own people. The workers' salaries were added to their investments. Mita established a credit union and Bible schools. Talented musically, she wrote several compositions and organized a marching band, the largest in the country, 150 young musicians who received free lessons. The Church still has a particularly strong ministry of music, with 35 members in a Harp Group, 75 members in a String Group, and a 35-member choir—all free to members, and comprised mostly of talented youth. There is also an unarmed volunteer Safety Corps with its own stations and a patrol car.

After Mita died, her adopted son, Aarón, born Teóphyllo Vargas Sein (b. 1921), took over and the Holy Spirit now speaks through him. He had already set up an apostolic college under his mother's guidance. Recently the female social worker, Rosinin Rodriquez Pérez (b. 1937), was added to the staff as vice-president, responsible for establishing a medical center, an Office for Counseling and Social Work, and many other facilities for members, especially seniors.

The Mita Church bases its beliefs on the Bible, attempting to return to the early simplicity of the first apostles. Its red, white, and blue flag symbolizes love, freedom, and unity. The women wear white suggesting purity and cleanliness. Preachers and deacons, both male and female, receive no salary and the Church accepts no money from beyond its members or its businesses.

The Mita Church has now expanded into the United States, Canada, Ecuador, Panama, Mexico, Columbia, Venezuela, Costa Rica, El Salvador, Curaçao, and Spain in addition to the Dominican Republic with hundreds of thousands of members in more than 300 congregations worldwide. In 2015, on the seventy-fifth anniversary of the first congregation, Hon. Alan Grayson of Florida recognized the Church in the United States House of Representatives with a congratulatory speech.[42]

THE ST. JOHN'S APOSTOLIC FAITH MISSION

In 2006, the St. John's Apostolic Faith Mission of South Africa celebrated a century since the church's founder Ma Christinah Mokotuli Nku (1894–1988) received her first vision. At Evanton in Sebokeng, east of Johannesburg,

where she built her church, there were three brass bands, choral singing by
seven choirs, and several speeches to celebrate the day.

"Alleluia," they sang:

> We have seen peace by mother Nku.
> She was given to us by the Almighty
> To gather all lost sheep.
> Mother Christinah Mokotuli Nku,
> The daughter of Boilbe,
> An amazing person.
> She brought salvation to the world.
> She received instructions from above.
> She healed the sick through prayers.
> People got life;
> The insane recovered;
> They sing alleluia.[43]

Prophet, healer, and church initiator, Christinah had been brought up in
the Dutch Reformed Church. Until she was 10 years old, she attended a
Methodist missionary school where she learned to read and write. She lived
with her older sister, helping to look after the children there. However,
her brother-in-law would whip her for spending so much time reading
the Bible, so she would sneak off to the mountains where she could hide
and read. Then when she was 12½ years old, she believed that God spoke
to her in visions.

She married Lazarus Nku and together they had three sons and five daughters. She began her ministry working in the slums of Johannesburg and crowds
made their way every day to her two-room dwelling for prayer at 5:00 and 9:00
a.m. and 3:00 and 7:00 p.m. Hundreds of persons reported being healed.[44]

In 1918, when she was working in a field, a burning coal "from heaven"
fell right in front of her and, in a third vision, she claims she heard a voice
announce that she was never to touch alcohol or work on Sunday. In 1924,
a voice in another vision told her to take bricks and build a church for God,
a church with 12 doors, at a specific place on a farm set aside for housing in
the west. It became one of the largest indigenous churches in South Africa.
In 1932, she was instructed—again in a vision—to wear a blue and white
belt and have her own services with designated church members at certain

times of the day. Blue and white became the colors for the uniforms of her church. Altogether she had a series of nine visions.

Her church services resembled those in other Pentecostal churches: scripture readings, hymns, preaching, and offerings were all part of the liturgy. People were encouraged to talk directly to God, and they knelt and loudly uttered their own prayers.

As her church grew, Christinah built schools for children, and began programs for youth and adults. Historian Linda Thomas wrote: "Nku was a pioneer, one of the few who initiated independent African churches, she also followed a stream of Africans who grew tired of being dominated by white Protestant Christianity and separated from mission churches to create new religious cosmotologies that blended Christian symbols and practices into well-established pre-colonial religious systems."[45]

An observer, historian Bengt Sundkler (1909–95), wrote that Ma Nku would pray over bottles of water that people would then use to heal or be healed by drinking the water or using it to wash. He remembered that "attending one of her yearly August meetings together with some ten thousand faithful, I realized that those people would claim, possibly without exception, that they were there because of having been healed by this woman, or because they were awaiting their opportunity for her healing touch."[46]

When Ma Nku was 78 years old, the church split into two factions over leadership, and although she disapproved, she realized at that time that she could do little about it. On her death, however, the various parties gathered together to try to effect a compromise. Ma Nku had prophesied the unification of the church. At the 2006 celebrations, one of her descendants said, "We must now show that she was a real prophet by uniting the church."

THE PILLAR OF FIRE

Mollie Alma Bridwell White (1862–1946), feminist, racist, fundamentalist, anti-Catholic, and the first female bishop in the United States, founded the Pillar of Fire Church in 1917 in Denver, Colorado. Five feet, eight inches tall, Alma was described as "almost terrifying in her intense earnestness." That was a behavioral change for Alma because as a young person she was very shy, and the "man-fearing spirit," as she called it in the story of her life, initially kept her from preaching.

Born in Kentucky, Alma became well educated and intensely spiritual; she began preaching in 1893 in the Methodist Church where her husband was the minister. "The enemy kept busy in the churches," Alma reported. "The pastors said it was a woman's place to stay at home and look after husband and children." The Methodists didn't like Alma's energetic style; however, she and her husband led revivals around the west until in 1901 they founded a fundamentalist Methodist sect, which in 1917 became known as the Pillar of Fire Church. Her husband supported her preaching even if the Methodist Church didn't. At one camp meeting in 1897 where her name had been left off the list of preachers because she was a woman, her husband gave her his five-minute allotted time spot and she preached for 50 minutes. As she said in 1904, "Seventeen years before, I was wrapped in the old ecclesiastical mantle and ready to lay my life down in sacrifice on the altar of the Methodist Church, but she made no provision for me to preach the Gospel and therefore it was in the mind of God to establish a new, soul-saving institution where equal opportunities should be given to both men and women to enter the ministry."[47]

Between 1893 and 1900, Alma conducted 3,000 revival services, traveling sometimes alone, sometimes with her husband, and sometimes with her two sons. She also began and supervised five missions in Colorado and Wyoming during this time. The media called her "Cromwell in skirts."[48]

Alma's husband, Kent, wanted to head the new church; she allowed him to be head of their marriage, but the church was to be hers. Consequently they split up. By the time of her death at age 84, Alma had expanded the church to 4,000 followers, 61 churches, 7 schools, 10 periodicals, and 2 broadcasting stations. In 1937, Alma Temple was dedicated in Denver, occupying 10 lots, an impressive building of lava stone and light gray brick. Two thousand people attended the opening service.

Followers worked full-time for the new church without a salary, living together in missions; the church provided for their material needs. They had to wear uniforms and Alma rejected all fancy clothes. "Where no change of sentiment is seen in regard to the wearing of gold and worldly apparel," she said, "the genuineness of one's profession may be seriously questioned." To raise money, they sold Pillar of Fire literature, including Alma's autobiographies. By 1918, they had sold 250,000 books door to door. Alma wrote more than 35 books and edited seven magazines. She was supportive of education for her followers and established three colleges, a seminary in Denver, and Christian schools throughout the country.

Alma was also a supporter of the Ku Klux Klan, believing that they could help liberate "white Protestant women," although many years later, she distanced herself from that racist organization.[49]

Aimee Semple McPherson disliked Alma. In a 1928 issue of *Time* magazine, Aimee is reported as saying, "Worst of all, there came a rival female evangelist from New Jersey, a resolute woman with the mien of an inspired laundress—the Reverend 'Bishop' Mrs. Mollie Alma White." Alma, however, regarded Aimee as a poacher on her preserves. Of Mary Baker Eddy of the Christian Science Church, Alma wrote, "The teachings of the so-called Christian Science Church ... have drawn multitudes from the orthodox faith, and blasted their hopes of heaven!"[50]

Alma disliked Roman Catholicism because of its treatment of women. "Rome hates any movement that tends to the uplifting and enlightenment of the female sex," she wrote in her book, *The Guardians of Liberty*. "When Christ came, he placed woman by the side of her husband and sons, but Rome ... is ... opposed to equal rights for the two sexes." Alma suggested that the Pillar of Fire Church set "the example of equality for the sexes ... by breaking the shackles that have held women in their bondage for ages." She celebrated women's suffrage and supported the country's Equal Rights Amendment. Religious and political equality for the sexes were a part of her church's creed and she often preached on women's place in church and state, with sermon titles such as "Emancipation of Women," and "Women's Place in Church and State." But it is difficult to understand how she put all her cultural beliefs together.[51]

She asked:

Should not old traditions and customs be forgotten, and every effort put forth in this the dawning of a new era to place woman in her intended sphere that she may help to start society on the upward grade? Women can never be made to feel their responsibility until they share in the ministry of God's Word, and take their place in the legislative bodies of the nation.[52]

In her 1980 book, *Women in American Religion*, Janet Wilson James describes Alma as a traditionalist in her idea of woman's place. But Alma's desire for women's position in society does not seem traditionalist; she insisted that women take an equal role to men. Both Alma's writings and her own life story stress that point.

After her death, Alma's children assumed the leadership of the Pillar of Fire Church, maintaining her ongoing commitment to women clergy. As she stated in 1944:

> ... man for the most part, has unchained his bulldogs and placed them to guard the gates where perchance women might find an entrance to the pulpit or to the halls of legislation. Men have charge of the gates, own the bulldogs, and their keepers, too, and any woman who tries to catch them off their guard, rise above her present status and presses her way in, will have a difficult task.[53]

THE LUMPA CHURCH

Alice Lenshina Mulenga Lubusha (1920–78) led one of the most famous movements in Africa, the Lumpa Church in Zambia. She had been christened Alice Mulenga Lubusha as a child, but she had herself rechristened Lenshina, meaning regina or queen.

Born in Northern Rhodesia (now Zambia), Alice, an ordinary middle-aged woman, believed that she had died after a serious illness, gone to heaven, and been told by God to return to earth, begin a church for Africans only, and destroy witchcraft and sorcery. At first, she stayed in the Presbyterian Church, but when she started baptizing men and women herself, the church decided she was overextending her responsibility.

Alice preached a Christian doctrine with baptism as the only ritual. As well as attacking witchcraft and sorcery, she condemned alcohol, tobacco, and polygamy. She believed in the sanctity of marriage, and the advancement of women. In his paper on the role of women in the church in Africa, Bishop Kasomo Daniel maintains that a church enforcing monogamy would have been attractive to unmarried women and women concerned with the future of their daughters.[54]

Alice turned against Holy Communion. She became the focus of a revival at the Lubwa mission, and gradually the revival became a church. In 1958, she had a grand temple built in her home town and, in 1955, it became known as the Lumpa Church. (In the Bemba dialect, Lumpa means "better than all others.") There was a pillar in the church upon which Jesus Christ was to descend on his Second Coming.

At the height of her popularity, about 1,000 Africans a week walked to her village of Sione (Zion), attended services in a huge brick building, and handed over their charms and amulets plus a small fee to absolve themselves from the influence of witchcraft. By the late 1950s Alice's religious movement had about 150,000 members and 119 houses of worship, draining the nearby Roman Catholic and Presbyterian churches. At one time, there were almost one million members. Alice exercised total control over her male and female preachers.

The Lumpans wrote their own spirited hymns in Bemba—about 400. They healed the sick and sheltered them in the church. Soon the church became wealthy; it had a chain of rural shops and a fleet of trucks and cars and the members were engaged in various building and agricultural projects.

By 1958, Alice was beginning to reject all earthly authority, refusing to register her church and pay taxes. The Lumpa members formed their own fortified villages, threatening the traditional authority of the chiefs because they refused to ask permission to erect homes. They set up their own law courts; they kept their children from attending government schools.

It should not be surprising that the church was considered a threat by the colonial northern Rhodesia government. The United National Independence Party (UNIP) started to compete for members. In July 1964, a 10-day gun battle broke out, killing between 1,000 and 2,000 people, including those wounded who died on their way to safety, mostly Lumpa congregants. It is said that the Lumpa were armed with spears, axes, and bows and arrows, against self-loading automatic rifles.[55] Many Lumpa members fled to the Congo near Mokambo where several thousand of them lived for many years. Alice surrendered to police that August; she and her husband were jailed. Her temple was destroyed, although the Lumpa Church continues today under various names, such as the New Jerusalem Church. The government threatened imprisonment for up to seven years for anyone assisting in any branch of the Lumpa Church.[56]

After Alice's death during house arrest, news reports began to refer to Alice and the Lumpa Church as primitive, religious fanatics, uneducated, evil, and uncivilized, but her initial intent had been to make Christianity more African and relevant to African people. Alice's body still lies in a tomb in the middle of her ruined cathedral.[57]

THE YOIDO FULL GOSPEL CHURCH

The largest church in the world, the Yoido Full Gospel Church in Seoul, Korea, began in Jashil Choi's (1915–89) living room.

Jashil and her mother attended a tent revival meeting when Jashil was 12 where they both were converted; Jashil later wrote her story, *I Was a Hallelujah Woman,* also known as *Hallelujah Lady,* perhaps a reference to The Salvation Army "Hallelujah Lasses." She became known as "Auntie Hallelujah."

Little is recorded of her early life. She was born in North Korea in Haeju City, moved to Seoul as an adult to open a business, and attended the Full Gospel Bible College when she was in her early 40s. There she met the young student Yonggi Cho, who would become her future church partner, helping to establish the Yoido Full Gospel Church, and her future son-in-law. As Yonggi Cho wrote in the preface to Jashil Choi's autobiography, "pastor Choi is the person whom I would never forget in my life. If she was not my personal companion, I would not be a pastor in the world's largest church."[58]

At one point in her life, Jashil Choi decided she had had enough. Having been in an unhappy marriage, with three children living with her ex-husband and a new mother, she went up a mountain with poisonous powder in her hand to end her life, but the wind blew the powder out of her hand, and she spent time in prayer instead. For the rest of her days, prayer and fasting would be the central part of her life and ministry. Many times, she would pray in tongues, even on the streetcar or in the street. As she wrote:[59]

> As people store up treasures, I will fast and pray to store Spiritual power so that I may heal those who are lonely and miserable sick people like epileptics, paralytics, consumptives, demonics, unbelievers, and Spiritual cripples whose faith is not in order. I decided to be a person who has the mission to drive away demons with desperate courage and heal all the sick people in spirit and flesh.[60]

Jashil initially thought her ministry would be with children, and she operated a Sunday service in her living room. Her first service, however, was attended by only six people, Jashil, her three children, Yonggi, and an elderly woman who wanted to get out of the rain. The pulpit was an apple box covered with a cloth. Jashil and Yonggi knocked on doors in the neighborhood, and eventually they had to hold services outdoors when her living room became too small to hold all the people. When it rained, they stood under a pine tree.

FIGURE 13.2 A recent Yoido Full Gospel Church (Assemblies of God) congregation, Seoul, Korea. Photo: Courtesy of the Yoido Full Gospel Church.

Eventually in 1956 she bought a battered marine tent for $50, the year before she graduated from the Bible College. She sold "personal ornaments" to pay for this and to cover debts, and she and Yonggi Cho ministered together. It was not long before the church membership grew to 1,000 in 1961, and soon it reached 18,000 under eight tents, even without a sign board.

The great growth in church membership was linked to a Pentecostal revival in the 1950s in Korea sparked by two American missionaries sent from the Assemblies of God Church in the States. Women were heavily involved; 70 per cent of Jashil's congregation was composed of women and today, they are assisted by elders, deacons, and deaconesses.

Jashil felt strongly moved to start a "prayer mountain," which she set up in a public cemetery in Osan-ri on a rise in the land close to the border of North Korea. Advised against that location, she persisted and soon was attracting people from all over Korea, Japan, and even the rest of the world, who would remain all day in prayer and fasting. Sometimes people would stay there for days. She was often successful in healing men and women through this ministry.

One of the strengths of the present Yoido Full Gospel Church is a cell system based on Methodism's early bands and classes. When a cell grows to 20 families, it is divided into two cells. As Yonggi points out, this is a way to mobilize lay people and an application of the Reformation theology of the priesthood of all believers. Cell leaders are trained and cells set up by geographical district helping church members get to know each other, but it only functions "where people rely on the work of the Holy Spirit." The members of the cells meet mid-week to worship and study the Bible. In 1995, 85 per cent of the cell leaders were women.[61]

By 1992, the church had a membership of 700,000 with several satellite churches throughout Seoul. In 2000, there were 171 associate pastors and 356 lay pastors. By 2007, the church needed to hold seven Sunday services that were translated into 16 languages. In 2017, the church had 410 pastors, 1,205 elders, 1,909 senior deacons, 8,567 senior deaconesses, and 49,615 regular deacons and deaconesses.

THE MAI (MOTHER) CHAZA CHURCH

Asked to leave the Methodist Church, Mother Chaza (1914–60) founded her own movement, partly Methodist and partly indigenous.

Born Theresa Nyamushanga in Buhera, Zimbabwe, she married Chiduza Chaza from Wedza, and together they had six children. A devout Methodist, she was active in that church's prayer groups, and the powerful independent women's *ruwadzan*, or Mothers' Union.

Theresa's life, however, was not easy. She was accused of causing her sister-in-law's death through witchcraft and was driven from her home. (Some reports claim that it was her brother-in-law's son who died.)[62] She became very ill in her late 30s, falling into a coma; her husband divorced her and sent her back to her family. She was reported to have died, and when she recovered after a few hours, it was thought by many people that she had been resurrected from the dead. She believed that God had commanded her to live a celibate life and become a faith healer, which she did, at first charging money for consultations. The Methodist Church asked her to stop and refused her request to have her own preaching circuit, so she set up her own, eventually occupying a position of power and prestige.

In 1954, Theresa relocated to the Seke Reserve, about 100 miles southeast of Harare. Several men and women flocked around her, and by the end of that year, a village of white round huts had sprung up, consisting of about 2,500 people, which became known as *Guta raJehovah* or City of God. By this time, Theresa was known as *Mai* or "Mother Chaza," an influential prophetess, a messenger from God, an angel, "Mother Savior," "Heavens," or "Lamb," even a reappearance of Christ. Her devotees came from South Africa, Botswana, Mozambique, Zambia, and Malawi, seeking healing. At some time, two huge brightly colored pillars were erected with the inscription, "GRJ: New Jerusalem."

Mother Chaza worked especially with barren women stigmatized in Africa for their condition, and was credited with great success. However, it was said that the women were told that if they did not conceive, it was because they lacked total commitment to God or they had not confessed every small sin they had committed from childhood. Mother Chaza also believed that women's infertility could result from men's sinful lifestyles. She insisted that those who came to her for healing renounce tobacco, alcohol, and pagan customs such as traditional medicines and charms. It was said that she could heal more than 8,000 people in the space of about two hours. Although she believed spiritual healing was superior, she was not opposed to hospital treatment as well.[63]

Mother Chaza's words and deeds were recorded in the *Guta raJehovah* Bible, which eventually supplanted the New Testament for her disciples. At one point, as many as 60,000 men and women were counted as her followers. It was rumored that at her funeral in 1960, she disappeared from her coffin as it was being lowered into the grave.

Mother Chaza is also credited with raising Chief Chitsunge's son, Shona, from the dead. Since Mother Chaza had healed his wife, when his son took sick and died, the chief asked that his son's body be taken to Mai Chaza. Other traditional healers had tried to help, but failed. Mai Chaza placed her hands on the dead boy's body, prayed, and he woke up.[64]

As the years separated her life from her followers, all sorts of stories began to circulate about her miraculous powers. One of her present disciples claims that he often saw her in company with angels and shows photographs to support this. She "had a human body," he says, but "she was actually God." Sect members believe that she is still alive in spirit and living in her large empty house, which they keep constantly cleaned. "There is no need for a successor," they claim.[65]

At the height of its popularity, the Mai Chaza Church had nearly one million members. Today, there are no more than 3,000 adherents. They still use Methodist hymns, although they have drifted away from Methodist theology.[66]

MOTHER LEAFY ANDERSON

Three young girls in New York, Kate Fox (1837–92) and her sisters Leah (1831–90) and Margaret (1833–93), are said to have originated the modern American spiritualist movement in 1848. The two youngest girls, living in what they thought was a haunted house in Hydesville, New York, decided to trick their parents and later their friends and neighbors with unexplained rapping and knocking. The eldest sister managed their appearances and the sisters became a sensation as spiritualist mediums. Forty years and numerous séances and exhibitions later, in 1888, they confessed their fraud: they were making the noises themselves, mostly with their legs and feet. The Fox sisters were discredited, but spiritualism continued, providing a professional option for women.

The spiritualist newspaper, *The Banner of Light*, printed a list of 300 lecturers in 1876; of them, 127 were women's names. By 1933, there were 222 black churches in New Orleans alone, of which 23 were "spiritual" churches, attracting members because of healing and prophecy.[67]

Reverend Jules Anderson, a minister in New Orleans in the 1990s, claimed that those churches weren't "spiritualist": "We're a spiritual church. Spiritualist would be a church that would deal with all types of spirits, good and evil, putting spells on people—to make people do certain things rather than for them to do things freely of their own will. In the Spiritual church, we mostly teach the doctrine of the Bible."[68] Nevertheless, there is a spiritualist tradition in New Orleans that some people trace to French-speaking Creoles. But most of the spiritualist churches there attribute their origin to Mother Leafy Anderson (1887–1927), a black woman with Indigenous ancestry from Wisconsin who worked as a religious leader in Chicago sometime before the 1920s and summoned up spirit guides. The New Orleans churches are somewhat different from other spiritualist churches in America, in that they involve spirit guides who are "symbols of protest and empowerment for largely low-income and working-class women." In the late 1980s, professor Claude F. Jacobs found about 50 small spiritualist churches still operating in New Orleans and mention of about 200 that had previously existed. Two-thirds of the church members were women.[69]

The members dance, spin, utter strange sounds, and writhe on the floor being "slain in the spirit," not unlike what happens in some Pentecostal churches. A certain spirit "takes control of a believer," or a member "works" with a spirit who serves as an intercessor between that person and God. One church member told Jacobs:

> When the spirit comes upon you … you can ask God for what you want while the spirit is [there]. Because the spirit is coming to intercede for you, to make things well for you…. When I'm in the spirit, if I'm dancing in the spirit, I'm asking. I'm working with my spirit. I know what to say, what to work with. See, when I finish dancing, I know what's going to happen.[70]

Spirit guides can be deceased relatives, New Testament men or women, Christian saints, or some partial manifestation of the Holy Spirit. Indigenous people are popular, such as Mother Leafy Anderson's spirit guide Black Hawk (1767–c.1838), a Native American Sauk and Fox tribe leader, Ma-ka-tai-me-she-kia-kiak. As one minister told Jacobs, "Each man got a spirit guide. Some folks know it and some folks don't. There's always a spirit to guide you some way or another and try to protect you from … evil forces." Anderson also introduced Father John, or Father Jones, and Queen Esther (492–c.460 BCE) from the Old Testament. Father Jones appeared to Anderson one dark and dreary night and instructed her how to master evil. She said that "Father Jones must have been a Bishop because he was the head man." However, she is also supposed to have called Father John a "great doctor," one of the most famous mid-nineteenth-century "practitioners of the Afro-Catholic syncretic cult." So, it is not clear which one was her spirit guide—Father John or Father Jones or both. While Mother Anderson leaned heavily on Black Hawk, New Orleans spiritualist churches were decorated with a mix of statues and icons of various saints such as the Virgin Mary, St. Anthony, St. Jude, St. Rita, and St. Raymond among others, and the churches celebrated saints' days as well as offering prayers to them.[71]

Anderson had gone to New Orleans when she was in her 20s or early 30s, deliberately to found a church reflecting women's lives. She had already established the Eternal Life Spiritualist Church in Chicago around 1913, and it is believed she also set up churches in St. Louis, New Jersey, and Indiana. The Chicago church grew into 11 other congregations in Chicago, Memphis, Little Rock, and Pensacola. Anderson had difficulty getting a license for her Eternal Life Christian Spiritualist Church in New Orleans until she gave a reading to a judge telling him things about himself and his family that were not widely known.[72]

There are few details of what took place at Leafy Anderson's church. An announcement in the *Louisiana Weekly* on 11 December 1926 listed a full schedule of activities at that time. There was a Sunday morning service at 6 a.m., and an evening service at 7:30 p.m. Tuesday nights were reserved for training others in spiritualism. There were also services on Thursday and Friday evenings at 8:00 p.m. Worship consisted of songs, scripture, prayer, a collection of readings and "phenomena" or predicting people's futures. There is no way of knowing if the hymns used the traditional words or if the lyrics were changed but they were sung to the music of a "red hot six-piece swing band." The services that featured Black Hawk varied from church to church but it was always at night and most of the lights were turned off. The music had a strong steady beat and there was some form of a Black Hawk chant: "Black Hawk is a watchman on the wall, He'll fight your battles on the wall," each phrase repeated several times.[73]

Little accurate information is known about Anderson's early life. Her obituary said that she was born in 1887 in Balboa, Wisconsin, but that town doesn't seem to have existed. A distant relative claims that she was born in Norfolk, Virginia, married an Anderson and had a son and two adopted children, one a baby left on her doorstep. Some say that she was divorced. She operated a lunch counter in Chicago between 1914 and 1917. When she went to New Orleans, she taught how to prophesy, heal, pray and see spirits, charging 85 to 100 students a dollar a lesson. Many of her students went on to found their own churches. She is supposed to have forbidden her students to use Jesus' name in prayer because "as a man, he was not important—he was merely the earthly body of a spirit," apparently forgetting that Black Hawk and her other spirit guides were male also.

She dressed lavishly in sequins, lace, expensive shoes, and lots of jewelry. "Sometimes she wore all white with a purple veil, but other times she wore a gold gown with a Black Hawk mantle over her shoulders. Once in a while she wore a man's full dress, but that was only for special occasions," according to a colleague and friend, Mother Doris. Anderson held dramatic events featuring historical plays, and dances on her roof with jazz bands. When she died around the age of 40 from complications brought on by a cold, her estate was worth only about us$109,000 in today's currency, although it was rumored that she had taken in a great amount of money from her collections.[74] It was also rumored that Anderson was a lesbian or a man posing as a woman. Mother Doris claimed that wasn't true. "She was as much a woman as I [am] … [I] know cause I nursed her when she was sick," Mother Doris said. "She had a breast like mine…. She was a natural woman."[75]

The seamstress and designer Bishop Efzelda Booker Coleman, another friend, noted that "She did a lot of good. She had a lot of, I guess you could call 'em, homes for abused women; she had centers and things that could give people lodging." It is reported that as she was dying, she said, "I am going away, but I am coming back and you shall know that I am here."[76]

Mother Catherine Seals (c.1887–c.1930), who regularly offered worshippers homemade castor oil to cure various problems, similar to Father John's medicines, had worked with Anderson at one point and may have separated over differences in style. Seals was opposed to abortion, calling her church The Temple of the Innocent Blood where she set up a sanctuary for unwed mothers. Like Mother Anderson, she taught students who then started out on their own, and also like Mother Anderson, little is known about her, except that she played the trombone. Music was a large part of her services, and traditional spirituals and hymns would ring out from her pulpit, such as "Just a Closer Walk with Thee" and "Precious Lord."[77]

Born sometime between 1887 and 1913 as Catherine Nanny Cowans, Seals lived first in Kentucky and then went to New Orleans where she worked as a housemaid. It is said that she married and divorced three times, each time to an abuser. Her last name may have been Fields or Jenkins, or perhaps these were married surnames. Taught Spiritualism by Mother Anderson, she bought a house on the outskirts of town, put up a 10-foot wall, and "got to work." She had a temple, a private ritual space, and a manger, an open air building that held more than 300 people and which she entered by the roof to make it look as if she were sent from heaven. She had about 500 lights blazing all over the place, a statue of "Jehovah," small clay sculptures, a Christian nativity scene, and a Nigerian serpent named Damballa. Most people had to trudge through knee-deep mud to get to her place but she was renowned for healing both black and white men and women. She sat on an ordinary chair at the edge of a platform at the entrance to her tent wearing a white robe and a red cape with a box of "shake of salt" [sic] in her hand. A white cockatoo would scream during her services and four mongrel dogs strode about with a donkey, a mother goat with her kid, and several sheep. By the 1920s, she had more than 10,000 followers.[78]

FIGURE 13.3 Mother Catherine Seals and members of her Spiritualist congregation in New Orleans, Louisiana, United States. Photo: Courtesy of the Hogan Jazz Archive.

Seals began healing services because she had been refused healing by a white faith healer. She received a vision from God that she was to heal herself, and then she used her power to heal others. After she became popular she would sleep in a brass bed surrounded by bodyguards; church members would come and pray over her while she slept.

The jazz funeral for Seals was one of the largest in the city's history, with thousands of people on the streets, and a write-up in *Time* magazine. The temple was kept alive for a few years, but it couldn't exist without her. At her death, at least half of her estate, worth only about US$58,000 in today's currency, was owed to creditors. What was left of her buildings disappeared during Hurricane Katrina in 2005, and archeologists recently dug the site along with the New Orleans African Museum.[79]

Seals's importance, and that of Mother Anderson, is not just that they were women founding churches, but that they were black women founding interracial churches. Because they avoided publicity, little is known about them, and what was known is almost forgotten, the details confused and colored by rumor.

FURTHER READING

PRIMARY

Dayton, Donald W. *"The Higher Christian Life": Sources for the Study of Holiness, Pentecostal, and Keswick Movements*. New York: Garland Publishing, 1985.

McPherson, Aimee Semple. *This Is That, Personal Experiences, Sermons and Writings of Aimee Semple McPherson*. Los Angeles: Echo Park Evangelistic Association, 1923.

—. *Divine Healing Sermons*. London: Forgotten Books, 2015.

Morgan, Amos. "Mother Crawford: A Profile" (2004). Accessed 21 September 2018, http://www.azusabooks.org/profile.shtml.

SECONDARY

Anderson, Allan H. *African Reformation: African Initiated Christianity in the Twentieth Century*. Trenton, NJ: Africa World Press, 2001.

Barrett, David A. *Schism and Renewal in Africa: An Analysis of Six Thousand Contemporary Religious Movements*. Nairobi, Kenya: Oxford University Press, 1968.

Bednarowski, Mary Farrell. "Outside the Mainstream: Women's Religion and Women Religious Leaders in Nineteenth-Century America." *Journal of American Academy of Religion* 48, no. 2 (June 1980): 207–31.

Berry, Jason. *The Spirit of Black Hawk: A Mystery of Africans and Indians*. Jackson, MS: University Press of Mississippi, 1995.

Daniel, Kasomo. "The Role of Women in the Church in Africa." *International Journal of Sociology and Anthropology* 2, no. 6 (June 2010): 126–39.

Drogus, Carol Ann. "Religious Change and Women's Status in Latin America." Working Paper #205, Kellogg Institute, March 1994.

"The Establishment of Pentecostalism in Korea (1928–1939)." N.d., n.p. https://dspace.library.uu.nl/hitstream/handle/1874/605/c5.pdf.

Houseal, Richard W. "Women Clergy in the Church of the Nazarene: An Analysis of Change from 1908 to 1995." MA thesis, University of Missouri-Kansas City, 1996.

Ingersol, Robert Stanley. "Burden of Dissent: Mary Lee Cagle and the Southern Holiness Movement." PhD diss., Duke University, 1989.

Jacobs, Claude F. "Spirit Guides and Possession in the New Orleans Black Spiritual Churches." *Journal of American Folklore* 102, no. 403 (1989): 45–56.

Kim, Ig-Jin. "History and Theology of Korean Pentecostalism: Sunbogeum (pure gospel) Pentecostalism." PhD diss., Utrecht University, 2003.

Lawless, Elaine J. *Handmaidens of the Lord: Pentecostal Women Preachers and Traditional Religions.* Philadelphia: University of Pennsylvania Press, 1988.

Levenduski, Cristine. *Peculiar Power.* Washington, DC: Smithsonian Institution, 1996.

Ma, Julie C. "Asian Women and Pentecostal Ministry." In *Asian and Pentecostal: The Charismatic Face of Christianity in Asia,* edited by Allan Anderson and Edmond Tang. Eugene, OR: WIPF & STOCK, 2011.

Mubvumbi, Paradzayi David. *Christianity and Traditional Religions of Zimbabwe.* Bloomington, IN: WestBow Press, 2016.

Payne, Leah. *Gender and Pentecostalism: Making a Female Ministry in the Early Twentieth Century.* New York: Palgrave Macmillan, 2015.

"The Rise of Pentecostalism." *Christian History* 17, no. 2.

Sanders, Cheryl J. "History of Women in the Pentecostal Movements." *Cyberjournal for Pentecostal-Charismatic Research*, 1996 PCCNA National Conference, Memphis, Tennessee, 1 October 1996.

Stanley, Susie Cunningham. *Feminist Pillar of Fire.* Cleveland: The Pilgrim Press, 1993.

—. "'Tell me the old, old story:' An Analysis of Autobiographies by Holiness Women." *Wesleyan Theological Journal* 29 (Spring-Fall 1994).

—. *Holy Boldness.* Knoxville, TN: University of Tennessee Press, 2002.

Tibbetts, Joel W. "Women Who Were Called: A Study of the Contributions to American Christianity of Ann Lee, Jemima Wilkinson, Mary Baker Eddy and Aimee Semple McPherson." PhD diss., Vanderbilt University, 1976.

NOTES

1 Mary Lee Cagle, as quoted in Ingersol, "Mary Lee Cagle: A Study in Women's History, Religion." The Cumberland Presbyterians had ordained Louisa Mariah Layman Woolsey (1862–1942) in 1889. She retired when she was 87.

2 Sanchez, "Your Daughters Shall Prophesy."

3 *The Grace and Peace Magazine*, published by the Church of the Nazarene, February 2011, mentions Grace George and Susie Sherman.

4 Mary Lee Cagle as quoted in Ingersol, "Mary Lee Cagle: A Study in Women's History, Religion."

5 Ingersol, "Mary Lee Cagle." Cagle had been brought up in the Cumberland Presbyterian Church, which ordained a woman, Louisa Mariah Layman Woolsey (1862–1952), in 1889.

6 Ingersol, "Whatever Happened to Fannie McDowell Hunter?" and "Mary Lee Cagle: A Study in Women's History, Religion."

7 Stanley, *Holy Boldness*, 84.

8 Mary Lee Cagle, as quoted in Ingersol, "Mary Lee Cagle: A Study in Women's History, Religion."

9 Stan Ingersol, Church of the Nazarene archivist, email conversation with the author, 13 July 2017.

10 Stanley, "Tell me the old, old Story," 17; Stanley, *Holy Boldness*, 15.

11 Stanley, "The Promise Fulfilled."

12 Ingersol, "The Deaconess in Nazarene History," 36.

13 Houseal, "Women Clergy in the Church of the Nazarene," esp. 23, 27.

14 McPherson, *This Is That*, 24; Tibbetts, "Women Who Were Called," 210; Walker, "A Chaste and Fervid Eloquence," 299.

15 McPherson, *This Is That*, 13.

16 McPherson, *Divine Healing Sermons*, preface.

17 McPherson, *This Is That*, 319.

18 McPherson, *This Is That*, 249.

19 "The Great I Am or I Was?" 34.

20 McPherson, *This Is That*, 97.

21 McPherson, *This Is That*, 118.

22 Payne, *Gender and Pentecostalism*, 93.

23 Payne, *Gender and Pentecostalism*, 92.

24 Tibbetts, "Women Who Were Called," 40.

25 *The New York Times*, as quoted in Tibbetts, "Women Who Were Called," 427.

26 Lawless, *God's Peculiar People*.

27 Payne, *Gender and Pentecostalism*, 124.

28 Tibbetts, "Women Who Were Called," 244f.

29 "Aimee Semple McPherson," in *Christian History*, n.d. The membership is recorded here as two million.

30 *Christian History*, 17, no. 2, 2.

31 Payne, *Gender and Pentecostalism*, 185n.

32 Payne, *Gender and Pentecostalism*, 123.

33 "Women in the Pentecostal Movement," Fuller Studio, n.d., n.p.

34 Sanders, "History of Women in the Pentecostal Movement," 1.

35 *Christian History*, 17, no. 2, 39.

36 *Christian History*, 17, no. 2, 3, 14.

37 Lawless, *Handmaidens of the Lord*, 7.

38 Drogus, "Religious Change and Women's Status in Latin America."

39 "The Establishment of Pentecostalism in Korea," 2. It is not known what a Methodist chanter would be unless it refers to a soloist, since *chanter* means to sing.

40 Grupo Editorial EPRL, *Encyclopedia de Puerto Rico*, 2014.

41 "Mita, Juanita Garcia Peraza," *Iglesia Congregación Mita.* ·

42 Grayson, "Recognizingthe Congregación Mita Church on Its 75th Anniversary."

43 Landman, "Christinah Nku and St John's," 1.

44 Quinn, *African Saints.*

45 Landman, "Christinah Nku and St. Johns," 13.

46 Landman, "Christinah Nku and St Johns," 13.

47 As quoted in Stanley, *Holy Boldness*, 169.

48 Le Casey, "Bishop White of Denver."

49 Hartley, "White, Alma Bridwell (1862–1946)."

50 *Time* magazine, 22 October 1928.

51 Stanley, *Feminist Pillar of Fire*, 96.

52 Stanley, "Tell me the old, old story," 20.

53 Stanley, *Feminist Pillar of Fire*, 121.

54 Daniel, "The Role of Women in the Church in Africa," 135.

55 "The Lumpa Massacre."

56 Brockman, *An African Biographical Dictionary.*

57 Anderson, *African Reformation*, 136ff.

58 Ma, "Asian Women and Pentecostal Ministry."

59 Kim, "History and Theology of Korean Pentecostalism," 110.

60 Kim, "History and Theology of Korean Pentecostalism," 111.

61 Kim, "History and Theology of Korean Pentecostalism," 137.

62 Dube, "Mai Chaza."

63 Chara, "Inside Mai Chaza's Shrine," 1.

64 Kupe, "A Woman Worth Knowing."

65 Chara, "Inside Mai Chaza's Shrine," 3.

66 Mubvumbi, *Christianity and Traditional Religions of Zimbabwe*, 72.

67 Bednarowski, "Outside the Mainstream"; Jacobs and Kaslow, *The Spiritual Churches of New Orleans*, xiii.

68 Jacobs and Kaslow, *The Spiritual Churches of New Orleans*, 17.

69 Jacobs, "Spirit Guides and Possession in the New Orleans Black Spiritual Churches," 45.

70 Jacobs, "Spirit Guides and Possession in the New Orleans Black Spiritual Churches," 47.

71 Jacobs, "Spirit Guides and Possession in the New Orleans Black Spiritual Churches," 48; Chireau, "Prophetess of the Spirits, Mother Leafy Anderson and the Black Spiritual Churches of New Orleans," 312.

72 "Leafy Anderson" in *Notable Black American Women.*

73 Jacobs and Kaslow, *The Spiritual Churches of New Orleans*, 35, 139; Berry, *The Spirit of Black Hawk*, 63.

74 Chireau, "Prophetess of the Spirits: Mother Leafy Anderson and the Black Spiritual Churches of New Orleans," 66f.

75 Berry, *The Spirit of Black Hawk*, 115.

76 Berry, *The Spirit of Black Hawk*, 115, 120.

77 Sanders, "Digging to Learn More about Mother Catherine Seals."

78 Sanders, "Digging to Learn More about Mother Catherine Seals."

79 Kaplan-Levenson, "Mother Catherine Seals and the Temple of the Innocent Blood"; "Leafy Anderson" in *Notable Black American Women*.

Chapter 14

THE MISSIONARY IMPULSE

ALTHOUGH SHE WAS ONLY 37 when she died, Ann "Nancy" Hasseltine Judson (1789–1826) was the most famous American missionary in the nineteenth century. In 1812, Ann and her husband Adoniram (1788–1850) sailed on the ship *Caravan* from Salem, Massachusetts, to India and Burma (present-day Myanmar) along with Harriet Atwood Newell (1793–1812), Harriet's husband Samuel (1784–1821), and a single male missionary, Luther Rice (1783–1836). Harriet was even younger than Ann when she died—at 19, from complications in childbirth. They had all been sent by the new Congregational Church missionary society—the American Board of Commissioners for Foreign Missions. However, when they reached Calcutta, both Judsons joined the Baptist Church and were re-baptized, horrifying the Congregational Church but resulting in the American Baptists quickly setting up their own missionary enterprise, the Baptist Society for Propagating the Gospel in India.[1]

The Judsons fled Calcutta as they were about to be deported to England, taking the first ship they could find which happened to be sailing for Burma. A maid that Adoniram had hired to be with Ann dropped dead the first day on the ship, and they sailed into a typhoon, but both Ann and Adoniram survived.

Ann's detailed letters home were reproduced in missionary magazines and even picked up by the secular press. She described the food they ate in Burma—mostly fish and rice. "There are no bread, potatoes, and butter and very little animal food," she wrote. She also explained the Hindu religion and the Burmese way of life as she saw it. Her goal was to change them. She wrote back home: "I desire no higher enjoyment in this life, than to be instrumental in leading some poor, ignorant females to the knowledge of the Saviour. To have a female praying society, consisting of those who were once in heathen darkness, is what my heart earnestly pants after."[2]

It was not an easy life. After nine years in Rangoon, they had made only 18 converts. In 1822, Ann returned home to the United States by herself because of illness, and in Baltimore was given a "course of mercury" for more than three weeks and the next year was bled more than five times; surprisingly, she got better. Then after her return to Burma, during the 1824–26 Burmese–British war, Adoniram was thrown in jail. Ann carried a newly born child through the jungle to his prison, where he was held for 17 months. She helped keep him alive with food and medicine, and when he was about to be executed, she pleaded for his life, eventually winning his freedom. Ann, however, died from a fever, weakened by smallpox.

Adoniram then married the widow Sarah Hall Boardman (1803–45), a translator, hymnist, and author who was already in Burma, the widow of another missionary who had died. Her language skills were so good that she was able to preach in Burmese. After she died en route to America, he married the writer and hymnist Emily Chubbuck (1817–54) and took her to help out in Burma. Emily wrote under the name Fanny Forester, and after she arrived in Burma in 1846, she wrote to a friend: "Frogs hop from my sleeves when I put them on, and lizards drop from the ceiling to the table when we are eating, and the floors are black with ants."[3]

Winnie Tovey (c.1922–?), a Methodist missionary wife in Mysore, India, described her life in the 1950s and 1960s as "wife, mother, hospital driver, physiotherapist, stenographer, librarian, sick visitor, church organist and food aid distributor." It was possible, she said, because "each servant had his or her own allotted duties and on no account was I allowed to cook or clean."[4]

But the missionaries got worn out, both the women and the men. Wives were at the greatest risk since childbirth was more dangerous than in more developed countries and maternal mortality was high. Loneliness was also a problem for missionary wives, who were often left to "grapple with the problems of a big station and bear the burdens of everything" when husbands were traveling. James Levi Barton (1855–1936), the secretary of the American Board of Commissioners for Foreign Missions, advised the missionaries to eat well and find proper accommodation:

It is the missionary's duty to invest his life in the way that will bring forth
the largest and most permanent results, and experience has proved that,
as a general thing, these results are not obtained by starving the body or
misusing it by unnecessary hardships. Or causing it to carry unnecessary
burdens, and thus wearing it out early in his [*sic*] career.[5]

Sarah Lanman Smith died in Syria, three years after she arrived there. She
had recognized the risks before she left: "I do not forget that the life of the
missionary is usually short, and that even before I reach the field of labor, I
may find a watery grave. Should I arrive there ... I shall live but a few years,
and that during those few I may accomplish but little for the benefit of those
immediately around me ... [but] I should not go in vain."[6]

Not only were the women's lives often in danger, but they were a dangerous force themselves, as well, both in the foreign country where they were
working and in America, for they challenged the place of women in societies
that had been set up for the convenience of men. In working for justice, they
questioned cultural norms such as foot binding in China, killing widows in
India and twin children in Africa, and also the social structure in America,
often demanding justice, education, and equality for all, especially women.

Many of the denominations set up their own missionary societies, both
general organizations and women's branches or women's independent groups.
Women also formed "mite societies" and "cent societies," taking their name
from the "two-mite" widow in the Bible whom Jesus commended for her
generosity (Mark 12:41–44; Luke 21:1–4), although the idea was supposedly
sparked during a dinner party in 1802 with the thought of giving up one
glass of wine and donating a penny a glass. The purpose was for women to
contribute their mites toward "so noble a design as diffusion of the gospel
light among the shades of darkness and superstition."[7]

Organized in 1869, the Woman's Missionary Society of the Methodist
Episcopal Church in the United States was set up to unite the women "in the
work of sending the gospel to women in heathen lands, through the agency
of female missionaries, teachers and Bible readers." Male missionaries had
realized that missionary women were absolutely essential to gain access to
women in these foreign lands, women who were kept out of sight to be seen
only by other women and their husbands; reaching and converting adult
Chinese women was the primary focus of this latest Woman's Missionary
Society. To achieve this, not only did they send out women missionaries,
but they set up schools primarily to train local "Bible women" who would

FIGURE 14.1 Considered the first missionary, a Samaritan woman known as Photina talks with Jesus at a well where she has gone to draw water (John 4:7-42). Afterwards, she runs to tell her neighbor about Jesus. Fresco from the catacomb on the Via Latina, Rome, Italy. Photo: Bridgeman Photos.

then visit and Christianize other local women by talking to them and reading passages from the scriptures. In 1888, a Bible woman for the Methodist Episcopal Church earned £50 a year while male missionaries were paid £150, about US$21,000 in today's currency. The concept of hiring local Bible women had originated in the slums of London in the 1860s where the writer and domestic missionary Ellen Henrietta Ranyard (1810–79), the founder of the Bible and Domestic Female Mission, had realized that upper-class women would not be welcomed in the poorer areas.[8]

Faced with poorly educated and not very literate "Bible women," the missionaries also recognized that they needed schools where "women may come and live for two or three months and be taught the truth." But no matter how little these local women knew about the Bible, they were quite active, obviously taking their jobs very seriously. In 1878, six Bible women in Shanghai made 972 visits, addressed 3,708 people directly, sold 36 books (presumably the Bible or parts of it), gave away 72 books, and read to 935 women. Another 3,708 people were contacted in some lesser way. Later, schools were organized to teach children, first boys and then girls; it was hoped that the children would take the gospel to their families after learning about it in school.[9]

How much the missionaries accomplished with these strategies is questionable. The educator Laura Askew Haygood (1845–1900), the first female missionary sent by the Methodist Woman's Missionary Society to China, where she worked for 16 years, wrote in 1887:

> Of Woman's Work, I am profoundly sorry that I have so little to report. It has been impossible during the year to do the work for mothers and families that we had hoped and planned. Our hearts have ached more than we can tell you, as again and again, in physical weakness, we have been obliged to turn away from open doors.[10]

The missionary Dora Hamilton, though, claimed in 1889 that they reached mothers through their pupils "in a way that claims at once their confidence and respect." It must be pointed out that the schools taught many more subjects than just the Bible and Christian thought and devotions. Homemaking of course was a topic for women and girls—sewing, knitting, embroidering, cooking, and so on—along with Chinese language and Chinese classics, geography, arithmetic, physiology, and music, which were fairly standard items. In addition, history, geology, chemistry, astronomy, zoology, and English were taught in some schools if possible. There were no uniform texts and generally students stayed only two or three years.

Perhaps one of the best tools for the missionary societies was their female doctors, women who became increasingly popular and gained access to the women who could not be approached by men. Not only did the doctors dispense badly needed medicines and medical care, but they were able to set up hospitals and train local nurses and eventually doctors. Clara Swain (1834–1910), the first female missionary doctor in the world and the Methodist Episcopal's first woman doctor sent to India in 1869, was particularly taken with the orphanages for girls and how quickly the little ones memorized the Bible verses they were given. Noting that it cost $30 a year to maintain a girl in the orphanage, she hoped that they would become Bible women or even doctors. Clara taught anatomy, physiology, and "*materia medica*" (the therapeutic properties of substances) to 17 women and girls the first year she was in Bareilly, India.

According to the letters Clara sent back to her friends and family in the United States, she was constantly dispensing medicines, the need for health care was so great. When prescriptions were given out at dispensaries, there were Bible verses printed in three languages in the package. Clara talked to her patients about Christianity, and held classes about the Bible as well as medicine and nursing. She founded the first mission hospital in Asia, reaching thousands of women patients. She was even invited to become the private court doctor for the Rajah of Rajputana and his wife the Rani. At that point, Clara was so worn out from her demanding work that she accepted. She wrote that she found them "noble and generous, and so kind and considerate that we can hardly realize that they are not Christians."

While she was at court, Clara was fascinated by a betrothal ceremony, the first part of a marriage ceremony for the Rani's two-and-a-half-year-old daughter, which cost 18,000 rupees or the equivalent of US$6,000 in 1895, noting that "people have their own customs." In her letters, Clara evinced a curious mixture of acceptance of the local lifestyle, and a firm belief that Christianity was much superior. She was still in the Rani's service when the girl was married at age 14. The wedding was attended by 7,900 people, who brought with them 2,000 horses, 1,900 camels, 12 elephants, and 78 pairs of bullocks to be fed by the state.

Clara felt tremendous compassion for the local people in this "dark land," and earlier had a difficult time denying any requests to travel for home care. In 1875 alone, she and her staff had treated 1,929 patients and gave out 5,000 prescriptions. In the year 1880, only five years later, they gave out 11,840 prescriptions and treated almost 6,000 patients. But one wonders where so much medicine came from. Clara offered some amusing and touching anecdotes about her work at the hospital. One woman arrived there with her husband, three children, a widowed sister, 12 servants, an ox-cart with their furniture, and a great deal of food, evidently planning to stay for a while. Clara accommodated them. Many of her patients traveled 20 to 30 miles to the hospital; one young woman had come 700 miles in the hope of being cured.[11]

The mission field at that time offered opportunities for North American and European women that were not open to them at home. They taught, exhorted, lectured, nursed, performed operations, and managed the construction and operation of hospitals and schools and other buildings. As the Canadian Methodist missionary Agnes Wintemute Coates (1864–1965) admitted, missionary work probably benefitted her far more than those she sought to help. However, by the end of its first decade in 1879, the Woman's Missionary Society alone had accomplished a phenomenal amount of activity around the world. It had sent out 38 missionaries to India, China, Japan, Mexico, Africa, Italy, and South America. It employed 200 Bible women and local teachers, had set up six hospitals and dispensaries, 15 boarding schools with 696 pupils, 15 day schools with 3,000 pupils, and supervised three orphanages and two homes for "friendless women," in the process offering care and training to women in countries where women had previously been required to stay at home.[12]

Mission was not only to exotic foreign fields, but local as well. In October 1800, 14 Baptist and Congregational women in Boston came together for prayer and fund-raising, forming the Boston Female Society for Missionary Purposes. They decided that they should look at home, at the state of their "own town":

> Viewing the destitute situation of a certain class of inhabitants, whose poverty forbids their appearing decent at public worship and of others who have abandoned themselves to every species of vice, ... we have thought it our duty to try the practicability of a new plan ... to the support of two missionaries ... to visit and labour with the above description of people....
> The calamity is a *public* calamity; the cause of virtue is a *public* cause.[13]

One of the more colorful local missionaries was Sophie Lichtenfels (1843–1919), "the scrubwoman." A German immigrant to New York City, Sophie had wanted to become a foreign missionary, but she was told she was too old. A gifted preacher but with a very strong accent, she told those she worked for as a cleaning lady that if they wanted her to work for them they would have to listen to her preach, too. For 12 years she said she prayed:

> "Oh Father, make me a foreign missionary. I want to go to foreign lands and preach." And Father says, "Sophie, stop. Where were you born?" "Germany Father." "Where are you now?" "In America." "Well aren't you a foreign missionary already? And who lives on the floor above you?" "A family of Swedes." "And on the floor above them?" "Why some Switzers." "And in the rear house are Italians, and a block away some Chinese? Do you think I will send you a thousand miles away to the foreigner and heathen when you have them all around...?"[14]

Saving the money she earned, Sophie was able to support a school boy in Japan and a teacher in the southern United States as well as preach to her neighbors. "So I was in Japan, down South, and here in New York," she reported, "preaching in three places like … I was triplets."

There have been Christian missionaries ever since the "great commission" in the New Testament given by Jesus as he ascended into heaven:

> And Jesus came and said to them, "All authority in heaven and on earth has been given to me. Go therefore and make disciples of all nations, baptizing them in the name of the Father and of the Holy Spirit, and teaching them to obey everything that I have commanded you. And remember, I am with you always, to the end of the age." (Matthew 28:18–20)

It has been suggested that the first missionary was the Samaritan woman at the well who ran to tell her people about Jesus after she met him and learned who he was (John 4:4–42). The disciples in the New Testament became missionaries—even when Jesus was still alive. Afterwards, women such as Mary Magdalene, Thecla, and Nino undertook mission journeys as they sought to convert men and women to Christianity. The abbess Lioba left England to help with missions in Germany. Religious orders such as the Ursuline Sisters took on missionary enterprises around the world; in the seventeenth century, they traveled to Quebec, and in the eighteenth to New Orleans.

Most of the more recent missionary women were sent out with the backing and support of a missionary society; some, however, went on their own. Serena Thorne Lake (1842–1902), the granddaughter of William and Mary Cowlin Thorne of the (Methodist) Bible Christian Church went to Australia as an independent evangelist, becoming the best-known woman preacher in that country; later, Mary's grandson went to China, marrying a fellow missionary.[15] Serena had preached for the first time in England when she was 18, and soon became a local preacher, but she wasn't able to support herself financially, so she became a traveling preacher in England and in Wales in 1862. However, when her family emigrated to Australia, she went with them and worked there as an evangelist for the Primitive Methodists, becoming so popular that when she was ill, there were public prayers for her recovery.

The Bible Christian Church asked her to open a mission in Queensland for them, but because she and another missionary were not compatible, she became a fundraiser for the Bible Christian missionary society instead. The *Bible Christian Magazine* reported on one of her talks:

> The young lady displayed none of the masculine manner that might have been anticipated from one of the fair sex placing herself in so prominent

a position, but opened the service in a very clear and articulate voice, without the slightest affectation … the words flowing from her lips with a marvelous rapidity and precision.[16]

The Bible Christians were so impressed with her abilities that they doubled her salary to £1 a week to go to Adelaide, where for 13 weeks she filled the 1,500-seat town hall. She married a Bible Christian minister she had known in England and continued preaching even with a family. The Bible Christian missionary society hoped to convert 100,000 people and raise £100,000 by the turn of the century, concentrating on home missions.

Meanwhile, Lois Anna Malpas (1858–1904) married Serena's nephew Samuel Thorne, and they moved to Chiao Tung as missionaries where "Mrs. Thorne was the pioneer of … women's work…. Her tall figure and the unusual sight of her 'big feet' contrasting so startlingly with the tiny mutilated lilly feet of the Chaotung women drew crowds of the latter to the mission house…. She spoke Chinese as possibly not a dozen missionaries could speak it in the whole of China."[17] Samuel died from typhoid, and Lois Anna eventually became ill herself and was called back to England. She worked there for the Primitive Methodists speaking at missionary meetings, but died at age 46, about 10 years short of the average age of life expectancy in England.

Women's missionary societies were also organized in most of the developed countries around the world. For example, in 1830, the Society for Promoting Female Education in China, India, and the East was founded in London—an interdenominational organization. First they sent £50 for "Miss Wallace's schools" in Malacca near Kuala Lumpur, Malaysia, and then they sent Eliza Amelia Thornton (c.1807–89) to help Miss Wallace. Missionaries had to stay for five years or repay their costs. Six months' notice was required if they planned to quit, and in the beginning, getting married was considered quitting.[18]

In 1858, British Methodist women had organized support of missions overseas with the Wesleyan Ladies' Committee for Amelioration of the Condition of Women in Heathen Countries, later changing its name to the Ladies' Mission Auxiliary. By 1912 they were supporting 93 missionaries. Methodist men, however, saw this as an incursion into men's work. Perhaps the women's official missionary hymn was not accidental:

Go labour on: 'tis not for naught
Thine earthly loss is heavenly gain;
Men heed thee, love thee, praise thee not,
The Master praises;—what are men?[19]

Most of the missionaries in the nineteenth century were ordained male ministers, preferably married. Their wives took care of them better than they would themselves, and the missionary society got two people for the price of one. By 1834, however, the Propagation of Female Education in the East recruited and trained single women to work as teachers in India and China. They sponsored a Miss Thornton in 1835 to go to Batavia in today's Jakarta, possibly a different Miss Thornton than Eliza Amelia. She stayed there for 11 years. In 1841, the Methodist Mary Twiddy (c.1814–?), a daughter of a minister, went to Ceylon to run a school; she married a missionary in South India. Between 1858 and 1862, the society recruited 11 teachers for British Honduras, India, Fiji, South Africa, and China.

By the end of the nineteenth century, more women than men were being recruited for mission work. By 1907, there were 2,481 women missionaries in China, of whom 1,038 were single. In societies where women were secluded, men could not approach them so women were needed, and men felt that the work was too important to be entrusted to missionary wives. Specially trained women were recruited who would see this as their life's work. Women were attracted to this; there were very few opportunities for them to have a profession and full-time paid work at home. When they came back on furlough or for good, Lois Thorne, who had been part of the China Inland Mission, and two couples, five single men, and eight single women who had also been sent in 1866 spoke at missionary meetings to attract money and more missionaries. By 1874, it was calculated that British missionaries in Chinese clothing were preaching 5,000 sermons and attending 4,000 public meetings a year throughout Britain.

Many women married with a missionary career in mind, caught up in the excitement of saving foreign women and their duty as Christians. Ann Hasseltine Judson, the first American woman on an overseas mission, had felt her heart "enlarged to pray for spiritual blessings for … the heathen world, and the African slaves. Felt a willingness to give myself away to Christ, to be disposed of as he pleases," she wrote in her diary. Sarah Hall (1803–45), who had joined the missionary team to Burma as the wife of George Boardman (1801–31), remained there after his death. Sarah Lanman Smith (1802–36) had saved up her money for the missionary cause long before she went to Syria. "I have thought lately," she wrote, "that if individuals from what are called the 'first families' of both sexes were to consecrate themselves to the work, it would give a new impulse to the cause." Harriet Lathrop Winslow (1796–1833) recorded a desire to become part of missionary work: "When I reflect on the multitudes of my fellow-creatures who are perishing for lack of vision and that I am living at ease without aiding in the promulgation of the Gospel, I am almost ready to wish myself a man that I might spend my life with the poor heathen."[20]

While at first only married women were sent out as missionaries with their husbands, eventually single women were well accepted. However, the discriminatory pay schedule that had existed in the local itinerants' work at home continued on the mission field. The Methodist male missionaries were paid $500/year in the 1850s; the first two single women sent to China received $300.

Annie Caroline Macdonald (1874–1931), a single woman who never married, has been ranked alongside such prominent people as Dag Hammarskjold (1905–61), Secretary-General of the United Nations, and the neurosurgeon Wilder Penfield (1891–1976). During the 1920s, she was the best-known foreign woman in Japan. Born in the small town of Wingham, Ontario, Canada, she grew up immersed in missions. Her mother was active in their Presbyterian Church mission organizations, both for adults and children. A brilliant student, Caroline graduated from university in mathematics and physics, unusual subjects for women in those days.

Caroline responded to an appeal from the World's Committee of the Young Women's Christian Association (YWCA) to begin an outreach to non-Christian women in Tokyo, Japan, in 1904. She immersed herself in the language and culture, taught Bible classes and English literature, and set up safe hostels for young women. But it was her work with prisoners that set her apart and gained her an international reputation as well as many converts. One of the young men in her classes murdered his wife and two young sons. Caroline visited him in jail every day, eventually changing his life and that of hundreds of others in prison, becoming known as "The White Angel of Tokyo." Though not a formal missionary, the Women's Missionary Society of the Presbyterian Church in Canada supported her. She even traveled to New York to learn as much as she could from leaders in criminology, social work, and prison reform.[21]

In recognition of her work, the emperor of Japan conferred on her the Sixth Order of the Sacred Treasure, and she became the first woman to receive an honorary Doctor of Laws from the University of Toronto in 1925. On her death, the prison governor in Japan, Arima Shirosuke, remarked that Caroline believed absolutely that every human being was a child of God, and her "effortless" practice of that faith put her "beyond every prejudice" of religion, race, or class. It is estimated that she helped more than 7,000 convicted criminals.[22]

In recent years, mission has taken many forms. Women such as Dr. Ruth Pfau, Maria Skobtsova, Dorothy Day, and Mother Teresa, for example, have all been recognized for the work they have done as a result of their deep Christian faith, but they have followed different paths. Their goal has not been to Christianize the world or even a small part of it, but simply to help others.

German-born Dr. Ruth Pfau (1929–2017) gave her life to defeating leprosy (Hansen's disease) in Pakistan. A convert to Roman Catholicism and a nun in the Society of Daughters of the Heart of Mary order, she was on her way to India in 1960 for a posting when a passport foul-up delayed her in Pakistan. She visited a leper colony in Karachi, and was so upset by what she saw that she joined the Marie Adelaide Leprosy Center in the Karachi slums. She soon turned it into the hub of a network of 157 medical centers that treated tens of thousands of lepers. Once leprosy was under control, the centers dealt with tuberculosis, blindness, and other diseases and disabilities. Born in Leipzig, Pfau was inspired to become a doctor after the death of her baby brother. She rejected marriage. "When you receive such a calling, you cannot turn it down, for it is not you who has made the choice," she said. "God has chosen you for himself."[23]

Maria Skobtsova (1891–1945), known as Mother Maria of Paris, born Elizaveta Yurievna Pilenko, a Russian noblewoman, poet, and nun, worked for the French Resistance during World War II. She believed in hospitality and loving her neighbor. "At the Last Judgment," she wrote, "I shall not be asked whether I was successful in my ascetic exercises, nor how many bows and prostrations I made. Instead I shall be asked, Did I feed the hungry, clothe the naked, visit the prisoners. That is all I shall be asked." Born to an aristocratic family in Riga, Latvia, she grew up an atheist in St. Petersburg but was gradually drawn into the church. She was accused of being a Bolshevik, and only because the judge was a former teacher of hers, she was saved; she ended up marrying the judge, her second marriage. Maria and her husband fled to Paris where she took up theological studies, divorced, and became a nun with the assurance that she would not be required to enter a monastery. Maria's house became a safe place for fleeing Jews. Eventually arrested, she died in Ravensbrück concentration camp.

Mother Teresa (1910–97) is known the world over. In 1979, she was awarded a $192,000 Nobel Peace Prize for the work she had done in Calcutta, India, where she founded the Missionaries of Charity, an organization devoted to helping those in need; she gave all the peace prize money to help the poor. "It is not how much we do," she wrote, "but how much love we put in the doing. It is not how much we give, but how much love we put in the giving."

Born in Skopje, Macedonia, she joined the Sisters of Loretto in Ireland, taking her name after St. Therese of Lisieux (1873–97), a Carmelite nun. Mother Teresa then went to India to teach, but was so overwhelmed with the poverty there that she founded a new order with the aim of caring for people nobody else was prepared to look after. "Love has to be put into action, and that action is service," she said. Consequently, in 1948 she left the convent to live full-time among the poor, and four years later opened a home for the dying, allowing them to die in dignity. Those in her hospices were given the religious rites appropriate for their religion; she never tried to convert anyone to her Roman Catholic faith. When she was asked how to promote world peace, she responded: "Go home and love your family."[24]

Dorothy Day's (1897–1980) friends and fellow workers were socialists, anarchists, and communists where she lived and worked in New York City, Oakland, California, and Chicago. Born in Brooklyn, she became a radical, a pacifist, and a bohemian, writing for *The Call* and *The Masses*, socialist papers, and in 1933, she co-founded *The Catholic Worker*, a newspaper that could be purchased for one cent, geared toward the homeless and the working poor. She had a daughter, although she never married, but she felt she should join the church to provide a better model for her child. Dorothy and a friend opened a house of hospitality to feed and shelter the poor and the homeless, and the one shelter grew to hundreds across the country.

Dorothy always led a life of civil disobedience and social service; she was jailed in 1917 for demonstrating outside the White House in Washington, DC, for women's suffrage. She protested against both World Wars, fascism, anti-Semitism, racism, the Vietnam War, and nuclear weapons. When she was 76 she was jailed for 10 days for walking a picket line with César Chávez, an American civil rights activist and labor leader.

In recent years, there has been a seismic shift in the churches' understanding of mission. The word missionary formerly brought to mind the picture of devout religious persons working in foreign lands, saving souls by converting "the natives" to their particular religious denomination or church and instructing and assisting them in every practical way, but always with the goal of Christianizing.[25]

Born in China to missionary parents, Katharine Boehner Hockin (1910–93) had to bridge two styles of mission. By the time she had become an adult, most churches respected the foreign country's right and responsibility to "discern what God's mission" was for them. Now, only if they are asked, do many First World churches participate in foreign mission. But it was a position forced on North American and European churches, to think in terms of other countries or churches as partners with many qualities and accomplishments to offer, rather than as ignorant "heathens" in a foreign land.

Katharine had been troubled by the dismissal of Indigenous cultures as pagan or heathen when she taught in the 1930s at the Ahousat Indian Residential School on Vancouver Island off the west coast of Canada, where the aim was to assimilate the Nootka people into white culture. Then, when she returned to China as a missionary in 1940 after a lengthy furlough, she was put under house arrest for two years because of recent hostility to Western religion and foreign residents as a result of the rise of communism in China and the beginning of the Cultural Revolution.

Once loved by her Chinese friends, she now had crowds shouting at her, "Teacher Hockin, the imperialist, international cultural spy.... She will answer to the people for her crimes!" As she said at the time, "If I were Chinese, I would have hated me too." She wrote, "I believe that in the events of this century the Western nations are under judgment.... I believe God judges all who misuse power." Later hired at the United Church Training School in Toronto (now the Centre for Christian Studies) when she returned to Canada, teaching missiology to men and women entering the professional paid ministry, she struggled to redefine the shape of mission. She had grown up participating in traditional missionary activity where her mother and father were respected evangelists but on Western terms.[26]

Although it has only been recently that most Western churches have discarded the feeling and attitude of superiority in mission activity, not all early missionaries were completely insensitive to the customs and culture of the countries where they were sent. For example, in some areas in China, missionaries seated men and women on different sides of the church, often with a screen between them, even though the missionaries themselves would have preferred everyone worshipping together in the same pews. The missionaries gave a lot to the countries where they were working. They built schools and hospitals and trained local nurses, doctors, and teachers, leaving a legacy of education and health care which benefitted the local population.

FURTHER READING

PRIMARY

Baker, Frances J. *The Story of the Foreign Missionary Society of the Episcopal Church, 1869–1895*. Cincinnati, OH: Curts & Jennings, 1898.

Judson, Ann Hasseltine, and James D. (James Davis) Knowles. *Memoir of Mrs. Ann H. Judson: Wife of the Rev. Adoniram Judson, missionary to Burma, including a history of the American Baptist mission in the Burman empire*. London: Wightman and Champ, 1829.

Skobtsova, Mother Maria. *Essential Writings*. Translated by Richard Pevear. Maryknoll, NY: Orbis, 2003.

Swain, Clara A. *A Glimpse of India*. New York: James Pott & Company, 1909.

SECONDARY

Beaver, R. Pierce. *American Protestant Women in World Mission*. Grand Rapids, MN: William B. Eerdmans, 1968.

Brouwer, Ruth Compton. *New Women for God: Canadian Presbyterian Women and India Missions 1876–1914*. Toronto: University of Toronto Press, 1990.

Gagan, Rosemary R. *A Sensitive Independence: Canadian Methodist Women Missionaries in Canada and the Orient, 1881–1925*. Montreal: McGill-Queen's University Press, 1992.

Keller, Rosemary Skinner, Louise L. Queen, and Hilah F. Thomas. *Women in New Worlds*. Vol. 2. Nashville, TN: Abingdon Press, 1982.

McNab, John. *They Went Forth*. Toronto: McClelland & Stewart, 1933.

Muggeridge, Malcolm. *Something Beautiful for God*. San Francisco: HarperOne, 1971.

Muir, Elizabeth Gillan, and Marilyn Färdig Whiteley. *Changing Roles of Women within the Christian Church in Canada*. Toronto: University of Toronto Press, 1995.

NOTES

1 Brumberg, "The Case of Ann Hasseltine Judson," 234f.
2 Brumberg, "The Case of Ann Hasseltine Judson," 242; Graves, "Judsons Find a Cheerless Home in Rangoon."
3 Claghorn, *Women Composers and Hymnists*.
4 Pritchard, "Methodist Women Abroad: Roles and Relationships," 3.

5   Pritchard, "Methodist Women Abroad: Roles and Relationships," 1.

6   Westerkamp, *Women and Religion in Early America, 1600–1850*, 149.

7   Armstrong and Armstrong, *The Baptists in America*, 278; Beaver, *American Protestant Women*, 13f.

8   "Women in the Uniting Church," para. 7.

9   Brumberg, "The Case of Ann Hasseltine Judson," 252f.

10 Brumberg, "The Case of Ann Hasseltine Judson," 258.

11 Swain, *A Glimpse of India*.

12 Baker, *The Story of the Woman's Foreign Missionary Society*, 34; Gagan, *A Sensitive Independence*, 212.

13 MacHaffie, ed., *Readings in Her Story*, 132.

14 McGarvey, "Sophie the Scrubwoman."

15 Lloyd, *Women and the Shaping of British Methodism*, 14f.

16 Lloyd, *Women and the Shaping of British Methodism*, 168.

17 Lloyd, *Women and the Shaping of British Methodism*, 207.

18 *Society for Promoting Female Education in the East Annual Report*, Missionary Periodical Data Base.

19 Lloyd, *Women and the Shaping of British Methodism*, 212.

20 Westerkamp, *Women and Religion in Early America 1600–1850*, 130ff.

21 Vaudry, "A. Caroline Macdonald of Japan."

22 Prang, *A Heart at Leisure from Itself*, 140ff.

23 Roberts, "Nun Worked to Contain Spread of Leprosy," S6.

24 "Biography Mother Teresa"; Muggeridge, *Something Beautiful for God*.

25 Blanchard, "From the Editor."

26 Centre for Christian Studies, "Imagine Church Differently"; Donnelly and Dau, *Katherine*, 12.

Chapter 15

WOMEN IN THE CHURCH TODAY

AFTER YEARS OF PREPARATION and discussion, the Church of England voted in 1992 to ordain women to the priesthood. Two hundred and nine male priests left the church, presumably to join the Roman Catholics. That church noted that there was no longer any hope of uniting with the Church of England because of this action. Nevertheless, in a ceremony in Bristol Cathedral in March 1994, 32 women were ordained as priests. While women such as Jane Hayward (b. 1952), a deacon at the neighboring St. Mary Redcliffe Church in the Church of England, said, "I'm so thrilled; I just think heaven and earth moved a little bit closer today," several men and women in the Church of England's pews across the country reacted strongly, both in favor of the motion and against it.[1] Here is a sample of their responses, though not representative of the membership:

A middle-aged woman: "Too many women are the breadwinners in the family; too many women are taking men's positions, to the detriment of men."

A man: "Women have the wonderful but exclusive role of bearing and nurturing children. This alone gives them status in society.... Thus it is important to preserve the function of men as patriarchs, counsellors, leaders, guiders, providers and protectors … if any self-esteem is to be preserved."

A middle-aged man in a group of rural parishes: "Now the human race isn't just male; now the priest, at the Eucharist is for all of us."

A man in an urban parish: "The ministry has definitely been enriched.… I feel guilty that for so many years I have never really considered how much the church could be losing by restricting women's ministry. Now I know."

From a woman: "The Anglican Church has no need of encouragement for division, but since you ask, this last year has hurt even more than I thought it might.… Jesus' Apostles were men.… For me it is no longer the Apostolic Church."

A man: "They'll want to be bishops next.… I can't imagine a woman bishop. I prefer a man."

An elderly woman wrote that she lives in fear of a woman priest giving her the sacrament when she is dying … a member of her family who had recently moved, now has to travel twenty miles to a "safe" church every Sunday.

A man who had changed his mind: "I hope and pray that those who are bigoted and intolerant may come to realize that christianity [sic] is about LOVE! … I cannot imagine any woman offering herself who did not feel she had a genuine vocation."[2]

The Anglican Church (i.e., the name of the Church of England in various countries around the world) had already ordained women. In 1984, a thousand people thronged into Westminster Abbey in London to celebrate the fortieth anniversary of the first ordination of a woman priest—Florence Li Tim-Oi (1907–92). Because of the impossibility of male priests traveling to Macau during World War II, Florence had been ordained as a deaconess in 1941 in Hong Kong, and was authorized to give the sacraments. Three years later, in 1944, she was ordained a priest to regularize her administration, but because of the controversy surrounding this appointment, she resigned her license until after the war, though not her priest's orders. Then in 1971, when the Anglican Church in Hong Kong ordained two other priests—Joyce Mary Bennett (1923–2015) from England and Jane Hwang Hsien Yuen (1917–97)—Florence was again officially recognized as a priest in that diocese. Hwang advocated in favor of women priests, noting in a sermon she preached in the United States in 1975 that "if humanity is to be fully represented before God in the priesthood, it is logical to suppose that the ministry which is not limited to people of one tribe or race should not be limited to one sex."[3]

Many other countries had ordained Anglican priests. Eleven women had been ordained in 1974 in the United States, known as "the Philadelphia Eleven," but they were considered to have been ordained irregularly by three retired Episcopal Church bishops, and there were four more in Washington ordained in 1975. These ordinations were regularized in 1976.

By the end of 1994, there were 1,340 ordained women priests and deacons and 10,808 ordained men in the Church of England and its overseas communions. The diaconate had been opened to women in 1987. In one year, more women than men were ordained—290 women and 273 men. And much as some had "feared," there have also been female bishops and even a female archbishop. In 2017, the *Anglican News Service* announced that the Right Reverend Kay Goldsworthy (b. 1956) had been elected Archbishop of Perth, the first woman to hold that office in the Anglican Church in Australia. Goldsworthy had been Australia's first bishop in 2008 and ordained earlier to the priesthood in 1992. There had been several bishops in other Anglican communions around the world by 2017 but no archbishops, except The Most Reverend Dr. Katherine Jefferts Schori (b. 1954), who was installed in 2006 as Presiding Bishop and Primate of the Episcopal Church in the United States, a position that is similar to archbishop in other Anglican communions.[4]

In the United States, female Episcopal Church bishops had been consecrated in 1989; a divorced African-American, Barbara Clementine Harris (1930–89), in the diocese of Massachusetts had been the first. Others were ordained the next year in New Zealand in 1990. Penelope Ann Bansall "Penny" Jamieson (b. 1942), the first bishop of New Zealand, said she wouldn't wish being a woman bishop on anyone. "The continuing subtle, even underground power of patriarchy, whether exercised by men or by women to destroy from a base of self-righteousness is truly appalling," she wrote. However, Canada,

FIGURE 15.1 The installation and induction of the Very Rev. Susanna Leigh Pain as the twenty-third dean of the Cathedral Church of St. Paul and incumbent of the parish of Sale in the Anglican diocese of Gippsland, Australia, on 3 September 2016, by Bishop Genieve Blackwell from Melbourne. Photo: Courtesy of the Anglican Church of Australia.

Ireland, South Africa, South India, Wales, and Cuba have all had female bishops as well as the Church of England.[5]

Even in recent decades, although becoming common, ordinations of Anglican women around the world still make headlines. "One for the Ladies," reported the press about Rev. Susanna Pain (b. 1957) who was soon to become the first female Dean of St. Paul's Cathedral in Sale, in the Anglican Diocese of Gippsland, Australia. Susanna had been ordained a deacon in Canberra in 1989, and a priest in December 1992. She was supposed to have been ordained along with 10 other women in February of that year, but a couple of male priests sought an injunction from the New South Wales Supreme Court in Australia, so the women had to wait several months.[6]

The Church of Ireland ordained its first three women priests in 1990, among them Janet Catterall (b. 1953), the first to serve in the Irish Republic, a former deacon in the Church of England. "At some point we all stopped counting [the number of women priests] and that's a great thing," Catterall says. "But I do think that when you have both women and men in ministry you have a completeness. It's not just men who were created in God's image, all humanity is."[7]

Most Christian churches now offer ecclesiastical equality to men and women. There is no question that the faces of church leaders have changed in the recent past. At the 2016 World Council of Churches assembly, Rev. Dr. Sharon Watkins (b. 1954), the head of the Christian Church (Disciples of Christ), pointed to the number of women delegates representing their churches contrasted with the "rows of men in dark suits and ties, most of them white" who would have been there 50 or 60 years earlier. There were at least 80 women from around the world in all colors and styles of dress.[8]

Kristine Greenaway (b. 1953), former director of the Office of Communications for the World Council of Churches in Geneva, notes, however, that the role of women in the global ecumenical movement varies enormously. Some women are equal partners with men; in other churches, women cannot be ordained.

For example, the Lutheran Church has had a long history of ordaining women in its various churches; the Lutheran Church in Denmark ordained women in 1948. By 1968, there were ordained women in Lutheran churches in Norway, Czechoslovakia, Sweden, France, and Germany; the Lutheran Church in America ordained its first minister, Elizabeth Alvina Platz (b. 1940), soon after, in 1970. There are about 30 female bishops in various Lutheran-member churches around the world at this time—the first, Maria Jepsen (b. 1945), elected Bishop of Hamburg in 1992. Much later, in 2013, Rev. Elizabeth Eaton (b. 1955) became the first presiding bishop of the four-million-member Evangelical Lutheran Church in America. Almost half of those ordained in that denomination between 2010 and 2015 were women. Yet, still in 2018, about 18 per cent of the Lutheran World Federation-member churches around the world did not ordain women. [9]

Greenaway also points to churches that once ordained women and now disallow it. But, she notes, there are things to celebrate: some global ecumenical networks have women moderators and more churches are ordaining women.

Today there are several prominent ecclesiastical women leaders around the world. Among them are Bishop Ellinah Ntombi Wamukoya (b. 1951), the first woman to be elected bishop in the Anglican Church of South Africa and on the African continent; Rev. Dr. Henriette Tabita Hutabarat-Lebang (b. 1952) of Indonesia, general secretary of the Christian Council of Asia; Dr. Agnes Regina Murei Abuom (b. 1949) from Kenya, moderator of the World Council of Churches; Dr. Isabel Apawo Phiri (b. 1957) from Malawi, deputy general secretary of the World Council of Churches; and Rev. Najla Abousawan Kassab (b. 1964) from Lebanon, president of the World Communion of Reformed Churches.

Bishop Wamukoya was involved in local politics as town clerk and head of the city council of Manzini, Swaziland as well as being a leader in the Anglican Church. She studied at universities in Botswana, Lesotho, and Swaziland, and was elected bishop of Swaziland with a two-thirds majority in 2012. David Dinkebogile (b. c. 1967), dean of the diocese of Christ the King, pointed out that Wamukoya was a bishop, "not a black woman, not an Anglican, not a Swazi woman," but she herself felt that the whole world would be watching to see if she could deliver. "I am going to try to represent the mother attribute of God," she told journalists; "a mother is a caring person but at the same time, a mother can be firm in doing whatever she is doing."[10]

An ordained pastor of the Toraja Church in Indonesia, Rev. Dr. Henriette Hutabarat-Lebang, the general secretary of the Christian Conference of Asia (2010) is extremely well educated like all of these outstanding women. She holds a Master of Arts and Doctor of Education degrees from the Presbyterian School of Christian Education and a Master of Divinity from the Jakarta Theological Seminary. The Christian Conference of Asia is made up of 95 member churches and 16 member councils in 17 countries representing 55 million Christians in Asia.[11]

A member of the Anglican Church of Kenya, and a former Africa President of the World Council of Churches, Dr. Agnes Regina Murei Abuom was elected moderator of the Central Committee of the World Council of Churches in 2013. As a child, Abuom had wanted to become a doctor, but "could not stomach dissection." Then she hoped to become a lawyer, but ended up studying education, development studies, and history. Becoming heavily involved in politics, she had to leave her native Kenya in 1976, lived in Sweden, then later worked with refugees in Sudan and as a tutor in Zimbabwe. She returned to Kenya in 1989, eventually working for the Anglican Church there. In 2017, she was awarded the Lambeth Cross for Ecumenism by the Archbishop of Canterbury.[12]

Abuom notes that she struggled enormously because she is a woman. "It was an issue of perseverance and determination," she says, "coupled with prayers, to discern the will of God" for her ministry. But, she notes, "the pilgrimage of women [in] leadership is [always] fraught with covert and overt forms of discrimination." Abuom believes that women bring a different approach than men to pastoral work: "Motherly love does in general permeate and not the raw competitive spirit for power so well exhibited by men," she writes.

The African theologian Dr. Isabel Apawo Phiri from Malawi, a former dean of the School of Religion at the University of KwaZulu Natal in South Africa, was elected Associate General Secretary for Public Witness and Diakonia for the World Council of Churches in 2012. She had been involved with the ecumenical movement for years and has a special interest in African women's theology. Now teaching at the University of Malawi, Phiri has authored and edited various works on religion and African women including *Women, Presbyterianism and Patriarchy: Religious Experience of Chewa Women in Malawi* (1997) and *African Women, Religion and Health: Essays in Honor of Mercy Amba Ewudziwa Oduyoye* (2012). Oduyoye (b. 1934) had served as deputy general secretary of the World Council of Churches, the first African woman from south of the Sahara to be in that position.

While several African women have achieved executive status in the church, Rev. Tseganesh Ayele (b. 1964) of the Ethiopian Evangelical Church, head of Women's Ministry at the Mekane Yesus Seminary in Ethiopia, notes that in the churches that have approved women's ordination, less than 1 per cent to about 15 per cent of those ordained are women. "If there were more women in ordained leadership positions, they would be able to reduce the doubts that women are capable of taking leadership positions and would be a role model," she says.[13]

President of the World Communion of Reformed Churches, Rev. Najla Kassab, a native of Lebanon, was given a preaching license in 2003 by the Evangelical Synod of Syria and Lebanon (Presbyterian), the first woman to be so recognized, and ordained in 2017, one of only two female ministers in her denomination. Speaking from the pulpit used by the Protestant Reformer Martin Luther in Wittenberg, Germany, she asked, "Why did it take so long" to have a woman in that pulpit? "This is not just a struggle of equality," she said. "It is a struggle of justice."[14]

Kassab counts herself fortunate that her family respected women, for she had to leave Lebanon to study for a Master of Divinity (although today women are able to earn that theological degree in her country). Later, when she was being considered for a preaching license, one male pastor in her church threatened to leave. Kassab understands that he thought he was doing the will of God, obeying a biblical injunction; she wondered if she was bringing trouble to the church. She concluded that she would "understand in love the position of this pastor." She notes that he changed his position and she changed as well. "It takes patience and focus to move forward. Anger makes us lose our wisdom," she notes. "Ordination is not a battle between men and women, but in partnership we can do change."[15]

The World Communion of Reformed Churches consists of more than 225 churches in over 110 countries. In the last elections, of the 22 members on the executive committee, 10 were men and 12 were women; 15 were ordained, and 7 were members of the laity. Of the 4 vice-presidents elected at the same time as Kassab, 3 were women, an ordained minister from the United States, a university professor from Indonesia, and a lawyer from Brazil.

Ordained women aren't the only women today who hold ecclesiastical positions in churches. Lay volunteers such as Dr. Marion Best (b. 1932) and Dr. Elisabeth Raiser (b. 1940) have made tremendous contributions to the world church.

Best served as the thirty-fifth moderator (head) of the United Church of Canada (1994–97) and vice-moderator of the World Council of Churches. She found tremendous support as a woman in her own denomination but realized how difficult it was for some of the women from other communions on the World Council. Best believes that women bring the value of "story" to their preaching and encourage parishioners to make connections between the biblical story and their own stories.

Raiser was president of the ecumenical Kirchentag in Berlin, a gathering of 100,000 participants, for 14 years, and elected president of the Ecumenical Forum of European Christian Women. A teacher and historian by profession, she never considered the study of theology or ordination, but occasionally is invited to the pulpit to preach. A Lutheran, Raiser has written about the history of women in the ecumenical movement: *With Love and Passion: Women's Life and Work in the Worldwide Church*.

Kristine Greenaway has held senior positions in the church. An experienced television producer, scriptwriter, and editor, she has served the World Communion Alliance of Reformed Churches as head of communications and was the first woman to hold the position of Director of Communications for the World Council of Churches where she served as editor in the Publications Office. She was also part-time head of the Consistoire Laurentian, an oversight body for the French-language and bilingual congregations in L'Église Unie du Canada (the United Church of Canada).

Most of these women have experienced discrimination in their church careers but they have managed to put those experiences behind them. The Very Reverend Lois Miriam Freeman Wilson (b. 1927), though, the first female moderator of the United Church of Canada from 1980 to 1982, the first female head of the Canadian Council of Churches (1976–79), and one of seven presidents of the World Council of Churches from 1983 to 1991, reminisced in her autobiography about some of the gender labeling that occurred in her career. Shortly after her ordination, she was asked to speak at a meeting and also bless the food before they ate. In the written agenda for that event was the following: "Grace: Lois Wilson, unless another [male] minister is present." After she was elected moderator of the United Church of Canada, she received many anonymous letters. One read, "Go home and look after your kids." (At that point, all her children were adults.) Another said, "Where are the men of the church that we have to resort to a woman moderator?" And, "Can't you do anything with your hair?" But even after she was ordained in 1965, married to a minister, Lois confessed that she herself often unconsciously bought into current cultural stereotypes.[16]

Wilson was the first of six recent female moderators in the United Church of Canada, which ordained its first female minister in 1936, Lydia Emelie Gruchy (1894–1992). Today there are roughly the same number of women in ministry as there are men in ministry in that denomination, which began as a 1925 union of mainly Methodist, Presbyterian, and Congregational Churches. Noticeable, though, is that there are more women ministering in rural churches than men—56 per cent of the women contrasted with 38 per cent of the men—and a greater percentage of men than women in urban and suburban churches. It would appear that some of the larger, more prosperous urban churches still feel more comfortable with a man in the pulpit.[17]

The Most Reverend Patricia Shaw Storey (b. 1960) laughs at some of the gender stereotyping she has experienced in her daily life. The first female bishop of the Church of Ireland, she was consecrated in 2013. Recently she went to deposit a check in a bank but was told that the bishop would have to endorse it himself. "I am he," she told the embarrassed teller. When she went to renew her driving license, the young man at the desk saw her address and said how impressed he was that she was married to the bishop. She explained that she was the bishop. She doesn't take offense at these gaffes, although she remarks that even today, people make assumptions

FIGURE 15.2 The Most Rev. Patricia Storey prior to her enthronement as bishop in St. Brigid's Cathedral, Kildare, Ireland, 14 December 2013. Bishop Storey was consecrated in Christ Church Cathedral, Dublin, 30 November 2013, and enthroned in two cathedrals the following month. An old rite calls for a "new" bishop to knock on the door of a cathedral three times with the base of "his" crozier as a sign of taking claim of the church. Photo: Courtesy of the Church of Ireland.

about women, and a woman at a senior level is still often mistaken for a secretary or "only" a wife.[18]

Originally from Belfast, Storey was ordained a deacon in 1998 and a priest the next year. When she was surprised at being asked to become a bishop, Dr. Richard Clarke (b. 1949), the Primate of the Church of Ireland, assured her that it was not a token appointment, that she was the right person for the job, that she "fitted the bill." The Church of Ireland had approved the ordination of women as priests and bishops in 1990, but today only just over 20 per cent are women, although about half of its deacons are female and almost 30 per cent of the students in their theological college are women.[19]

Many denominations just weren't prepared for female leaders, especially ministers. The Presbyterian minister Cynthia Campbell (b. 1948), a former president of McCormick Theological Seminary in Chicago, remembers her ordination certificate in 1974 had an "s" added to a printed "he." An IBM Selectric typewriter had been used to type "her" over "his."

The Uniting Church in Australia, also a union of Congregational, Methodist, and most of the Presbyterian Church (1977), has ordained women for almost a century, with the first woman ordained in the Congregational Church in 1927, Winifred Kiek (1884–1975). The social worker and theologian Dr. Deidre Palmer (b. 1956), president-elect in 2018, is the second female president of that denomination. She has been the moderator for the Synod of South Australia and a professor of Christian Education at Flinders University. Palmer believes that every member of the church is called to minister, "to engage in Christian discipleship in the world."[20]

The Right Reverend Helga Haugland Byfuglien (b. 1950), the first female presiding bishop of the Church of Norway, was also one of the first women ordained in that Church. She considers that her mother was her best female role model: a widow at age 38 with six children. "She was wise and strong, a leader of the congregation, but not self-serving. That is my way, too," Haugland notes.[21]

The Church of South India has also ordained women as priests since 1976; there are around 120 in that communion today. In 2013, the church ordained its first woman bishop, a former nun, the Rev. Sister Eggoni Pushpa Lalitha (b. 1956). Comprising more than four million members, the Church of South India (CSI) is a union of several traditions including Anglican, Methodist, Congregational, Presbyterian, and Reformed. Pushpa Lalitha said she has often faced bias against women in leadership. "Be it any institution," she noted, "women are always given second-rung treatment. We need to change that by promoting values that teach us not to discriminate and treat all humans the same." Pushpa Lalitha made a vow of celibacy when she was in college; her parents had dedicated her to God's service even before her birth.[22]

Pushpa Lalitha is the second female bishop in Asia. Aliveli S. Katakshamma (1936–97) was consecrated bishop of the Lutheran Church in Asia just months before she died in 1997. It had been a "proud moment" for the Lutheran Church when she was ordained, "breaking the male bastion and male dominated tradition," said the head of the women's desk for the Good Samaritan Evangelical Lutheran Church.[23]

The students and faculty at theological colleges are also changing their appearance. While they were generally all male not many years ago, today there are sometimes more female students than male. One year recently at Emmanuel College, part of the University of Toronto, all the ministerial candidates were women. Today, there are five women and one man on the faculty, with eight female sessional lecturers and four male. Significantly, the opposite is true of the current professors *emeriti*: seven male and three female. Not all theological colleges, however, are so feminized. For example, the Nazarene

Theological College at the University of Manchester in England has a female principal, but there are only four female faculty members, contrasted with thirteen males including guest lecturers.

But perhaps the most remarkable shift in women's position in the church today is the presence of Roman Catholic women priests, not that the pope agrees. During a press conference in November 2016, Pope Francis (b. 1936) reaffirmed the Roman Catholic Church's position on ordaining women:

> "Saint Pope John Paul II had the last clear word on this and it stands, this stands," Francis said in his initial response to journalists, referring to a 1994 document stating that women could never join the priesthood. "But for ever, for ever? Never, never?" a reporter asked in a follow-up question.... Francis replied: "If we read carefully the declaration by Saint John Paul II, it is going in that direction."[24]

Indeed, the Vatican is resolutely opposed to the ordination of women. In 2010, the Vatican named pedophilia and the ordination of women as two of the gravest crimes against the Catholic Church, and in 2011, Pope Benedict XVI (b. 1927) removed an Australian bishop, William M. Morris, for suggesting in a pastoral letter that he would be open to women's ordination. The next year, Father Roy Bourgeois, a Nobel Peace Prize nominee, was dismissed from the Maryknoll Fathers and Brothers after 44 years because of his continued support of women priests. In 2008, after he took part in the ordination of his activist friend Janice Sevre-Duszynska (b. 1950), he was told to recant his support of women priests but he refused. Later, he was part of a panel of speakers following a showing of *Pink Smoke over the Vatican* at Barnard College in New York City, an award-winning video tracing the history of women's journey to ordination. Bourgeois was then dismissed.[25]

While the door may have been closed to the ordination of women as priests, Pope Francis did not rule out the possibility of ordaining women as deacons. In response to a question at a town hall-style meeting in 2016 with heads of 900 women's religious orders, he claimed that he would appoint an official commission to study the issue. But the Catholic reporter Kristina Keneally from *The Guardian* is not optimistic. "There is zero chance that this study (similar to earlier studies) is going to find some theological basis that women can be ordained permanent deacons," she wrote.[26]

However, the Association of Roman Catholic Women Priests (ARCWP) and the Roman Catholic Women Priests (RCWP) are two streams of an organization dedicated to ordaining qualified women as deacons, priests, and bishops in the Roman Catholic Church around the world. The groups affirm that women's baptism is spiritually equal to that of men. While their goal is similar to that of male ordination, their approach is different; they are working toward a new "**paradigm**" that is "egalitarian and empowered ministry in a community of learners that includes contemporary theology, wholistic spirituality, sacramental ministry and action on behalf of justice, peace and healing."[27]

Now more than 250 strong, the women priest movement began on the Danube in 2002. A male bishop, then in good standing in the Roman Catholic Church, ordained seven women from the United States and Europe over international waters to avoid interference. The bishop had already ordained his wife. The bishop was excommunicated; the women were given a period to repent for this "most serious offence." But because the women "gave no indication of amendment or repentance," they were excommunicated also. The women responded that they were "not leaving the church. They were leading the church." A year later, two women were ordained as bishops. Somehow, the Vatican understands this as "an affront to the dignity of women."[28]

Many of the ordained women are former nuns. All of them are theologically and sacramentally trained, some through the not-for-profit People's Catholic Seminary, an online certificate and professional development program founded by Dr. Bridget Mary Meehan (b. 1948) and Dr. Mary Theresa Streck (b. 1947) both from the ARCWP. The women priests and bishops are well educated, and as the journalist Ross Anderson notes, "The group is composed mostly of middle-age and older women, many of them married with children and grandchildren—hardly a radical organization."

For example, Catherine O'Connor (b. 1961) in Pickering, Canada, holds a Master of Divinity degree and is a registered social worker. At age four, she felt called by God to be a priest, so she later decided to work in the Anglican Church. But brought up a Roman Catholic, she didn't feel the Anglican Church was quite right for her. She was elated when she heard about the "Danube Seven." She was ordained by the RCWP in 2013.

Judy Dahl (b. 1949) of Cape George, Washington, was eight years old when she was certain that she, too, was called to become a priest. But it was only in 2016 that her dream came true and she was ordained a Roman Catholic priest. Judy had belonged to a cloistered Benedictine convent for three years; then when she realized the convent was not for her, she became a flight attendant for more than a decade. A lesbian with two children, she joined the Metropolitan Community Church, becoming an ordained minister there for 30 years. With a Master of Divinity from Iliff School of Theology and a doctorate from San Francisco Theological Seminary she was well trained for that position. She also supervised 37 churches with 85 ministers in the southwestern United States. Judy worked with Cuban refugees and later directed a global program for LGBTQ people in Africa and Asia. Eventually she found the RCWP and is now an ordained priest in the Roman Catholic Church where she feels she really belongs. Even with her educational background and ministry experience, she was required to take 10 more theological courses and complete a psychological assessment before she could become a priest.[29]

Other people are working to change the Catholic Church from within, Dahl notes, and she respects those efforts. But she still feels called to do more. When women around the world are taking their rightful place in business and politics and in other churches, her mission is to address "one of the last bastions of misogyny on the planet."[30]

Ordained as a priest in 2010, Olga Lucia Alvarez Benjumea (b. 1941) from Medellin, Columbia, the first Latin American to be ordained by the ARCWP, was also well prepared to become a bishop in 2015. Educated by the Dominican Sisters of the Presentation, she did missionary work with indigenous and Afro-Columbian communities and was secretary of the Latin American Episcopal Council at Medellin in 1968 (CELAM; *Consejo Episcopal Latinoamericano*). She studied pastoral ministry, higher catechesis, and liberation theology in addition to taking biblical and religious courses. A member of the Collective of Ecumenical Bible Scholars (CEDEMI; *Centro Educacional da Emilia*), Olga has written several books and articles on theology. Her main ministry today is with women ex-convicts and the Association of Families of the Disappeared (ASFADDES; *La Asociación de Familiares de Detanidos Desaparecidos Asfaddes*).[31]

Male ecclesiastics say they are the representatives of Christ, Olga remarks. "There's no basis for that. We have all been created in the image of God. We are all equal…. It's not about power, it's about service," she says.[32] The women priests' mandate is entirely service-oriented: equality for women in the church includes decision-making and ordination; ministry with the poor and the marginalized; living the spiritual and social justice tradition of the church serving inclusive communities; and actively and openly participating in non-violent movements for peace and justice. Olga quotes Eleanor

FIGURE 15.3   Rev. Janice Sevre-Duszynska in Rome, March 2013, two days before Pope Francis was elected. Sevre-Duszynska was representing the Association of Roman Catholic Women Priests (ARCWP). Photo: Courtesy of AP France.

Roosevelt (1884–1962), who said: "It isn't enough to talk about peace, one must believe it; and it isn't enough to believe in it, one must work for it."

Everyone is welcome at the women priests' services: divorced and remarried men and women who are excluded from the regular Roman Catholic Church, as well as LGBTQ people. People could be excommunicated just for attending, but the people come. A 35-year-old mother said, "I choke back tears every time" she attends one of their services. "I did some research and found out what these women are doing is totally legit because they can claim apostolic succession … that means it's real." A male non-Catholic goes as a show of solidarity: "It's a beautiful thing that's happening here. These women are very brave," he says. Father Roy Bourgeois, the Roman Catholic priest who attended the ordination as priest of Janice Sevre-Duszynska in the United States in 2008 commented: "It is our conscience that compels us to be here today. How can we speak out against the injustice of our country's foreign policy in Latin America and Iraq if we are silent about the injustice of our own church here at home?"[33]

Two other women priests should be noted: lawyer and author Kathleen Maria Macpherson (b. 1944), ordained in the American Catholic Church in the United States (ACCUS) in 2011, a small independent Catholic denomination not subject to the rules and regulations of the Roman Catholic Church, and in which clergy support themselves through ministerial and secular jobs; and Ludmilla Javorová (b. 1932), a Czechoslovakian woman, ordained a priest in 1970 by Bishop Felix Maria Davidek (1921–88) of the underground Catholic Church Koinótés. During the Communist era in Czechoslovakia, Catholic orders were banned and existing clergy were jailed, sent to labor camps, forced into military service, or murdered. There was an urgent need to ordain qualified men and women to the priesthood. It is thought that four other women were also ordained but their identities are not known today.

FURTHER READING

PRIMARY

Leading. ARCWP Newsletters, Orlando Park, Illinois, 2017.

Melton, J. Gordon. *The Churches Speak on Women's Ordination*. Detroit: Gale Research, 1991.

Wilson, Lois. *Turning the World Upside Down: A Memoir*. Toronto: Doubleday Canada, 1989.

SECONDARY

Hart, Jules, dir. *Pink Smoke over the Vatican*. Eve Goddess Films, 2013. DVD.

Wakeman, Hilary, ed. *Women Priests: The First Years*. London: Darton, Longman and Todd, 1996.

Winter, Miriam Therese. *Out of the Depths: The Story of Ludmila Javorova, Ordained Roman Catholic Priest*. New York: The Crossroad Publishing Company, 2001.

NOTES

1 Brown, "Send Down Your Holy Spirit upon Your Servant Angela."

2 Wakeman, *Women Priests*, 1–26.

3 Diocesan Press Service, "Hong Kong Priest Visits Southern Ohio."

4 Lusted, *Women's Roles in Religion*, 11.

5 "First Female Archbishop Elected in Australia"; Brewerton, "Penny Jamieson, Biography."

6 Harris, "One for the Ladies."

7 Butler, "The First Female Priest Ordained in Ireland Discusses the Influence of Women Priests in the Anglican Ministry." Today approximately one-fifth of all ministers in the Church of Ireland are women.

8 Greenaway, "The Faces of Global Ecumenical Leaders Have Changed." Approximately one-third of all ministers in the Disciples of Christ are women and the first woman minister in that denomination was Clara Celestia Hale Babcock (1850–1925), ordained in 1888.

9 Evangelical Lutheran Church in America, "ELCA Celebrates 45 Years of Ordaining Women"; Houston, "Lutheran Women in Ministry."

10 "Swaziland's Ellinah Wamukya Becomes Africa's First Female Bishop"; Ghosh, "African Anglicans Ordain First Female Bishop as Church of England Prepares Vote on Matter."

11 "Rev. Dr. Henriette Hutabarat Lebang, General Secretary of CCA," *Christian Conference of Asia*, 2011.

12 A Discussion with Agnes Abuom, Executive Committee, World Council of Churches. Berkley Center for Religion, Peace and World Affairs, 3 July 2009.

13 Guyer, "Based on Discussions with Ordained Women in Ghana, Ethiopia, Malawi and Zimbabwe."

14 Eckert, "Incoming President Najla Kassab Speaks of Gender Equality and Justice." In the United States, the first Presbyterian woman was ordained in 1956—Margaret Towner (b. 1925). Today approximately one-third of the ministers in that denomination in the US are female (OGA Communications).

15 Najla Kassab, email conversations with the author, September–October, 2017.

16 Wilson, *Turning the World Upside Down*, 45, 132.

17 Susan Jackson, email to the author, 20 June 2017.

18 McCann, "Church of Ireland Bishop Pat Storey Mistaken for Secretary."

19 O'Brien, "A First among Equals"; "List of Clergy," Church of Ireland, 2017.

20 President-elect profile, "Hearts on Fire," 14th Triennial Assembly, Uniting Church in Australia, 2015. Today approximately 32 per cent of the ministers in the Uniting Church of Australia are women, according to Christine Gordon.

21 Greenaway, "Bishop Helga Haugland Byfuglien"; "Church of Norway's Presiding Bishop to Open Leiv Erickson Festival."

22 Arora, "First Anglican Woman Bishop in India Says Critics Have Been Silent."

23 "Death of Asia's First Woman Bishop Mourned by Indian Lutherans."

24 Kirchgaessner, "Pope Francis Says Women Will Never Be Roman Catholic Priests."

25 Hart, dir., *Pink Smoke over the Vatican*; Rev. Janice Sevre-Duszynska, email to the author, 12 October 2017.

26 Kirchgaessner and Sherwood, "Pope Francis to Consider Ordaining Women as Deacons"; Keneally, "Pope Francis Is a Master at Playing the Crowd."

27 Janice Sevre-Dusynska, email to the author, 9 September 2017; a retired teacher, Janice is working on a Doctor of Ministry. Connolly and Willan, "Vatican Casts Out 'Ordained' Women."

28 Connolly and Willan, "Vatican Casts Out 'Ordained' Women"; Janice Sevre-Duszynska, telephone conversation with the author, September 2017.

29 Anderson, "Ordination of Renegade Priest."

30 Anderson, "Ordination of Renegade Priest."

31 Olga Lucia Alvarez, email conversations with the author, September–October 2017.

32 "Latin America's First Women Priests Challenge Church."

33 Fornasiero, "Two Ordained Women Priests Challenging Rome in Toronto."

CONCLUSION

OVER THE CENTURIES, WOMEN have been apostles and deacons, priests and presbyters, preachers and prophets, bishops and archbishops, abbesses and canonesses, missionaries and itinerants, ministers and evangelists, and maybe even a pope. Women have written theology and devotions, sermons and homilies, inspirational biographies, church music, hymns, and convent rules. They have interpreted scripture. Women have preached, taught, healed, baptized, and served communion or the Eucharist. Women have founded Sunday Schools, theological colleges, hospitals, orphanages, schools, churches, abbeys, convents, religious orders and denominations, and administered these organizations. And there are so many other roles that have not even been considered in this study because of length constraint, such as organists and choir conductors, lay readers, and study group leaders.

It should not be surprising that women were so active in the church. Women have formed the majority of the members in the Christian Church from its beginning. Even recently, in 2001, a national church survey for the Uniting Church in Australia found that 61 per cent of church attendees were women, 39 per cent male.[1]

Why then do most people not know about these capable women? They have been legion.

One reason is that as often as women became ecclesiastical leaders, they were put down, enclosed in convents and kept invisible, thrown in jail or put under house arrest, burnt at the stake, or drowned. Official histories omitted their stories entirely, or devoted only a line or two to their life and work. Their obituaries neglected to mention any of their church activity, often deliberately. In spite of the greater number of women in churches, it has been male ecclesiastics who have recorded the histories, written the rules, and exercised control.

While a few men supported these impressive women, most church ecclesiastics and others noted that the women were operating beyond their allotted sphere and fixed occupation in life, a sphere determined by men, but supposedly created and dictated by the deity. This was the women's main crime: they were acting as if they were men. They had usurped men's place and role both in the church and in society.

There are numerous examples of this in every century, as illustrated in the chapters in this study. For example, in the early years of Christianity it was considered "dangerous" for women to baptize or teach in church for it was deemed "contrary to custom," the custom being that it was men's work. It was never clear where the danger lay! As Tertullian wrote about women in the Montanist sect, "They do all kinds of things they shouldn't do," such as baptizing men. The missionary-martyr Thecla operated in the sphere supposedly restricted to men, traveling in men's clothes and performing men's work, preaching, baptizing, and healing; she had to be rescued and hidden inside a mountain. The fourth-century deaconess-abbess Olympias was engaged in duties that "belong fitly to a man," setting up and administering monastic communities with her vast wealth. In the fifth century, it was said that women were taking part in "all matters imputed to the offices of the male sex, to which they do not belong," teaching, preaching, baptizing, and instructing in theology.

Joan of Arc believed that she could access God or her "voices" directly; the church was firm that she should have checked with her local male priest first. Women were supposed to be enclosed—in a convent or an anchorhold or a home, not running around a battlefield winning battles. Confined, women would be safely kept from taking on men's work. When they traveled about they were perceived as a threat. As a Dominican told the highly skilled Cathar debater Esclarmonde, "Go tend your distaff, madam, it is no business of yours" to discuss theology. It was understood by the church to be a male preserve. The thirteenth/fourteenth-century Pope John XXII noted that a good Beguine stayed inside four walls and did not discuss theology.

In the seventeenth century, Mary Ward's efforts to train children and mothers in the Catholic faith met with stern resistance from the Catholic Church she was trying to save. It was never known that women could undertake apostolic work the Catholic Church responded; women were meddling in a male preserve, the conversion of England. In the nineteenth-century mission fields, men often felt women were intruding into their area of work. Even the Freewill Baptists in America, with their more liberal attitudes such as supporting the ordination of women, noted that women "should not be meddling with those affairs which are peculiarly designed for the transaction of men." Time and time again, women were castigated for entering into areas of church work where they were told they were not entitled to be and especially where they were not wanted.

The irony, of course, is that in the early church, women had tried to become "manly" to be saved, denying their femininity and espousing asceticism. But becoming a "man" in that sense was quite different from taking on "man's work."

At one time in the Middle East, the area where Christianity began, the gods were women and women held superior positions in much of society. Sun goddesses were worshipped in Canaan, Anatolia, Arabia, Australia, and among the northern first peoples, the Japanese, and the Khasis of India. Centuries ago in Sumer, Babylon, Egypt, and other parts of Africa, Australia, and China there were stories of goddesses who created the earth and the heavens. The earliest law, government, medicine, agriculture, architecture, metallurgy, wheeled vehicles, ceramics, textiles, and written language were originally developed in countries that worshipped the goddess.[2]

Christianity, however, grew out of the Jewish tradition when it worshipped a male God. Worship of the goddess was anathema, and women had few or no privileges. Other cultures where the first Christian churches developed were also male oriented and the Christian Church fell under their influence. Jesus was a Jew and would have been expected to follow the rules of his society, although there are numerous examples recorded in the New Testament where he broke with the traditions that limited women's roles. It was inevitable, however, that churches would assume the surrounding cultural patriarchy and misogyny after his death, although in every century prominent well-educated women could be found in secular society. A few of these are listed in the timeline at the back of this book.

We need to note, however, that over the years, in many denominations and churches led by the transforming power of the Holy Spirit, women's call to ministry was accepted and encouraged. Leadership was based on prophetic authority rather than priestly authority, which is anchored in tradition. Unfortunately, over time, these progressive churches often became hierarchical and institutionalized, influenced by surrounding cultural mores, with theological colleges not open to women and other requirements for ministry accessible only to men; gradually, women were relegated to subordinate supportive positions.[3] For example, one can find this phenomenon in groups such as the Bible Christians and Primitive Methodists within the Methodist tradition. There were some exceptions: in earlier periods, some mystics were allowed to maintain a direct "pipeline" to God; their spirituality was considered feminine, and their voices were often seen as prophetically inspired.

Fortunately today, there are many outstanding women around the world who have taken their place in leadership in their denominations; witness especially those mentioned in chapter 15 of this book. Although many of them suffered discrimination in their religious and ecclesiastical journeys, the future looks promising for women. The whole Christian Church may yet offer equal opportunities for all.

One further question remains to be asked in the history of the Christian Church. What would the history of the church have looked like if Mary Magdalene had won over the disciple Peter?

NOTES

1 "Women in the Uniting Church: By a Partial, Prejudiced, and Ignorant Historian (to Quote the Immortal Jane)," para. 1.
2 Stone, *When God Was a Woman.*
3 Sanchez, "Your Daughters Shall Prophesy," 17ff.

APPENDIX: TIMELINE

SELECTED WOMEN AND EVENTS

BCE

Anna, mother of Mary, grandmother of Jesus?

1–100 CE

Alce, Apphia, Claudia, Lydia, Mary,
Nympha, Priscilla, Tavia, and
others, heads of house churches

Anna, Philip's four daughters and
others, prophets

Assia, Lydia, Jesus' sisters

Elizabeth, Mary (Jacobe), Jesus' aunts,

Euodia, Photina (Samaritan),
Prisca/Priscilla, Syntyche,
Tryphosa, and others, evangelists

Joanna, Martha, Mary of Bethany,
Mary (James and Joses's mother),
Mary wife of Cleophas, Salome,
Sarah, Susanna, and others, disciples

c.4 BCE–c.33 CE: Jesus of Nazareth
lived and worked

15–59: Agrippina II, ruler of the
Roman Empire

b. 20: Pamphile, Greek female
essayist and historian

64–313: Intermittent persecution of
Christians

70: Brigh Brigaid, Irish lawyer
interested in women's rights

Junia, apostle
Mary Magdala/Magdalene/Miriam
 (c.10 BCE–c.74 CE), apostle to
 the apostles
Julia, Olympas, and others, church
 workers
Phoebe, Tryphaena, and others,
 order of deacons
Mary, mother of Jesus
Tabitha/Dorcas and others, order
 of widows
Thecla and others, missionaries
Veronica, woman healed by Jesus
Helena, disciple of Simon Magus
Lois, Timothy's mother; Eunice,
 Timothy's grandmother

100–200

Ammia, Prisca, Quintilla, prophets
Marianne, Maximilla (?–179), lead-
 ers of Gnostic churches
Grapte, in charge of women in the
 church
Women in the orders of virgins,
 widows, deacons
Women writers

113: Suetonius writes *De Viris
 Illustribus* (*Concerning Famous Men*)
c.157–217: Julia Domna, well-
 educated female Roman regent
166–67: Plague in Europe

200–300

Perpetua (?–202) and Felicitas
 (?–202), martyrs
Antony/Anthony's sister and
 others, nuns
Catherine (?–307) and others,
 intellectuals
Cleopatra, Eugenia (?–258), Drusiana,
 Sara, and others, ascetics
Helena (246/50–327/30), mother of
 Constantine, built churches

d. 235: Julia Mamaea, led troops in
 battle in Roman territory
180–222: Julia Soaemias, Head of
 Roman Senaculum and army
240–75: Zenobia, queen of
 Palmyrine Empire, Syria

Maria, sister of Pachomius, head
of male and female convents
Women presbyters

300–400

Alexandra, Blaesilla (364–84),
Eustochium (368–419), Syncletica
(c.270–c.350), Theodora, Sara,
and others, ascetics
Egeria and others, pilgrims
Elisanthia, Fabiola (?–399),
Macrina (c.330–c.379), Marina,
Marcella (325–410), Melania the
Elder (350–410), Melania the
Younger (c.383–439), Paula (347–
404), found/head monasteries,
convents, hostels, hospitals
Lucilla, leader in Donatist sect
Nino/Nina (c.296–c.335) and
others, evangelists
Mary of Egypt (344–421), penitent
prostitute
Olympias (c.368–c.408), Palladia,
Pentadia, Procla, Martyria, and
others, deacons
Women canonesses

306–53: Faltonia Betitia Proba, Latin
Roman Christian poet
313: Decriminalization of
Christians: Edict of Milan
c.350–415: Hypatia, philosopher,
astronomer, mathematician,
professor
366: Augustine is supposed to have
invented prayer beads
fl. 398: Sylvia of Aquitaine, extensive letter writer

400–500

Bishop Brigid/Bridget of Ireland
(453–523)
Clothilde (475–545), Susan, Cyra,
Marana, and others, ascetics
Genovefa (419–512) and others,
virgins
Principia and others, students
Theodora and others, teachers
Women continue as presbyters,
priests, elders, deacons, widows,
virgins

399–453: Pulcheria, virtual ruler of
Eastern Empire for 40 years
400–460: Eudocia, writer and founder
of University at Constantinople
476: Rome falls, virtual end of
Western Roman Empire

500–600

Caesaria II and others, abbesses

Monegundis (?–570), Radegund/e (520–87), and others founded convents, hospices, monasteries, and hospitals

Glodesind of Metz, abbess (?–608)

Women continue as deacons and presbyters

512: Arabic alphabet is invented

542: Plagues throughout Europe and North Africa

543: Worldwide earthquakes

570: Mohammed is born, founder of Islam

600–700

Hilda of Whitby (c.614–80), abbess in England

Aethelthyrth (636–79) founds a monastery at Alftham, England, is succeeded as abbess by Sexburga (640–99), Ermenhild, and Werburg (?–700)

d. 612: Bertha of England, established first church at Canterbury

624–705: Wu Zetian, empress of China, Tang Dynasty

c.658–80: Caedmon's Hymn, England

700–800

Bishop Theodora/Theoda

Abbess Lioba (710–82) of England travels to Germany as a missionary for Boniface

Evidence of women presbyters and deaconesses

730: Intense power struggle between Emperor Leo III and pope

752–803: Irene, ruler of Eastern Roman Empire

800–900

Pope Joan?

Abbess Kassiani (c.805–65), celebrated Byzantine poet, hymnist, and musician

895–968: Queen Maude, established hospitals, churches, abbeys

891: Anglo-Saxon Chronicles, history of England

900–1000

The Bogomils allow women to preach and take other ecclesiastical roles

Canoness Hroswitha of Gandersheim (c.935–c.1002) writes poetry, prose, drama, history

?–932: Lady Uallach, Irish poet

?–995: Libana, Spanish poet, philosopher, musician

1000: Fear of the end of the world and a Last Judgment

The abbesses at Gandersheim
are allowed to rule their own
kingdom; Matilda (955–99) and
others have their own army
Evidence of women deacons

1000–1100

Double monastery at Fontevrault
and in other places administered
by the abbess
Gregorian reforms result in severe
disparagement of women

1046–1115: Mathilde of Tuscany,
built churches, hospitals, baths
1054: East-West schism in
Christian Church
1083: Anna Comnena, Byzantine
historian, physician, medical writer
1091–1150: Adelaide of Suza, leads
an army in Italy

1100–1200

Christina of Markyate
(c.1097–c.1161), consecrated virgin,
recluse, anchoress, nun, and abbess
Hildegard of Bingen (1098–1179),
writer and preacher, sage,
prophet, and mystic
Abbess Héloïse (1101–64) establishes
a school of theology
Cathar women appear in Europe
Waldensian women appear in Europe
Beguines continue into the twentieth century
Abbesses at Quedlinburg and
Gandersheim mint their own
coinage

d. 1127: Frau Ava, composed biblical stories in German
d. 1127: Thoma, wrote books on
grammar and jurisprudence
fl. 1140: Almucs de Castenau,
female French troubadour and
writer

1200–1300

Ancrene Wisse, anonymous rule for anchorites

Albigensian Crusade against the Cathars (1209–29)

The Guglielmites: Guglielma (c.1210–81), Maifreda Visconti da Pirovano (?–1300)

Gertrude the Great (1256–1302), writer and mystic

The Humiliati flourish

Chiara Offreduccio (St. Clare of Assisi: 1194–1253), the first woman to write a set of monastic guidelines

fl. 1200: Ckaricia, painter, manuscript illuminator

1213–90: Devorguilla, founded Balliol College at Oxford

d. 1249: Bettisia Gozzadini, studied law disguised as a man

1300–1400

Mystics such as Bridget of Sweden (1303–73), founder of the Bridgettines

Julian of Norwich (c.1342–c.1416), mystic and anchoress

Margery Kempe (1373–1438), mystic, writes autobiography in vernacular

Women scribes in convents

1300–60: Elizabeth Stagel, historian, writer

fl. 1321: Francesca of Salerno, had a degree in surgery

1347–61: Black Death

1374: *Concerning Famous Women* by Giovanni Boccaccio

1378–1417: Two rival popes at the same time

1400–1500

Joan of Arc (c.1412–31)

Malleus Maleficarum, manual for witch hunters, 1487

The Lollards flourish in England

Women judges permitted in Unity of the Brethren Church

The Taborites allowed leadership positions for women

1453: Gutenberg prints the Bible

1492: Columbus sails to America

1500–1600

Angela Merici (1474–1540) founds the Ursuline order

Women leaders in the Anabaptist Church throughout Europe

1517: Martin Luther posts theses, beginning Protestant Reformation

1533–1603: Elizabeth I, queen of England

1536–41: Henry VIII disbands monasteries, convents etc.

1563: Roman Catholic Counter-Reformation begins

1600–1700

Salem witch trials in the United States; all witch trials end

Mary Ward (1585–1645) and her English Ladies open schools for girls

Ursuline sister Marie de L'Incarnation (1599–1672) leads expedition to Quebec

Louise de Marillac (1591–1660) begins the Company of the Daughters of Charity with Marguerite Naseau (1594–1633)

Margaret Askew Fell Fox (1614–1702) co-founds the Quakers (Society of Friends)

Jane Ward Lead (1624–1704) leads the Philadelphian Society in London

Mexican Juana de la Cruz (1651–95), the greatest writer in the Spanish-speaking world, dies broken in the Convent of San Jeronimo

Baptist Church begins with women allowed to be deacons; Catherine Scott is the first female Baptist preacher of many in the United States

1608: Galileo Galilei constructs a telescope

1691: First slaves in Virginia, United States

1700: Unmarried women taxed in Berlin

1700–1800

Ursuline sister Marie Tranchepain (1680–1733) leads expedition to New Orleans

Ann Lee (1736–84) founds the Shakers (the United Society of Believers in Christ's Second Coming)

Women leaders in the Moravian Church in Europe and North America

Women leaders and preachers in the Methodist Church gradually supported by John Wesley (1703–91)

Jemima Wilkinson (1752–1819) founds the Society of Universal Friends

1700s: John Wesley encourages women preachers

1718–72: Women's suffrage in Sweden

1750–1825: Bluestockings: educated, intellectual women

1766: Czarina Catherine the Great grants freedom of religion in Russia

1789–99: French Revolution

1792: Abolition of slave trade in Great Britain

1792: Mary Wollstonecraft: *A Vindication of the Rights of Woman*

1800–1900

Female Primitive Methodist and Bible Christian preachers in England and North America

Ann "Nancy" Hasseltine Judson (1789–1826) and Harriet Newell (1793–1812) sail from the United States to India and Burma (present-day Myanmar) as missionaries

Elizabeth Cady Stanton (1815–1902), biblical exegete, writer, feminist

Women ordained in Church of the Brethren, Church of God (Anderson, Indiana), some Baptist Churches in the United States (Clarissa Danforth [1792–1855] ordained in 1815 in the Freewill Baptist Church)

1820–1910: Florence Nightingale, founder of modern nursing

1829: Suttee abolished in British India

1834: Sewing machine invented

1861: Mrs. Beeton's *Book of Household Management*

1861–65: American Civil War

1865: First carpet sweeper

1869: Women could vote in Wyoming Territory, United States

1881: Women property owners could vote in Isle of Man (Great Britain)

1888: First beauty contest

1893: Women's suffrage in New Zealand

Ellen Gould Harmon White
(1827–1915) founds the Seventh-
Day Adventist Church
Mary Morse Baker Eddy (1821–
1910) founds Christian Science
(the Church of Christ Scientist)
Catherine Mumford Booth (1829–
90) co-founds The Salvation
Army
Clara Swain (1834–1910), the first
female missionary doctor, goes
to India from the United States
Antoinette Brown Blackwell
(1825–1921) ordained in the
Congregational Church in 1853

1900–2000

Mollie Alma Bridwell White (1862–
1946) founds the Pillar of Fire
Church, becomes the first female
bishop in the United States
Mary Lee Wasson Cagle (1864–
1955) co-founds the Church of
the Nazarene
Mother Leafy Anderson (1887–1927)
founds spiritualist churches in the
United States; other women found
other spiritualist churches
Aimee Elizabeth Kennedy Semple
(1890–1944) founds the Foursquare
Gospel Church; several other
women found Pentecostal churches
Ma Christina Mokotuli Nku
(1894–1988) founds the St. John's
Apostolic Faith Mission
Juanita Garcia Peraza (1897–1970)
co-founds the Mita Congregation

1902: Suffrage for most women in
Australia
1903: First Nobel Prize for Marie
Sklodowska Curie (1867–1934)
1904: Woman arrested in New York
for smoking in public
1907: First Woman's Day in United
States
1914–18: World War I
1916: Margaret Sanger's book on
birth control
1917: Bobbed hair accepted for
women
1920: Suffrage for women in
United States
1939–1945: World War II
1945: Gnostic Gospel texts found at
Nag Hammadi, Egypt
1969: "Trouser" outfits acceptable
for women

Jashil Choi (1915–89) co-founds the Yoido Full Gospel Church

Mother Chaza (1914–60) founds the Mai Chaza Church

Alice Lenshina Nulenga Lubusha (1920–78) founds the Lumpa Church

Ludmilla Javorová (b. 1932) is ordained a Roman Catholic priest in Czechoslovakia

Most of the Protestant Churches, the Church of England, and the Anglican Churches around the world ordain women

The World Council of Churches, the World Communion of Reformed Churches, and the Christian Conference of Asia elect women leaders

Doctrines of the Assumption of the Blessed Virgin Mary into Heaven and the Queenship of Mary in the Roman Catholic Church

1976: Women's Bank, New York City

2000–Present

The Association of Roman Catholic Women Priests (ARCWP) and the Roman Catholic Women Priests (RCWP) are formed, ordaining Roman Catholic women as deacons, priests, and bishops

The American Catholic Church in the United States (ACCUS) ordains women

GLOSSARY

Abbess/Abbey: The head of an abbey, a building or complex of religious buildings, generally a home for nuns.

Agape: A simple Christian ritual meal separate from the Eucharist, sometimes called a "love-feast."

Altar: A central table or small structure in a church for religious purposes.

Anchorite/anchoress/anchorhold: Someone who lives alone for religious reasons, in an anchorhold, a small cell usually walled up but with small openings.

Apocryphal: Possibly made up or not true.

Archbishop: An ecclesiastical position or office.

Ascetic/asceticism: One who practices extreme self-denial or self-mortification for religious reasons.

Basilica: A Christian church.

Baptism: A religious rite accompanied by immersion of a person in water or sprinkling of water on a person.

Bible: The Christian scriptures consisting of the Old and New Testaments.

Bishop: An ecclesiastical office or position.

Call: A religious vocation or calling, initiated by a feeling or manifestation of a call.

Camp meeting: A religious meeting lasting several days usually held in the open air or in a tent.

Canon: A collection of official religious books considered genuine; in Christianity, the canon is the Bible; an ecclesiastical office.

Canon/canoness: A person living in a community under a religious rule but without a perpetual vow.

Cantor: A person who sings solo verses or passages in a religious ceremony.

Catechism: A summary of the principles or beliefs of a Christian community.

Cenobite/coenobitic: A member of a religious group living with others, contrasted with a hermit or recluse who lives alone.

Christ: A title by which Christians refer to Jesus.

Church Fathers: Early Christian male theologians.

Church Mothers: A recent designation for early Christian female writers and theologians.

Churching: A blessing given to mothers in some churches after the birth of a child.

Circuit: A specific itinerary consisting of several preaching places, usually covering a great distance.

Cistercians: A religious order founded in 1098.

Confessor: A priest who hears confessions and gives absolution and spiritual counsel.

Consecrate: A solemn rite for people or for objects for worship.

Convent: A community of sisters or nuns or the building in which they live.

Cope: An ecclesiastical vestment, a long mantle or cloak.

Cowl: A long hooded garment with wide sleeves.

Crucifixion: The execution of a person by nailing or binding them to a large cross.

Dark Ages: An artificial period in history considered to be approximately 400–1000 CE, suggesting ignorance and barbarism.

Deacon/deaconess: An office in the Christian church generally involving service of some kind.

Desert Mother: Female Christian ascetics living in the desert in the fourth and fifth centuries.

Dominicans: A religious order founded by the Spanish priest Dominic of Caleruega, approved by the pope in 1216.

East/Eastern Church: Generally, any of the churches of the former Byzantine Empire owing allegiance to the Orthodox Church.

Ecclesiastic: A member of the clergy; a church officer.

Ecumenical: Relating to most or all the Christian churches in the world.

Elder: A member of the clergy in the Christian Church who may or may not be ordained.

Encyclical: A papal letter generally sent to all bishops.

Eucharist/Communion/Lord's Supper: The central rite of the Christian Church commemorating the Last Supper that Jesus and his disciples ate together.

Evangelist: A person who tries to convert others, usually by preaching.

Eve: In the Old Testament in Genesis, the woman who disobeyed God by taking an apple from a tree in the Garden of Eden. Her partner was Adam.

Exegete/exegesis: One who analyzes and explains a text; an explanation of a text.

Exhort/exhorter: In the Christian Church, one who speaks of his/her personal religious experience after the main preacher.

Franciscans: A religious order founded in 1209 by Francis of Assisi.

Gnostic/Gnosticism: From ancient Greek meaning knowledge; a group of ideas or churches in the first and second centuries with specific Gnostic theology.

Gospels: The records of the teaching and life of Jesus, the first four books of the New Testament in the Bible.

Heresiologist: A person who studies heresies or theologies or churches not considered orthodox by the church in power.

Heretic: A person who believes in a theology different from that of the church in power.

Hermeneutic: An interpretation or explanation of a text.

Hermit/recluse: A person who lives alone for religious reasons contrasted with those who live in religious communities.

Herod: Herod the Great (73 BCE–4 BCE), king of Judea.

Holiness movement: A movement begun in the nineteenth century that held that people could achieve Christian perfection, based on the ministry of the Holy Spirit.

Holy Land: Land roughly between the Jordan River and the Mediterranean Sea where Jesus lived and preached.

Holy Spirit: The third person of the Trinity but in an unseen spirit form; God the Father, God the Son and God the Holy Spirit, three manifestations of the one being.

Itinerant: A minister who rode or walked around a large circuit, rather than remaining in one fixed preaching spot.

Jesuits: A scholarly religious order founded in 1534, also known as the Society of Jesus.

Jesus: A first-century religious figure from Nazareth c.4 BCE to c.33 CE, central to Christianity.

Love-feast: A meal or symbolic meal eaten in common with other Christians, following the practice of the early Christians.

Messiah: A future figure to be king of God's kingdom and rule the Jewish people; in Christianity, Jesus was the expected Messiah.

Middle Ages: Often considered the period between the fall of the Roman Empire and the fall of Constantinople, from the fifth century to the fifteenth.

Minister: An ecclesiastical office, generally in Protestant churches.

Misogynist: Someone who hates women.

Missionary: A person sent into another area to covert others.

Miter: A tall headdress worn by bishops and other ecclesiastics.

Monastery: A building or complex of buildings, the home of monastics, often male.

Order: A community or group of communities set apart and living according to principles determined by its founder.

Ordination: An act or ceremony conferring holy orders.

Orthodox Church: A Christian denomination or denominations with a patriarch in Constantinople/Istanbul as head.

Paradigm: An example, model, or pattern.

Pastorate: The period or office or physical area of responsibility of a pastor/minister/priest.

Patriarch: The head of the Orthodox churches.

Pentecostal: A movement generally, but not always, within Protestant Christianity that emphasizes personal experience of God through the Holy Spirit, often involving speaking in tongues.

Pilgrim/Pilgrimage: A traveler on a journey or pilgrimage to a holy place.

Postulant: A candidate generally seeking permission to enter a religious order.

Prelate: A bishop or other ecclesiastical officer.

Presbyter: An elder or minister of the Christian church.

Priest: A religious leader authorized to perform the religious sacraments.

Prioress: Head of a religious house or priory, generally below an abbess.

Prophet: An inspired teacher or proclaimer of the will of God.

Protestant Reformation: A movement considered to have begun with Martin Luther's *Ninety-Five Theses* in 1517, resulting in a split between Protestantism and the Roman Catholic Church.

Protracted meeting: A religious meeting lasting for a long time, generally several days.

Religious (as a noun): A person bound by monastic vows.

Renaissance: A cultural rebirth in Europe roughly from the middle of the fourteenth century to the seventeenth.

Revival: A religious awakening, a renewed interest in religion.

Rosary: In the Roman Catholic Church, a string of beads used for devotions.

Sacrament: A religious ceremony in Christian churches regarded as an outward sign of inward divine grace, e.g. baptism.

Sacristy: A room in a church where a priest prepares for worship and religious vestments are kept.

Scripture: The sacred writings of the Bible.

Separatists: A group of Church of England members who wanted to break away from that church.

Sermon: A talk on a religious subject as part of a religious service.

Speaking in tongues: Glossolalia or speaking in tongues is a phenomenon in which people speak in a language previously unknown to them but which can be interpreted by someone else.

St. Paul: An apostle, first known as Saul, but when converted to Christianity became Paul.

Stigmata: In the Christian tradition, marks that appear mysteriously on a person's body similar to the wounds left on Jesus' body after his crucifixion.

Tabernacle: a place or house of worship, especially one designed for a large congregation.

Tertiary: A lay associate of certain monastic movements.

Theologian: One who talks/writes about God or other religious matters.

West/Western Church: That part of the Christian Church associated with Rome as contrasted to Constantinople/Istanbul.

WORKS CITED

PRIMARY SOURCES

Abbott, Walter M., ed. *The Documents of Vatican II*, Volume 4. Translated by Very Rev. Msgr. Joseph Gallagher. El Monte, CA: New Win Publishers, 1966.

"Acts of Perpetua and Felicitas." In *The Anti-Nicene Fathers*, edited by Philip Schaff et al., translated by Marcus Dods, 699–706. Peabody, MA: Hendrickson Publishers, 1996.

Andreacchi, Grace. "Hadewijch of Brabant and the High Palace of Love." *Amazing Grace Magazine*, 29 January 2011. https://graceandreacchi.blogspot.com/2011/01/hadewijch-and-high-palace-of-love.html.

Apostolic Constitutiones, III, 375–380 CE. N.p. Anti-Nicene Fathers Collection.

Baker Eddy, Mary. *Retrospection and Introspection*. Boston, MA: Trustees of Will of M.B.E., 1891.

Benedict XVI. "Saint Bridget of Sweden." General Audience, St. Peter's Square, Rome, 27 October 2010.

—. "On St Catherine of Genoa," General Audience, St. Peter's Square, Rome, 12 January 2011.

Biddle, E. *The Trumpet of the Lord Sounded Forth unto these Three Nations*. London: n.p., 1662.

Braithwaite, Deborah. "An Account of Rachel Wilson's Religious Visit to Friends in America Carefully Transcribed from her Manuscript for the Information and

Benefit of her Children and Near Relatives." London: Library of the Religious Society of Friends, c.1827.

Choi, Jashil, with Yong-gi Cho, Johnny Neung H. Lee, and Junhee Kim. *Hallelujah Lady*. Seoul, Korea: KIATS, 2009.

"A Confession of the Faith of Several Churches of Christ." *The Reformed Reader Committed to Historic Baptist and Reformed Belief*. London, England, 1646.

Cyprian. "To Pomponius, Concerning Some Virgins." Epistle 61. *New Advent, Roman Catholic Church*, http://www.newadvent.org/.

The Didascalia Apostolorum. Translated by Margaret Dunlop Gibson. London C.J. Clay & Sons, 1903.

Documents of the Christian Church. Edited by Henry Bettenson. London: Oxford University Press, 1963.

Epiphanius. *Panarion. 403*. Translated by Frank Williams. Leidein: E.J. Brill, 1987.

Fell, Margaret. "Women's Speaking Justified, Proved, and Allowed by the Scriptures, All such as speak by the Spirit and Power of the Lord Jesus. And how Women were the first that Preached the Tidings of the Resurrection of Jesus, and were sent by Christ's own Command before he Ascended to the Father, John 20.17." London: n.p., 1666.

Glover, Mary Baker (Eddy). *Science and Health*. Boston, MA: Christian Science Publishing Company, 1875.

Gow, Andrew Colin, Robert B. Desjardins, and François V. Pageau, eds. and trans. *The Arras Witch Treatises*. Old Main, Philadelphia: Penn State University Press, 2016.

Grimlaicus, *Rule for Solitaries*. Translated with an Introduction and Notes by Andrew Thornton. Collegeville, MN: Liturgical Press, 2011.

Hennecke, Edgar, and Wilhelm Schneemelcher, eds. *New Testament Apocrypha, Vol. II*. Translated by R. McL. Wilson. Philadelphia: The Westminster Press, 1964.

Madigan, Kevin, and Carolyn Osiek, eds. and trans. *Ordained Women in the Early Church: A Documentary History*. Baltimore: The Johns Hopkins University Press, 2005.

Marshall, Joyce, ed. and trans. *The Selected Letters of Marie de L'Incarnation*. Toronto: Oxford University Press, 1967.

Melton, J. Gordon. *The Churches Speak On Women's Ordination*. Detroit: Gale Research, 1991.

The New Testament, The New Revised Standard Version, 1989.

Oden, Amy, ed. *In Her Words, Women's Writings in the History of Christian Thought*. London: SPCK, 1995.

"The Ordination of Edith Hill, Minutes of the meeting convened for the ordination of the pastor-elect—Miss Edith Hill." American Baptist Churches USA, 1894.

Pius XII. *Ad Caeli Reginem*. Encyclical, St. Peter's Basilica, Rome, 11 October 1954.

St. Athanasius of Alexandria. *The Paradise of the Holy Fathers, Vols. 1 & 2*. Translated by Ernest A. Wallis Budge. London: Chatto & Windus, 1907.

St. Thomas Aquinas. *Summa Theologica*. Translated by the Fathers of the English Dominican Province. Benzinger Brothers, 1947.

Tanner, Norman P., ed. "Text of the Trial in Norwich of Hawisa Mone." In *Heresy Trials in the Diocese of Norwich 1428–31*. Royal Historical Society Westminster Diocesan Archives, 1977.

Tertullian. "On the Apparel of Women." In *Anti-Nicene Fathers, Vol. IX*, edited by A. Menzies. New York: Christian Literature Co., 1896.

—. "Treatise on Marriage and Remarriage." In *Ancient Christian Writers*. Translated by William P. LeSaint. Westminster, MD: Newman Press, 1951.

Twain, Mark [Samuel Clemens]. *Christian Science*. New York: Harper & Brothers, 1907.

White, Ellen G. *Testimonies*. Vol. 1, 1855–1868. E.G. White Library, The Gilead Institute of America, n.d.

Wilson, Lois. *Turning the World Upside Down: A Memoir*. Toronto: Doubleday Canada, 1989.

SECONDARY SOURCES

"Abigail Roberts." In *Portraits of American Women in Religion*. Philadelphia: The Library Company of Philadelphia, 2005.

Abrahamsen, Valarie. "Women at Philippi: The Pagan and Christian Evidence." *Journal of Feminist Studies in Religion* 3, no. 2 (1987): 17–30.

"An Abstract of the Life of Margaret Fell." Gwynedd Friends Meeting Historical Notes, based on *An Abstract of the Sufferings of the People Called Quakers, For the Testimony of a Good Conscience, from the Time of Their being first distinguished by the NAME Taken from Original Records, and other Authentick Accounts, Vol. I*. London: Assigns of J. Sowles, 1733.

"Aimee Semple McPherson." *Christian History*, Issue 58, 1988.

Anderson, Ross. "Ordination of Renegade Priest: 'I am ready.'" *Port Townsend Leader and Chimes*, 10 August 2016.

Ankerberg, John. "Should the Catholic Church Elevate Mary's Status to Co-Redeemer, Mediator of All Graces, and Advocate of Mankind?" Ankerberg Theological Research Institute, 2016. https//.www.jashow.org/articles.

Armstrong, O.K., and Marjorie Armstrong. *The Baptists in America*. New York: Doubleday, 1979.

Arora, Vishal. "First Anglican Woman Bishop in India Says Critics Have Been Silent." *Religion News Service*, 3 October 2013.

Atkins, Pamela. "Hannah Ball, Friend of John Wesley and Founder of the First Sunday School." *My Methodist History*. Accessed 24 September 2018, http://www.mymethodisthistory.org.uk/page/hannah_ball.

Atkinson, Clarissa W.A. *Mystic and Pilgrim*. Ithaca, NY: Cornell University Press, 1983.

Audisio, Gabriel. *Preachers by Night*. Translated by Claire Davison. Leiden: Brill, 2007.

Bacon, Margaret Hope. *Mothers of Feminism: The Story of Quaker Women in America*. San Francisco: Harper & Row, 1986.

Bailey, Judith Bledsoe. "Nancy Towle, 1796–1876: Faithful Child of God." MA thesis, College of William and Mary, Williamsburg, Virginia, April 2000.

Bainton, Roland H. *Women of the Reformation: From Spain to Scandinavia*. Minneapolis: Augsburg Publishing House, 1977.

Baker Eddy, Mary. *Science and Health*. Boston: Christian Science Publishing, 1875.

Bardsley, Sandy. *Women's Roles in the Middle Ages*. Westport, CT: Greenwood Press, 2007.

Bednarowski, Mary Farrell. "Outside the Mainstream: Women's Religion and Women Religious Leaders in Nineteenth-Century America." *Journal of American Academy of Religion* 48, no. 2 (June 1980): 207–31.

Bell, D.G. "Allowed Irregularities: Women Preachers in the Early 19th-Century Maritimes." *Acadiensis: Journal of the History of the Atlantic Region* 30, no. 2 (2001).

Bell, Rudolph M. *Holy Anorexia*. Epilogue by William N. Davis. Chicago: University of Chicago Press, 1985.

Bell, Susan Groag, ed. *Women: From the Greeks to the French Revolution*. Belmont, CA: Wadsworth Publishing Company, 1973.

—. "Medieval Women Book Owners: Arbiters of Lay Piety and Ambassador of Culture." *Signs* 7, no. 4 (Summer 1982): 742–68.

Bennett, H.S. *Six Medieval Men & Women*. New York: Atheneum, 1962.

"Béziers Massacre." *Christian History Institute*, 22 July 2017.

Billington, Louis. "Female Laborers in the Church: Women Preachers in the Northeastern United States, 1790–1840." *Journal of American Studies* 19, no. 3 (December 1985): 369–94.

"Biography Mother Teresa." *Biography Online*. Accessed 24 September 2018, https://www.biographyonline.net/nobelprize/mother_teresa.html.

Blanchard, Mary Bergan. "From the Editor." *Leading* 1 (Summer 2017).

Brakke, David. *Demons and the Making of a Monk: Spiritual Combat in Early Christianity*. Cambridge, MA: Harvard University Press, 2006.

Brekus, Catherine A. *Strangers and Pilgrims: Female Preaching in America, 1740–1845*. Chapel Hill: University of North Carolina Press, 1998.

—. "Female Preaching in Early Nineteenth-Century America." The Center for Christian Ethics at Baylor University, 2009. https://www.baylor.edu/content/services/document.php/98759.pdf.

Brenon, Anne. "The Voice of the Good Women." In *Women Preachers and Prophets through Two Millennia of Christianity*, edited by Beverly Mayne Kienzle and Pamela J. Walker, translated by Janice Valls-Russell. Berkeley: University of California Press, 1998.

Brereton, Virginia Lieson, and Christa Ressmeyer Klein. "American Women in Ministry." In *Women in American Religion*, edited by Janet Wilson James. Philadelphia: University of Pennsylvania Press, 1980.

Brewerton, Emma. "Penny Jamieson, Biography." *New Zealand History.* Accessed 24 September 2018, http://nzhistory.govt.nz/people/dr-penny-jamieson.

Brockman, Norbert C. *An African Biographical Dictionary*. Santa Barbara, CA: Grey House Publishing, 1994.

Brown, Andrew. "Send Down Your Holy Spirit upon Your Servant Angela: History Is Made as the Church of England Ordained Its First Women Priests." *The Independent*, March 1994.

Brown, Charles E. "Women Preachers." *The Gospel Trumpet*, 27 May 1939, 5.

Brumberg, Joan Jacobs. "The Case of Ann Hasseltine Judson." In *Women in New Worlds: Historical Perspectives on the Wesleyan Tradition*. Vol. 2. Edited by Hilah Frances Thomas, Rosemary Skinner Keller, and Louise L. Queen. Nashville, TN: Abingdon Press, 1982.

Butler, Jonathan de Burca. "The First Female Priest Ordained in Ireland Discusses the Influence of Women Priests in the Anglican Ministry." *Irish Examiner*, 26 November 2015. https://irishexamner.com.

Byers, A.L. "Sarah Smith." *Gospel Trumpet*, 28 February 1920, 5–6.

Bynum, Caroline Walker. *Holy Feast and Holy Fast: The Religious Significance of Food to Medieval Women*. Berkeley: University of California Press, 1982.

Cahill, Thomas. *Mysteries of the Middle Ages: The Rise of Feminism, Science, and Art from the Cults of Catholic Europe*. New York: Nan & Talese, 2006.

Campbell, Joan Cecelia. *Phoebe, Patron and Emissary*. Collegeville, MN: Liturgical Press, 2009.

Carroll, Michael P. *The Cult of the Virgin Mary*. Princeton: Princeton University Press, 1986.

Cartwright, Jane. "The Desire to Corrupt: Convent and Community in Medieval Wales." In *Medieval Women in Their Communities*, edited by Diane Watt. Cardiff: University of Wales Press, 1997.

Casey, Lee. "Bishop White of Denver—A Cromwell in Skirts." *Denver Rocky Mountain News*, 28 June 1946, 14.

"Catherine Booth." *Christian History* 26 (1990).

Centre for Christian Studies. "Imagine Church Differently." 7 June 2016. http://ccsonline.ca.

Chabot, Marie-Emanuel. "Guyart Marie, *dite* Marie de L'Incarnation." *Dictionary of Canadian Biography.* Vol. 1. University of Toronto/Université Laval, 1966.

Chara, Tendai. "Inside Mai Chaza's Shrine." *Sunday Mail Reporter*, 28 August 2016, 1.

Charles River Editors. *Pope Joan: The Indestructible Legend of the Catholic Church's First and Only Female Pontiff.* San Bernardino, CA: Charles River Editors, 2017.

Chicago, Judy. *The Dinner Party: A Symbol of Our Heritage.* New York: Anchor Books, 1979.

Chireau, Yvonne. "Prophetess of the Spirits: Mother Leafy Anderson and the Black Spiritual Churches of New Orleans." In *Women Preachers and Prophets through Two Millennia of Christianity*, edited by Beverly Mayne Kienzle and Pamela J. Walker. Berkeley: University of California Press, 1998.

Chryssavgis, John. *In The Heart of the Desert: The Spirituality of the Desert Fathers and Mothers.* Bloomington, IN: World Wisdom, 2008.

Church of the Brethren General Board. "Resolution on 50 Years of Women's Ordination in the Church of the Brethren." 9 March 2008. www.brethren.org/about/statements/2008-womens-ordination.pdf.

"Church of Norway's Presiding Bishop to Open Leiv Erickson Festival." *Metro Lutheran*, 28 September 2012. metrolutheran.org/2012/.../church-of-norway's-presiding-bishop-to-open-leiv-eriksso.

Claghorn, Gene. *Women Composers and Hymnists: A Concise Bibliographical Dictionary.* Metuchen, NJ: Scarecrow Press, 1984.

Cloke, Gillian. *"This Female Man of God": Women and Spiritual Power in the Patristic Age, AD 350–450.* London: Routledge, 1995.

Connolly, Kate, and Philip Willan. "Vatican Casts Out 'Ordained' Women." *The Guardian*, 6 August 2002.

Corfield, Kenneth. "Elizabeth Heyrick: Radical Quaker." In *Religion in the Lives of English Women 1760–1930*, edited by Gail Malmgreen. Bloomington: Indiana University Press, 1986.

Corrington, Gail. "Anorexia, Asceticism and Autonomy: Self-Control as Liberation and Transcendence." *Journal of Feminist Studies in Religion* 2, no. 2 (Fall 1986): 51–61.

Couperus, Molleurus. "The Significance of Ellen White's Head Injury." *Adventist Currents* 1, no. 6 (June 1985).

Crosfield, Helen G. *Margaret Fox of Swarthmoor Hall.* Bishopsgate: Headley Brothers, 1913.

Cross, Donna Woolfolk. *Pope Joan: A Novel.* New York: Broadway Books, 2009.

Cunneen, Sally. *In Search of Mary*. New York: Ballantine Books, 1996.

Cyrus, Cynthia J. *The Scribes for Women's Convents in Late Medieval Germany*. Toronto: University of Toronto Press, 2009.

Dahl, Sarah E. "That Most Familiar Story." *Christian History* 83 (Summer 2004).

Damo-Santiago, Corazon. "Saint Rose of Viterbo: Mystic Street Preacher." *Business Mirror*, 3 September 2016.

Dayton, Donald, ed. *The Higher Christian Life: A Bibliographical Overview*. Shrewsbury, MA: Garland Publishers, 1971.

de Pisan, Christine. *Ditié de Jeanne d'Arc*. Edited by Angus J. Kennedy and Kenneth Varty, translated by L. Shopkow. Oxford: Society for the Study of Medieval Language and Literature, 1977.

Deane, Jennifer Kolpacoff. *A History of Medieval Heresy and Inquisition*. Plymouth, UK: Bowman and Littlefield, 2011.

"Death of Asia's First Woman Bishop Mourned by Indian Lutherans." *UCA News*, 1 November 1997.

Deboick, Sophia L. "The Friendly Recluse: Medieval Hermits Were the Agony Aunts of Their Day." *History Today*, June 2017.

Deen, Edith. *All of the Women of the Bible*. New York: Harper & Row, 1955.

Dimont, Max. *Jews, God and History*. New York: Penguin, 1994.

Diniejko, Andrzej. "Catherine Mumford Booth: The 'Mother' of the Salvation Army and an Early Christian Feminist." *The Victorian Web*. www.victorianweb.org/religion/sa3.html.

Diocesan Press Service. "Hong Kong Priest Visits Southern Ohio." The Archives of the Episcopal Church, 28 May 1975.

"A Discussion with Agnes Abuom, Executive Committee, World Council of Churches." Berkeley Center for Religion, Peace and World Affairs, 3 July 2009. https://berkleycenter.georgetown.edu/.../a-discussion-with-agnes-abuom-executive-co.

Dolan, Autumn. "A Revival of Female Spirituality: Adaptations of Nuns' Rules during the Hiberno-Frankish Monastic Movement." *Medieval Feminist Forum* 46, no. 1 (2010): 38–62.

Donnelly, Mary Rose, and Heather Dau. *Katharine*. Winfield, BC: Wood Lake Books, 1992.

Dorland, Arthur G. *The Quakers in Canada: A History*. Toronto: The Ryerson Press, 1968.

Dronke, Peter. *Women Writers of the Middle Ages*. Cambridge: Cambridge University Press, 1985.

Dube, Lilian. "Mai Chaza: An African Christian Story of Gender, Healing and

Power" (2008). Accessed 24 September 2018, https://core.ac.uk/download/pdf/43167445.pdf.

Dunn, Mary Maples. "Latest Light on Women of Light." In *Witnesses for Change: Quaker Women over Three Centuries*, edited by Elisabeth Potts Brown and Susan Mosher Stuard. New Brunswick, NJ: Rutgers University Press, 1989.

Dunning, Brian. "Pope Joan." *Skeptoid Podcast* #353, 12 March 2013.

Durso, Pamela R. "Learning from Baptist History: The Migration of Baptist Women to Other Denominations." *EthicsDaily*, 17 March 2009.

—. "She-Preachers, Sisters, and Messengers from the Lord: British Baptist Women, 1609–1700," *Baptist History and Heritage* 49, no. 1 (Spring 2014).

East, David. "'Lightly Esteemed by Men': The Last Years of Sarah Mallet, one of Mr. Wesley's Female Preachers." *Methodist History* 42, no. 1 (October 2003): 58–63.

Eckenstein, Lina. "Harrad and the Garden of Delights." In *Women: From the Greeks to the French Revolution*, edited by Susan Groag Bell. Belmont, CA: Wadsworth Publishing Company, 1973.

—. "Woman under Monasticism." In *Women: From the Greeks to the French Revolution*, edited by Susan Groag Bell. Belmont, CA: Wadsworth Publishing Company, 1973.

Eckert, Amy. "Incoming President Najla Kassab Speaks of Gender Equality and Justice." World Communion of Reformed Churches, July 2017.

Elm, Susanna. *"Virgins of God": The Making of Asceticism in Late Antiquity.* Oxford: Clarendon Press, 1994.

Evangelical Lutheran Church in America. "ELCA Celebrates 45 Years of Ordaining Women." 19 November 2015. https://www.elca.org/News-and-Events/7798.

Everhart, Janet S. "Maggie Newton Van Cott." In *Women in New Worlds: Historical Perspectives on the Wesleyan Tradition*. Vol. 2. Edited by Rosemary Skinner Keller, Louise L. Queen, and Hilah F. Thomas. Nashville, TN: Abingdon, 1982.

Fanous, Samuale, and Henrietta Leyser, eds. *Christina of Markyate: A Twelfth Century Holy Woman.* London: Routledge, 2005.

Ferrante, Joan. *Epistolae: Medieval Women's Letters*. Columbia Center for New Media, Teaching and Learning, 2004. https://epistolae.ctl.columbia.edu.

Fiorenza, Elizabeth Schüssler. Lecture Delivered at the McGill University Faculty of Religious Studies, Montreal, QC, 1982.

—. *In Memory of Her: A Feminist Theological Reconstruction of Christian Origins*. New York: The Crossroad Publishing Company, 1983.

"First Female Archbishop Elected in Australia." *Anglican News Service*, 20 August 2017. www.anglicannews.org/news/2017/08.

Fornasiero, Nancy. "Two Ordained Women Priests Challenging Rome in Toronto." *The Toronto Star*, 20 July 2014. https://www.thestar.com/news/insight/2014/07/20/two_ordained_women_priests_challenging_rome_in_toronto.html.

Fox, Stuart. "St. Rose Died of Heart Attack, Analysis of Mummy Shows." *Live Science*, 10 June 2010. https://www.livescience.com.

Franklin, Stephen E. "Typhon: A Chronology of the Holocene Period." http://www.lordbalto.com/neros/default.htm.

Freeman, Curtis W. "Visionary Women among Early Baptists." *Baptist Quarterly* (January 2010). https://divinity.duke.edu/sites/divinity.duke.edu/files/documents/faculty-freeman/visionary-women-among-early-baptists.pdf.

Ghosh, Palash. "African Anglicans Ordain First Female Bishop as Church of England Prepares Vote on Matter." *International Business Times*, 20 November 2012. https://www.ibtimes.com/african-anglicans-ordain-first-female-bishop-church-england-prepares-vote-matter-892574.

Gies, Frances, and Joseph Gies. *Women in the Middle Ages: The Lives of Real Women in a Vibrant Age of Transition*. New York: Barnes and Noble, 1980.

Graves, Dan. "Judsons Find a Cheerless Home in Rangoon." *Christian History Institute*, 13 July 2017.

Grayson, Hon. Alan. "Recognizing the Congregación Mita Church on its 75th Anniversary." *Congressional Record—Extension of Remarks*, 23 October 2015.

Greenaway, Kristine. "Bishop Helga Haugland Byfuglien: Presiding with Faith and Clarity." World Council of Churches. Press Release, June 2016.

—. "The Faces of Global Ecumenical Leaders Have Changed, Says American Woman Church Leader." World Council of Churches. Press Release, June 2016.

Grupo Editorial EPRL. *Encyclopedia de Puerto Rico*. San Juan, Puerto Rico: National Endowment of the Humanities, 2014.

Guiley, Rosemary Ellen. *The Encyclopedia of Witches and Witchcraft*. New York: Facts on File, 1989.

Guyer, Rev. Janet. "Based on Discussions with Ordained Women in Ghana, Ethiopia, Malawi and Zimbabwe, Ordination of African Women." *Presbyterian Mission*, 15 April 2016.

"G.W." *The Primitive Methodist Magazine* 64, 1 January 1883.

Haines, Lee M. "Women in Ministry: A Biblical Historical Perspective," 28 January 2012. https://www.Wesleyanholinesswomenclergy.org/women-in-ministry.

Hammack, Mary L. "Women of the Early Church: A Gallery." *Christian History* 17 (1988).

Hardesty, Nancy. *Great Women of Faith*. Nashville, TN: Abingdon, 1980.

—. "Minister as Prophet? Or as Mother?" In *Women in New Worlds: Historical Perspectives on the Wesleyan Tradition*. Vol. 1. Edited by Rosemary Skinner Keller and Hilah F. Thomas. Nashville, TN: Abingdon, 1981.

Harmon, Nolan B. *Encyclopedia of World Methodism*. Nashville, TN: United Methodist Publishing House, 1974.

Harris, Eleri. "One for the Ladies: 20 Years of Women's Ordination in Australia." *ABC Canberra*, 9 March 2012.

Hartley, Cathy. *A Historical Dictionary of Women*. Kobo Books, 2003.

—. "White, Alma Bridwell (1862–1946)." *A Historical Dictionary of Women*. Kobo Books, 2003.

—. "White, Ellen Gould (1827–1915)." *A Historical Dictionary of Women*. Kobo Books, 2003.

Higginbotham, Ann R. "Respectable Sinners: Salvation Army Rescue Work with Unmarried Mothers, 1884–1914." In *Religion in the Lives of English Women 1760–1930*, edited by Gail Malmgreen. Bloomington: Indiana University Press, 1986.

Hoag, Gary. "Jacques de Vitryon the Women of the Beguine Movement," 27 July 2011. *Generosity Monk*. https://generositymonk.com/2011/07/17/jacques-de-vitry-on-the-women-of-the-beguine-movement/.

Hodder, Delbert H., M.D. "Visions or Partial-Complex Seizures?" *Evangelica* 2, no. 5 (November 1981).

Hooton, Elizabeth. "In Pursuit of the King." In *English Women's Voices*, edited by Charlotte F. Otten. Gainesville: University Press of Florida, 1992.

Hoover, Peter. *Behold The Lamb: The Story of the Moravian Church*. N.p.: Crossreach Publications, 2016.

Houston, Jennifer. "Lutheran Women in Ministry." Accessed 24 September 2018, https://secure.wideopen.net/ltsg_s/ltsg-images/revartpdf/Ministry.pdf.

Howard, Evan B. "Getting Away to It All: The Place of Withdrawal in Fourth Century Monasticism and Postmodern Christianity." *Spirituality Shoppe*, 6. Accessed 24 September 2018, https://spiritualityshoppe.org/getting-away-to-it-all-the-place-of-withdrawal-in-fourth-century-monasticism-and-postmodern-Christianity.

Ide, Arthur Frederick. *Woman as Priest, Bishop & Laity, in the Early Catholic Church to 440 A.D.* Mesquite, TX: Ide House, 1984.

Ingersol, Robert Stanley. "The Deaconess in Nazarene History." *Herald of Holiness* 73 (1984).

—. "Mary Lee Cagle: A Study in Women's History, Religion." *Wesleyan Theological Journal* 28 (Spring–Fall 1993).

—. "Mary Lee Cagle." *Encyclopedia of Alabama*. 1 December 2008. http://www.
    encyclopediaofalabama.org/article/h-1875.

—. "Whatever Happened to Fannie McDowell Hunter?" International
    Headquarters of the Church of the Nazarene. 28 January 2012. https://www.
    weleyanholinesswomenclergy.org/category/ingersolstan/.

Jacobs, Claude F., and Andrew J. Kaslow. *The Spiritual Churches of New Orleans:
    Origins, Beliefs, and Rituals of an African-American Religion*. Knoxville, TN:
    University of Tennessee Press, 1991.

"Jacques de Vitry," *Catholic Encyclopedia*. New York: Robert Appleton Company.

Jansen, Katherine Ludwig. "Maria Magdalena: Apostolorum Apostola." In *Women
    Preachers and Prophets through Two Millennia of Christianity*, edited by Beverley
    Mayne Kienzle and Pamela J. Walker. Berkeley: University of California Press, 1998.

—. *The Making of the Magdalen: Preaching and Popular Devotion in the Later Middle
    Ages*. Princeton: Princeton University Press, 2000.

Jeffrey, David Lyle. "Where'd That Come From?" *Christian History* 83 (Summer 2000).

—. "Hail Mary, Her Moment of Obedience Triggered Two Millennia of Reverence."
    Christian History 83 (Summer 2004).

Jennings, Daniel R., ed. "Ancient and Medieval References to Montanism."
    Accessed 24 September 2018, http://danielrjennings.org/
    AncientReferencesToMontanism.html.

Johnson, Brenda. "Hrotsvit of Gandersheim: Tenth Century Poet and Playwright."
    Mount Saint Agnes Theological Centre for Women. Baltimore, Maryland.

Johnston, Emma. "Marguerite Porete: A Post Mortem." In *Worshipping Women:
    Misogyny and Mysticism in the Middle Ages*, edited by John O. Warn and
    Francesca C. Bussey. Sydney, Australia: University of Sydney Press, 1997.

Kaelber, Lutz. "Weavers into Heretics? The Social Organization of Early-Thirteenth-
    Century Catharism in Comparative Perspective." *Social Science History* 21, no.1
    (1997): 111–37.

Kaplan-Levenson, Laine. "Mother Catherine Seals and the Temple of the Innocent
    Blood." 1 December 2016.

Kasten, Patricia. "Locked Up Forever in the Wall of a Church." *The Compass*,
    September 2013.

Keller, Rosemary Skinner, Rosemary Radford Ruether, and Marie Cantlon.
    Encyclopedia of Women and Religion in North America. Bloomington: Indiana
    University Press, 2006.

Keller-Lapp, Heidi. "Floating Cloisters and Heroic Women: French Ursuline
    Missionaries, 1639–1744." *World History Connected* 4, no. 3 (2004). http://
    worldhistoryconnected.press.uillinois.edu/4.3/lapp.html.

Keneally, Kristina. "Pope Francis Is a Master at Playing the Crowd. But We Won't Get Female Deacons." *The Guardian*, 16 May 2016. https://www.theguardian.com/commentisfree/2016/may/16/pope-francis-is-a-master-at-playing-to-the-crowd-but-we-wont-get-female-deacons.

Kenworthy-Browne, Christina, ed. *Mary Ward 1585–1645: "A Briefe Relation" with Autobiographical Fragments and a Selection of Letters*. Suffolk, UK: Boydell & Brewer, 2008.

Kernohan, R.D. *An Alliance across the Alps: Britain and Italy's Waldensians*. Waddington, Scotland: The Handsel Press, 2005.

Kidder, Annemarie S. *Women, Celibacy and the Church*. New York: Crossroad Publishing, 2003.

Kienzle, Beverly Mayne, and Pamela J. Walker, eds. *Women Preachers and Prophets through Two Millennia of Christianity*. Berkeley, CA: University of California Press, 1998.

—. "The Prostitute-Preacher, Patterns of Polemic against Medieval Waldensian Women Preachers." In *Women Preachers and Prophets through Two Millennia of Christianity*, edited by Beverly Mayne Kienzle and Pamela J. Walker. Berkeley, CA: University of California Press, 1998.

King, Karen L. *The Gospel of Mary of Magdala: Jesus and the First Woman Apostle*. Farmington, MN: Polebridge Press, 2003.

—. "Women in Ancient Christianity: The New Discoveries." *Frontline*. PBS.org. Accessed 28 September 2018, https://www.pbs.org/wgbh/pages/frontline/shows/religion/first/women.html.

King, Margot H. "The Desert Mothers: A Survey of the Feminine Anchoretic Tradition in Western Europe." *Vox Benedictina*, 1980.

—. *The Desert Mothers: A Survey of the Feminine Anchoretic Tradition in Western Europe*. Toronto: Peregrina Publishers, 1989.

Kirchgaessner, Stephanie. "Pope Francis Says Women Will Never Be Roman Catholic Priests." *The Guardian*, 1 November 2016. https://www.theguardian.com/world/2016/nov/01/pope-francis-women-never-roman-catholic-priests-church.

Kirchgaessner, Stephanie, and Harriet Sherwood. "Pope Francis to Consider Ordaining Women as Deacons." *The Guardian*, 12 May 2016. https://www.theguardian.com/world/2016/may/12/pope-francis-consider-ordaining-women-female-deacons-catholic-church-commission.

Knight, Charles. *Biography: or, Third Division of the English Encyclopedia*. London: Bradbury, Evans & Co., 1867.

Kraemer, Ross Shepard, ed. *Maenads, Martyrs, Matrons, Monastics: A Sourcebook on Women's Religions in the Greco-Roman World*. Philadelphia: Fortress Press, 1988.

—. *Her Share of the Blessings: Women's Religions among Pagan Jews and Christians in the Greco-Roman World*. New York: Oxford University Press, 1992.

Kroeger, Catherine. "The Neglected History of Women in the Early Church." *Christian History*, April 2016.

Kupe, Lovejoy. "A Woman Worth Knowing: Mai Chaza Founder of Guta Ra Jehovah." *Onward Christian Radio*, 30 September 2015.

Laird, Rebecca. *Ordained Women in the Church of the Nazarene*. Kansas City: Nazarene Publishing House, 1993.

Lambert, Tim. "A Brief History of Life Expectancy in Britain." Accessed 24 September 2018, www.localhistories.org/life.html.

Landman, Christina. "Christinah Nku and St. Johns: A Hundred Years Later." *Studia Historiae Ecclesiasticae* 32, no. 3 (2006): 1–32.

"Latin America's First Women Priests Challenge Church." *IIUM TODAY*, 2 April 2015. news.iium.eduin .my/2015/04/02/latin-americas-first-women-priests-challenge-church/.

Lawless, Elaine J. *God's Peculiar People: Women's Voices & Folk Tradition in a Pentecostal Church*. Lexington: University Press of Kentucky, 1988.

"Leafy Anderson." In *Notable Black American Women*, edited by Jessie Carney Smith and Shirelle Phelps. Detroit: Gale Research, 1992.

Le Casey. "Bishop White of Denver—A Cromwell in Skirts." *Denver Rocky Mountain News*, 28 June 1946.

Levenduski, Cristine. *Peculiar Power*. Washington, DC: Smithsonian Institution, 1996.

Levterov, Theodore N. *The Development of the Seventh-day Adventist Understanding of Ellen G. White's Prophetic Gift, 1844–1889*. New York: Peter Lang Publishing, 2015.

Lierheimer, Linda. "Preaching or Teaching? Defining the Ursuline Mission in Seventeenth-Century France." In *Women Preachers and Prophets through Two Millennia of Christianity*, edited by Beverly Mayne Kienzle and Pamela J. Walker. Berkeley, CA: University of California Press, 1998.

"The Life of St. Nina, Equal to the Apostles, Enlightener of Georgia." *The St. Nina Quarterly: A Journal Exploring the Ministry of Women in the Eastern Orthodox Church*. Accessed 24 September 2018, www.stnina.org/st-nina/her-life/life-st-nina-equal-apostles.

Lloyd, Jennifer. *Women and the Shaping of British Methodism: Persistent Preachers 1807–1907*. Manchester: Manchester University Press, 2009.

Loveless, Dr. Alton E. "Clarissa H. Danforth Richmond." In *Free Will Baptist Women Ministers and Early Leaders*. Columbus, OH: FWB Publications, 2016.

Lowther, W.K. *The Lausiac History of Palladius*, Chapter LXI, "Melania the Younger."

London: Society for Promoting Christian Knowledge, 1918. Accessed from *Forgotten Books*, 24 September 2018, file:///C:/Users/User/Downloads/TheLausiacHistoryofPalladius_10036468.pdf.

"The Lumpa Massacre." *Zambian Economist*, 27 March 2010. www.zambian-economist.com/2010/03/lumpa-massacre.html.

Lusted, Marcia Amidon. *Women's Roles in Religion*. Edina, MN: ABDO Publishing, 2011.

MacHaffie, Barbara J., ed. *Readings in Her Story: Women in Christian Tradition*. Minneapolis, MN: Fortress Press, 1992.

Mack, Phyllis. "In a Female Voice: Preaching and Politics in Eighteenth-Century British Quakerism." In *Women Preachers and Prophets through Two Millennia of Christianity*, edited by Beverly Mayne Kienzle and Pamela J. Walker. Berkeley: University of California Press, 1998.

MacLean, Maggie. "Julia Foote: Female Preacher in the Civil War Era." *Civil War Women*, 12 October 2007. https://www.civilwarwomenblog.com/julia-foote/.

"Macrina the Younger (c.327–390)." *Tentmaker Ministries*. Accessed 24 September 2018, www.tentmaker.org/biographies/macrina.htm.

Macy, Gary. *The Hidden History of Women's Ordination: Female Clergy in the Medieval West*. Oxford: Oxford University Press, 2007.

—. "The Ministry of Ordained Women." *Oxford Scholarship Online*, January 2008. www.oxfordscholarship.com/view/10.1093/.../acprof-9780195189704-chapter-3.

"Maeyken Wens's Heritage." *Christian History Institute*, 5 October 2017.

Malvern, Marjorie M. *Venus in Sackcloth: The Magdalen's Origin and Metamorphoses*. Edwardsville, IL: Southern Illinois University Press, 1975.

Manners, Emily. *Elizabeth Hooton, First Quaker Woman Preacher*. London: Headley Brothers, 1914.

Mar, Alex. "The Rebel Virgins and Desert Mothers Who Have Been Written Out of Christianity's Early History." *Atlas Obscura*, 21 January 2016. https://www.atlasobscura.com/articles/the-rebel-virgins-and-desert-mothers-who-have-been-written-out-of-christianitys-early-history.

Martimort, Aimé-Georges. *Deaconesses: An Historical Survey*. Translated by K.D. Whitehead. San Francisco: Ignatius Press, 1986.

Martin, John H. "Saints, Sinners and Reformers: The Burned-Over District Re-Visited." *The Crooked Lake Review* (Fall 2005).

"The Martyrdom of Saints Perpetua and Felicitas." *Frontline*. PBS.org. Accessed 24 September 2018, https://www.pbs.org/wgbh/pages/frontline/shows/religion/maps/primary/perpetua.html.

Matter, E. Ann. "My Sister, My Spouse: Woman-Identified Women in Medieval

Christianity." *Journal of Feminist Studies in Religion* 2, no. 2 (Fall 1986): 81–93.

Mayeski, Marie Anne. *Women at the Table: Three Medieval Theologians*. Collegeville, MN: Liturgical Press, 2004.

McAvoy, Liz Herbert. "Uncovering the Saintly Anchoress: Myths of Medieval Anchoritism and the Reclusion of Katherine of Audley." *Women's History Review* 22 (2013): 801–19.

McBeth, Leon. *The First Baptist Church of Dallas*. Grand Rapids, MI: Zondervan Publishing, 1968.

McCann, Nuala. "Church of Ireland Bishop Pat Storey Mistaken for Secretary." *BBC News*, 8 September 2017. https://www.bbc.com/news/uk-northern-ireland-41200218.

McCutcheon, Lillie. "God Is an Equal Opportunity Employer." *Vital Christianity* 109, no. 4 (May 1989).

McDonald, Jean. "Mary Baker Eddy and the Nineteenth Century Public Woman: A Feminist Reappraisal." *Journal of Feminist Studies* (Spring 1986).

McGarvey, Patty. "Sophie the Scrubwoman." *Foundations Alliance Heritage*. Accessed 21 September 2018, https://www.cmalliance.org/alife/sophie-the-scrubwoman/.

McGinn, Bernard. *The Flowering of Mysticism*. New York: Crossroad Publishing, 1998.

McKenzie, Donald. "An Early Tribute to Women Preachers." *Canadian Methodist Historical Society Newsletter* (Fall 1996).

Memling, Hans. "Did You Know? The Seven Joys of Mary." *Christian History* 83 (Summer 2004).

Meyer, Charles R. "Ordained Women in the Early Church." *Chicago Studies* 4 (1965): 285–308.

Mick, Kenneth. "A Bastion of Feminine Equality? Women's Roles in the Waldensian Movement." University of Massachusetts Amherst, 2014.

Minnis, Alastair, and Rosalynn Voaden, eds. *Medieval Holy Women in the Christian Tradition c.1110–1500*. Turnhout, Belgium: Brepols, 2010.

"Mita, Juanita Garcia Peraza." *Iglesia Congregación Mita*. Accessed 24 September 2018, https://www.congregacionmita.org/html/espanol/mita.html.

Monter, E. William. "The Pedestal and the Stake: Courtly Love and Witchcraft." In *Becoming Visible Women in European History*, edited by Renate Bridenthal and Claudia Koonz. Boston: Houghton Mifflin Company, 1977.

Mother Gavrilia. *The Ascetics of Love*. Athens: Tertios Publishers, 2008.

Mouczko, Marg. "Working Women in the NT: Priscilla, Lydia and Phoebe." *New Life*, 5. https://margmowczko.com/likewise-women-likewise-husbands/.

Muir, Elizabeth Gillan. "Thecla and Friends: Woman in the New Testament Apocrypha." Unpublished research paper, McGill University, 1981.

Murray, Margaret. *The Witch-cult in Western Europe.* Oxford: Clarendon Press, 1921.

"New System Elects a Pope." *Christian History Institute*, 1 November 2017.

Newsome, Carol A., and Sharon H. Ringer, eds. *The Women's Bible Commentary.* London: Westminster/John Knox Press, 1992.

Numbers, Ronald. *Prophetess of Health: Ellen G White and the Origins of Seventh-Day Adventist Health Reform.* Knoxville: University of Tennessee Press, 1992.

"Nuns, Spinsters, and Single Women in Early Modern Europe." *Radcliffe Centennial News,* January 1980.

O'Brien, Martin. "A First among Equals." *The Irish Catholic,* 2013.

"The Outrage." *Boston Evening Transcript,* 13 August 1834.

Oyer, John S., and Robert S. Kreider. *Mirror of the Martyrs.* Intercourse, PA: Good Books, n.d.

Pederson, Rena. *The Lost Apostle, Searching for the Truth about Junia.* San Francisco: Jossey-Bass, 2006.

Pegg, Mark Gregory. "On Cathars, Albigenses, and Good Men of Languedoc." *Journal of Medieval History* 27 (2001): 181–95.

—. "Albigenses in the Antipodes: An Australian and the Cathars." *Journal of Religious History* 35, no. 4 (December 2011): 577–600.

Pernoud, Régine. *The Retrial of Joan of Arc; The Evidence at the Trial for Her Rehabilitation 1450–1456.* Translated by J.M. Cohen. New York: Harcourt, Brace, 1955.

Pernoud, Régine, and Marie-Véronique Clin. *Jeanne d'Arc.* Paris: Fayard, 1986.

Perotta, Louise Bourassa. *Saint Joseph: His Life and His Role in the Church Today.* Huntington, IN: Our Sunday Visitor, 2000.

Petroff, Elizabeth Alvilda. *Medieval Women's Visionary Literature.* New York: Oxford University Press, 1986.

Power, Eileen. *Medieval Women.* Cambridge: Cambridge University Press, 1971.

Prang, Margaret. *A Heart at Leisure from Itself.* Vancouver: UBC Press, 2002.

President-Elect Profile. "Hearts on Fire." 14th Triennial Assembly Report, Uniting Church in Australia, 2015.

Prioli, Carmine A. "The Ursuline Outrage." *American Heritage* 33, no. 2 (February/March 182): 101–5.

Pritchard, John R. "Methodist Women Abroad: Roles and Relationships" (2011). Accessed 24 September 2018, http://www.methodistheritage.org.uk/missionary-history-pritchard-methodist-women-abroad-2011.pdf.

Quaker Faith and Practice: The Book of Christian Discipline of the Yearly Meeting of the Religious Society of Friends (Quakers) in Britain. Quaker Books, May 1995.

Quinn, Frederick. *African Saints: Saints, Martyrs, and Holy People from the Continent of Africa*. New York: Crossroads Publishing, 2002.

Ramik, Vincent L. *The Ramik Report Memorandum of Law Literary Property Rights 1790–1915*. Spotsyvalia, VA: Diller, Ramik & Wight, 1981.

Reames, Sherry L. "The Legend of Mary Magdalen, Penitent and Apostle." In *Middle English Legends of Women Saints*, edited by Shelly L. Reams, Martha G. Blalock, and Wendy R. Larson. Kalamazoo, MI: Medieval Institute Publications, 2003.

Rebenich, Stefan. *Jerome*. London: Routledge, 2002.

"Religious Nuns in Medieval Europe: Women of Action" (2005). *Clio Project*. Accessed 17 September 2018, www.clioproject.org/files/PDF/Medieval_Nuns_Lesson.pdf.

Ricci, Carla. *Mary Magdalene and Many Others*. Minneapolis: Fortress Press, 1994.

Richardson, Herbert W. Lecture. Faculty of Religious Studies, McGill University, 1981.

Roberts, Sam. "Nun Worked to Contain Spread of Leprosy." *Globe and Mail*, 17 August 2017, S6.

Robo, Etienne, "The Holiness of Saint Joan of Arc." Catholic Truth Society, Eternal Word Television Network, London, England. Accessed 24 September 2018, www.ewtn.com/library/mary/joan1.htm.

Roffe, David. "St. Aethelthryth and the Monastery of Alftham." Accessed 24 September 2018, http://www.roffe.co.uk/alftham.htm.

Rogers, Albert N. "Personality Profile: Rev. Elizabeth Fitz Randolph." *Sabbath Recorder* 202, no. 6 (June 1980).

Rossi, Mary Ann. "Priesthood, Precedent and Prejudice: On Recovering the Women Priests of Early Christianity." *Journal of Feminist Studies* 7, no. 1 (1991): 73–94.

Ruether, Rosemary Radford. *Mary: The Feminine Face of the Church*. Philadelphia: The Westminster Press, 1977.

Russell, Jeffrey B. *Witchcraft in the Middle Ages*. Ithaca, NY: Cornell University Press, 1972.

—. *A History of Witchcraft, Sorcerers, Heretics and Pagans*. London: Thames and Hudson, 1980.

Sanchez, Michelle. "Your Daughters Shall Prophesy: The Rise of Women's Ordination in the Holiness Tradition." *Priscilla Papers* 24, no. 4 (Autumn 2010).

Sanders, Mark. "Digging to Learn More about Mother Catherine Seals." *New Orleans Magazine*, April 2011.

Scheck, Thomas P., ed. and trans. *Origen of Alexandria: Commentary on the Epistle to the Romans*. Washington, DC: Catholic University of America Press, 2002.

Schmidt, Kimberly D., Diane Zimmerman Umble, and Steven D. Reschly, eds. *Strangers at Home: Amish and Mennonite Women in History*. Baltimore: The Johns Hopkins University Press, 2002.

S.C.S. "Who Were the Beguines?" *The Economist*, 12 May 2013.

Shahar, Shulamith. *Women in a Medieval Heretical Sect: Agnes and Huguette the Waldensians*. Translated by Yael Lotan. Rochester, NY: Boydell Press, 2001.

Short, Colin C. "Portraits of Some Female Bible Christian Ministers." Methodist Family History, Memorabilia and Research, 14 April 2015. www.mybiblechristians.org.uk/content/.../portraits-female-bible-christian-ministers.

Simmonds Gemma. "Mary Ward: Then and Now." *Thinking Faith*. Accessed 24 September 2018, https://www.thinkingfaith.org/articles/20100122_1.htm.

Slick, Matt. "Was Junia in Romans 16:7 a Female Apostle in Authority?" *The Christian Apologetics and Research Ministry*, 25 April 2008. https://carm.org/junia-apostle.

Smith, Sir William, and Henry Wace. *A Dictionary of Christian Biography, Literature, Sects and Doctrine during the First Eight Centuries*. Vol. 3. London: John Murray, 1882.

Society for Promoting Female Education in the East Annual Report. Missionary Periodical Data Base. Accessed 24 September 2018, https://archiveshub.jisc.ac.uk/data/gb150-fes.

Stanley, John E. "Doctrinal Dialogue." Research article, Anderson University School of Theology, June 2009.

Stanley, Susie C. *Holy Boldness*. Knoxville, TN: University of Tennessee Press, 2002.

—. "The Promise Fulfilled: Women's Ministries in the Wesleyan/Holiness Movement." *Wesleyan Holiness Women's Clergy*. Accessed 24 September 2018, https://www.wesleyanholinesswomenclergy.org/the-promise-fulfilled-womens-ministries-in-the-wesleyanholiness-movement/.

—. "The Promise Fulfilled: Women's Ministries in the Wesleyan/Holiness Movement." In *Religious Institutions and Women's Leadership: New Roles Inside the Mainstream*, edited by Catherine Wessinger. Columbia: University of South Carolina Press, 1996.

Stanton, Elizabeth Cady, and the Coalition on Women and Religion. *The Woman's Bible*. New York: European Publishing Company, 1898.

Stone, Merlin. *When God Was a Woman*. New York: Harcourt Brace Jovanovich, 1976.

Strege, Merle. "Church of God." *Foundations*, May 1989.

—. *The Wisdom of the Beguines*. Katonack, NY: Sisters of Benedict, St. Placid Priory, 2014.

"Swaziland's Ellinah Wamukya Becomes Africa's First Female Bishop." *Episcopal News Service*, 19 November 2012. https://www.episcopalnewsservice.org/2012/11/page/3/.

Swidler, Leonard. *Biblical Affirmations of Women*. Philadelphia: The Westminster Press, 1979.

Tarvers, Josephine Koster. "'Thys ys my mystrys boke': English Women as Readers and Writers in Late Medieval England." In *The Uses of Manuscripts in Literary*

Studies, Essays in Memory of Judson Boyce Allen, edited by Charlotte Cook Morse, Penelope Reed Doob, and Marjorie Curry Woods. Kalamazoo, MI: Western Michigan University Press, 1992.

Tibbetts, Joel W. "Women Who Were Called: A Study of the Contributions to American Christianity of Ann Lee, Jemima Wilkinson, Mary Baker Eddy and Aimee Semple McPherson." PhD diss., Vanderbilt University, 1976.

Tice, Paul. "The Bogomils: Europe's Forgotten Gnostics." *New Dawn Magazine*, January–February 2008.

Torjesen, Karen Jo. *When Women Were Priests*. San Francisco: Harper Publishing, 1993.

—. "The Early Christian Orans: An Artistic Representation of Women's Liturgical Prayer and Prophesy." In *Women Preachers and Prophets through Two Millennia of Christianity*, edited by Beverly Mayne Kienzle and Pamela J. Walker. Berkeley: University of California Press, 1998.

Trask, Willard, ed. and trans. *Joan of Arc: In Her Own Words*. New York: Turtle Point Press, 1996.

Turpin, Joanne. *Women in Church History: 20 Stories for 20 Centuries*. Cincinnati, OH: St. Anthony Messenger Press, 1990.

Umble, Jeni Hiett. "Anabaptist Women in Augsburg." In *Strangers at Home: Amish and Mennonite Women in History*, edited by Kimberly D. Schmidt, Diane Zimmerman Umble, and Steven D. Reschly. Baltimore: The Johns Hopkins University Press, 2002.

Underhill, Evelyn. *The Essentials of Mysticism and Other Essays*. London: J.M. Dent & Sons, 1920.

"United Presbyterian Church." *San Francisco Call* 99, no. 23 (23 December 1905).

Vasilev, Georgi. "Bogomils, Cathars, and Lollards and the High Social Position of Women During the Middle Ages." *Facta Universitatis Series Philosophy and Sociology* 2, no. 7 (2000).

Vaudry, John P. "A. Caroline Macdonald of Japan." *Renewal Fellowship*, 13 February 2001.

"A Waldensian Timeline." *The Reformation*. Accessed 15 August 2018, http://thereformation.info/waldensian_time_line.htm.

Walker, Pamela J. "A Chaste and Fervid Eloquence." In *Women Preachers and Prophets through Two Millennia of Christianity*, edited by Beverly Mayne Kienzle and Pamela J. Walker. Berkeley: University of California Press, 1998.

Warren, Ann K. *Anchorites and Their Patrons in Medieval England*. Berkeley: University of California Press, 1985.

Webber, Robert. "Second Eve." *Christian History* 83 (Summer 2004).

Webster, D.R. "Order and Abbey at Fontevrault." In *The Catholic Encyclopedia*. Vol. 6. New York: Robert Appleton Company, 1909.

Wellesley, Mary, and Peter Toth. "Kassia: A Bold and Beautiful Byzantine Poet." *Medieval Manuscripts Blog*, March 2016. blogs.bl.uk/digitisedmanuscripts/2016/03/kassia.html.

Westerkamp, Marilyn J. *Women and Religion in Early America, 1600–1850: The Puritan and Evangelical Traditions*. New York: Routledge, 1999.

White, Ellen G. "Proper Education." *The Health Reformer*. Battle Creek: The Health Reform Institute, 1895.

Whiteley, Marilyn Färdig. *Canadian Methodist Women 1766–1925: Marys, Marthas, Mothers in Israel*. Waterloo, ON: Wilfrid Laurier University Press, 2006.

Wigger, John H. *Taking Heaven by Storm: Methodism and the Rise of Popular Christianity in America*. Chicago: University of Illinois Press, 2001.

Wijngaards, John. *No Women in Holy Orders: The Women Deacons of the Early Church*. Norwich, UK: Canterbury Press, 2002.

—. "The Ancient Diaconate of Women Was a Sacrament." *Wijngaards Institute for Catholic Research*. Accessed 24 September 2018, www.womendeacons.org/rite-ancient-diaconate-of-women-was-a-sacrament/.

Williams, Manon. "From the Holy Land to the Cloister: The Decline of Female Ascetic Pilgrimages in the Early Medieval West (c.350–615)." MA thesis, University of Colorado, Boulder, 2015.

"Woman Speaks of Scriptures." *San Francisco Call* 99, no. 3 (4 December 1905).

"Women in the Heart of God (8): Women's Roles in the Early Church." *A Christian Think Tank* (updated November 2005). Accessed 24 September 2018, http://christianthinktank.com/fem08.html.

"Women in the Pentecostal Movement." *Fuller Studio*. Accessed 24 September 2018, https://fullerstudio.fuller.edu/women-in-the-pentecostal-movement/.

"Women in the Uniting Church: By a Partial, Prejudiced, and Ignorant Historian (to Quote the Immortal Jane)." *Rev Doc Geek* (blog), 22 June 2013. https://revdocgeek.com/2013/06/22/women-in-the-uniting-church-by-a-partial-prejudiced-ignorant-historian-to-quote-the-immortal-jane/.

Wordsworth, William. "Ecclesiastical Sonnets, XIV: 'The Waldenses.'" In *The Poetical Works of Wordsworth*, edited by Ernest de Selincourt. London: Oxford University Press, 1951.

OTHER SOURCES

Email and/or telephone conversations (June–October 2017) with women in church
    leadership including Dr. Agnes Regina Murei Abuom, World Council of
    Churches; Dr. Marion Best, the United Church of Canada; Canon Janet
    Catterall, Church of Ireland; Kristine Greenaway, World Council of Churches;
    Susan Jackson, the United Church of Canada; Rev. Najla Kassab, World
    Communion of Reformed Churches; Rev. Kathleen Macpherson, ACCUS; the
    Very Rev. Susanna Pain; Dr. Deidre Palmer, Uniting Church in Australia;
    Dr. Isabel Phiri, World Council of Churches; Dr. Elisabeth Raiser, Kirchentag;
    Sister Elizabeth Rolfe-Thomas, Sisterhood of St. John the Divine; the Most
    Rev. Patricia Storey, Church of Ireland; Bishop Olga Lucia Alvarez, Bishop
    Michele Birch-Conery, Bishop Bridget Mary Meehan, Rev. Janice Sevre-
    Duszynska, and Rev. Suzanne Theil, Association of Roman Catholic Women
    Priests.

INDEX